Praise for *The Punishment Monopoly*

"In a reckoning with the past that explains the horrors of the present, anthropologist Pem Buck digs into tales of her ancestors and historical archives to weave an unforgettable story of the rise and reproduction of the family, private property, and the punitive state. The secret global history of the United States revealed in this masterwork is a must-read for knowing the world, then and now."

—**ALISSE WATERSTON**, author, *My Father's Wars: Migration, Memory, and the Violence of a Century*

"Through the lens of family members, and those with whom they interacted, Pem Davidson Buck allows the reader to flesh out the structures of domination, inequality, the restrictions of gender, race, religious conflict, warfare, and notions of property present in the British Isles, West Africa, and mainland North America from the seventeenth century through contemporary times. A great book."

—**YVONNE JONES**, Associate Professor of Anthropology, University of Louisville

"In the United States, we often assume that social theory of the state—specifically as an entity that has jealously gathered unto itself the power to kill—belongs on the other side of the Atlantic. Pem Buck's work shows, through a revelatory 400-hundred year historical anthropology of her own family, that the U.S. has its own genealogy of state violence."

—**EDWARD E. BAPTIST**, Cornell University; author, *The Half Has Never Been Told: Slavery and the Making of American Capitalism*

"In an extraordinary combination of state-theory and genealogical analysis, this book exposes the rarely acknowledged relationships between the right to punish and processes of accumulation of capital and dispossession in U.S. history. Pem Buck's book is an outstanding contribution to political theory, American history, kinship studies, reflexive anthropology, and studies in culture and power."

—**NINA GLICK SCHILLER**, Emeritus Professor, Social Anthropology, University of Manchester, University of New Hampshire; co-editor, *Anthropological Theory*

"This book is a major feat in historical interpretation. It un-silences important aspects of the U.S. past and present through its intersectional approach to multicultural contact and interaction; the intricate workings of colonial power continued into the present day; the dehumanizing effects of indenture, genocide, and enslavement in a class and racially stratified social order that came to be organized around white privilege and supremacy, heteropatriarchy, and punishment. Like no other book I've read, Buck's remarkable counter-storytelling brings the insights of an ethnographer and creative writer to her tales about her Scottish ancestors, whose privileges depended on the dispossession, displacement, and enslavement of others. Throughout the history she narrates, from colonial Jamestown to the current-day Fergusons and Standing Rocks, her analysis of statecraft, the power to punish, and ordinary people's resistance is accessible, theoretically engaging, and methodologically honest."

—**FAYE V. HARRISON**, Professor of African American Studies and Anthropology, University of Illinois, Champaign-Urbana; author, *Outsider Within: Reworking Anthropology in the Global Age*

The Punishment Monopoly

Tales of My Ancestors, Dispossession, and the Building of the United States

by PEM DAVIDSON BUCK

MONTHLY REVIEW PRESS

New York

Library of Congress Cataloging-in-Publication Data:
available from the publsiher

ISBN pbk: 978-158367-832-9
ISBN cloth: 978-158367-833-6

Portions of previously published articles have been incorporated into
various chapters: "The Violence of the Status Quo: Michael Brown, Ferguson, and
Tanks," *Anthropology News* 55(9): 2015; "Stating Punishment: The Struggle over the
Right to Punish," *North American Dialogue* 17(1):31-43, 2014; "The Strange Birth
and Continuing Life of the U.S. as a Slaving Republic: Race, Unfree Labor, and the
State," *Anthropological Theory* 17(2):159-191, 2017,
https://doi.org/10.1177/1463499617713137.

Typeset in Bulmer Monotype

Monthly Review Press, New York
monthlyreview.org

5 4 3 2 1

Contents

Timeline | 6

Acknowledgments | 7

Introduction: Ancestor Tales | 11

1—Tales of a Mythical Ancestor, Punishment, and Diarchy | 24

2—Ancestor Tales of Dispossession and a Revolt
of the Unfree | 55

3—Ancestor Tales of Slavery, Slaving, and Women with Voice | 85

4—Ancestor Tales of the Revolt that Happened
and One that Didn't | 109

5—Ancestor Tales of the Logic of a Slave Society | 141

6—Ancestor Tales of the Birth of a Slaving Republic | 171

7—Ancestor Tales of the Dispossession of Women, the Domination
of Men, and the Definition of Liberty | 205

8—Ancestor Tales of Life in a Capitalist Slaving Republic | 235

9—Tales of the Present | 270

Appendices | 307

Genealogy Chart of Ancestors | 312

Notes | 313

Bibliography | 397

Index | 429

Timeline

1607–1620	X Radford to Jamestown
1645?	Birth of Bruen Radford
1652	John Radford to Virginia
1665	George Radford born in Henrico Co., VA
1670?	Birth of Sarah McDavid in Scotland; perhaps mother of Alexander Davidson I
1675	Death of John Radford
1687	Death of Bruen Radford
1690?	Alexander I born in Scotland
1718–1728?	Birth of Venis in Igboland (Nigeria)
1717	Sarah Ellis born in Middlesex Co., VA
1717–1720?	Alexander I arrives in Virginia from Scotland
1730–1745?	Venis arrives in Virginia from Biafra
1727	Death of Hezekiah Ellis, father of Sarah Ellis
1733–1743?	Marriage of Alexander I and Sarah Ellis
1744	Birth of Alexander II (some dispute but generally accepted)
1745	First records of Alexander I (in Spotsylvania Co., VA)
1748	Death of Alexander Davidson I (Spotsylvania Co., VA)
c.1752	Death of Sarah Ellis Davidson (Spotsylvania Co., VA)
1766	Death of William Ellis, brother of Sarah Ellis Davidson
1767?	Marriage of Alexander II and Anna Bridges (perhaps in Prince William Co., VA)
1771	Alexander II and Anna are in Orange Co., NC (in what later became Caswell Co.)
1777–1778	Alexander II and Anna move to Tryon Co., NC (in what later became Rutherford and then Cleveland Co.)
1782 or 1783	Death of Anna Bridges Davidson
1783	Marriage of Alexander II to Mary Ellis (sometimes referred to as Mary Ellis Jones, a widow)
1796	Alexander II ordained
1797	Alexander II and Mary move to Warren Co., KY (in what later became Barren Co.)
1814	Benjamin Radford I and family move to Christian Co., KY
1817	Alexander II dies
1824	Elijah Davidson ordained
1831–1834	Families of Hezekiah and Elijah Davidson and Benjamin Radford II move to Illinois
1849	Mary Ellis Davidson dies

Acknowledgments

The first sentences of *The Punishment Monopoly* were written early one fall morning of 2012 on the porch of a little camping cabin my husband and I had rented, along with a horse stall, for a weekend of driving my Haflinger horse and cart on the rugged trails of East Fork, Tennessee. But the book actually had its birth years earlier, although I didn't know it then, when my foster sister, Deborah St. Amant Narboni, and I began tracking down Davidson ancestry together, until cancer finally stopped her. She was an honorary Davidson, and a wonderful buddy for what we termed "our adventures." So it is she whom I must first acknowledge.

Much of my research involved trips to the Filson Historical Society in Louisville, Kentucky, where the librarians were both helpful and extremely patient with my repeated requests for volumes stored in back rooms. Without interlibrary loans much of my research would have been impossible—my thanks in particular to Sarah Jones of the Elizabethtown Community and Technical College Library for all her effort in tracking down obscure volumes. My thanks also to the South Central Kentucky Cultural Center in Glasgow, Kentucky, to the Hart County Historical Society, to the County Clerk's Offices of Barren County, Kentucky, and of Spotsylvania County, Virginia, and to the curators at the Dingwall Museum in Dingwall, Scotland. Without the clues provided by the anonymous family researchers who made their discoveries public on Ancestry.com—accurate or not—the task of searching out Davidson and Radford genealogy would have been much harder. Elizabethtown Community and Technical College has supported my efforts, funding trips to American Anthropological Association meetings until my retirement, where I presented papers analyzing and theorizing issues related to various chapters, receiving valuable feedback and encouragement. After my retirement, support continued in the form of Professor Emerita access to college facilities and the use of my old office. Donna Hester, secretary to the Social and Behavioral Sciences Division, was both a source of good cheer and a resource in my attempts to untangle computer messes. Perhaps most important in this list of the institutions I wish to acknowledge is the Association of Black Anthropologists, my intellectual home within anthropology, a vital source of support, stimulation, and critique.

My approach to *The Punishment Monopoly* has benefitted immensely from my involvement with a group of anthropologists who have taken the issue of mass incarceration head on, connecting it to the state, to governance, and to local communities. I am particularly grateful to Mieka Polanco, Karen Williams, Andrea Morrell, and to the participants in sessions related to incarceration at the American Anthropological Association meetings in 2008, 2011, 2014, and 2017. Melissa Burch's suggestions of books and articles, many of which now appear in my bibliography, were extremely helpful. My thanks to Nina Glick Schiller, editor at *Anthropological Theory*, for raising my consciousness of the way in which the concept of dispossession was central to my writing. Derrick Hodge's critique of the introduction and first chapter was invaluable, as was Rachel Buck Pradeep's support of the route I eventually took for the introduction. Then there is Vicki Reenstra, the cousin who told me about her family mythology, instigating my pursuit of Radfords, Jamestown, and Powhatans, and who, along with Jonathan Davidson, encouraged me in "chasing the ancestors."

Contextualizing those ancestors and the documents that carry clues to their lives would have been impossible without the scholars— anthropologists, historians, sociologists, philosophers—on whose work I have depended. I owe a huge debt of gratitude to the people who gave me their support throughout the whole long process of writing this book. Faye Harrison's support has been foundational for me as an anthropologist, first at the University of Louisville, where her teaching and guidance set me on the anthropological trajectory I have pursued ever since, and later as colleague and friend. Yvonne Jones made research trips to Louisville a pleasure, both for her hospitality, which included long evenings discussing a huge range of anthropological subjects (and not so anthropological subjects—although she generally brought anthropological theory to bear on them as well), and for her critique of and support for every chapter I wrote. Naomi Buck Palagi did a marvelous job of copy editing and commenting. Ann Kingsolver's friendship and encouragement over many years, starting long before I had conceived of this book, has mattered enormously. And she did a marathon read of the book, with numerous perceptive comments and suggestions, for which I am deeply grateful. By the time she was done, I felt it was safe to send the book off to Monthly Review Press.

And at Monthly Review Press, my book and I were taken in hand by a wonderful team. My thanks in particular to Martin Paddio, who shepherded me through the publication process with patience and good humor. Gloria Jacobs was both editor and interlocutor, with both a fine eye for detail and an overview of the project as a whole that led her to ask searching questions and push me to address issues I had sidestepped. Working with her was both eye-opening and fun.

Last, but very far from least, is the support and the intellectual stimulation of my family, Rachel Buck Pradeep, Naomi Buck Palagi, Jason Palagi, and most important of all, David Buck, who debated issues with me, read every word, often many times in varying iterations, without whom this book would not exist.

May the next generation of my Davidson and Radford descendants, Janakhi and Rose Pradeep, Nicolas and Callista Palagi, find a world in which *The Punishment Monopoly* is no longer relevant.

Ancestor Tales

S omewhere, just where and when I'm not sure, but surely in Scotland, a swaddled baby cries in his mother's arms. Who his parents were, I don't know, but I do know his name. He is Alexander Davidson. The year might be 1690, and the place might be Dingwall, in the Scottish Highlands. He most likely joined the Jacobite rebellion against the British Crown as a young man, and being on the losing side, found himself, willingly or not, crossing the Atlantic to the Chesapeake Bay, most likely sold as an indentured servant, most likely sometime in the decade after 1715. Davidson genealogy refers to him as Alexander I.

Some eighty years earlier, long before Alexander's birth, a man with the last name of Radford was puking up his guts on one of the first ships bound for Jamestown, one of the "lesser sort" in a company of "gentlemen adventurers" headed for a world they considered new— and ripe for exploitation.[1] I have a cousin whose family mythology says his name was Benjamin. But perhaps the ancestral Radford really arrived much later, in 1652, and was named John. Whenever that first Radford arrived, though, he surely puked; ships hadn't changed much in the intervening forty or so years. If he arrived on the earlier date, the first Radford was probably young, and most likely in some form of indentured servitude. If he came just a couple of years later, he might well have had to choose between the gallows and the years of servitude in the colonies.

When the first Radford arrives in the Chesapeake, the Powhatan are the dominant polity in that world, which they consider anything but new. They have been consolidating their power through the late 1500s and early 1600s, and now have a paramount chief, Wahunsonacock, whose reach and demands for tribute are becoming ever more extensive.

And, somewhere and sometime in Africa, war captives are sold, who, like that early Radford, would become some of the first non-Native people to enter the world of the Powhatan. Perhaps it was two of their descendants who are known, at least by whites, as Venis and Adam, and are held enslaved in the 1740s by that baby boy born in Dingwall, Scotland. More likely, however, they, or their parents or grandparents, arrived well after the first Africans at Jamestown. Africans arrived by ones and twos during the early years, and it wasn't until after 1680 that they were brought and bought in large numbers. Statistically, Venis and Adam most likely arrived in the early to mid-eighteenth century. So they will enter this story after those early Radfords. And many years later, people who might be their descendants, Judah and Depha and eleven others, will enter the story, enslaved in the household of Alexander's son.

Finally, there is Sarah Ellis, the last of the "founding generation" to enter these tales. She is a second- or third-generation English Virginian, born in 1717 in Christ Church Parish of Middlesex County. Most of her life is a bit of a mystery to me, hidden as it is, like that of most women, from official view under the "cover" of their husbands and fathers. Rules of coverture kept women, for the most part, off tax lists and out of the records of county court orders and of judicial proceedings. They are counted but nameless in early census documents. Regardless of whatever managerial power or influence they might have had in their own families and communities, it was mostly husbands and fathers and brothers who carried out public business. So, women don't show up much in the records we can search today, making their lives even harder to document than the lives of men of that time. But what is clear is that Sarah later marries that baby born in Scotland, Alexander I, and that she bears a son, and dies in her mid-thirties. Alexander II, her son, marries and moves his family to North Carolina just before the Revolution, and then moves on to the Barrens of central Kentucky just after it became a state of the fledgling United States. Alexander I and Sarah Ellis are my seventh-generation grandparents; that first Radford is my eleventh-generation grandfather.

So it is these people and their descendants who will carry these ancestor tales—first Radfords, whom I will rudely abandon as soon as there are Davidsons to follow in Virginia. It was my father's identification with Scotland, and my own curiosity about Davidson family mythology, that started this search, and that, rather than the story of the Radfords, is the track I will be following. But I will equally rudely abandon the Davidsons in the 1820s, just before my great-great-great-grandparents, Alexander II's son Hezekiah and Eleanor Wilson Davidson, left Kentucky. The final chapter of this book, having left the ancestors, does a fast forward to the present, following the themes of these tales, so that the past can illuminate some of the most contentious issues of the twenty-first century.

I HAD HEARD ALL MY LIFE, growing up in Pennsylvania, that "we were abolitionists in Kentucky," and that my ancestors had left Kentucky about when Lincoln did. There was also the story that my father's great-uncle Ben Radford (the third of that name) had watched Abraham Lincoln playing horseshoes in Illinois when Lincoln was a young lawyer. It turns out that none of this is exactly true. It was Uncle Ben's father-in-law who did the watching.[2] Lincoln left Kentucky considerably before the Davidsons did. Were they abolitionists? Well, that question will take some unraveling when we get to Kentucky in these tales.

Ancestor tales had never impressed me much, and even when I moved to Kentucky myself, and even when I wrote *Worked to the Bone: Race, Class, Power, and Privilege in Kentucky*, an anthropological history focused on the two central Kentucky counties where I live and work, I continued to ignore that family history.[3] *Ignore* is actually the wrong word; it never crossed my mind to wonder whether my family history had any relevance to the book I was writing. And I had at that time no idea that my Davidson ancestors had settled less than an hour's drive from where I now live—Hezekiah and Eleanor had lived in my own county. Coincidence?!

The story I am weaving now is, in a sense, my attempt to place that family history within the context of the understandings of class and race—particularly whiteness—that I developed in my first book. This included what I thought of as my search for my "one black drop," which I was sure must exist somewhere among all those European ancestors. I never found it, though it quite likely is there, given the flexibility in the early days of colonial Virginia of what we now call race.

But more important, my goal is to use that family history as a vehicle for talking about the right to use force, and how that relates to the formation of governmental structures called "states"—entities that claim and enforce a monopoly on the use of force to exercise punishment. For ultimately, the state must punish to be a state, and, bottom line, this is what states and the force they control are for—to protect the ability of the few to set people up so that they have little choice but to hand over to them the value of the work they do. The citizens of some states have fought, with some degree of success, to limit or mitigate exploitation, and as a result states have varied enormously in the degree of security they provide for those who cooperate. But ultimately all depend on their power to punish those who don't.

Using family history to do this will be tricky. This will be a story partially constructed from known facts, and partially a story constructed from likelihoods—a fiction, but not a baseless fiction. I don't *know*, for instance, that in 1607 or even in 1652, a Radford was seasick on a ship bound for Jamestown. I do know that many people on those boats were, and my Radford might well have been one of them.[4] And though I can know little of the men, I know even less of the women, and less again of the enslaved, of Venis and Adam and the others listed in my ancestors' inventories. So this will be a creative reconstruction, a tale that illustrates not really *my* family history, but the history of many families as forming states that claimed from them the right to punish.

This story will start with the people who were there first, and in whose hands rested the fate of the ancestral Radford, if he actually arrived early, and of the others who arrived to risk their lives to create wealth for the already wealthy investors of the Virginia Company—safe, for the most part, in England.[5] In that early period of colonial encroachment, two corporate not-quite-states confronted each other as Powhatan aristocrats decided how to deal with the Virginia Company's officers and vice versa, and as both attempted to spread their use of force beyond the confines of their own groups. Even as they pushed outward to absorb more land and people, however, that use of force was contested within each polity. Punishment was contested both by those who suffered from it and by those who wished to gain the right to punish—to rule—for themselves. To clarify, "polity" is a term I will use frequently because it indicates a political, resource-managing, self-governing entity but leaves its actual form of organization ambiguous, and thus is very useful in talking about the process of state formation.

The struggle over the use of force within the Virginia English polity had, by John Radford's arrival in 1652, become central and would in twenty years lead to Bacon's Rebellion, a class-based uprising in which exploited Africans and English workers joined together against the elites who exploited them. In the aftermath of that rebellion, the racial distinctions were legally constructed that eventually justified hereditary racial slavery for those who would be defined by African descent, and enabled continued poverty for many of the others, now defined as white. Thus, separated by race, they were not likely to join again in a class-based challenge to the elites' right to exploit—a classic example of divide and conquer.

That racialized distinction would endure despite the fact that enslaved Africans and English indentured servants did much the same work and lived in comparable physical misery, both exploited by the planter elites. By Alexander's time these distinctions set indentured people, including probably Alexander himself during his first years in Virginia, apart from enslaved people like Venis and Adam. While John Radford may well have been involved in Bacon's Rebellion—most people in Virginia were—by the time Alexander Davidson arrived, the rights of free white men to own and punish the enslaved and to temporarily own and (within some limits) punish the indentured were well established. Alexander, however, if he was in fact indentured and subject to his owner's punishment, lived through that period of servitude and became free, unlike Venis and Adam, whom he later owned and had the right to punish, with whips if he so chose. As a father and husband, he also had the right to punish his wife, Sarah, as well as their children—a right that enslaved husbands and fathers could not claim.

BEFORE I CAN GO ON, I NEED to explain why I keep referring to states, force, and punishment. There has been much theorizing about what "states" are, and I will address those issues in the last chapter, for the very idea of a "state" is problematic. For now, however, I am referring to the state as a territory held under one governing entity, be it a kingdom, a dictatorship, or a democratic republic. Beginning with Weber, social theorists have generally argued that coercion and a monopoly on the use of force are central foundational processes in all states.[6] States are, by definition, stratified, with some categories of people having far greater access to resources than others.[7] The state uses force as needed to control inhabitants and to control/defend borders. The inhabitants of the territory, or at least most of them, believe that the use of force is legitimate; it is the state's right and obligation. The state authorizes agents to make laws, make demands, regulate behavior, and, when necessary for enforcement, exert force. Those who resist will undergo punishment that is itself authorized by the state and carried out by agents of the state. The primary beneficiaries of the monopoly on the use of force are a subset of the population, the elite, and, to a lesser extent, those on whom they depend—their agents in using state power to enforce stratification. Stratification, in turn, enables wealth extraction—and wealth extraction is the basic point of state formation. Wealth extraction requires categories of people who are powerless to prevent the expropriation of the fruits of their labor. The power to punish is the essential tool that makes this feedback loop possible.[8]

Thus, states are about inequality, about making it possible for some few to gain wealth off the labors of the many, and the threat of punishment is an important component in convincing people to cooperate. Most people would prefer to keep the value of their labor for themselves, but the state apparatus provides the force to convince even the recalcitrant that they cannot do so. The state enforces the rights of individuals to own or control property, the resources people need to produce food and goods—the means of production. In enforcing those rights, the state at the same time enforces the propertyless condition—the dispossession—of many people. So, in enforcing the rights of property, the state also fulfills its other critical function: the supply and control of a cheap labor force to do the work of making wealth for others.

In these tales, we will see the state protecting the rights of the elite to own huge amounts of land and to use the labor of the dispossessed for their own benefit. In the early colonies, that dispossession applied only to those who were enslaved and indentured, but soon spread to many more people, people who were legally free. This is why force is required: to make sure that there are enough people without property who will go hungry unless they turn their labor over to someone else in return for wages or at least for a way to eat, and to be able to punish those who don't cooperate or threaten to upset the system. How else would an elite "persuade" other people to make them rich? How else can wealth trickle up into the hands of the very few? In fact, people do at times revolt and resist, despite punishment, on a regular basis. Sufficiently organized, they sometimes force concessions, though punishment means that only rarely are they able to change the basic structure of inequality.

So when I refer to "the state," I am referring to an entity that has the legitimate right to exert force both in relation to its borders and in relation to its inhabitants. Such entities are "sovereign." The United States was becoming a modern nation-state by the time my ancestors left the East Coast and arrived in Kentucky. Modern nation-states claim that their sovereignty, their right of self-determination, their right to demand loyalty and obedience and thus their right to use force to punish—their right to exist at all—is based on the existence of a homogenous "nation," a "people" who share the same values, culture, language, and history.[9] Getting seriously disparate peoples to conceive of themselves as a nation, to legitimize the existence of the state, has been an ongoing challenge—and still is, as documented by the present furor promoted by the descendants of some immigrants over the acceptance of other immigrants as part of the state.

IN FACILITATING WEALTH EXTRACTION, the state acts as what sociologist Charles Tilly calls a "protection racket"—something that is often euphemistically referred to as the "social contract."[10] The state provides "protection" to citizens, and in return the citizens allow themselves to be exploited. The state may also provide benefits for some of the population in the form of a rising standard of living, helping to ensure their allegiance. This means that the legitimacy of a state in the eyes of its more protected citizens rests largely on its control of the use of force. The state, to fulfill its side of the contract, must be effective in maintaining an "orderly" society. It must provide its citizens the local peace they need to raise families with at least minimal success and to produce the surplus needed to fulfill elite demands, all without the fear of additional extractions of surplus by marauding neighbors or outsiders. Belief in that contract is part of what Edward Herman and Noam Chomsky have called "the manufacture of consent"—the orchestration of beliefs and fears that get people to accept, and ideally not even recognize, elite rule and their own exploitation.[11] But if Tilly's "protection racket" is to work, citizens must believe they need protection—otherwise they might keep for themselves the value they produce, refusing to pay for protection. So, if there is no real external enemy, no threat of war or invasion, something fearsome will have to be invented. Certain people can be framed as dangerous, in need of punishment to protect everyone else. Punishing the already compliant, the "us," won't work. It is "them," those Others who are framed as enemies. I will introduce several such enemies in these tales, ranging from witches to those so framed today—women with babies, criminals,

Muslims, and immigrants—all of whom supposedly threaten the security of the compliant clients of the protectors. I will show how "the law" creates criminals, and how the state and its media allies foster fear of certain groups, telling us how dangerous they are in an attempt to manufacture consent. That the state provides protection in the face of fear gives it legitimacy in the eyes of many of its citizens. That the state created the fear in the first place remains invisible to most.[12]

The power to punish allows the state to make clear what happens to the noncompliant. The state itself, just like a Mafia boss running a protection racket, must be feared. So "governments decide how much punishment they want, and these decisions are in no simple way related to the crime rate."[13] Punishment provides the state with the opportunity to use certain bodies to produce "shock and awe," spectacular displays of power over life and death. Executions and imprisonment, decisions to withhold life-supporting services such as healthcare, welfare, education, as well as the ability to declare exceptions to those rules, all demonstrate that the state is indeed sovereign, both to its own people and to other states.[14] As Achille Mbembe says, "The ultimate expression of sovereignty resides, to a large degree, in the power and capacity to dictate who may live and who must die."[15] Steve Martinot states, "The prisoner is the means by which the state produces its overarching power. . . . The prisoner is the sign of the state's presumed political legitimacy."[16] The stories of my ancestors offer numerous examples of how spectacular punishment and the demonstration of sovereignty are linked.

Ultimately, then, a state to be a state has to punish. It can't just *claim* a monopoly on the use of force; it can't just say, "Hey folks, we, the state officials, are the only ones who can use force, so we are in charge of punishing anyone who needs it. And if you try, we'll punish you too. Somebody stole your stuff, report it to us and we'll punish the thief. We are the only ones who can use force, with a couple of specified exceptions." Very few people will buy into that, unless it is demonstrably true. The state has to prove its monopoly by actually using force to punish. And the force must be based on laws, no matter how unequal, to justify that use of force.

The state demonstrates its monopoly by punishing a carefully selected few, those defined as "Other"—as not real or rightful members of the polity and therefore inferior—by the majority of citizens. Selecting Others ensures that the punishing does not cause the majority to question the legitimacy of elite rule. Making this selection may well require another aspect of sovereignty, the ability to declare a de facto or de jure exception, thus getting people to accept that the standard rules, including those of human decency and state protection, don't apply to these Others.[17]

Well-managed punishment produces a display of the state's power over life and death—currently in the relentless grinding of the wheels of the legal system, but in the earlier stages of state formation through the public administration of intense pain: whippings, amputations, and sometimes the dismemberment and annihilation of offending bodies. The fate of a few Scottish Jacobite rebels—a fate Alexander I avoided, though he was probably one of those rebels—makes this clear. They were drawn and quartered: first hung by the neck, cut down while still alive, their innards ripped from their living bodies, and then literally pulled apart by horses tied to their four limbs. The shrieks of one victim, Archibald Burnet, could be heard a mile away.[18] It would be hard to misunderstand the warning being delivered. The Powhatan likewise provided spectacular, lengthy, and agonizing deaths, but, unlike English executions, those deaths were considered to be an honor for worthy enemy captives. Ordinary Powhatan criminals were merely beaten to death with cudgels on a sacrificial rock altar.[19]

Foucault, in *Discipline and Punish*, begins with an unforgettable description of punishment by drawing and quartering in France.[20] Like the English punishment of Archibald Burnet, it was performed by a state in which the power to carry out such a killing was monopolized by the king. With the development of a modern state, however, spectacular punishments waned, and a "different physics of power" emerged,[21] in which punishment had to appear to be a result of laws that reflected nature—the natural consequence of crime, rather than merely a king's prerogative.[22] Discipline, not painful punishment, was meant to create productive subjects who, though bowing to sovereign power, remained unable to recognize their own subservience. Foucault takes the sovereignty that is built on the power to punish as his starting point. However, there is a prehistory to that starting point. Polities moving in directions that eventually lead to what we call states fight long and hard to gain the power to punish, wresting it out of the hands of local people. As a ruling elite becomes stronger, it more and more effectively prevents less powerful individuals or groups from defining and punishing transgressions. Thus gaining a monopoly on punishment is integral to state-making and is required if states are to exist at all. As a polity concentrates punishment in fewer and fewer hands it becomes more state-like, enabling a feedback loop in which greater punishing power allows greater dispossession and a greater concentration of wealth—those hallmarks of a state. In this process Davidsons and Radfords gradually lost their rights to punish as the US state became stronger, preventing any but state-authorized agents from punishing. Sovereignty thus rests at base in the control of punishment. The tales in this book will follow that development.

Throughout this history, other nations surrounded Radfords and Davidsons, all claiming their rights as unconquered, though diminished, autonomous sovereign polities. We can presume the Davidsons were aware of Cherokee and Shawnee struggles to create or maintain sovereignty, just as early Radfords must have been aware of Powhatan and other East Coast nations' claims to sovereign status. Native Americans, in signing treaties at various times with the US, British, French, and Spanish governments, reserved to themselves territory they continued to claim and certain rights concerning the use of force within those borders. At least in the early days of Radford history, both parties conceived of those treaties as agreements between equal sovereign entities. But by the time Alexander Davidson arrived in Virginia, the conception of Native American polities as equal to colonial entities had disappeared on the East Coast, although it was still relevant west of the Appalachians. The Shawnee leader Tecumseh envisioned another sovereign Native polity north of Kentucky, in the Old Northwest, a vision he came surprisingly close to realizing. I say "surprisingly" because our present understanding of history generally leads us to see such efforts as doomed from their inception because they weren't on what we see as the inevitable trajectory that led to the United States in its present form. But, had Tecumseh succeeded, that Native polity would have been a sovereign state, controlling the use of force within its own borders; it would have had the right to punish those within its borders as it saw fit; and it would have exercised the right to regulate and defend its own borders in relation to other states.[23]

THE FOUNDATION OF A STATE'S sovereignty is its monopoly on the use of force internally to control the population and externally to maintain borders. That control depends on the power of a governing elite, a power it could not acquire without dispossession, and punishment is what allows dispossession to exist, with the wealth of the few built on the labor of the many. And that wealth, in turn, feeds the power to use force.

While some who do the work of wealth-making lead reasonably comfortable lives, those who do the hardest and arguably the most productive and important work lead lives of struggle and suffering. This was true of the enslaved, and it is still true. Without the use of force and punishment, it is hard to imagine how the seriously dispossessed, leading lives of deprivation, loss, and exhaustion, could be kept from revolting. Davidsons and Radfords, from Jamestown to Kentucky, were directly involved in the US history of state-making, in the inequality that entailed, and in the capitalism that both depended on and enabled it. Capitalism depends on acquiring labor and resources through dispossession—through the literal taking of people and land to prime the pump of capitalist accumulation. Rosa Luxemburg said long ago that capitalism always requires something from outside capitalism.[24] That "something extra from outside" sets off the chain of accumulation. You will see it frequently in these tales. It involves using people and land or other resources that have not come by way of capitalist social relations. This use is not legitimized by paying wages or by purchase; it is the stealing of people, coerced labor, the theft of land, conquest to gain control of critical resources. Acquiring them requires force, chicanery, or dispossession, or all three, and the whole process is enabled by a state that ideologically legitimizes such behavior, that when necessary employs military might, and that provides the necessary policing and punishing needed to maintain it. This is as true today as it was in the days of the slave trade and the colonial plundering of Native American lives and resources.

To talk about dispossession and punishment, about who has the power to punish whom, and how gaining exclusive right to determine punishing is the mark of a sovereign state, I use stories of the intertwining lives of my paternal ancestors, Davidsons and Radfords, with the peoples they encountered, owned, and fought, African and Native American, Scottish and English. All in these tales were caught up in the struggles to establish and maintain sovereignty over a wider and wider area and over more and more people, more and more of whom were dispossessed. That struggle, which eventually led to the formation of the United States, has left its mark on the country today and shapes continuing efforts to mark and legitimize sovereignty. In a world the Native people came to say had been "turned upside down" there was nothing inevitable about the outcome—either then or now.[25]

CHAPTER 1

Tales of a Mythical Ancestor, Punishment, and Diarchy

Back when I began envisioning this book, I assumed my cousin's family mythology was that elusive concept called "truth." We believed that our first Radford ancestor was named Benjamin, one of the early settlers at Jamestown. And "early" we all took to mean within the first few shiploads. My cousin, visiting Jamestown with her children and husband, swears she saw the name Radford engraved on a monument. But when I began genealogical research as well as research on early Jamestown, I found no Radford. Eventually my husband and I went to Jamestown. We had a lovely vacation, and I learned a lot about Jamestown and life there for the English—though much less for the Powhatan—but found no Radford on a monument or anywhere else. It wasn't until several years later that I ran across what might be the source of the mythology of Benjamin Radford, in an old book on the history of Christian County, Kentucky, where the Radfords who were part of my family eventually moved. There, in black and white, it refers to Benjamin Radford, "one of the first Jamestown settlers in 1607."[1] And yet, according to the records of Jamestown, no such person existed. Further, if he did exist, there is no link between him and John Radford, who really did arrive in 1652, and thus is very unlikely to have been the son of a supposed Benjamin of 1607. Family history, I think, has gotten garbled and created a more glorious past for itself than reality warrants.

So, a dilemma. I had become hooked on the research I had begun on sovereignty, state formation, and punishment as they related both to the Powhatan and the English at Jamestown, and to the role of religious authority in both systems. What we now call the relationship between church and state seemed critical to both, and to the later Jacobite rebellion that propelled Alexander Davidson to the colonies. But still, I had no Radford available to ground this discussion. My solution: let us suppose, for the sake of this chapter, that family mythology is right. Some Radford arrived in Jamestown between 1607 and 1620. We'll call him X Radford, not Benjamin, since it is another century and a half before the name shows up in family records. After all, there were unnamed people—John Smith's account refers to "divers others" after naming the more important people—who came with that first expedition and on later ships.[2] So we will pretend there was an X, just so I can write about the Powhatan and early Jamestown.

When X would have arrived, the struggle over control of the use of force, and with it the ability to enforce the right to punish, was in crisis for both Powhatan and English. We'll pick up the story later, with the John Radford of 1652, who is documented—although there is some doubt about whether the genealogical links are all correctly in place to make my cousin and me his many-generations-later granddaughters. And then again, there is the "so what?" If those Radfords weren't our ancestors, they certainly were somebody's, and the weaving of the tale of punishment in state formation can be carried by someone else's ancestors just as well as by my own. The "truth" in this tale is obviously already having a hard time.

And there is another area where truth is going to have a hard time. I want to talk about what was going on with the Powhatan at the time X Radford would have shown up on the Chesapeake Bay. But all we have to go on is what anthropologists, archaeologists, and historians have pieced together. Their work has had to depend largely on what people like John Smith, or what someone like X himself, said about the Powhatan. We have the perceptions of those English who kept records, wrote reports or letters, or wrote books for public consumption—much of it propaganda—about Virginia, Jamestown, and the Powhatan. What the Powhatan had to say about their lives, their social structure, and about the English, is recorded only as interpreted through English eyes, obviously not the most reliable source. Archaeologists, anthropologists, and historians today strive to interpret the documents and the clues left buried in the ground, crosschecking back and forth.[3] Do clues from one discipline support or contradict theories developed in another? How can we use those clues to interpret what might have been going on when, for example, Pocahontas threw her body over John Smith, assuming his account is true? From here on, I will use what we do seem to know about the Powhatan, but bear in mind there are inevitably varying interpretations and disagreements among the experts. So what I am going to do in this chapter is interpret all these interpretations to tell a story of states, almost states, punishment, and two peoples at the time when X Radford—himself an interpretation—might have dragged his exhausted, and perhaps hopeful, perhaps horrified, body through the surf and stood on shaky legs on Powhatan territory.

THE POWHATAN ALREADY HAD extensive knowledge of European people in the early 1600s when X Radford would have arrived. Spaniards had been coming and going for nearly a century, trading, looking for gold, hiding out in secluded bays to avoid English pirates, being shipwrecked and taken in by various Powhatan towns, presumably mixing themselves into the gene pool, preaching Catholicism, and occasionally killing and getting killed. Several high-ranking Powhatan had gone to Spain and brought their knowledge back with them. A bit later the English were also roving around the edges of Powhatan society, although, being mostly Protestants, they weren't preaching Catholicism. Unlike the Spaniards, they began trying to establish forts that would act as trading centers and would support the English pirates who were after the gold carried by Spanish ships—the

Spaniards, being at that time far more powerful than the English, had already grabbed the most lucrative lands for extracting gold and silver from local people in Central and South America. [4] The Powhatan would have observed the English at Roanoke twenty-five years before X arrived, and surely found the observations instructive for the analysis of English norms and hierarchy. Even closer observation would have been possible if, as one theory has it, those English who disappeared when they abandoned the colony threw in their lot with one of the northern Chesapeake chiefdoms. [5] Joining a native polity was certainly a choice a lot of people at Jamestown made, much to the disgust of those in charge!

So, when X and the rest would have shown up, Wahunsonacock, the king, paramount chief, ruler, emperor—the English word to translate *mamanatowick* depends a lot on how you understand Powhatan social structure—would have had a pretty good idea of how to use them in his ongoing conquest of independent chiefdoms on the Chesapeake. The polity over which he presided, Tsenacommacoh, was now much larger than it had been when he inherited it. Each conquered chiefdom became a unit within the larger polity; its former chief, or *werowance*, became a subchief under the *mamanatowick*. What the conquered people thought of this we can only guess, but there is at least a little evidence of revolt, and Wahunsonacock did have much less control in the newly conquered outlying territories than at the core of Tsenacommacoh. He demanded tribute from conquered areas, largely of luxury goods like pearls and copper, the items that represented wealth and power, and used it to position himself at the center of the regional trade among polities to the north and west of Tsenacommacoh.

He planned to position the English in this network, apparently as a tributary entity, like the conquered chiefdoms. The English had brought a lot of copper with them—kettles, chains, and medallions, for instance. [6] And Wahunsonacock had real leverage over the English—they couldn't feed themselves and were utterly dependent on Powhatan women, the farmers, for their survival. X Radford and the rest sent to labor at Jamestown pretty effectively refused to grow food, and looked for gold instead. This move gained them the opprobrium of the powers that be—the authorities at Jamestown and the investors in the Virginia Company—who described them as lazy, the "very scumme of the Land."[7] It took the institution of martial law and spectacular punishing to get them working at all. We'll get to why X and others would have behaved so apparently stupidly, but for now, my focus is on the fact that the English remained dependent on trading for corn, and used a lot of copper to make those transactions. Which of course played directly into Wahunsonacock's hands; he controlled this massive influx of copper.

But he didn't control it alone. He was not the sole ruler, sovereign in his own right. In most instances he couldn't exercise the authority required to punish on his own. He was dependent on the religious authority provided by his partner in sovereignty, the priest, or *quiyoughcosough*. What the Powhatan had, and what the English and the rest of Europe had until not too long before X Radford left it, is a form of governance called diarchy, or dual sovereignty.

Diarchy has been a widespread, highly complex and sophisticated form of governance, in which sovereignty is carried out through the convergence of spiritual authority and worldly power.[8] Diarchy means joint rule, usually by a priest and a king, who are complementary (but inherently unequal) representatives of religious authority and secular power. One legitimizes action, the other acts. The priest (for instance, the pope for the English until 1534 when Henry VIII made himself head of the church, or the priest for the Powhatan) speaks for the gods and legitimizes the king's exercise of power. The king or queen carries out the will of the gods as expressed by the priest; his or her actions are defined as legitimate because they carry meaning within a religious context. When people have to hand over crops, or money, or wealth items to elites— lords, aristocrats, kings—they need a good solid reason for believing that they are doing the right thing, especially if they have to work extremely hard or half-starve themselves and their children in order to give enough. While this degree of exploitation wasn't the case for the Powhatan, if Wahunsonacock had his way that might have changed.

Religious ideas about the will of the gods can go a long way toward convincing people. And if they object, or if they steal or otherwise mess with the orderly regulation of wealth and behavior, there is the threat of punishment, well advertised in spectacular public displays of maimings or deaths. It becomes quite obvious that you should think twice before taking the risk of similar treatment. However, making such punishment acceptable to those punished and to their families and communities, so that they submit to this treatment without revolt, is not easy. And here again, the king—the secular power—is dependent on the priest as the spiritual legitimizer. If the king as punisher is merely the tool to interpret and carry out the will of the gods, then he *has* to punish or he himself will be upsetting the gods, and all will suffer. So, the punishing becomes sacred—a sacrifice for the gods to keep them benevolent—disobedience to the king is sacrilege, a sin, and the whole social hierarchy, with its extraction of wealth for the few from the work of the many, gains a sacred aura, ordained by the gods.

Now, to make this all work, ordinary people can't know much about the spiritual forces. Otherwise, they wouldn't need priests to tell them what offends the gods and what might regain their protection. In societies that are not so unequal, where there is no wealthy elite, where everyone has the right to use the resources they need—as probably the chiefdoms included in Tsenacommacoh had been several generations earlier—religious knowledge is pretty widely available to all. Nobody needs special priests, and thus there is no way of holding the will of the gods over people's heads. But as a society consolidates power in fewer hands, knowledge of the spiritual forces becomes secret, passed on and accessible only to specially trained and appointed religious authorities. In both diarchic England and diarchic Tsenacommacoh the religious authorities made a lot of the decisions about who had transgressed against the gods and the social order, and thus about who needed to be punished. But the priest can't punish alone, any more than the king can; the priest can't actually force people to submit to punishment. It is the king who has guards and armies—people to carry out violence. So the priest, though superior to the king, is nevertheless dependent on the king for material support—food, shelter, temple maintenance, and protection—and because the priest has no coercive power and cannot carry out the wishes of the gods without the king. Neither can function without the other. Without the priest, however, the king has no right to exist: the king's legitimacy and ability to rule come from the priest.[9]

For both the English and the Powhatan, the sacred was the source of all authority.[10] The Church for the English, the shaman for the Powhatan, spoke for that authority. In England, as in other Christian-ruled countries, it had, until the Reformation, taken the Pope or his representative to perform the ceremony that made a king a king. Consecration made him king "by the grace of God," no longer merely a natural human, and invested him with the power to act.[11] Thus for centuries in England, as in other countries ruled by Christians, sovereignty was a two-part enterprise, with the king exercising power, but only by the authority granted him by God by way of the Church.[12]

For aristocrats, both English in the centuries preceding Jamestown and Powhatan shortly before Jamestown, diarchy had been a useful tool, lending spiritual authority to their accumulation of wealth through tribute in money or valuables and through requiring labor or produce from ordinary people who had nothing to give but their labor or the fruits of that labor. The hierarchy that determined who gave to whom, and everyone's position in it, was set by birth; it was God-given and natural. The spiritual authority in dual sovereignty does not necessarily have to provide justification for the extraction of wealth by an elite. However, if state formation is underway, the structure of dual sovereignty is easily amenable to that role. Threats to the legitimacy of the developing state and to elite extraction of wealth can be defined as sin, an offense to the gods and a threat to the well-being of the people. The king is then *obliged* to take action. The secular power carries out the punishment of sin, backed by the legitimizing spiritual authority, so that challenges to elite rule are less likely. Both the developing Powhatan empire and the English feudal state were based on such ideas.

However, as the kings in Europe in the centuries leading up to Jamestown generally began trying to get more of the wealth produced by ordinary people, this system became an annoyance. Although the backing of the Church was critical to the king's legitimacy in exercising what force he could, there was a downside for kings and lords. Lower-level elites and the Church could keep too much of the wealth, so less got passed up the hierarchy to the king. In a diarchic structure, economic and political elites don't have full control even if they do own the means of production; religious elites carry considerable influence and are in a position to manipulate the ideology that supports the power of kings and lords, potentially a threat to elite control. The king must, like Wahunsonacock, rule within the bounds of tradition and live up to the expectations of the priesthood and nobility for religiously defined correct kingly behavior—he is, to some extent, held in check by their interpretation of what a godly king should do.

In the old English feudal structures, control was exercised locally; punishing power was in the hands of local lords, authorized by the local church. The state in this system was a weak one, without a full monopoly on the use of force, and the religious institution was particularly strong, as least in comparison with modern states.[13] Since successful exploitation depends on the ability to punish, the power to punish would have to move into the hands of the king if the king were to exploit directly, rather than through regional lords. To take more for himself, a king needed to curtail the power of the local lords.[14] So when a king wanted to strengthen his position, a very likely consequence was an ongoing struggle among king, lords, and church over who has the right to punish, along with an interconnected struggle between strong church and weak state, between pope and king.[15]

In England, the feudal system of control broke down as the Crown began to break the power of the local lords, but when, as a result, lords could no longer enforce punishment, the king had a law and order issue.[16] The king did not have a secure grip on the use of violence and therefore couldn't punish effectively enough to keep public order, and was as dependent on honor, magnificent display, and the pageantry of office as on force to maintain his position—as was Wahunsonacock.[17] Both had a plurality, not a monopoly, on punishment and on the use of force it entails, although punishing power in England was consolidated further up the hierarchy than it had been in the Powhatan polity before Wahunsonacock's manipulations of the system.[18]

WHEN THE ENGLISH FIRST ENCOUNTERED Wahunsonacock and his entourage, they described him as imperial, ruling over a large number of subordinate polities, with all the splendor and power they associated with kingly behavior. He was a man of regal bearing surrounded by a deeply respectful populace who regarded him with "great fear and adoration," a man of a "Majestie . . . which oftentimes strkyes awe and sufficient wonder in our [English] people."[19] There is no doubt that they saw him as royal in the same sense that they saw their own King James. Had they arrived maybe a hundred years earlier, things would have been different. They would have found instead of Tsenacommacoh a number of small independent chiefdoms, each with its own diarchic structure. Each would have its own werowance and priest exercising joint sovereignty, together making decisions about punishment and war, and collecting tribute. A lot of that tribute would have returned to the commoners who produced it, in exchange for labor, and as feasts and as gifts associated with assembling a fighting force when needed. Other gifts would have been acquired through trade; the werowance would in turn give them to high-ranking people, thus helping to ensure their loyalty.

However, sometime before Wahunsonacock, this structure had begun to change—there are a lot of arguments among scholars as to why, but it does appear that trade with Europeans or the presence of a few colonies did not initiate the change.[20] However, once started, the consolidation of small chiefdoms into larger polities may have accelerated through a kind of ripple effect related to the European presence. Those polities that had to deal most directly with Europeans may have consolidated in defense; or perhaps consolidation occurred because gaining control of trade with Europeans gave one polity the clout to conquer the neighbors. For thousands of years, control of trade had enabled some polities to gain dominance over others. Their power had waxed and waned over the course of history, just as happened in Europe, Asia, Africa, and South America. The arrival of Europeans was at first just another source of potential trade and power. But as one polity became stronger, others may have also consolidated power, a kind of Cold War effect: if you have dangerous neighbors gaining strength, you may try to keep up. Another theory about the Powhatan consolidation is that epidemics of European diseases preceded the actual arrival of the English in the Chesapeake, and that with such a diminished population, a werowance needed to control more people to gather enough tribute. However, there is no actual evidence either way about whether epidemics had hit the Chesapeake chiefdoms.[21]

For whatever reason, by the time Wahunsonacock inherited his position, he reigned over at least six chiefdoms, not just one. From that base, he went on, through conquest, negotiation, and intimidation to control almost the entire Chesapeake Bay region, thirty-some chiefdoms. He became the imperial figure who so impressed English people like X, laborers and gentlemen alike. Tsenacommacoh was on the verge of state formation, one of the most complex polities on the East Coast of North America at that time, perhaps in all of what is now the United States.[22] Getting to that point, however, meant some real changes in social structure and with them the growth of the solidified class structure that characterizes states.[23]

INEQUALITY WAS SOLIDIFYING INTO inherited class in Tsenacommacoh by the time X arrived. There were clear distinctions between chiefly families, the respected and wealthy families of the "better sort" as the English put it, commoners, and "the poor."[24] These distinctions existed even though all free members of the polity had rights to use land for farming as portioned out by the local werowance, and all could hunt in the territory claimed by the polity. There were also servants, although little is said about who they were, and there were slaves who were war captives. Local werowances, who once had shared sovereignty only with their priests, now were no longer independent; they and their priests were inserted into the new, larger hierarchy somewhere below the top. Perhaps there was a certain amount of resentment at the loss of sovereignty. Again, we don't really know.

Within this system Wahunsonacock as *mamanatowick* was the paramount secular authority. He didn't yet have a true monopoly on the use of force, although in the early 1600s he was making progress on this front. The first step in the process was to get punishing into the hands of the local elite families and out of the hands of clan leaders and individuals. He was shifting punishment, particularly for murder and stealing, to local werowances who were answerable to him, who owed him tribute and ideally obedience. In some cases, it appears that he actually bypassed the local werowance and priest to take charge of punishing himself. Acting as judge is a very concrete demonstration of authority.[25]

Before the English arrived, Wahunsonacock had gained a "plurality," rather than a monopoly, on the use of force. While absolute in the sense that what he ordered did happen, including punishment, subchiefs also had the ability to punish on their own authority, although they could not override Powhatan. Local werowances could still punish on the authority of their priests, and clan leaders and even individuals could take revenge for personal affronts.[26] Nevertheless, by coming closer to confining punishment to elites he could control, Wahunsonacock clustered punishers higher up the hierarchy, closer to himself. People were losing local control of punishment. This was a dramatic extension of power over local people, a move toward the monopoly on force that is part of state-making.

But whenever power to punish is being concentrated, there must be beliefs to legitimize it, beliefs that make people's behavior, good or bad, a matter of concern, not just to their neighbors and kin, the people directly affected by it, but to a larger polity. Additionally, punishment needs to be defined as the correct response to transgression. Antisocial behavior in non-state societies gets dealt with by peer pressure, by manipulation on the part of local elders and leaders to bring about a change in an individual's behavior, or maybe even by a locally-sanctioned killing. The goal is not punishment, but the restoration of community balance. To centralize the power to punish, that goal has to change. Certain behaviors must be redefined as a transgression worthy of punishment—retribution becomes the goal, not just the restoration of community balance. The behavior of individuals has to be made to carry meaning beyond the local group, so that transgressions can no longer be dealt with locally. An individual's behavior becomes relevant to a much larger entity ruled by those gaining power within the developing state, who may feel their ability to extract wealth is threatened by certain behaviors that they therefore define as transgressions.

The Powhatan legitimized this move by a very common shift, gradually establishing an elite-controlled religion. Earlier beliefs could then be extended to claim that certain behaviors were so offensive to the gods that their protection could be withdrawn, not just from the offending individual or local group, but from the entire polity. Thus the authority for this transition came from a higher source, from the gods. Expanding the earlier diarchic structure, so that transgression came under its purview—not under the purview of clan or neighbors, with issues of revenge and honor to be handled, not by those who were injured, but by authorities representative of the polity-wide hierarchy—helped to accomplish this goal. Whether such a shift means that actual perpetrators are more or less likely to be the ones picked for punishment is an open question, but it is clear that the decision is now made by people further up the hierarchy. Priests can identify the behavior relating to the entire polity that will offend the spiritual forces. Punishment becomes a religiously mandated sacrifice, performed for the benefit of the entire polity, to be handled by the spiritual and secular power of the polity itself. A king or a paramount chief in this system is merely the tool to interpret and carry out the will of the gods, and his power comes directly from the religious authorities. The king's exercise of power thus takes on a sacred aspect, and disobedience takes on the aura of "sacrilegious transgression"; there is a corresponding "sacralization" of the social order itself. [27]

Transgressive behavior becomes more a sin than a crime, an offense to the gods, not to the state, and such sins are seen as indeed threatening the entire polity, not just the local group, through displeasing the gods or upsetting the balance of spiritual forces. Mixed in and disguised by the mantle of sin is behavior that is actually threatening to the elite ability to extract wealth. Refusing to give tribute, for instance, becomes an offense against the gods, as does a king's refusal to redistribute some (usually relatively small) portion of that wealth in rituals that promote the well-being of society.[28] Beliefs about sin, figuratively speaking, provide a smoke screen.

The belief that Powhatan gods spoke directly only to priests, and the priests spoke only to werowances and influential men, strengthened the process of consolidation. Priests, as in other diarchies, were the most powerful individuals in the Powhatan empire. This despite the fact that Wahunsonacock was seen as half god. It was the priests, not the king, who would know, by way of the gods, if you committed a wrong, and would single you out for sacrifice. Priests thus played a role in directing the use of force internally as punishment. Additionally, personal disobedience to Wahunsonacock or to subchiefs was punishable with a beating or clubbing to death on a sacrificial stone.[29] That stealing became punishable by death administered by the werowance perhaps reflects the importance that personal wealth played in Powhatan society. Stealing was much more than merely taking someone else's stuff. Taking someone's corn, beads, or copper was seen as a threat to the entire social hierarchy, since it shifted wealth, thereby potentially shifting status. Thus it was as reprehensible as murder, which, by shifting people, likewise threatened the social hierarchy. As the Powhatan social structure became more stratified, both theft and murder could no longer be a matter for individuals to deal with. It was perhaps for this reason that punishing those transgressions became a chiefly function. As if all this was not adequate, the disobedient could look forward to a tormented afterlife, at least according to some accounts.[30]

As Wahunsonacock gained greater control of punishing, he made himself more and more central to people's lives. The *mamanatowick* was beginning to matter even more than the local werowance, who now had to look further up the hierarchy. At the same time, Wahunsonacock began shifting the focus of the aggression men were trained from babyhood to exhibit in defense of their honor. Men now vied with one another for reputations as great hunters, able to give the gifts of skins that satisfied the increasing demand for tribute.[31] Warfare was another important component of this shift. War in service of the expanding Powhatan empire became the focus of aggression and a source of great prestige. Distinguishing yourself on the battlefield, like being a great hunter, began to replace feuding as the proper way to prove your honor and manhood—aggression was to be expressed externally in war. Internally within the polity, aggression was to be expressed only in competition that served to enrich Wahunsonacock and enable him to exert greater power. Men's definitions of honor began to mean loyalty to the Powhatan polity and thus to Wahunsonacock.[32] Wahunsonacock, in other words, was moving toward a monopoly on the use of force within Tsenacommacoh.

THESE INTERNAL DEVELOPMENTS, realigning aggression and loyalty, were intertwined with war and conquest. Externally Wahunsonacock was also increasing his ability to use force. His conquest of surrounding polities depended on mobilizing large armies, and that in turn depended on collecting tribute, particularly of wealth items. Charles Tilly, in his analysis of European states, emphasizes the importance of war in making state formation possible; Wahunsonacock's strategy serves as an illustration of this principle.[33] How important punishing was in mobilizing his armies is not clear.[34] But as his empire expanded, so did his access to tribute, thus giving him the wherewithal to recruit larger armies, thus allowing him to expand further or tighten control. A vicious or a benevolent circle, depending on your point of view.

In the early 1600s Wahunsonacock's control over this empire was not complete, and its boundaries were not fixed. It was tightest in the core areas that he ruled by bloodright. There absolute obedience could be directly enforced with swift violence—whole communities were sometimes wiped out. The punishing consequences of disobedience must have been obvious to their neighbors. This degree of control was much harder to accomplish in the periphery where he ruled only through conquest and control of trade.[35] In conquest as in internal affairs, Wahunsonacock had to act within Powhatan customary law. He was dependent on the legitimizing approval of his priests, his primary councilors, for the use of force externally as well as internally. Priests had the final say in a declaration of war.[36]

There was an additional religious dimension to war. Diarchy in a wide range of societies regularly obliges a king to provide sacrificial victims to ensure the life, the general well-being, of the community. Sacrificial punishment was of significant religious benefit to the polity, protecting it and bringing the approval of the gods. War captives supplemented sinners as sacrificial victims. Thus the king's exercise of the use of force, both externally in conquest and internally in punishing, was justified religiously as sacrifice needed to keep the favor of the gods for the benefit of all. Not coincidentally, sacrifice strengthened the position of an extractive elite. For the Powhatan, providing sacrifices, whether war captives or transgressors, was the most important thing a king did for the general welfare.[37] Sacrificial deaths benefited the polity spiritually, and as anthropologist Margaret Williamson points out, the elimination of transgressors and enemy captives enabled the elimination of threats to the order the king was expected to provide.

With the religious legitimacy for war comes an added benefit—the king or paramount chief can claim legitimacy for protecting people from dangerous enemies. Wahunsonacock, well before Jamestown, appears to have embarked in this direction, using war with enemies to create dangerous Others, and thus people's need for protection. He could then use the resulting need for war as legitimation for collecting tribute from these Others, some of which he passed on to the subchiefs who fought for him.[38] It was that tribute, recycled, and his monopoly on the copper trade, that enabled him to extend his conquests—all legitimized by the production of human sacrifices, spectacularly punished enemies.

Building the Powhatan empire must have led to changing relationships among priests. Each chief, some of whom were women, was associated with particular priests, and as a chief was conquered and subordinated, his or her priests would probably have been subordinated in some sense to Wahunsonacock's priests. The structure of diarchy as it affected daily lives may have changed correspondingly, so that the local representatives of the sacred lost their power as final authority.[39] Local people's loyalty would then shift more effectively toward Wahunsonacock and his priests, particularly as they became the ultimate punishing authorities.

FOR MANY OF THOSE AT JAMESTOWN, having experienced the chaos in England resulting from the gradual development of capitalism and the disputes between church and state, and now confronted with more chaotic conditions, Powhatan communities must have been tempting. Many, in the early years in Jamestown, wrote home about Powhatan social structure with its order, hierarchy, obedience, and reverence for their king, which seemed to exemplify all that they felt their own society in England and in Virginia had recently lost.[40] Maybe X was one of those who ran away to join the Powhatan.

So, looking at the English—weak, disorganized, dying at an enormous rate, and loaded with copper—Wahunsonacock and his priests must have seen a marvelous opportunity and taken action accordingly. John Smith would have seemed to the Powhatan to be the secular power, the active partner in a diarchy. Captain Christopher Newport, the highest authority in Jamestown, like the Powhatan priests, did not travel much, and appeared to be the spiritual authority, judging and legitimizing John Smith's activities outside the fort. Smith was captured and put through a ritual that may well have been intended to make him into the werowance of a territory that was offered for the use of the English. Located near Wahunsonacock's principal town, it could be easily subjected to surveillance.[41]

Pocahontas's legendary move to save Smith from actual execution by throwing her body over his was instead probably part of this process, a symbolic death and rebirth as kin in her lineage. Powhatan social structure was matrilineal, so women would have been necessary in placing him within that structure. Pocahontas, a youngster at the time, would have been acting as a representative of her matrilineage— perhaps obeying the older women in it, working in concert with her father, Wahunsonacock. He couldn't induct Smith into his own matrilineage, but Pocahontas could bring him into her mother's. He could then be treated as the English werowance. Wahunsonacock sometimes removed the werowance of a conquered chiefdom and installed a new one with ties to himself. Smith's position would have been similar.[42] Smith, as English werowance, would be expected to submit to Powhatan expectations, copper would flow to Wahunsonacock, and the English would quit misbehaving, cease killing and stealing, and conduct proper exchanges of gifts according to status.

The English, knowing little of Powhatan norms and social structure, and with a very different understanding of governing and kinship, didn't get it. Furthermore, they believed they were in charge, despite the respect they had for Powhatan elites. Wahunsonacock, according to their orders from England, was to swear allegiance to the English Crown and acknowledge that his right to rule came to him from James I of England. Ultimately, an even weightier problem was that the English were there simply to make a profit for the English investors. They somehow had to extract wealth from the Powhatan and other Native polities to transfer to England.

AND THAT THE ENGLISH NEEDED to make a profit was why X Radford would have been standing on sea-weary shaky legs on Powhatan territory, fresh off the boat. Growing tobacco on the Chesapeake was like growing money: it served as currency in Virginia. And as an export crop to sell to England, it was proving to be far more profitable than hunting for gold or trading with the Powhatan. But to grow much tobacco, landholders needed more than their own labor, and there was a severe shortage of labor in the colony. Thus, the importation of indentured servants, followed by a very few Africans. Perhaps X was hopeful, perhaps horrified, about what might lie ahead, but even more likely he was emotionally exhausted, simply putting one foot in front of the other in a numb acceptance of fate. If he was typical, he had most likely already been traumatized by life in England. So we need to take a look at the life he left behind.

The "quickening pace of commercial and agrarian capitalism" in England meant that X Radford would have lived in a society undergoing dispossession—landholders absorbing into large-scale agricultural holdings the commons and waste land once used for foraging and pasturing by tenants and villagers.[43] This process, known as the enclosure movement, resulted in massive unemployment as the land people had depended on was fenced in by private landowners bent on profit. The poverty that typically accompanies the dispossession that capitalism engenders was rampant. Those who did manage to stay on the land as tenants had little left after landowners took their bite. Consequently, "the ranks of the poor steadily swelled." [44] Capitalism, though causing dispossession, was insufficiently developed to absorb all the dispossessed as wage labor—those who, like our invented X Radford, were suffering the direct or indirect effects of the enclosure movement. Cities did offer some opportunity for employment, but not nearly enough for all who needed it. People apprenticed their children and indentured themselves to work for years in return for nothing but food and a place to sleep, and sometimes the training that might allow them, with luck, to set up eventually in a skilled craft.

Hunger and illness took an enormous toll. For those at the bottom of the social hierarchy, the consequences were devastating. Many resorted to petty theft in an attempt to keep body and soul together, to feed their children, simply to survive. Women had the additional option of prostitution, and many took it. Others wandered, hoping for work, and sometimes getting a little, as they went from town to town. But, cutting off virtually the last option, the Poor Laws of the 1500s made wandering without visible support illegal. It was called vagrancy, and, like theft, meant you risked joining those in the already overflowing prisons. Some chose "voluntary" exile instead. Poverty made risking Virginia, selling yourself for (usually) seven years, look like a reasonable choice. [45] Few chose to go because they were ambitious and hopeful; they went in hope of staying alive—an ironic hope, given the extraordinary death rate in Jamestown. By 1624, all but 1,200 of the 6,700 colonists sent to Virginia were dead. [46] Perhaps they would have chosen differently had they been better informed, but staying in England was hardly a healthy option either. Yet even the likelihood of starvation in England did not produce enough willing volunteers to satisfy Virginia planters' desire for labor; death in Virginia was too likely. [47]

Meanwhile, as more and more people were driven into poverty, the charity burden on parish coffers became heavier and heavier. English politicians, some of the Virginia Company investors, and some of the Jamestown gentry, began to suggest that they could relieve England's problems—rising crime, vagrancy, prostitution—by sending the glut of the dispossessed, the poor, and the unemployed to the colonies. Hence, involuntary workers joined the so-called voluntary transfer of England's dispossessed to the colonies.[48] The gentry who supported this proposal insisted the dispossessed would work off their punishment and become useful, docile, and eventually free and productive members of an orderly society. Not everyone was in favor of this solution. Some Jamestown leaders protested that more "scum" was not what they needed—they had enough trouble controlling the ones they already had. To be sure, in the early days they had at least as much trouble controlling the "swaggering great" as the laborers; all pretty much refused to work for the good of the Virginia Company investors in England.[49] But in any case, the proposal took hold.

Force would be needed, given that not enough people were "volunteering" to go. So laws and policies were established to provide it, including the criminalization of vagrancy, the punishment of Scots and Irish "traitors," and the elevation of petty crimes to hanging offenses— eventually there were 300 crimes carrying a death penalty. Since the king had no authority to sentence people to transportation, it was offered as a "merciful" option. The poor were swept up on vagrancy charges; prisons were emptied of able-bodied inmates. The poor thus joined the criminal—although as historian Peter Linebaugh makes clear, that was often a meaningless distinction since it was impossible for so many to survive legally.[50] The entire way of life of the dispossessed—the poor, the jobless, the homeless— had been made illegal.

Killing two birds with one stone, England both unloaded its increasingly restive poor and provided Jamestown planters with dispossessed laborers—assuming they didn't die.[51] Children were among the first to go under this system. Orphans were indentured, transferred from overcrowded orphanages and poorhouses to ships' captains who sold their indentures in the colonies, a whole shipload in 1619, and some 1,400 to 1,500 in 1627 alone. It is very unlikely that X Radford would have been one of them—only 12 of the first 300 children lived more than three years, and if I consider my cousin's family mythology true for the sake of this chapter, then he obviously lived long enough to reproduce.[52]

More likely, his master brought him as a servant; even more likely, he was one of the poor on an investor's estate, sent as a Virginia Company laborer, with or without his consent. Or he might have been accused of vagrancy or theft. Or he might have been kidnapped. Once the headright system was established in 1618, bringing indentured servants to the colonies became a source of wealth. "Headright" meant that whoever paid the shipping fee for a servant could claim 50 acres from the Virginia Company and, after 1624, from the Crown. Kidnapping quickly became profitable, and joined the legalized methods of providing more workers.

Even if X were one of those who went voluntarily, the choice to go would have reflected his assessment of the conditions under which he was living. For younger sons of the middling gentry, the decision was often based on a lack of financial opportunities: primogeniture laws meant that eldest sons inherited their father's entire estate, leaving younger sons to fend for themselves. For them the propaganda about Virginia and the wealth to be found there might well have been attractive. (Few women made that choice, and in the beginning few women were sent involuntarily.) Absconding to Virginia was also a way for embroiled younger gentry to escape debt or avoid the clutches of the law. But if X had been one of these, he would have been listed on one of the ship rosters of those early years, and far less likely to be among the many nameless and voiceless in the annals of Jamestown history.

CONDITIONS IN JAMESTOWN WOULD certainly not have relieved X Radford.[53] I am going to make an assumption here about X and the others who so infuriated Jamestown leaders and investors by their refusal to work. Their refusal was so intense that had not John Smith and his successors instituted martial law and adopted the spectacular punishments for minor infractions that were already common in England (and among the Powhatan), the colony might have disappeared. My assumption is that these refusers were not stupid or irrational people, nor particularly greedy or lazy, or as unaccustomed to hard work as they are often described. After all, even soft-handed gentry are quite capable of changing their ways and developing cal-luses if that is obviously the only way to stay alive. Most accounts of Jamestown are written with an underlying assumption that the right thing (for the English at the time) was to make a success of Jamestown—that such success would best serve the interests of English people sent to work in the colony. With this assumption, their refusal to work appears misguided at best, and the leaders appear to have been right, even heroic, in their draconian efforts to force people to work to save themselves. I tend to be suspicious of accounts that assume that leaders who kill, jail, and maim are acting for the good of "the people" rather than for the good of an elite who thereby gain a relatively docile population who permit the orderly extraction of wealth from their labor. And I tend also to be suspicious of accounts that portray those from whom wealth is being extracted as irrational when they don't cooperate.

As I have shown, forcing people into docility requires control of punishment, which requires a monopoly on the use of force. Ultimately, it requires the punishing institutions that only a state has the power to provide. The English at Jamestown were backed by a state, but it was a relatively weak one, and it certainly was a distant one. The assump-tion that leaders designated by elites would know what was best for the good of all disappeared. Indeed, the whole hierarchy of duty to one's superiors fell apart without the class and gender structures that had locked people into obedience in England. To me it seems obvi-ous that, without the accustomed channels to obedience, leaders in Virginia would have looked quite different to many of the laborers and even to some of the gentry. And since access to land was denied in the colony, the incentive of hope for a better future was cut off. I don't think it would have been at all evident to X and many others that their best interests lay with a successful Jamestown colony and happy investors in England. Especially when they saw what looked to them like paradise—orderly Powhatan fields and villages, and people who apparently loved and honored their leaders, leaders who returned that honor with unparalleled (in English experience) generosity. That the Powhatan were moving toward the centralized control of punishing that characterizes a state would not have been immediately evident, or perhaps even recognized as relevant. Either Jamestown leaders had to reconstruct state power or fail in their duty to organize the production of wealth for the elites. And without the social structures that normally would legitimize state power, they had nothing to resort to but the raw use of force to punish, and punish they did—publicly, painfully, and lengthily. They also tried to harness the authority that had been created out of ritual and spirituality in England as religion, state, and stratification had developed hand in hand.[54] Attending church services twice daily was mandatory; once martial law was established in 1612 by the new acting governor, Sir Thomas Dale, missing church three times meant execution. As did blasphemy: in what was presumably seen as a fitting punishment, one man's tongue was run through by a red-hot poker, after which he was chained to a tree until he died.[55] The colony itself was said to be God's will, bringing Christianity to Native people and glory and wealth to England, God's favored nation.

That none of this was too convincing is clear. By 1612, forty to fifty men had deserted, about 10 percent of those still alive, off to marry and live with Powhatan people. Six others had attempted to reach the Spanish in Florida.[56] To keep a workforce it became necessary to make joining the Indians or trading with them another crime punishable by death, as was fornication. Considering the lack of English women in the colony, this must have referred to sex with Powhatan women, which was often manipulated to Powhatan advantage. English men could be lured into death traps or perhaps coaxed into an alliance through connection with women who were part of Wahunsonacock's entourage.[57] Many other infractions were likewise subject to the death penalty, often administered to elicit maximum fear among the spectators. Lesser infractions involved whipping or such inventive punishments as lying all night with your back arched and your heels tied together and drawn backwards toward your head.[58] That so many ran off to the Indians, and that it was deemed necessary to so intensely punish those English who, in various ways, consorted with Indians, is testament to the opinion of many at Jamestown: striving for a successful colony was not in their best interests.

Indeed, there was good reason, beyond the harsh punishments, to hold this opinion. Jamestown itself was an unhealthy, swampy site, with dirty water; death from malnutrition, combined with malaria and the intestinal "bloody flux," was rampant and gruesome.[59] In addition, leaders very quickly decided that conflict with the Powhatan was preferable to cooperation, raiding better than trading, especially when it turned out that the Chesapeake didn't have gold or other items of great value to the English. Trade, therefore, wasn't going to provide the wealth the Virginia Company investors required. But corn grown by Powhatan women was desperately needed, and it quickly became easiest to get it by raiding. So life in the colony was threatened not just by disease, but also by angry Powhatan, as well as by punishment from English leaders. And once tobacco became established as an immensely valuable, but also immensely labor-intensive, crop, laborers began to die of overwork and malnutrition, or even of being whipped to death. If you were one of the convicts shipped after 1619, your indenture, as directed by the Privy Council, was to constrain you to "such heavy and painful works as such servitude shall be a greater terror than death itself."[60] And life for non-convict indentured servants was scarcely better; indenture was a form of temporary slavery. You became a piece of property that could be sold or passed on to heirs.[61] But more of this in the next chapter.

For someone like X, indenture would have been a dismal prospect, with very little to weigh on the other side of the balance. Supposing the colony survived, what was in it for him? At the end of the contracted seven years of labor, you were to receive a share in the Virginia Company—that is, assuming you lived that long, which at first was highly unlikely. As was the prospect of actually receiving anything of value. When the first arrivals came to the end of their contracts, a share in the Virginia Company was worthless. Instead, small parcels of land were made available—company land, on which you could be a tenant. People Governor Dale favored were designated as "farmers," and had to give two and a half barrels of corn per acre and 30 days' service to the company each year, while "laborers" instead owed eleven months service per year.[62] This would have borne little resemblance to freedom for either group. Those who did not run away and finished their indenture but rejected the Company's continued control of them could (somehow) return to England—or join the Powhatan.

By 1616, keeping a labor force had become a real problem. It required some way of providing better options—a lure to keep people tied in, and again land proved to be the only viable (in the eyes of the elite) resource. Ending the indenture system, or even making it less oppressive, was apparently not on the table. Instead, the Company set aside land to be available for private ownership, with the payment of "quitrent," a kind of real estate tax. The headright system gave rights to land for however many head (of people) you brought to the colony. This meant that any of the free people who were already there could increase their holdings by 50 acres for each person whose way they paid—which in practice frequently meant buying an indentured servant from the ship's captain who had provided the servant's passage, and thus acquiring the headright. In addition, it was now possible to own a private plantation, or to form syndicates to own a plantation. Until 1624, when the Virginia Company was dissolved, the Company also reserved land for its own use, and brought over sharecropping tenants to work it.[63]

ONE MORE STEP WAS CRITICAl in controlling recalcitrant colonists, beyond providing the hope of land and the wealth that went with large-scale tobacco growing. I mentioned earlier that the gender relations that helped control men and kept them tied into the class hierarchy had fallen apart at Jamestown. This had to be mended. Originally Jamestown was to be a trading post, along the lines of those established by Europeans in Africa and Asia. It was not to be a colony in the sense of families making a life there. It was simply to be the point at which wealth would be extracted from the local inhabitants. The problem was that there was no wealth to extract, or at least nothing that the English recognized as wealth (the Powhatan, with their flourishing exchange of wealth items, must have found this an odd attitude!). The only way for the colony to provide its investors with wealth was by becoming an agricultural outpost. But that entailed settled people doing the labor themselves, rather than simply taking wealth from Indians.

Settling people, convincing them that the long-term investment of hard labor and of capital in making land productive for tobacco was worth it, required giving them private ownership of land, or at least the prospect of it. For such long-term commitment, simply turning loose a bunch of able-bodied young men wasn't going to work. Women were needed, who would produce children, and even more important, would "civilize" the men and persuade them that cooperation in the present, in the hope of a better future, was worth it.[64] Women, in other words, would restore the structures of patriarchy. And patriarchy is at least as much about controlling subordinate men as about controlling women. A man who is poor, who is dominated by other men, but who can go home to be king of his castle, where he rules and is served, is more likely to acquiesce to the orderly extraction of wealth and to the class structure that places him toward the bottom. The raw use of force in punishing can then ease off. In Virginia, in a sense, families would act as hostages, as a guarantee of men's good behavior. Obedience because you don't want to jeopardize your family's chances of rising in the social structure feels voluntary, quite different from obedience because of fear of a horrifying punishment. And that is especially true if you have the right to punish your family and servants. The feeling that you are in control at home can enhance your feelings of self-worth, which may well be battered outside the home.

So the Virginia Company decided to reconstruct the patriarchal social hierarchy that prevailed in England.[65] And Powhatan women definitely wouldn't do as wives in a patriarchal system. Powhatan women expected, and got, a significant degree of equality with men. Their voices, particularly as elders in their matrilineal clans, were heard and influenced political decisions. Inheritance of position went through the female line, giving women leverage in relation to brothers and uncles and fathers and husbands. Some women were werowances. "[I]n the Powhatan world," says historian Helen Rountree, "women... were considered intelligent, autonomous human beings just as the men were."[66] Definitely not good submissive wife material. Whether the Virginia Company officials considered making it legal to marry Powhatan women I don't know, but it certainly seems unlikely. Instead, in 1620 the Company began shipping boatloads of poor and desperate women to Jamestown to be sold, as indentured servants were, but as wives instead of servants—another form of unfree labor. The going rate was 120 pounds of tobacco, paid by the husband to the ship's captain, six times the cost of a male servant. This was so profitable that one company official set up a joint-stock company simply to sell women in the colony.[67]

Perhaps eventually X Radford might have seen land ownership as a real possibility. Perhaps he dreamed of buying a wife. At this point, perhaps he would have decided to throw in his lot with the colony. That certainly was the hope of the planters, who by now were deeply committed to tobacco and desperately needed a labor force if they were to grow rich off the land they had acquired through the headright system. If X didn't return to England, if X didn't join the Indians, if X worked hard as an indentured servant—in other words, if he bought into the system because he believed, however mistakenly, that he might someday be a planter, then he would be part of the docile labor force the Company, and the planters, required. As we shall see in the next chapter, this system, although temporarily successful, soon failed. Revolt was in the air, and it wasn't just English people who revolted. They were joined by the Africans who by that time were laboring in the tobacco fields with them, and undoubtedly by many of Powhatan ancestry who were also held in servitude.[68]

Perhaps at some point X did gain land. If he gained more than he could work himself, and since the point of getting more land is increased production, then he would need an exploitable labor force to reap the benefits of ownership. Perhaps he began importing indentured servants himself. Or perhaps he owned a grandparent of Venis, who, over a century later, would be held enslaved by Alexander Davidson I. If any of this happened, then X would have been developing a stake in the colony; he would be far more likely to "behave." He would have been sucked into supporting the budding state mechanisms that guaranteed his ownership of private property. The state's militia would defend his property rights against both Powhatan claimants and the English poor and landless dispossessed, against even his own indentured servants should they revolt. And his right to punish those servants was guaranteed by the state. At the first meeting of the Virginia House of Burgesses, masters were given the right to punish servants, with whipping and added years of servitude explicitly included.[69] Punishment is clearly on the agenda of a state in formation. However, the colony, even with the backing of the Crown and Parliament, did not have a monopoly on the use of force. Even X had the right to use force to control his servants, not just his wife and children. This was a long way from being a strong state.

AND THE POWHATAN WERE DETERMINED to keep the colony weak. There are arguments about what happened in 1622. Was it a genocidal massacre by the Powhatan against the English—a desperate failed attempt to remove from the land the rapacious invaders who by now were arriving in droves and clearly had no intention of anything but total control of more and more land, making life more and more difficult for the Powhatan? Or was it instead a blow against an upstart and recalcitrant subject population delivered by a people who saw themselves as dominant and sovereign? Were the English people who needed to be punished and taught to behave—as Wahunsonacock had occasionally done with other upstart polities? In any case, in 1622 close to a third of the English population was killed in a carefully orchestrated attack in which the Powhatan and their allies imitated English behavior and killed women and children as well as men—but unlike the English, they spared Africans.[70]

Opechancanough, a brother of the now aged Wahunsonacock, acting as the secular power, had apparently spent several years planning this move. Indians had up to this point been coming and going fairly freely in Jamestown and in outlying farms and plantations. Despite the laws, there was actually a great deal of illicit trading, largely corn for copper, iron tools, and guns.[71] And the English had apprenticed Powhatan children, claiming to be teaching them a trade, but generally treating them as indentured servants. This was a situation Powhatan parents soon recognized and vigorously resisted, but by this time, poverty was becoming an issue for some Powhatan people. They were being dispossessed—the English were stealing their corn or were preventing them from using their former clan land. Some became servants, working for the English.[72] Altogether, the Powhatan presence was pervasive. It was these people, along with an unusual number of Powhatan men, pretending to arrive for trading, who, on the morning of March 22, 1622, suddenly grabbed knives, hoes, their own hidden weapons, and attacked simultaneously many English settlements.[73]

The colony was a mere 1,200 English and 23 Africans several years after the attack. Nearly a third of the colony had been killed; it took 1,100 arrivals, given the generally high death rate, to bring the population back to its pre-attack level.[74] Although recovery and growth came relatively quickly as shiploads of people continued to arrive, the attack of 1622 was emotionally a turning point for the English. Far from accepting Powhatan punishment and becoming well-behaved subjects, any lingering doubts about Indian virtues, any thoughts of coexistence, any doubts about their God-given right to sovereignty, all disappeared. The right to punish Powhatan became, in English eyes, critical to establishing their own sovereignty—just as the Powhatan had apparently viewed punishing the English. The English ability to take this stance (which many had long advocated) grew as the colony finally began to produce more of its own food. With the English no longer dependent on Powhatan corn, who had the right to punish those who became a serious bone of contention. The polity that could punish members of the other demonstrated its dominance and, for the English, made it possible to get more work out of Powhatan servants and slaves and out of the unfree laborers sent from England and Africa.[75] Even worse, the English challenged Powhatan sovereignty by attempting to take over the punishing of Powhatan who had transgressed against each other.[76]

The struggle went on for several decades, with the English having declared all-out extermination of Indians as the only viable policy—a policy that left them without powerful nearby allies and thus vulnerable to the attacks mounted later by the Susquehanna and then the Seneca.

The structures that support state power grew for the English and diminished for the Powhatan. Former subject peoples of Tsenacommacoh separated into individual polities, no longer under centralized control. Clan elders and local werowances regained some of their former authority. They took back control of their own punishing, or at least fought with the English, not with the former Tsenacommacoh authorities, over who had the right to punish offenses of one Indian against another.[77]

By the end of the 1600s, long after Wahunsonacock's death, the English actually gained the power to enforce laws that gave them the right to adjudicate quarrels among the Powhatan. But before that, Opechancanough, in what perhaps was a desperate last attempt to assert sovereignty and the right to use force to punish, attacked again in 1644. This time 4 to 5 percent of the now much larger English population of about 10,000 was killed.[78] English retaliation was ferocious. Thereafter Powhatan culture continued for a bit, but largely in isolated areas, out of English sight and direct influence—and indeed Powhatan identity continues today.[79] But Powhatan sovereignty was gone. Tsenacommacoh never became a state, and was never again to challenge English elites' rights to exploit land and labor, protected by the state structures of control and punishment.

DESPITE THE REMOVAL OF THE POWHATAN threat, the colonial state structures remained weak; opposition by local elites could force the governor and council to back down or skirt issues that had no local support. In 1619, the General Assembly had mandated tithes to provide support for the church and its parsons and required church surveillance of parishioners (and all Virginia colonists were legally parishioners).[80] The state was enlisting the church in its attempts to control and punish. But at the same time, since the church was controlled by local elites, as we shall see in the next chapter, de facto this move allowed those local elites to wrest power from families and neighbors, who, even so, continued to play a major role in the policing of behavior by reporting and testifying.

Throughout the 1620s the state remained so weak that its authority could be enforced only through the continuation of the horrific punishments that John Smith and then Thomas Dale had relied on—it was either that or give in, evading the challenges posed by disgruntled people. Those dramatic and public punishments are a sign of a weak state, not a strong one whose authority is unquestioned. Authority over ordinary people was strengthened in 1634 by establishing the county court system, which gave power to local elites and only indirectly to the state itself. Justices of the peace had the power to adjudicate a wide range of behaviors deemed illegal or immoral. This process of shifting power to punish from groups of neighbors who policed themselves into the hands of local elites was ongoing. It meant that women lost much of the control over who was to be punished that they had had earlier, when they policed each other and witnessed for or against each other in the court of public opinion, and, if it came to that, in the courthouse where men had to listen to their testimony about other women.[81]

Men also lost some control. In 1662, for instance, in John Radford's day, the General Assembly allowed men to ask the court to have their wives ducked (a procedure a bit like waterboarding) instead of fined.[82] This was done under the guise of both relieving husbands of the burden of paying the fines imposed on wives convicted of slander and of backing up men's often rather tenuous grip on authority over their wives. It did, perhaps, increase men's leverage over their wives, but at the same time it gave the court, and thus local elites, the right to intervene in the husband's right to punish. In other words, state formation was gradually shifting control of punishment from local informal groups into the hands of a few powerful people—paralleling Wahunsonacock's move to shift power from local elders to subchiefs.

The diminished Powhatan presence did not at all mean the end of other powerful Indian nations. The next Native challenge was not long in coming. And this time, accompanying war between Native and English polities, was rebellion within the English polity. Local elites tried to wrest power from the colonial government, and a desperate workforce rebelled against the exploitative system those local elites espoused.

What happened to X we don't know. Maybe he made it through the Powhatan punishing attacks. If so, maybe he participated as an old man in the next uprising. But from here John Radford can pick up this tale.

CHAPTER 2

Ancestor Tales of Dispossession and a Revolt of the Unfree

So here we leave imaginary X's and turn to Radfords who aren't imaginary, but will nevertheless have to be imagined, for their presence in the historical record, itself fragmentary, in the wills, the land titles, the court cases, is fleeting indeed. You see their shadows, the occasional historical marks their feet left on the sands of time. But who they were, why those marks were left, what the substance was that made those shadows, that will all have to be imagined. Historically, anthropologically, and sociologically placed, imagining, of course, chasing a reality that did once exist, and that lives on in the underpinnings of our world today.

This ancestral Radford is real, that is, John not Benjamin. John is my ancestor because seven generations later his descendant, Elizabeth Radford, married Thomas Davidson, great-grandson of the Alexander who crossed the ocean. It was her brother, my father's great-uncle Ben—who, according to family mythology, watched an up-and-coming young lawyer named Abraham Lincoln play horseshoes.

So, what was this John Radford doing at age fifty-seven, heading for Virginia? We know he did indeed do that, an old man for those days, far older than the usual immigrant, voluntary or involuntary. We know because his mark is there, in the historical record. Why he did it, we will have to imagine. First, his mark: in 1652, Thomas Todd claimed 450 acres of what was once part of a Native polity, on Winter Harbor, on the coast in what is now Gloucester County, Virginia. Todd got the right (in English eyes) to those acres by claiming John Radford as a headright, along with headrights for seven other people. To make that claim, Todd would have paid the ship's captain for their passage. In return, the eight should have become Todd's indentured servants, owing him their labor for a contracted number of years—in essence they were selling themselves to him for a limited term.[1] However, it is unlikely that John was in fact indentured. I appear, at least on the Radford side of the family, to be descended from relative privilege from the moment this ancestral Radford set foot on invaded but not yet fully conquered Virginia soil.

I say "privilege" because the next we know of John is the shadow of activity that could not have occurred if he were indentured, and indicates that he had some kind of head start. He bought land, 160 acres in Northumberland County, from a man named Martin Cole in 1654, just about a year and a half after his arrival. The court record of the sale refers to him as "Gent," an appellation reserved for those with money and position.[2] He clearly did not go through the standard procedure, which involved surviving indenture, then renting, and finally years later, with luck, for rental conditions were terrible, buying land and marrying.[3] This was the common pattern for those indentured servants who actually succeeded in becoming planters themselves—and high school history to the contrary, not too many made it that far. Indeed, between the founding of Jamestown and the American Revolution, only one-fifth of the indentured servants who arrived in British North America became independent, as either farmers or artisans. The rest either died before they became free or became day laborers or paupers.[4]

Perhaps at this point I should make it clear that the privilege I am talking about here did not include the white privilege that, looking back from the vantage of the present, we might be inclined to read into John Radford's experience of life in Virginia. What he had was class privilege and male privilege; whiteness in and of itself had not yet been legislated—and enforced with punishment—into privilege during the initial tightening of control over the exploited and resisting workforce that is characteristic of state formation. By the time John's (probable) son Bruen died in (probably) 1687, however, whiteness had begun to mean privilege, particularly for the relatively well-to-do.[5] By the time Bruen's (probable) son George died, five decades after Bruen, however, whiteness conveyed some degree of privilege over free blacks to even the poorest and the unfree indentured, who could successfully claim an identity as English.

The laws that created difference between the two were, as we shall see, tightened after English and Africans revolted together, and were designed to control poor whites just as much as to control Africans. The key was being able to *claim* that it was the English part of your ancestry that identified you. Bear in mind that by this time there had been several generations of intermixture among English, Native American, and African, whose status ranged from freedom to varying degrees of servitude in a society which at first did not have strict racial lines. That mixture was the result of marriage, of unmarried consensual sex, and of rape performed primarily by English men, all of it producing numerous people of mixed ancestry. Before approximately 1670, there were few Africans in Virginia, and most of them, for most of those early decades, were in some form of indenture, very different from the slavery Venis and Adam would experience in the mid-1700s. There was not a clear and dramatic difference between English and African indenture; exploitation for both was frequently severe; and being white in itself brought no particular privilege until toward the end of the 1600s. So, it wasn't whiteness that brought John Radford his bit of privilege compared to Africans or other English. It was class.

That class privilege came to him from England, for John Radford was a surgeon—a "chyruegeon [*sic*]"—as the records of one court controversy indicate.[6] Medical fees, at least in 1664, were described as "exorbitant," so his income in Virginia may have been high.[7] Perhaps he actually paid for his own transportation, thus acquiring a headright for himself, but the ship's captain might have lied, claiming he had borne John's transportation costs, was given a headright for John, and sold it to Thomas Todd. Or perhaps John himself sold his headright to Todd, or perhaps Todd simply put together a list of names and claimed to have paid their transportation. In none of these cases would John have been actually indentured. Colonial authorities turned a blind eye to much of this maneuvering of headrights, some of which was clearly fraudulent, some in a legally gray area, but all certainly common—and it led to the wealthy, who could buy up many headrights, accumulating immense estates, often scattered over several counties, and to a corresponding land shortage for those coming out of indenture.[8]

By 1652, the catastrophic death rate of the early years had eased a little, but life was very far from secure. For newcomers, getting land was becoming harder and harder, and without it there were few ways to make a living. Tobacco was the only viable export crop, but it brought inconsistent returns. Even worse, tobacco was literally money, used to settle debts, make purchases, and pay tithes. Without land, you couldn't grow money, and marriage would be unlikely. Indeed, 20 to 30 percent of men never married.[9] Many people coming to the end of their indentures found themselves stuck, unable to move upward in the Virginia hierarchy.[10] Deep poverty was increasing. Early deaths were normal. In Middlesex County, research by Darrett and Anita Rutman revealed that as late as 1689 sixty percent of children had lost one parent by age thirteen. Thirty-seven percent had lost both by the time they were eighteen, by which time girls might themselves be married. [11]

WE NEED A DIGRESSION HERE. This idea of private property, that some could own land, on which all depended for life itself, to the exclusion of others, was a new idea on the Chesapeake, as it was for all Native polities. But it was an old idea to the English; indeed, the right to private property, or the dispossession from it, was the reason many of them had ended up on the Chesapeake. X Radford carried that tale of dispossession for us in England. In Virginia, as in England, the remains of the diarchic structure legitimized both ownership and its flipside, dispossession. Local parishes in Virginia, rather than church courts, as in England, regulated land rights. And by regulating property and inheritance, the church actually regulated who had the right to make a living and how they did it. John Nelson, in a study of the Anglican Church in colonial Virginia, describes the system of governance as joint parish/county.[12] The parish vestry consisted of twelve men, almost invariably representatives of the most powerful local families, plus the minister. Everyone, regardless of religion, paid the heavy parish levies that supported church and minister. As in England, a vague sense of the old commons made the parish responsible for the welfare of those in it. This meant, de facto, that the parish was responsible for people it kept dispossessed by its enforcement of property rights. Parish charity was a major expense.

The parish kept the land records and validated the boundaries of private property, every four years organizing "processioning," in which members of the community were chosen to walk all boundaries, renew boundary marks as necessary, and settle any disputes—all accompanied, apparently, with a bit of conviviality, judging by at least one parish bill for ale. [13] This was the church validating ownership—and by extension, validating landlessness for everyone else. Disputes that couldn't be settled amicably through church intervention were turned over to the secular authority, the county court, with its ability to apply force if needed. Not only did the church validate the control of land, but it also, under the guise of responsibility for "poor relief," played an important role in validating the use of labor. The parish "bound out" poor and orphan children, by the early 1700s at the rate of hundreds annually, who were thus legally obligated to provide free labor until adulthood for the family to which they were bound, in return for food and shelter and education (at least for the more fortunate).[14] All this was exacerbated by Virginia's dependence, not on mixed farming by individual families, as was common in the Northern colonies, but on tobacco, an extremely labor-intensive export crop that doubled as money, and grew well in Virginia's climate.

Tellingly, it was on the monuments to these two pillars of governance, the church and the courthouse/jail (the jail was often in the courthouse basement, with a pillory out front), that the elites lavished money and care, generally with at least a modicum of consent from those who paid the levies that made such impressive buildings possible. This control was all in the hands of local elites. Theoretically, some were appointed by and answerable to the governor, who was appointed by the king, but typically the governor rubber-stamped local selections for the county courts and for parish ministers. And if he didn't, the local elites were quite capable of strategically ignoring him.[15] Wresting power out of their hands and into the hands of the state would turn out to be bloody, involving war, executions, and the English navy.

DIGRESSION FINISHED, BACK TO John Radford and the possible sale of his headright to Thomas Todd—and however Todd got that land, his right to it was legitimized by the church and enforced by the state. If John sold his headright, the sale could have enabled him to do as many did: leave to go and join relatives and connections in the colony. Darrett and Anita Rutman's extensive study of the area just south of the Rappahannock River (which eventually became Middlesex and Essex counties), where there were many Radford connections, shows this pattern clearly—just about everybody lived within fairly easy reach of relatives or people with whom they had had long-term connections.[16] John, however, went a bit farther up the coast, to Northumberland County, on the north side of the Wicomoco River. He did have connections there, through Martin Cole and a possible cousin, Roger Radford. Traveling to Middlesex by boat would have been a long trip. Cross-country would have been even harder, although by the 1650s, there were a few roads, ferries, and bridges in the regions that had been settled by English the longest.

Ferries and bridges marked a very different way of life for the English compared to the Powhatan. For the Powhatan rivers and streams had been connectors, and all had equal access. Everyone had canoes, so all could use the rivers and streams for traveling. Transportation of people and goods by canoe was quick and easy, far easier than cross-country travel. For at least some of the English, however, rivers quickly became barriers. Given the disparities in wealth and possessions, many would have been boatless.[17] In the 1650s, horses were fairly rare;

transportation by road often meant on foot. For those with boats, or who were connected with those with boats, the rivers were a lifeline to economic well-being. The well-to-do bought or patented land on the rivers; planters in the backcountry, without river access, were dependent on the big planters on the rivers for commercial connections to Jamestown for the sale of their tobacco.

So here was John, buying land from Martin Cole on the north shore of the Wicomoco—land with river access. He remained linked with the network of Rappahannock connections, however, despite the distance, through Martin Cole, who was a relative of Francys Cole, a wealthy planter on the south side of the Rappahannock. Francys was himself connected to Rowland Burnham, an even wealthier planter, whose son John was one of the elite that rebels later imprisoned. In addition to the wealth he inherited from his father, John Burnham was both a planter and one of the few Middlesex merchants. He exported tobacco to England and filled return voyages with English goods ordered mostly by the local gentry, as well as some merchandise for general sale. He is referred to as "Lt. Coll" (for colonel) and was a justice.[18] High status indeed.

This whole set of connections appears to have been available to John through Roger Radford, his probable cousin, who was closely connected with Francys Cole, perhaps having been indentured to him previously. These connections appear to have carried over into the next generation, via John's (probable) son, Bruen Radford, and Rowland's son, John Burnham. Bruen appeared at John Burnham's deathbed, signed his will, and inherited a substantial sum of money from him.[19] His appearance to pay his respects to his dying patron reflected the attention a client owed his patron—and turned out to be well worth the trip he most likely made from Essex downriver by boat or by road to Middlesex. This was a common pattern in early Virginia, with the less powerful man dependent on the backing of the more influential merchants or wealthy planters, who might themselves be clients of even more powerful men. In return, the client would give service and loyalty, backing the patron's economic and political strategies.[20]

These networks of patron-client relationships helped make local elite governance possible. Clients were, to greater or lesser extents, dependent on patrons. Men like John Burnham had power not just as merchants and planters, but also had a surprising degree of influence over access to land, having patented enormous tracts. Their speculation paid off as they rented, and sometimes eventually sold, to newcomers and freed indentured servants. As centers of financial networks, they had at least some degree of influence over the lesser planters, like Francys and Martin, who were dependent on them, and who in turn had their lesser dependents—people like the Radfords. [21] In addition, these were the men who were authorized by the church, as vestry members, to wield the legitimizing spiritual power of the church and, as justices, to wield the secular use of force. From the Powhatan perspective, this certainly would have been a subversion of dual sovereignty; too much of both spiritual and secular power was in overlapping hands. Wahunsonacock himself, however, with his expansionist, perhaps imperial, ambitions, might well have understood the benefits. From the English perspective, the institutions were separate but the overlap made that separation workable; one institution would not stymie the other.

A BIT OF AN ASIDE IS CALLED FOR here, about those shadowy figures in the historical record. It is often extremely difficult to tell for sure who is who when looking at court records and even at wills. People named children for parents and grandparents and siblings, so often there are several people of the same name, who may or may not be related, or may even be the same person. Is the John Radford who bought land in Northumberland the same John Radford who earlier testified in a murder trial? In this example, there is reason to think they are one and the same—in both cases, Martin Cole is also involved.[22] And it is possible that this John Radford is not actually my ancestor, despite Radford family researchers who think he is, or that Bruen is not really his son. From the start, Bruen is elusive in the historical record. It isn't clear that John is his father, nor, for that matter, that George Radford is his son, but starting with George the record that connects me to the Radford line is pretty clear. For John and Bruen there is very little evidence—no records of marriage or birth, for instance—which may indicate I've got it wrong, or it may simply be that the verifying records, as is often the case, were destroyed in rebellions, wars, or accidental fires. So what I am saying about all these ancestors must be accompanied by the caveat that, despite my best efforts at detective work, I may have gotten people mixed up. However, for the sake of the story I will go ahead, for after all, this is not only a family story, but the story of punishment and dispossession. For that, it doesn't matter whether I have the ancestors quite right.

THE VIRGINIA THAT JOHN RADFORD encountered was far from a peaceful place or a land of opportunity. English policy toward the Powhatan and then toward other neighboring polities added another layer of difficulty to the life of the English in Virginia. It had been only thirty years since Opechancanough and the Powhatan had killed off nearly a third of all the English in Virginia, and just eight years previously had again tried to punish the English into proper behavior, killing about four percent of the population. By 1652, when John Radford arrived, the Powhatan were no longer a force to be reckoned with. However, the expansion of the Iroquois, whose imperial ambitions challenged those of the English and the French, was realigning the East Coast Native nations, both geographically and politically.[23] Iroquois conquest pushed other nations, particularly the Susquehanna, up against English settlement in Virginia, predictably leading to conflict with land-hungry English.

Most white Virginians had come to define all Indians as enemies, even those like the Pamunkey, who were allied with colonial governor Berkeley's government. Berkeley was all for alliances and trade with Indians—but legally monopolized that trade for himself and his cronies, and was called an Indian-lover by poorer English. Consequently, most English Virginians, wanting land, opted not for alliance and trade but for incessant low-level warfare, with occasional flare-ups, along the outer reaches of the colony. And they bitterly resented Berkeley's failure to provide reasonable protection, despite demanding increased tithes for forts. Those forts were supposedly to protect them, but instead were placed to protect elite holdings, while at the same time Berkeley forbade the local populace from forming militias to protect themselves. It was these resentments that eventually, along with landlessness and poverty among both English and Africans, free and unfree, led to class warfare in the bloody rebellion of 1676. And in the aftermath of the rebellion elites centralized power as they regained control, particularly the power to punish. [24] In 1652, those resentments were already bubbling noticeably.

A COMMENT ON THE UNDERSTANDING of colonial history is in order. Scholars have made it dramatically clear that Native American nations were major players in colonial history. [25] During the first century and a half the colonies had less military might than many of the surrounding native polities. And the English were competing for colonies with other Europeans—French, Spanish, Dutch. On their own, without Native allies, the English colonies were too weak to protect themselves against other Native attacks or to hold off other Europeans. And just as European polities fought with one another, so also did Indian polities. Alliances made sense on both sides for defensive purposes, but also for trade and for leverage in maneuvering through complex inter- and intra-polity rivalries. Native Americans, like the English, acted in their own interests, in relation to both other Indian polities and to European polities. They were far from being passive victims of European aggression. And the European states were far from being all-conquering. Even their guns did not convey a clear advantage over the bow and arrow. [26] Colonies frequently invited tribes to settle close by, or formed close trading partnerships and military alliances. [27]

As we will see in a later chapter, pan-Indian organizing did not become a reality until sometime in the mid-1700s. Nevertheless, Indian resistance toward the end of the 1600s was fierce. This is the time when numerous Indian nations united in King Philip's War against the English in New England (and although the English in Virginia probably didn't know it, the Pueblos were on the verge of their 1680 revolt in which they successfully tossed out the Spanish). Closer to home, the Iroquois had imperial ambitions themselves, and were extending their reach into the Virginia colonial periphery, bringing into question the continued viability of the English and, elsewhere, the French hold on eastern North America. The English were unable to protect themselves against either the French or Indians and certainly not against both at once. They were eventually forced into alliance under Iroquois terms that successfully confined the English to the eastern seaboard, behind a frontier that gradually moved west, but at a speed held well in check by Native American military power.[28] That system held from 1676 for well over a hundred years, finally dying with Tecumseh's death in the War of 1812 and the demise of any real possibility of a sovereign Indian state with frontiers that the US state would have to respect. But that is getting ahead of the story.

SO WE COME AT LAST TO THE PUZZLE of John's presence in the Chesapeake at age fifty-seven. What was going on in England that made the risks of Virginia attractive to an elderly surgeon, presumably moderately well off, who apparently had a seven-year-old son to care for? Why would anyone voluntarily take such risks, even someone who could avoid indenture, as John did? The answer we were taught in school, "They came voluntarily to better themselves, worked for free for a while to pay back their passage, and then, joining those who were already free and independent, helped make this the land of the free and the home of the brave" is, as we have seen, a serious whitewash. Many English, like Africans, came at the point of a gun. They were rebels captured and exiled, they were vagrants, or hungry, they were criminals, they were kidnapped (a 1680 report says 10,000 were "spirited" annually).[29] They were street children and orphans rounded up and shipped off. Or they were women so desperate that they were willing to be sold as wives for 120 pounds of tobacco. The headright system, of course, made procuring servants to ship to the colonies, legally or illegally, a lucrative business. The school version also whitewashes what happened to indentured servants once they were in the colonies. Life for most was one long misery; life after indenture, if you survived that long, was for many so desperate that at the time of John Radford's arrival, small-scale revolts were becoming common, long before the eruption of the widespread rebellion of 1676.[30]

So what were the conditions in England that might have driven John Radford to Virginia? There is no identifiable record of his early life in England—or if there is, I haven't found it—except that he was probably born in Devon, the son of Robert Radford and possibly Alice Leigh. Given the lack of facts, all I can do is put together a likely scenario of maybes, grounded in the history of the times.

When the imagined X Radford headed to Virginia, England, unlike Tsenacommacoh, was already a state, but a relatively weak one, without a clear grip on the right to use force and to keep others from using it.[31] The Crown's attempts to consolidate that grip had been a source of bitter contention for a century or more and, shortly before John Radford's departure, erupted in a civil war and a royal beheading— Charles I was executed in 1649. Eruptions continued as the English Crown, like Wahunsonacock, struggled to control its borders, particularly with Scotland, a struggle that eventually propelled Alexander Davidson to the Chesapeake. However, unlike the Powhatan strategy, English kings were trying to tame diarchy, to become the dominant partner. The sword, not the church, would determine how and when force would be used, both in war and in punishment. The priest would be the servant of the king; the interests of the state, as defined by the king, would no longer be held hostage to legitimation by the church. What eventually resulted from these power struggles was what is now called a "modern" state, with both the internal use of force to punish and the external use of force to make war and control borders in secular hands.

Both Radfords and, a little later, Alexander Davidson, would have been living with the chaos, both religious and political, created by the power struggle between church and king. And at the same time, they would have been living with the not unrelated chaos that accompanied the deepening grip of capitalism on both economic and social relations. Native Americans who traveled to England invariably were shocked by the desperate poverty they saw there, and commented on the hypocrisy of the claim that Christian civilization was superior to their more egalitarian social systems.[32] The power and right to exploit was shifting; people without birthright to status, power, or wealth, merchants and entrepreneurs, now had access to all three—and were bent on enhancing their grasp.[33] Without a feudal birthright to the use of people's labor, the rising capitalist class was increasingly dependent on hiring workers, people dispossessed, as we have seen. Those dispossessed were desperate enough to take the abysmally small wages employers offered instead of the payment they preferred, in kind or in the right to use land, or in room and board, with token money perhaps added.

The religious arguments, though often appearing intensely esoteric, actually were pragmatic justifications for particular economic and political positions; arguments about Natural Law, or about the King's Two Bodies, had real consequences in terms of shifts in the right to exploit, to punish, to exercise force, to rule.[34] They stood in for and expressed both the political and the economic malaise of the times. At the base of these arguments was the question of the source of the king's sovereignty and thus his right to wield the power of the sword. All agreed it came ultimately from God, but did it go from God to the people (or to the aristocrats only, by bloodright) and, by their consent, to the king, or did it go to the church, and through the authority of the church to the king, or did it go directly to the king? The answer to that question had enormous implications: was the king answerable to the people? The arguments were often massively involuted—but nevertheless, they mattered. And these arguments may have led to John's decision. He left during Cromwell's rule, shortly after Charles I was beheaded, a time when many Royalists fled to Virginia.[35] If John was one of the Royalists, he may well have been one who believed sovereignty came to the king directly from God, in opposition to the position taken by Cromwell. Practically speaking, being on the losing side, he may have been subject to persecution, maybe in real danger, maybe simply unable to continue to make a living.

The claim that the king's sovereignty comes directly from God without the mediation of the church provided a way around the restraints on the power of the English king, restraints such as the diarchic structures that empowered the religious elites, as we saw in chapter 1, and power grabs by lesser lords and rising capitalists. Monarchy, not diarchy, became a kingly goal. And absolute monarchy was even better, in which the two roles, priest and king or council and king, are rolled into a single authority, a monarch who is head of both church and state, who both speaks for and interprets the gods, *and* exercises the power to carry out their wishes and to punish those who don't comply.[36] But in consolidating power this way, legitimizing spiritual authority is lost, and a king's claim to both roles can be a pretty transparent power grab. That problem becomes particularly acute as the shift to capitalism supports the rise of a wealthy merchant class with no birthright claim to power. This merchant class exercises considerable economic power and is inclined to question the infallibility of the policies of an unrestrained monarch. As indeed they did for several centuries, with some backing the power of the church against the king, and others the power of the people against the king.

This seesawing kept England in turmoil for a few centuries, with one of its high points coming in 1534 when Henry VIII declared himself both head of state and head of church, giving him sufficient power to gain a greater monopoly on the use of force by reining in the great aristocrats' private armies.[37] A shift in address marked his heightened sovereignty: he was "Your Majesty," no longer "Your Grace," king by the grace of God.[38] Diarchic forms remained, though with some redistribution of roles. Monasteries were confiscated and the state took over the former monastic roles of education and charity—much of the social control function was now backed directly by the state's ability to exert force.[39]

HERE WE TURN AGAIN TO VIRGINIA and Radfords, with, I hope, some sense of the ideas that were swirling around in the intellectual soup of the England in which X and John Radford had lived. Those who came first to Jamestown, people like X, tended to see the king as merely God's lieutenant, with other lesser lieutenants. With John, or at least with many of the people who fled Cromwell, came a more absolutist vision of monarchy, one to which Henry VIII had subscribed, and for which Charles I lost his head. The monarchy was restored after John left for Virginia. Charles II reigned, and despite the enhanced position of Parliament and of the King's Council, the possibility of absolutism again arose. With this changing of the guard, there was a new flood of refugees headed for Virginia. This time they were escaping royal punishment for supporting Cromwell. Members of the rising capitalist middle class and low-level aristocrats, they had seen in Cromwell and the religious beliefs that vested sovereignty in the people the possibility of public policy that resonated with their own desire for greater power and independence. These were people like Nathaniel Bacon, who eventually became a leader of the rebellion against Governor Berkeley and his autocratic rule.

The discontent that eventually led to rebellion was simmering when Bruen may have arrived as a seven-year-old with his father in 1652. Bruen is well situated, in time and space, to pick up the story of punishing, sovereignty, and state formation, a thread that weaves its way through Bacon's Rebellion of 1676 and its aftermath. He actually first shows up in the historical records in 1680 at age thirty-five, at John Burnham's bedside. His probable son George, apparently his only child, was born in Henrico County in 1665, when Bruen would have been twenty, and though there is no record of Bruen himself in Henrico, George spent at least some time as an adult living there with his wife, judging by the fact that his children were born there. There is no record of Bruen's marriage. This could be just a case of missing records, of course, and many are missing in Henrico. Even so, one would still expect some mention of a wife in someone's will or in land transactions, in which the wife had to sign away her dower rights in the land to make a sale legal. Or a record of her death, or of her remarriage after Bruen died at age forty-two. Since there was still a shortage of English women in Virginia at this time, it is improbable that if she did exist, she didn't remarry. Most widows did, and many men managed to get land by marrying widows who inherited or held a lifetime estate from their first husbands. That Bruen may have remained unmarried, as did John's probable cousin Roger and many other men, was not particularly unusual, given the shortage of women.[40] Or perhaps there was a marriage, but the wife died in childbirth almost immediately, thereby having little time to leave traces in the historical record.

Alternatively, perhaps George's mother was one of the many other Radfords, unrelated to John or Bruen (in which case they are not related to me). Her last name would have gone to him if George were one of the many babies described as a "bastard" because an appropriate man had not made the appropriate claim—marriage—on his mother's body and reproductive capacity. Most frequently such children were born to indentured servants, who needed their master's permission to marry, were sometimes abused by their masters, or sometimes simply fell in love with someone they were unable to marry.[41] However, if George had an unmarried mother who was English, free or not, there would most likely have been some record. English women were brought to court and punished for bearing a child outside of marriage, or even for having a child too soon after marriage, since the child was conceived without the appropriate legal claim on the mother's reproductive capacity.[42] They were whipped or fined, depending on the woman's "quality," and called into church wrapped in a white sheet to beg for forgiveness and reentry into the church community. On top of that, servant women had two and a half years added to their indenture. Men were sometimes sued, sometimes forced to marry the mother. Without a marriage and therefore without support for mother or child, the child was taken to be raised by a family, often indentured or apprenticed and thus free labor, with early expenses paid by the court. Hence, the insistence on marriage—it saved the county tax money. So, either the records are missing or George's mother wasn't English.

Perhaps George was the result of a loving—or a forced—relationship with a Native American or African woman who was perhaps enslaved, perhaps free, perhaps herself the product of one of the early not-so-uncommon cross-race alliances. If so, Bruen must have acknowledged

George as his son and given him the Radford name. If George's mother were a member of one of the matrilineal native nations, George would also have been an acknowledged member of his mother's matrilineage.[43] There is no indication that George was not considered white, regardless of his actual ancestry. Bruen, who at least later was reasonably well established, and was the son of someone designated as "gent," would have had the power to ensure that the English part of George's ancestry determined his identity.

Although there is no record of his owning either land or people, Bruen must have been reasonably well respected in that nest of Radford connections on the Rappahannock. After all, he signed John Burnham's will. He served on juries, did appraisals of estates, and acted as an agent in the sale of Tappahannock Mill.[44] These are low-level positions, but were rarely given to men without property.[45]

Assuming Bruen was already living in what was then Rappahannock and later became Essex County before he first shows up in the records in 1680, he would have been in the thick of the bloody upheaval of Bacon's Rebellion of 1676. Which side he would have been on is a question. John Burnham, apparently his patron, sided with Berkeley and the old established elite who ran the colony; rebels eventually burned him out. So Bruen might have followed his patron's lead. But not many among the ordinary people in Rappahannock, or elsewhere, sided with Berkeley. Tappahannock itself was a center of opposition to Berkeley.[46] So, statistically, Bruen is more likely to have been at least nominally one of the rebels, although probably not one of those who joined Bacon's army, since that army was composed mainly of laborers, free and unfree, and the poor. He may well have been one of the relatively well-off who backed away when, as Webb describes, the revolt shifted from merely challenging Berkeley's rule and his failure to undertake what many saw as the obviously necessary genocide of the surrounding Indians.[47] Instead it became a real revolt of slaves, servants, and the poor but free, challenging the entire established social hierarchy, including disobeying the king's representatives and fighting the king's military.

THE CAUSES OF THE SIMMERING discontent that underlay Bacon's Rebellion are linked to the strategies that are often used to get people to agree to work for next to nothing, as was happening to indentured workers in Virginia. Until 1675 over half the population was unfree and English.[48] Life-term servitude, slavery as opposed to indenture, was growing only slowly during this time. The death rate was so high that it did not make sense to buy people for a lifelong stint of forced labor until toward the end of the century. Buying a lifetime of servitude was expensive, and it was an investment you might well lose through death long before the initial expense was paid off. Buying people for a shorter term through indenture meant you stood a better chance of making back your investment, as the Rutmans and Edmund Morgan both explain.[49] In some areas, the unfree English labor force was supplemented by Indians, who could have been enslaved "legally" according to English standards, often by other Indian nations, in "just wars" fomented by the English, with other tribes.[50] Although that unfree labor force was largely English, there were many whose status was ambiguous. After all, several generations had passed since the English and Africans began contributing to the Native gene pool of the Chesapeake.

So the English state provided dispossessed workers, but how was the state to maintain that dispossession in Virginia, so that people would work even though the state was weak, too weak to dispossess completely either Native people or ordinary English colonists? As we have seen, land was available and granted through headright. Nor could the state prevent people from squatting on the outer edges of English settlement, although Native polities did maintain limits to that process. It takes a strong state to keep land monopolized in the hands of the few in the face of demands to the contrary, and the Crown's government in Virginia was unable to do so during the first decades of English settlement in the early 1600s. Nevertheless, Jamestown tobacco planters needed a labor supply—dispossessed people.[51]

So to keep them dispossessed, the state stepped in again. Indenture was a legally enforced contract—you were technically in debt to whoever paid your passage until you had served your time. With state oversight weak and distant, local state actors, the elites who ran the local governments in the name of the Crown and nominally under its jurisdiction, enforced the system. It was local elites who saw that runaways were legally caught and whipped and who oversaw the contracts by which indentured servants were forced to work and were sold or transferred through inheritance from one owner to another.[52] Those same local elites adjudicated disputes between owner and servant. Servants could not take up land by purchase or headright, even though it was available. They were kept dispossessed until the indenture was completed.

However, given a state too weak to force people into lifelong servitude and given also that more tobacco growers clearing more land was profitable for the Crown, land was at first often provided after indenture. But by the 1630s, land was becoming a commodity to be bought and sold, rather than held from the Crown with an annual quitrent to maintain an individual's right to a particular piece of land. And by the 1650s, servants ending their indentures could no longer count on getting the fifty acres their contracts specified.[53] Land was either too expensive for newly freed servants to buy, or it was simply unavailable except on the dangerous frontiers. Many either continued as laborers or became tenants required to grow tobacco, making barely enough after taxes and rent to keep themselves alive.[54] Dispossession thus functioned more permanently by privatizing land through state policies that made it possible for a few wealthy landholders, as well as London merchant/investors, to own enormous tracts and to pass them on legally to their heirs.[55] As land became less available, and owners could sell for whatever price they could get, another string was added to the dispossession bow: it was okay to refuse people land to feed themselves if they couldn't pay the required amount.[56]

In other words, during the 1650s and 1660s, the foundation for a capitalist system of private ownership of the means of production, permanent dispossession, and wage or tenant labor for most men had been laid and was gradually solidifying. The expected progression to landownership for servants surviving indenture was no longer secure. Instead of the prospect of moving up the colonial hierarchy as independent planters, workers saw lifelong dependence as wage laborers, or worse. But honorable manhood required independence, land, and wife—property and patriarchy—and attaining either independence or wife was nearly impossible without land.[57] In other words, the class structure was not sufficiently developed to cause English laborers— still the majority of the workforce—to accept landlessness as normal and permanent wage labor as an honorable way to head a household. This left the relatively few Africans and the many English, who existed on a wide continuum of statuses ranging from more or less enslaved to more or less free, deeply angry—landless, desperate, and often armed. It was they, Africans and English, indentured, enslaved, or poor, who eventually became the backbone of the army of Bacon's Rebellion.[58] But it was not they who actually orchestrated the rebellion.

Discontent had been heating up for a number of years, sometimes breaking out into organized resistance.[59] There were a number of sore points, the most intense of which was rampant poverty for the many in an increasingly rigid class structure. In addition, there were issues angering people across the class spectrum, not just African and English unfree workers or the newly freed and frustrated. There was the declining price of tobacco. Then Berkeley's Assembly restricted the vote in 1670, so that only property owners and householders, not all free men, determined who would be assemblymen.[60] In 1673, the elites were exempted from payment of taxes, while for average planters taxes took between one-quarter and one-half of their annual income, leaving them close to starvation in bad years and their laborers likely even closer.[61] There was additional taxation for forts that appeared to be placed to protect elite estates from Indian attack but left smaller outlying planters vulnerable.

All this came close to a boil when Indian attacks increased (in response to considerable provocation), just before the start of Bacon's Rebellion. Most of the deaths from these attacks occurred in Rappahannock and other frontier areas. In Rappahannock there was a dramatic increase in the number of wills proved in court during and right after this period, presumably reflecting the heightened death rate.[62] It is easy to see why a later formal complaint to the king's commissioners stated, "Poore Rappahannock lies a bleeding."[63] The pot actually boiled over in 1676. Susquehanna Indians from over the border in Maryland, in a revenge attack, killed thirty-six English in Rappahannock, not too far from Tappahannock, where Bruen might have been living. Indians also attacked at the head of the James River, in Henrico. Webb argues that this invasion, when combined with all the other discontents, was instrumental in making the colony so unstable that Bacon was able to pull off his rebellion.[64] The state could neither force people into obedience nor defend them, clearly failing in the use of force both externally and internally, thus leaving its sovereignty subject to question.[65]

Whether Bruen, maybe with fifteen-year-old George, was still in Henrico or already at Tappahannock, he must have felt vulnerable. That vulnerability might have inclined him to side with Nathaniel Bacon, a recently arrived landholder and member of the minor British aristocracy, who resented his geographic marginalization on the dangerous colonial frontier and perhaps also the power of low-born, newly rich planters under Governor Berkeley's rule. With Berkeley denying the right to take up arms independently against the Indians, and failing to send adequate militia defense, Nathaniel Bacon apparently saw his chance to claim status for himself. Lacking power to oppose the elite land monopoly, colonists had largely taken out their anger at lack of land on Native people, who, in effect, were enforcing the elite's monopoly on land by keeping new colonists from spreading west. Bacon used that anger and then redirected it against Berkeley, who governed with very little reference to the authority of the Crown, and with very little reference to the desires of the frontier elites who rose to lead the rebellion.[66] Bacon's plan included a genocidal attack on Native people, which he would parlay into regime change in Jamestown. Frontier elites like Bacon would replace the old established elites like royal governor Berkeley and his allies, as the Crown's government.[67]

Bacon organized an army, went with the army to Jamestown, and intimidated Berkeley into giving him a legalizing military commission. He led his army against all Indians, including English allies. He terrorized Berkeley's administration into permitting new elections in which all free men voted, and was elected to the Assembly along with a lot of other men from the colony's periphery—not the entrenched

Tidewater elites who were Berkeley's cronies. Together they passed laws that at least paid lip service to dismantling elite institutionalized power and proposed that defense of the periphery be paid for by the sale of Indian captives as slaves. But feeling that the essential power structure was unchanged, the rebels then turned on Berkeley's militia and Berkeley in turn declared Bacon a traitor. Bacon and his army attacked and burned Jamestown in response and advocated a changed relationship to the Crown that might have amounted to independence from England. Bacon eventually died of fever; British ships and then the navy finally put down the rebellion. By the end, six hundred to a thousand English and an even larger number of Indians were dead in the Indian-English conflict. An uncounted number more died from the direct and indirect results of the English-English Rebellion.[68]

The fascinating part of all this to me is not Bacon or Berkeley, despite all the attention they have received. What interests me is the way in which the exploited laborers latched on to Bacon's power grab and attempted to turn it to their own purposes. Together the people Berkeley quite accurately described as "poor, armed and desperate," both free and unfree, English and African (and probably some Native), demanded and fought for freedom, land, a voice, and even talked "openly of sharing men's estates among themselves"—land redistribution, that perennial bugbear of the elite.[69] Those who were most committed to the armed struggle—the poor and the unfree, Virginia's labor force—did indeed have a vision of a different kind of Virginia, not a Virginia in which one set of ruling elites was exchanged for another. Four hundred of them held out to the very end against what had become improbable odds, and ultimately the final one hundred fighters, all unfree, eighty of them African, succumbed to trickery and the false offer of freedom.[70] In essence, that motley army of poor, dispossessed, and desperate English and Africans had hijacked the rebellion and repurposed it, pushing Bacon, in order to keep their support, into demanding land reform or redistribution and a voice in government.[71]

It might make sense to think of the whole rebellion as two overlapping revolts. One was a revolt of middling planters fed up with Indian attacks and Berkeley's "Indian-lover" policies and corrupt taxation, led by newly arrived wannabes who believed their aristocratic heritage gave them both the ability and the birthright to rule, as opposed to the nouveaux riches who surrounded Berkeley.[72] The other was a revolt of the unfree and the poor that took advantage of the chaos of the first rebellion and the structure provided by the rebels' army to rise against the whole system of exploitation. That they rose up together would have been no surprise—African and English laborers worked together and often resisted masters together. To a significant extent they identified with one another as exploited laborers. In fact, one-tenth of Virginia's unfree Africans joined the rebellion, and English and African unfree workers made up two-thirds of Bacon's field army—they *were* the rebellion in a very real sense.[73] This is what made the rebellion particularly threatening. It was no mere shift of power among elites, the substitution of one set of elites for another—although that certainly seems to be what Bacon and the planters who followed him had in mind.

From the point of view of the English Crown, both sides were problematic challenges to its increasingly imperial ambitions. Berkeley needed to be removed for two reasons. First, because he intended a more or less autonomous Virginia ruled as a private fiefdom for himself and his cronies, not an imperially governed province within an empire. And second, because his policies were so inept that the resistance they aroused made Virginia practically ungovernable by anybody—and an "orderly" society is required for wealth creation.[74] Bacon, on the other hand, depending on how you read him, might have intended to undo the social hierarchy that made for the unimpeded flow of wealth toward the elite. Or he might have intended to substitute himself and his wannabes at the top of that lucrative hierarchy, at the head of a still more or less autonomous Virginia only nominally under Crown control. But in either case, from the Crown's perspective, both Berkeley and those who had rebelled against him needed to be brought to heel.

CONTROL OF PUNISHMENT QUICKLY became the critical issue at stake in the aftermath of Bacon's Rebellion. It even raised its head during the rebellion, as Bacon attempted to take away from Berkeley

the control of punishing friendly Indians by advocating they be outlawed and thus removed from Berkeley's "protection."[75] After the
rebellion, Berkeley, in the months after the last unfree laborer had been
returned to captivity and before he himself was recalled to England
and removed from power, went on a punishing rampage, executing,
whipping, and extracting huge fines. Bruen doesn't appear on the
lists of those punished, and neither do any of the other people from
the Radford connections on the Rappahannock. John Burnham, of
course, was a Berkeley supporter, his property "much worsted" and
himself imprisoned by Baconians.[76] Berkeley supporters like Burnham
were not subject to punishment. And many low-level rebels also went
unpunished and simply returned to life as normal—even Berkeley
couldn't punish nearly the whole population of Virginians.[77] But it
seemed like he was trying. According to some accounts, King Charles
commented: "The old fool has taken more lives in that naked country
than I did for the murder of my father."[78]

Just as the English and Powhatan had fought earlier over the right
to punish, Berkeley and the king's commissioners, sent to Virginia to
establish the Crown's sovereignty and return Virginia to governability, eventually fought over who was going to control the punishing of
the rebels. Turning back to the Introduction a moment to explain the
importance of this struggle, theorist Achille Mbembe said, "The ultimate expression of sovereignty resides, to a large degree, in the power
and capacity to dictate who may live and who must die."[79] If the Crown
was to establish itself as the legitimate ruler, forming Virginia as a province under the sovereignty of the English state, then gaining control
of punishing was critical. The Crown, not Berkeley, must determine
"who may live and who must die," who must be a prisoner and who
may be free.

Because Berkeley was on a punishing rampage, the Crown simply
taking over the punishing wasn't much of an option: Virginians wouldn't
be able to distinguish between Berkeley and the Crown. Since deciding which people may live and be free is just as much an expression of
sovereignty as is killing them, the Crown pardoned just about everyone involved in the revolt who had survived Berkeley's punishment

(although it reneged on the promise of freedom that had been used to trick the last of the rebels into surrendering) and hauled Berkeley back to England. That pardon proclamation was posted all over the colony, "announcing the advent of royal government."[80] The king was now sovereign; it was evident that he, not Berkeley, determined who would live and who would die. The force required to back that sovereignty was evident in the presence of well over a thousand British military personnel garrisoned in Jamestown. Virginians did indeed notice the difference, especially when the commissioners followed the Crown's instructions and held hearings to investigate and right the policies that had led to the revolt. The colonists largely preferred sovereignty held by a distant king to a sovereignty held by Berkeley's exploitative cohorts. That is, most planters, including the elites who had supported Bacon, preferred the king's sovereignty.[81]

What the poor and unfree thought is another matter. All free men, regardless of property ownership, had briefly had the right to vote as part of the laws passed by Nathaniel Bacon and the other new assemblymen elected during the rebellion. Once the rebellion was quashed and Berkeley was temporarily back in power, that law and others that leaned toward a leveling of inequality were all repealed. Those property requirements remained in place until well into the 1800s. In the mid-1700s, only about fifteen percent of the Virginia white population could vote, and in 1723, all Indians and all people with identified African ancestry, regardless of property, were disenfranchised.[82]

So the Crown succeeded in ending Berkeley's relatively independent government of the colony, put down the rebellion, and denied most of the demands of the dispossessed. At the same time, it met some of the rebel leaders' demands by making entrance into the governing elite more accessible to a wider range of white, property-owning men.[83] Though the better-off had backed down, and even poorer planters— property owners and thus voters—were pacified, the threat of a workers' revolt remained, as the frightened planters well knew. The Crown, having removed Berkeley, had instructed the Virginia elites that their system of labor control was inadequate—it would take an army to keep such desperate workers under control, and the Crown was not about to pay for even the troops still in Virginia.[84] Even though the elite had been brought to heel and made to pay taxes like everyone else, supporting an army would require taxing even more heavily. Considering that planters, large and small, were already up in arms, this was hardly a viable option.

Since the state was not strong enough to turn the mass of laborers permanently into the extremely exploitable people the planters wanted without maintaining an army to prevent revolt, planters needed a different strategy to control their entire English, African, and Native workforce. Poor English must never again join with African workers in revolt, for that had been the true backbone of the most threatening aspect of Bacon's Rebellion. Their solution was what makes Bacon's Rebellion a watershed in American history, leaving a legacy that haunts the country today.[85]

THAT SOLUTION, THE STRATEGIES ADOPTED to prevent another rebellion, shifted Virginia from being a society with slaves, one in which only a few people were actually enslaved, to a slave society, one in which slavery was the central organizing principle of the social structure.[86] The principal labor force, those most seriously exploited, would no longer be English—the state couldn't compel their labor on a permanent basis without provoking revolt. The timing of this shift coincided with a changing attitude among England's elites. For the colony's first half-century its system of dependence on English labor worked. But by the 1660s or so the calculus was shifting. London elites now wanted to keep the poor as wageworkers in England. They began to claim that "only the poor can make wealth." And "fewness of people is real poverty."[87] Sending the poor off to indenture in the colonies no longer made economic sense to England's elites.

And an English workforce had a huge disadvantage as far as planters were concerned. Over the previous centuries, England's working class, members of the polity, had won some rights, and they took those rights with them to the colonies. Meager though they were, they did limit the planters' ability to exploit. English could be indentured, but not enslaved. Servants had the right to take planters to court for excessive cruelty or violation of contract, and occasionally the courts actually upheld their rights. Whatever rights Africans had gained in their polities of origin, however, did not apply in the colonies, so they were more exploitable.[88] Armed and angry English colonists couldn't be kept from appropriating land and attempting to keep them landless clearly was dangerous. The gradual invention of racialized chattel slavery of non-English Others became the answer to supplying labor in the context of a relatively weak state, a context we will come back to in several more of these ancestor tales.

To make this solution work, English workers had to learn to see themselves as totally, irreconcilably, different from other workers, a difference that could not be made to disappear by conversion to Christianity or by learning the English language and English ways, a permanent difference that would make joint cooperative action practically impossible. That difference was the contrived concept of race. Divide and rule requires a wedge with which to divide, and whiteness was invented to provide that wedge. That process created white privilege and whiteness itself as a separate identifiable category—though who was white, given several generations of mixture, was often dependent on having sufficient power to claim that English was the ancestry that counted. The shift meant that your most basic identity, along with gender, was that you were white, not English, not Christian. That new identity carried the advantage that it could exclude Christian Africans and also be expanded to include a wider range of Europeans, not just the English.

Divide and rule may well have been cheaper than maintaining a permanent army to control the labor force, but the punishment a weak elite needed to use when moving further toward state formation meant it was not cheap in terms of lives lost, as historian Lerone Bennett makes clear in describing the decades after the rebellion in both the South and the North (which, like the South, also depended on unfree black and white labor, though to a lesser degree):

> The whole system of separation and subordination rested on official state terror. The exigencies of the situation required men to kill

some white people to keep them white and to kill many blacks to keep them black. In the North and South, men and women were maimed, tortured, and murdered in a comprehensive campaign of mass conditioning. The severed heads of black and white rebels were impaled on poles along the road as warnings to black people and white people, and opponents of the status quo were starved to death in chains and roasted slowly over open fires. Some rebels were branded; others were castrated. This exemplary cruelty, which was carried out as a deliberate process of mass education, was an inherent part of the new system. [89]

In the aftermath of the rebellion, legislation enhancing the already existing but often ambiguous legal differences between African and English, between slavery and indenture, accelerated dramatically. In the other North American colonies, laws surrounding slavery and racial differentiation gradually tightened as well. Those laws created the necessary difference between black and white.

In Virginia punishment for whites who ran away was worse if they ran with blacks than with whites, for instance. Interracial alliance and cooperation became dangerous, and whiteness became the wedge for dividing and ruling the entire labor force.[90] Whiteness became a real material advantage. White privilege gave whites the illusion that they had something to gain from supporting the regime that provided their racial privilege—but at the cost of accepting their own lesser, but real, exploitation and continued class subservience.

The privilege was also real. Whites were free, or had the expectation of freedom after indenture. Since they couldn't be enslaved, they were far less likely to be blackmailed into submission by threats to enslaved loved ones. They could whip blacks; they could testify against other whites in court. White servants could own possessions such as livestock, whereas slaves could have their possessions appropriated by their owners. White servants could take cases of mistreatment to court, and sometimes actually did. In 1675, land ownership was formally limited to whites. Whites could own guns, and were to receive a gun when they were freed. Gun ownership was thus a symbol of freedom as well as a symbol of racial distinction that denied blacks the possibility of membership in the racial fraternity of military manhood. Even free blacks were excluded from the militia in 1723.[91]

Laws like these and those that disenfranchised free people of color were gradually tightened to include anyone identified as being of African descent. New laws made slavery more clearly heritable through the mother, so that children of enslaved women were born enslaved, even when the father was white. Those laws were sharpened with laws that punished with banishment white women who had sex with black men.[92] Such laws prevented the further development of a free biracial population; you would be either white and free or black and enslaved. Thus, slavery was slowly turned into the inherited racial slavery that became the cornerstone of the colonial, and then US, economy, North as well as South. Toward the end of his life, Bruen Radford might have begun to feel the effects of white privilege in addition to class and male privilege. By the time his son George was an adult, however, whiteness and white privilege would have been as natural to his identity as being male. Lives, mostly black, continue to be lost to maintain that wedge, which continues to enable the system of divide and rule that serves elite interests. The legacy of Bacon's Rebellion is still with us.

THE LEGACY OF BACON'S REBELLION is still with us also in that it led to the next step in state formation. In the process of both laying to rest the rebellion and undermining the solidarity of the unfree and the poor, control of punishing became further centralized. As we saw earlier, back in X Radford's day establishment of the court system in 1634 had, to some extent, taken control of punishment from neighbors who policed one another and from the church, and placed it in the hands of local elites who ran the courts and frequently defied the governor and council. There was a running battle between local elites and the regional elites who, with the governor, nominally governed the colony. With the takeover by the Crown in the aftermath of Bacon's Rebellion, both lost power relative to the Crown. It is hardly surprising that war led to another step in state formation, with greater coercive power on the part of the state—we saw this effect after the events of 9/11.[93] In Virginia, the governor-general, appointed by the king, would now be answerable only to the king, not to the elected legislature or to a council composed of other colonial elites, as governors had previously been. Virginia's laws were now subject to royal approval or veto. The wealthy had to pay taxes. The Crown's court, with Crown-appointed justices, gained greater jurisdiction—thus control of punishment was moved a bit further out of local elite hands.[94]

So long as slavery remained, poor whites and enslaved Africans stood little chance of uniting in revolt. Divide and rule worked, and the elite no longer feared a white uprising. But the enhanced control of the colony by the Crown and of the workforce by the elites came at a price—the shift from indenture to slavery meant an exponential increase in the number of enslaved Africans in Virginia, and with that shift came a new fear: slave revolt. Enslaved Africans were being imported after Bacon's Rebellion in ever-increasing numbers, and the earlier ambiguities that somewhat mitigated African servitude had been legislated out of existence. As Governor Spotswood warned in 1710, "Freedom Wears a Cap which Can without a Tongue Call Together all Those who Long to Shake off The Fetters of Slavery and Such an Insurrection would surely be attended with Most Dreadfull Consequences."[95] And indeed, resistance and revolt among the enslaved was endemic.[96]

This was a new Virginia, one where whites, at least for a while, were no longer to be feared. Instead, the fear of black revolt and the use of black labor shaped all lives, white as well as black. And Indians, with military power and diplomatic skill, continued to limit white expansion and at the same time mediated, and fought in, the imperial struggles of competing European states. This was not the world of X or John Radford. Instead this was a world in which George Radford and Ann Massey, who became his wife, inherited privilege and where Alexander Davidson, marrying Sarah Ellis, eventually adopted it, owning Venis and Adam. So we turn to their story, the story of Venis and Adam and Davidsons, and the continuing struggle over punishment and dispossession.

CHAPTER 3

Ancestor Tales of Slavery, Slaving, and Women with Voice

FEB 13, 1748

...APPRAISED YE ESTATE OF ALEXANDER DAVIDSON:

As follows: Negro woman named Venis 30.0.0
One Negro boy named Adam 25.0.0

Into the story now come two sets of people propelled to Virginia by the two elite uses of force in the pursuit of power and wealth: war and punishment.[1] The first set were Africans, a "Negro woman named Venis" and a boy named Adam. Africans were captured in wars between rival kingdoms, wars defined by the Christian religious hierarchies and the English state as "just," making it legally and religiously acceptable to sell those taken captive. Or, equally justified by African elites, they were taken to pay off debts, to punish misbehavior, or handed over as religious sacrifices.[2] The second set now entering the story were Scottish Jacobites, including Alexander Davidson, "choosing" to be sold, also with the approval of Christian religious hierarchies and the English state, rather than risk execution as punishment for participation, willingly or not, in a war between elites contending for sovereignty. Alexander,

Venis, and Adam were all unfree laborers, but unlike Venis and Adam, Alexander's servitude was temporary, probably for seven years. He died eventually as the owner of the unfree laborers listed in the appraisal of his estate. His ownership gave him the freedom to punish; he was the recipient of the benefits of the now well-established racialized difference between indenture and slavery, between whites who could not be enslaved and Africans and Indians who could.[3]

So first, Venis and her life in Igboland; then, in chapter 4, Alexander and his flight from Scotland. Finally, in chapter 5, Sarah Ellis enters the story. Born in Virginia, she became Alexander's wife, and so starts the intertwining of the stories, Igbo, Scottish, and English Virginian, free and enslaved in a slave society.

"VENIS," A NAME TO WHICH SHE SURELY answered, but quite likely not her own. "Negro," a well-honed legal identity by 1748 but quite likely not the one she was born with. "Woman," another well-honed legal identity but quite likely carrying implications far different from those where she was born. Thirty pounds, a monetary value placing her worth above all else Alexander owned, higher than a boy's, and many times that of the cattle she was appraised with at Alexander's death. It is likely, according to statistical analysis, that, described as a "woman," not a "girl" or a "wench," or an "old woman" and valued at thirty pounds, she was somewhere between twenty and thirty years old at the time of the estate evaluation. Adam, as a "boy," could have been anywhere between childhood and twenty years of age, but given his above-average evaluation for a "boy," he was quite likely in his late teens.[4] Venis could have been his mother . . . or not. Alexander died intestate, so there is not even a will that might have indicated the relationship between Venis and Adam and might have given clues to where she came from, or what was to happen to her after Alexander's death. So that is all I know of her—a brief surfacing in a court record in Spotsylvania County, Virginia, but otherwise invisible, despite living a life every bit as real as that of those Radfords and Davidsons whose traces are far more visible.

What follows is therefore fiction, at least as far as the actual person is concerned who was identified as "Venis" by those who held her enslaved in Virginia. But what happened to nine and a half million people, including Venis, and what they themselves did, in Africa and in the Americas, is not fiction, and it is that story I want to tell about punishment and state formation and people's lives.[5] So I am briefly borrowing Venis to be the central character who carries us from her life as a very young woman in what is now Nigeria to becoming a human commodity in the hands of Aro traders from the southeastern edge of what is now called Igboland, where I am assuming she lived.[6] Apparently deemed unsuitable for purchase into a wealthy Aro or Igbo household, she would have been sold to English traders on the coastal Bight of Biafra sometime around 1730 or a bit after.[7] Eventually she found herself the property of Alexander, perhaps a gift or a purchase to relieve Sarah, Alexander's wife, of the female outdoor physical labor that marked a white Virginia family's lower-class status. The contrast between these two ways of life, that of the Igbo town and of the recently formed Spotsylvania County, must have been stark, despite the fact that people lived enslaved in both.

Obviously, I have just made an enormous leap, from a mere entry in the appraisal of an estate to statements about who Venis was and where she came from. That leap is based purely on probabilities. About sixty percent of the people shipped to Virginia in the early 1700s were Igbo—or at least that is how the English identified them, perhaps less than accurately—and the numbers shipped from Biafra increased with time. The result was that most of the people growing tobacco in the Chesapeake had arrived on ships coming from ports on the Bight of Biafra, and most Igbo being shipped out of Africa were shipped from the Bight.[8] Though in general many more men than women were sold to the Americas rather than kept as domestic slaves locally, an unusually high proportion of the people shipped from the Bight were women.[9] This all makes it somewhat more likely that Venis came from Igboland rather than elsewhere in West Africa. If so, then she probably went through the hands of the Aro, as did a great many Igbo.[10] The Aro traders from the periphery of Igboland organized the slave trade through the Bight during this period, using a highly developed network for creating debtors and criminals for sale, as well as for wars and raids to produce captives who could be sold.

Actually, Venis could have been born in Virginia. Africans who survived shipment to Virginia in the 1700s generally lived long enough to reproduce.[11] This was very different from what happened to Africans (and English indentured servants) who were shipped to the West Indies. There, conditions were so awful that it took three imports to raise the population permanently by one—they died too fast, and women were mostly too overworked and underfed for successful pregnancies.[12] So if Venis's parents had arrived in Virginia in the early 1700s, they could well have lived to produce a healthy baby who would also survive. I'm guessing that this is not what happened, however, judging by her name. Owners commonly gave African arrivals classical names such as Caesar or Pluto, much as owners might name a dog or horse. Baptismal records in one Virginia parish rarely include such names. Babies born in Virginia to Africans were named by their parents, with the owner's consent, or by negotiating with the owner, who had ultimate naming rights, and were often recorded with names that were diminutives of English names—Tom, not Thomas, Betty, not Elizabeth. African names were quite rare, although the family may have used them privately.[13] So it is likely that Venis (or Venus) was named for a Roman goddess after her arrival; Adam, with a common English name, on the other hand, was probably born in Virginia. As for the timing of her arrival, there were importation peaks in Virginia in 1725, with 3,500 people, and in 1735, with 3,000.[14] Of these, at least 1,600 a year came from Biafra.[15]

AFRICANS WERE AT FIRST ONLY ONE of several sources of coerced unfree labor in the developing Atlantic world, but by the 1700s they were the primary source. Enslaved Africans by then had outstripped the temporarily enslaved English indentured and enslaved Native Americans. Trading in human lives was hardly new; the business of the production and sale of unfree labor was probably the world's first globalized business. Arguably, it was at the epicenter of a developing capitalism and funded the take-off of the Industrial Revolution. [16]

But long before capitalism had anything to do with it, people were selling each other all over the world.[17] Slavery was often the punishment for crime. Often, particularly in somewhat less stratified societies, this slavery was tempered with some rights and with the possibility of earning freedom, as it was for Igbo household slaves before the burgeoning of the Atlantic slave trade in the 1600s.[18]

War captives were sold pretty much wherever people fought wars and had social structures that were sufficiently unequal that one person could benefit from the labor of others—labor in either sense of the word, whether the labor of reproduction or the labor of production. Male war captives were bought and sold in societies able to mount such a believable threat of force that owners assumed these well-trained fighters, now enslaved, would be too intimidated to kill them in their sleep. Greece and Rome, for instance, pulled this off, but there were male war captives in smaller numbers throughout much of Europe, along with many other people in various forms of unfree labor—serfs in Europe, "untouchables" in India, bound peasants in China.[19] Coerced labor was the basis of wealth creation in all societies whose elites could muster the force to get away with it. However, in societies where the use of force was less centralized, where rapid and sure punishment by some form of police or military action wasn't available, most male war captives were killed, often with ceremony.[20] At least some groups of Venis's Igbo, for instance, gained respect by bringing home the heads of men they killed in war for ceremonial display—they didn't leave them rotting dishonorably in public on posts as the English were wont to do.[21]

Women and children captured in war or raids were a far safer bet. Women could be quickly tethered by children, particularly if their children were given rights within the household or kin group that owned them. This was quite common in societies where having a large household and many kin and clients gave status. "Wealth in people" was what counted, as it did for the Powhatan, and as we will encounter again in the Scottish Highlands. Being able to support lots of followers marked the abundance you controlled.[22] A bought woman could provide domestic labor; her children, fathered by men of the household, could be absorbed into the kin group or could be freed to become grateful retainers or clients. In some cases, she could also be eventually freed to function as an additional wife. For women, none of this was particularly unusual around the world, except in Europe with its formal and unusual insistence on monogamy—supplemented by rampant prostitution, kept women, and considerable winking at infidelity, at least among the elite and for men more generally.

Thus, that many African societies had slaves, like much of the rest of the world, should be no surprise. Most were women, but there were also men who were born as slaves or who were captured as children. Slaves performed a wide variety of tasks, from mining to farming to accounting to transportation to soldiering. The Igbo apparently had relatively few slaves, unlike some of their neighbors.[23] But even where slavery was more common in polities in what became Nigeria, it was not the basis of the political and economic structure of these polities in the 1700s. That changed in some areas after the British outlawed the Atlantic slave trade in 1807 and African elites needed another source of income. They turned to plantation production, such as the palm oil industry in Nigeria. So African elites continued buying and selling slaves, but instead of selling them to American elites, they used the slaves' labor themselves.[24] This, of course, is long after Venis or her ancestors had left Africa. In her time and place, it was the Aro who organized the trade that would have carried Venis to the coast, to be used elsewhere.

IF VENIS ARRIVED IN VIRGINIA in her late teens or early twenties, the most common age for enslavement, she would have been old enough to have been thoroughly involved in the life of the Igbo village from which she came. Unfortunately for my story there was very little contemporary reporting about Igbo life in the 1700s. Although a lot was written by contemporary Africans and Europeans about the coastal kingdoms through whose ports Igbo captives were shipped, hardly anything was written about the inland villages where they had been captured. Europeans waited on the coast for African traders to deliver people to purchase, having negotiated the permission to do so with the local kings, who taxed them and restricted their movements.[25] Not that the European traders had much interest in going up the rivers of the Niger Delta to capture or purchase slaves themselves. They thought the coast was healthier.

The result was that African kings and traders determined the form taken by the slave trade just as much as did the Europeans. For a while Europeans recognized African sovereignties, just as they had recognized Powhatan sovereignty.[26] Africans maintained the political independence of what is now Nigeria into the mid-1800s, when the British began establishing protectorates. The first Europeans did not see anything at all of Igboland until 1830. And it wasn't until the end of the 1800s that they penetrated much beyond the rivers. Missionaries were operating in what they referred to as that "Citadel of Satan" by the mid-1800s, but when the British declared a Protectorate over all of what is now southern Nigeria in 1906, there were still sections of the Igbo interior that had yet to see a European.[27] Thus for Venis's time there are no recorded Igbo oral histories, no missionary reports, no travelers' tales, no European traders to describe Igboland markets; nor did the international traders and historians from the Mediterranean world have much to say, although they did earlier.

There are detailed reports on the earlier medieval kingdoms of West Africa; the wealth, the kings, and the markets of kingdoms such as Ghana impressed Muslim historians. Many of them, writing between 900 and 1500 CE, were armchair travelers who had never been to Africa. They drew on the knowledge of merchants who crossed the Sahara, following the spread of Islam, to reach the burgeoning markets for gold and people in Africa and the Mediterranean.[28] Igboland was largely left out of these accounts. It had no great kingdoms; the Aro trade network had not yet developed; it had no gold; it wasn't sufficiently unequal to produce large numbers of saleable people. Even its kola nuts were not the type preferred by Muslims to the north.[29] Igboland remained "pagan" and off the map as far as both Muslims and Christians were concerned.

And while some enslaved Igbo in the Americas certainly learned to write, they didn't have the freedom to spend time detailing their lives in Igboland. Of those who gained their freedom, only Olaudah Equiano wrote a narrative that includes a description of Igboland, the land from which he was captured as a child in approximately 1756, perhaps a couple of decades after Venis might have been shipped from the Bight of Biafra. His narrative is the only real, albeit limited, source of knowledge about Igbo life in the 1700s.[30] So to get a picture of Venis's life before she was enslaved, and how she might have come to be enslaved, we have to depend on reading backwards into history. Accounts began trickling in during the late 1800s, and in the mid-1900s anthropologists were sent by the British to give British administrators advice on controlling these people, whose women had a terrible tendency to "riot" with "savage passions" in "frenzied mobs" against British restrictions on women's autonomy.[31]

Reading backward this way, assuming that little has changed in 150 or so years, is often an iffy proposition. The temptation to do this is particularly dangerous when we assume that so-called primitive people—Powhatan, Igbo—led a stagnant tradition-bound life, with no new ideas, no coming and going of peoples and powers, no realignments of neighboring polities, a "people without history."[32] In the case of the Igbo, however, we can be somewhat more confident about reading backwards—Equiano's account provides a baseline against which to compare. More recent historians and anthropologists have therefore been able to use oral history as another source. People who were themselves quite elderly in the 1970s and 1980s told the histories they had learned as children from grandparents and great-grandparents. Those oral histories give a window onto life at the end of the 1800s. With caution, we can say that many attributes of late nineteenth- and early twentieth-century Igbo life do appear to be consistent with Equiano's recollections, or more likely with the knowledge he acquired from other Igbo as an adult and included in his memoir.[33] We can glean a bit more because kingdoms surrounding Igboland recorded their own histories, at least in terms of kings and conquests and migrations.

African, African American, European, and Euro-American historians and anthropologists have used all these sources to piece together a picture of Igboland in the 1700s. Their analysis depends on the older texts as well as on the more recent number-crunching computer analyses of census materials, shipping reports, days spent loading people at particular ports, and a wide array of other data. Needless to say, the perspective is no longer primarily colonialist. Since Igbo culture varied considerably from village to village, and since there is no way of knowing which might have been Venis's home, I have tried to make a generalized composite picture of Igboland in the early 1700s and of the life Venis might have led.[34]

POWER AND AUTHORITY AMONG the Igbo were widely dispersed, and the power to punish was held in thoroughly local hands. Many small autonomous polities, in other words, held sovereignty, and there was nothing resembling a "state." For the British, of course, this later became the source of massive headaches as they attempted to demonstrate their sovereignty by consolidating the power to punish in their own hands.

In Venis's time, the power of the coastal kingdoms still held off the British, who thus had little direct effect on Igboland. Parts of Igboland were to some extent under the sway of the Igala, others under that of the kingdom of Benin, while Nri, another kingdom, had for a time a significant influence over northern Igboland, particularly in religious matters. There was considerable variety in the details of Igbo social structure, partially because of these differing influences, and partially because there was no overall governing or organizing structure; instead the Igbo shared certain aspects of culture.[35] Basically, Igbo village-groups were autonomous groups of kin, organized into corporate lineages, and "governed" by elders in council and a number of separate organizations, all more or less cooperating and playing complementary functions. All controlled the punishing related to their own functions, and all were dependent on the acceptance of their rulings for enforcement.[36] Village-groups in some areas did have a highest-ranking leader, called an *eze*, sometimes referred to in English as king. However, the eze was chosen by the elders, could be removed, and was under the guidance of the council.[37] Thus, there was no king with power, no kingdom, and no centralized use of force. This is not to say the Igbo were thoroughly egalitarian. Some people had more wealth and power and influence than others, but gaining that prestige depended on giving away wealth. A certain amount of leveling was built into the system—you gave away much of your wealth, trading it in for prestige.[38] Age mattered, as did seniority in the lineage system. Age and seniority got you respect; combined with talent they could get you influence and some power.

Venis most likely grew up in a large compound—a cluster of family buildings.[39] One would have been her father's public room, where he received visitors and carried on business, with his bedroom in back. Each of his wives would have had her own house, with garden land behind it and her own farmland farther away, outside the compound. In essence, each wife had her own sub-compound. The oldest son of the senior wife would inherit the compound and its land. Other sons inherited the land that had been allotted to their mother. This meant there was frequently a land shortage, and younger sons often moved out to establish their own compounds on unused patrilineage land. Or brothers could continue to share a compound. Having the land and organization to keep a large compound going, with lots of people in it, was a sign of prosperity and status.[40]

Near Venis's family compound would be others headed by men who were close relatives of her father—forming other branches of the same patrilineage. If a branch died out, the land reverted to the patrilineage. The village itself would contain several such patrilineages, with highest status held by the patrilineage descended from the first son of the senior wife of the original village founder. Within each patrilineage, highest status went to the senior branch. Then there was one further level of organization: villages were part of village-groups, that is, several villages that saw themselves as related. The village-group was the largest cooperating unit in Igboland, carrying out some rituals together, coordinating rotating market days, and to some extent creating laws that applied to the entire village group. "Laws" on any level, however, were really a matter of consensus. The elders in council, after hearing what everyone who wanted to put their oar in had to say, could make a ruling. Everyone there could even approve of the ruling. But if people on a day-to-day basis ignored it, it would gradually fade away. [41]

Now, if you are like me, and like some of the anthropologists and historians who have written about Igboland, you have been subconsciously picturing men carrying out all this governance. [42] That picture would be wrong, though. Wrong in two ways. Women as biological females did hold considerable authority. Beyond that, women could become men, fill positions that had to be held by men, and carry the authority that biological men typically held in those roles. [43]

So first, women as biological women. Each village and village group had an organization of the women who lived there—the women who had married into the patrilineages. The villages were exogamous—you had to marry an outsider, and on marrying, women moved to the husband's village. So Venis's mother would have been a member of the organization of patrilineage wives. As such, she would have helped settle disputes among the members, participating in judging and fining if necessary, but more often mediating. Most important, women were the traders, and the organization of wives ran the market, regulating prices and setting rules that men had to abide by. [44] In cases of desperation the organization might decide that all the members would go on strike together, refusing to cook, refusing to have sex, maybe picking up and all going back to their natal village. The husbands apparently gave in without much fuss.

Venis herself would have belonged to another organization—the multigenerational organization of patrilineage daughters. Patrilineage daughters had serious clout. As a group, they could decide to discipline the men of their patrilineage, all of whom would have sisters and cousins, women of their own generation and above, among the members of the organization of patrilineage daughters. Abusive husbands might find themselves punished by their lineage sisters. If the men were threatening to go to war with another village-group, the organization of patrilineage daughters, with members married into many different villages, mediated the quarrel. They likewise mediated disputes between individuals. A village dispute that couldn't be settled at the village level might be referred for judgment to the organization of village-group patrilineage daughters. They might also decide to "sit on a man," going to his compound en masse, hollering insults, exposing their private parts—the ultimate insult—and generally creating an enormously humiliating ruckus.[45] Patrilineage men, reportedly, were quite reluctant to get in wrong with the women of the patrilineage. Actually, Venis's mother would have belonged to both these organizations, attending meetings of the patrilineage wives in her marital village, and travelling to different villages for meetings of the organization of patrilineage daughters. Meetings rotated among the homes of married members, and so the organization formed a network of connections between all the villages into which women of the patrilineage had married.

Religion provided other forms of enormous prestige and authority for biological women. The senior woman of a patrilineage was revered; her status was greater than that of the senior man, and her word carried greater authority. The senior woman of a patrilineage branch, within her own branch, was likewise revered, although in terms of the whole patrilineage her position was of lesser importance than that of senior women of more senior branches. Such women carried a semi-sacred aura, as, to some extent, did all elderly women and men. Beyond purely age and seniority—both ascribed characteristics—was the possibility of achieving another form of status. Wealthy women, whose exceptional ability to acquire wealth proved that the goddess had chosen them, would pay the costs of taking on the title of *ekwe.* In some parts of Igboland, these titled women functioned as the community's final court of justice and law enforcement.[46] The most senior ekwe of a village-group, the *agba ekwe,* held "the most central political position" in the village-group, with vetoing rights in village and village-group assemblies.[47] She was second in rank only to the local goddess, and while there were also titles that men could take, and some gained such widespread influence that they were called *eze*—king-like—they could be challenged, be questioned, even lose status. This could not happen to the agba ekwe.[48]

Anthropologists call this whole system, in which men and women had parallel positions and powers within their own sex, a dual-sex system.[49] Each sex had its areas of authority in relation to the village as a whole, and each had its own internal systems of organization. For men, the age-grade system was critical. Men went through life in cohorts, each cohort with its own leadership, and cohorts took on a succession of different responsibilities as they aged. Aged men who also were talented as informal leaders and in their own economic endeavors carried the greatest authority in the general village meetings.[50] Additionally, men could raise their status through the acquisition of wealth and of titles.

So far, we have been talking about men and women in the roles assigned to them, or available to them, as members of their biological sex. In that system, in daily life, men probably did have somewhat greater power and access to wealth than women did. Husbands had somewhat more power than wives. Only men could perform in masquerade as spirits who patrolled the village and brought people to judgment before the village council. It was men who received most of the bridewealth when a daughter married. Men of the patrilineage and its branches controlled land and houses; men controlled the crops (yams and palm oil) that produced the greatest profits and status. Women, farming a husband's land, did largely control the crops they grew, but more of their crops went to feed their families, and when sold they didn't bring in as much, so routes to prestige for women through wealth were a bit more difficult to traverse than they were for men. [51]

However, this isn't the end of the story. Women could sometimes *become* men and as men take positions of authority, controlling land or people, or both.[52] That they were not biological men did continue to matter, however. They were not "full men"; like many biological men, they were only regular men—men who had not been successful enough to acquire the right to perform as a supernatural in masquerade. They could not, through mask, costume, and dance, perform as a spirit. [53] Despite that restriction, a woman could become a husband; she could marry a wife in what anthropologists call woman-woman marriage and become a female husband. The women who became female husbands were especially likely to be wealthy and without children from their own marriage, and thus in need of heirs, but this choice was available to any woman with ambition and the resources to pay bridewealth. Readers who are steeped in American culture might assume this describes a lesbian relationship, but woman-woman marriage had nothing to do with sex between the two women. Instead it had to do with gaining a workforce and children for the female husband—and thus access to status, wealth, perhaps *ekwe* titles, and heirs.

Perhaps Venis was the daughter of a woman married to a female husband. Probably she wasn't, since more women were married to men than to women, but let's just suppose for a moment. Her "father," not the sperm donor, but the person who paid the bridewealth that validated her mother's marriage and who fulfilled the responsibilities of a father toward her, would be the female husband. By paying bridewealth, the female husband laid claim to the children born to the wife, in the same way that any man did in paying bridewealth. Some anthropologists say that bridewealth isn't really about claiming a wife. Instead, it is about claiming the children the wife has, regardless of who the biological father might be. Perhaps a way to think of it is that the husband is laying claim to the fruits of her womb, not necessarily to sole insemination rights. Among the Igbo and many other societies, in a divorce, the woman's family returned the bridewealth, and the husband had no claim on later children. [54]

Let me add that for the Igbo at least (for there were numerous African and Native American societies that legitimized some version of woman-woman marriage) adultery in any marriage was a serious offense against the gods.[55] A wife in a woman-woman marriage, however, was expected to produce children for her female husband, and thus did—discreetly—have sex with a lover who at least sometimes was acknowledged by the female husband, while sex with anyone else would be considered adultery. In any case the lover would never be able to lay claim to the children. He had not paid the bridewealth, so they were not his children. Alternatively, a wealthy woman could also formally marry a wife "for her brother" or even for a slave or former slave. She paid the bridewealth, the woman acted as a wife for the man, perhaps one of his many wives, but the children belonged to the woman who had paid bridewealth. She was their father. A woman could also become a man if her father formally declared she was a man, making her a male daughter. Men without sons might take this step in order to have an heir, so that the lineage branch did not die out. In this case, the male daughter would not marry, but might have children, or might marry a woman. In either case, the lineage would carry on through her, so the land would not revert to the patrilineage. [56]

As male daughters or as female husbands, women gained authority over people and labor. Getting the wealth together to provide bride-wealth for a marriage would be more difficult for a woman than for a man. But if she succeeded, she had made an investment that could be expected to pay off. She would have increased her labor force with a wife, enabling her to accumulate wealth. So having a wife enhanced her ability to handle the enormous costs of the feasting and gifting entailed in taking on a title that would raise her status. As men, such women participated in village councils with authority equal to that of a biological man. They could take male titles, expect service and respect within family and lineage as a man, and have a public house in the compound surrounded by the houses of their wives and perhaps sons.

Although there is a great deal of literature supporting this description of the role of female men, one authority, Ugo Nwokeji, maintains that becoming male in this way was not part of Igbo culture in the 1700s, and thus Venis would have known nothing of this kind of gender flex-ibility. Instead, Nwokeji says, women could and did buy slaves, rather than marry wives.[57] Given the way in which Igboland household slaves became incorporated into both production and reproduction, in many ways gaining something of the status of wives and lineage members, it seems that there could have been considerable slippage between the two positions. Nwokeji says that it was the British objection to slav-ery after its abolition that made colonized Igbo female husbands claim that what they were practicing was a traditional form of marriage, not slavery. However, before colonization a woman simply owning a slave did not become a man. That gender became more flexible under the British seems highly improbable, given their extreme inflexibility on matters of sex and gender, and the way British colonialism typically destroyed whatever power women held, as it did for the Igbo.[58]

This is the context in which Venis would have grown up, expecting as she aged to gain status, perhaps wealth, perhaps wives. She would certainly have expected to exercise a certain amount of autonomy and initiative, to live a life where her own work directly benefited her and those around her, to whom she was bound by kinship, duty, and, we can hope, affection. That is not the life she lived, however.

BY THE TIME VENIS MIGHT HAVE been in her teens the Aro had expanded their trade network throughout Igboland from the base they had established at Arochukwu, near the border of what became Cameroon.[59] Their focus by this time was on the provision of saleable people for the Atlantic slave trade, rather than for the smaller trade north across the Sahara. Nwokeji describes their spread as a trade diaspora.[60] Aro merchant lineages set up in many Igbo towns, often establishing their own separate ward. Others started new Aro towns, often attracting a diverse group of non-Aro from around the region.[61] The slave trade through the Bight of Biafra was an African affair, shaped by the social structure and cultural values of the various African societies involved. Although Aro traders were taking advantage of English demand, the slave trade didn't become an English business until the traders reached the coast with their captives.[62] Nor, in the Bight of Biafra, was it Muslim, as Americans often assume, although it certainly was in other areas.

The Aro used the existing systems for producing saleable people and modified those systems to take advantage of the growing English demand for slaves.[63] Local wars produced captives; some of these wars were apparently fomented by the Aro, much as the English fomented wars between Native American polities for the same purpose.[64] Raids, not rising to the level of war between polities, but specifically for the purpose of stealing people to sell to the Aro, were another source of captives, mostly carried out by non-Aro in need of income. Kidnapping was extremely common—that is what happened to Olaudah Equiano.

Pawning people was part of the existing system before the Atlantic slave trade. You could even pawn yourself or someone over whom you had power. Junior members of lineages often found themselves pawned, as did children and slaves. Pawns were given in exchange for a loan. Theoretically, pawns would return to freedom once they paid off the debt and sometimes they did. Pawns worked part of the Igbo four-day week for the owner, part for themselves. With luck, they accumulated enough during the days that belonged to them to eventually pay off the debt. Or the family that had pawned them might later redeem them. Without luck, the pawn might be sold to pay off the rest of the debt, or might simply remain a pawn forever.[65] Poverty and sometimes famine were quite real in war-torn areas of Igboland by the 1800s—a point of similarity between Venis's home and Scotland, the home of Alexander Davidson, her owner-to-be.[66]

Thus debt was common, an incentive for pawning and, as the Atlantic slave trade grew, for kidnapping and raiding among those who could pull it off. Alternatively, needy parents sometimes sold their children to pay off debt or in hopes that the child would now have enough to eat. It is unlikely that this happened to Venis; people sold by their parents for economic reasons were usually bought and kept as domestic slaves, rather than sold into the Atlantic trade.[67] Nonetheless, Venis could have been caught up by any of these systems for producing slaves.

Another possibility: perhaps Venis was trapped in the "justice" system. That system played a critical role in the slave trade; punishment provided unfree labor, as it did in England with indenture. At this point, we need to make a digression, back to village governance in Igboland, but also back to the concept of dual sovereignty, to see how the Aro did not simply use the existing social control system, but enhanced it, or perhaps changed it so dramatically that it was to all intents and purposes a new system.

IN TALKING ABOUT HOW IGBO VILLAGES worked, I described only a part of their system of governance, the secular part, with some intimations of the role of religion. However, anthropologists

seem to agree that "the real rulers of Igbo towns were the ancestors or spirits, and that the living persons who acted as rulers were
merely the agents of these divinities."[68] Reminiscent of dual sovereignty for the Powhatan and for the early English, Igbo priests had
great authority.[69] They determined the desires of the spirits or gods
through divination, and in consultation with the elders decided
what should be done. The outcome was then declared to the village.
These invisible divine beings made their presence very real, mani-
fested sometimes by strange noises in the night and regularly in the
performance of masquerades. Displeasing them caused sickness, bad
luck, or death for individuals, for lineages, or for whole villages.[70] It
thus behooved everyone to avoid those specific behaviors that could
bring supernatural disaster, major offenses such as murder, adultery,
incest (which included sex between people born in the same village),
or sex after the birth of a child before the woman had had a period
(if the result was a birth, she was punished by being buried alive
and the baby was thrown away). Seizing and selling the child of a
member of your own village was another such offense, punished by
hanging.[71] Unauthorized viewing of the secret and sacred masquerade costumes was another. Land disputes that couldn't be settled by
mediation were also under the purview of the priests. As in England
and in Virginia's parish processioning, control of land, the validation
of who had the right to use a particular bit of land, was so critical to
the entire social structure that it was overseen by sacred authority.
Igbo priests used divination to determine who was right in such disputes. Apparently, the priest often concluded that both were wrong
and redrew the boundaries.[72]

Other offenses, such as stealing, were merely against the law but
did not offend the gods.[73] Traditionally, when a violator was caught
red-handed those involved administered punishment instantly. Some
thieves were buried alive; other forms of execution, or beating, were
also possible. Less severe offenses against human law, such as refusal
to return the bridewealth in a case of divorce, unpaid debts, or fights
in which someone was injured, required less severe punishment. Fines
or various forms of restitution were common. In cases that were not

clear-cut, a group of elders would act as arbitrators. If they didn't reach an agreement or if the defendant refused to cooperate with the judgment, either party could call for a trial at a meeting of the whole village. Judges would be appointed, everyone who wanted to express an opinion was given their say, and if necessary, the priest would consult spiritual beings through divination. For less dramatic offenses the secular organizations concerned, for instance the men's age-grade cohorts or the organization of patrilineage wives, did the judging and punishing.[74] These organizations generally imposed fines of some sort, which were paid into the organization itself and used both for feasting and for division among the organization members.

Some Igbo villages had oracles they consulted through their priests.[75] The Igbo generally assumed that illness, death, and disasters were the result of violations that displeased the gods, and oracles could tell you what you needed to do to remove the pollution that was the cause of your problems. A class of slaves served these oracles and their shrines, supervised by the shrine priest, carrying out religious duties, sometimes mediating disputes, and sometimes enforcing the priest's decisions. Some authors have described this as a caste system; others disagree.[76] In any case, a possible sacrifice was to provide a slave for the shrine. You could buy a slave for this purpose, or you could volunteer yourself or a family member. You could take refuge at a shrine in a neighboring village to escape capital punishment—but in exchange for your life, you became a slave in service to the shrine. War captives could do the same to avoid being sold into the trans-Sahara slave trade. Traditionally, such slaves served for life and were not sold away.[77] Their situation was different from that of household slaves. Freedom was not a possibility; they could marry only among themselves; and their children would be slaves. They were in many ways an outcast group; but they were also under the protection of the god of the shrine they served. They could marry, were often provided with land, and had a share of the food donated at the god's shrine.[78]

Aro traders used Igbo secular punishment as a source of saleable people. A heavy fine for a poor person could lead to debt, and thus to pawning and possible slavery. As the Atlantic slave trade gained momentum, slavery became a more common Igbo punishment for crime—and selling criminals to the Aro was profitable. The Aro began to use their oracle to produce even more saleable people by tweaking the system of offenses against the gods by "spreading the belief in the dangers of abominations and taboo violations," such as a woman climbing a tree or a child whose lower teeth came in before the upper ones.[79] The Aro at Arochukwu had what neighboring people believed was a particularly powerful oracle, and some non-Aro traveled there for difficult cases of either crime or disaster. Using their oracle, the Aro enhanced this system out of all recognition, producing saleable people by defining many more offenses against the gods than the Igbo had previously recognized.

Whether the Aro devised their strategy with malice aforethought and a cynical manipulation of religion is a matter of dispute. But regardless, their oracle was "one of the most effective agencies of Aro domination."[80] Members of the Aro trade network established a shrine to their oracle in each of their villages and town wards spread around Igboland. The Aro themselves were not seen as conquerors, but they did expect, insist upon, and receive high status, setting themselves apart from local people. Northrup and Nwokeji both believe that maintaining that Aro identity was critical to their ability to dominate the trading networks of Igboland.[81] That a trade diaspora could pull this off is, as Nwokeji points out, unusual. The respect in which their oracle was held may have contributed to their status—the Aro were the "children of god." So also, surely, did their military prowess, their alliances, and their trade relationship with Europeans.[82] Meddling with an Aro trader was definitely not a good idea.

The Aro themselves didn't consult the Arochukwu oracle for judgment; according to Nwokeji they "knew better than to expose themselves to the . . . ruse." [83] Instead, the Aro had an organization, the *Ekpe* society, which handled their disputes, provided law enforcement, oversaw credit, and provided financial security for transactions between themselves and various European traders. The society guaranteed the trust system of credit by which European traders advanced trade goods to coastal traders, who in turn advanced them to the Aro, who eventually repaid the original trader with slaves.[84]

The Aro high status made it possible for them to encourage non-Aro to consult the oracle. They purposely spread belief in the laws they promulgated, according to Nwokeji, claiming that violators needed to be sent to the shrine at Arochukwu, "manipulating information and local people's fears."[85] Only sacrifice could alleviate the consequences of violations. And the presence of illness or other problems proved that someone, perhaps unwittingly or perhaps in secret, had committed an offense. The priests were needed to detect the offender. They usually chose someone the people involved could accept as the violator, either because they believed divination proved guilt or because the person chosen was believable as a violator.[86] The violation may in fact have been real, or the fact of illness could be taken as proof that a violation had occurred, regardless of facts. Ultimately, someone had to accept responsibility and perform the sacrifice/punishment that would remove the impurity and its threat.

Like the British turning petty crimes into serious offenses in order to provide convicts who would volunteer for indenture, the Aro oracle, and sometimes village elders, prescribed slavery for quite minor offenses as demand grew on the coast.[87] Meeting the cost of sacrifices to remove the deadly threat of spiritual displeasure drove more and more people into debt, creating more pawns or causing people to volunteer themselves or others as slaves for the oracle. On top of that, the oracle frequently indicated that slavery was the only option for the offender. Many of those who were enslaved to the shrine no longer served the oracle for life, as they had previously. Instead, they were never seen again. People believed the oracle "ate" its victims. Really, they were handed off into the Atlantic slave trade through the Aro trade network. Just how many slaves the Aro oracle produced, how many more were acquired through local punishing and sacrificing, and how these methods might have ranked in comparison to kidnapping and raiding is a matter of debate.[88] Perhaps Venis was one of those powerless people handed over by a relative to appease the gods and save a lineage or a village from disaster.

REGARDLESS OF HOW VENIS MIGHT have found herself in the hands of Aro traders, it would certainly have been through an exercise of power. Force would have been behind her trip to the coast—force exerted by kin, by an owner if she was already enslaved or pawned, by the gods through their agents the priests, by military might, or clandestine kidnappers. But it is hard to conceive of a less centralized system for the exercise of force. No individual, no group, had a monopoly on the control of punishment (the exercise of force internally in a polity) or on the control of a military (for a polity's external use of force), whether in the Aro trade network or in Igbo villages. Igbo village-groups were autonomous little polities. The power to punish, on which governance ultimately depended, was atomized, with bits held by various secular organizations believed to have religious legitimation, and other bits held directly by a variety of representatives of the sacred. Control of the use of force externally was likewise atomized. For the Igbo there was no state, or anything even resembling a state.[89]

In Venis's time, the British did not claim sovereignty over Igboland, and neither did the Aro. Yet it is hard to imagine that the slave trade could have gotten off the ground without the power of a state behind it to finance the use of force it required. Applying force came at a price, at both the European and the African end: manacles, ships, crews, some form of credit, food, guards, holding facilities on the coast, and warehouses for goods to trade into the interior. In the interior, transport canoes and their crews, credit, war matèriel, food for captives and captors, guards to prevent escape and to prevent raids by rival slavers bent on theft—all of this cost something in money or goods, and all of it required careful organization and legitimation.[90] The Aro and local kings provided the African organization, credit, and protection for the trade, while European investors had state backing, and in the case of the English the navy, the granting of a royal monopoly to select investors, and a stable banking system. This was all part of what the historian Sven Beckert calls "war capitalism," a term he finds far more accurate than the more usual "mercantilism" for a description of a system of merchant capitalism directly dependent on military might.[91]

Although the question of "stateness" for the Aro is complicated, it seems clear that in order to manage trade they needed some of the functions normally performed by a state. While some argue that the Aro had no state, power was slightly more centralized than among the Igbo; some historians argue that the court, the Ekpe society, and officials at Arochukwu performed some state-like organizational functions.[92] There was someone identified as a king at Arochukwu after 1650. However, a council actually controlled the king's power. Without the council, the king could not act.[93] The council and king together did perform at least one function of a state, that of providing a source of extremely cheap labor for elite use in wealth creation. The Aro needed that labor in order to carry on their wide range of trading functions. This need expanded as the slave trade expanded, and the Aro council and king provided support for the expansion of Aro trade, kick-starting the process by sending a consul to each outlying Aro post, along with the retinue required to administer the connection between that post and the rest of the network. This connection was a major piece of Aro success in dominating trade in people and other commodities. Private enterprise took over later, and along with it a resort to far more violence.[94]

European states also were obliged to provide cheap labor and, like the Aro, subsidized the trade in unfree people, providing in various ways the subsidies and policies that initially nourished the trade in laborers. For the British, this meant providing people who would be desperate enough to "volunteer" to sell themselves as indentured servants, as Alexander Davidson did, but it also meant making conditions as favorable as possible for those engaged in the slave trade. The Crown gave the Royal African Company, a joint-stock company of mostly private investors, a monopoly on the British trade in people from Africa and goods to Africa. Thus investors were far less likely to lose their investment in the required infrastructure—for instance, the ships and warehouses they funded before transporting and selling a single African whose sale would provide some return on their investment. Once the trade was well started, more private investors wanted a piece of the action, and in 1698, the Royal African Company lost its royal monopoly.[95] It began charging other traders for the use of its forts on the coast.

So I am imagining Venis, transported for private profit with state connivance, arriving on Powhatan land from which the Powhatan had largely been removed, likewise for private profit and with state connivance. There she would have been sold for private profit, to be herself a source of private profit, with state connivance, in the hands of Alexander Davidson, who had himself been transported and used a number of years earlier for private profit with state connivance. Punishment or fear of it in the case of Alexander, possibly in the case of Venis, but certainly in the case of many enslaved Africans, was what enabled making them into a source of profit.

CHAPTER 4

Ancestor Tales of the Revolt That Happened
and One That Didn't

For telling Alexander I's story there are just enough facts to play with, far more than for Venis, but nowhere near enough to create a truth. We can speculate, we can do "most likely," and we can create a picture of the world in which he was an actor. To do it we have to cross the ocean again, this time to the Scottish Highlands. And so we did, my husband and I, both of us now retired and able to do such things. Like our earlier trip to Jamestown in search of an elusive Benjamin Radford, things didn't turn out quite as expected. To even begin work on Alexander in Scotland, I had made an executive decision about who his parents were most likely to be. I had found, among family researchers, frequent mention of an Alexander Davidson, married to a Sarah McDavid in 1689, with a son named Alexander born a year later. And I found reference to an Alexander Davidson in Dingwall, in the Highlands. So that was my starting point—I thought I had Alexander I's parents.[1] I went to Scotland, and to Dingwall, and discovered that there were numerous Alexander Davidsons, none of whom seemed to fit. Even worse, the one I had picked had gone through several wives, none of them named Sarah McDavid. I still have no idea who Alexander I's parents were and thus no idea about my actual ancestor, the Alexander Davidson who did appear in Virginia, having left Scotland, and from whom I am descended. In fact, I know no more about who my ancestors in Scotland were than I did before I went there.

Before I knew all this, however, I had gotten hooked on early Dingwall history, as I had done with the Powhatan and early Jamestown, and that is a story I want to tell. And as luck would have it, there are several studies of the Dingwall area that focus on the time around Alexander's birth, which means I have grist for the story I want to tell.[2] Maybe my Alexander who went to Virginia did come from Dingwall, maybe not. He quite likely did come from the Highlands, however, given that he was a Davidson—the Davidsons were a Highland clan, and there were lots of them around Dingwall. So for the sake of the story, truth will again have to be flexible; if what I relate didn't happen to my ancestor, it certainly did to lots of other people. For Alexander I's father, I will just have to make do with an X Davidson to go along with X Radford. And for his mother? I can't even do "Mrs. Davidson," because women in Scotland didn't change their names at marriage. Maybe I'll just stick with Sarah McDavid—it's as good a name as any, and after all, she may have been his mother even if the Alexander Davidson I had in mind was not his father.

So, in this story X Davidson and Sarah McDavid lived in Dingwall, just north and west of Inverness, a town with "a thousand years" of history. I will assume that they had a son, Alexander I, born in 1690. He was much later described in old Kentucky church records as a Jacobite exile.[3] Thus he would have been one of the many who fought in three major rebellions between 1690 and 1745 to restore James VII and the Stuart succession to the throne after their removal in 1688. And I know he was in Virginia by sometime in the early 1740s, because his son Alexander II was born there. That timing means that he most likely left Scotland after the 1715 Jacobite uprising, and I will use those two facts to frame my Davidson-in-Scotland story.[4]

With that framework—inaccurate though it may be—we can now go to Dingwall and to the Firth of Cromarty, where Clan Davidson had migrated, probably after being decimated by the Camerons in the Battle of Invernahavon at the end of the 1300s, after which, as Davidson clan historian Alan McNie asserts, and my father loved to quote, the clan was "of small account."[5]

NOW, ABOUT CLANS. I've got to describe their basic structure in order to explain the changes and the wars that sent Alexander off to Virginia. However, most studies of Scottish history and social structure have focused on the Lowlands, while those few that do focus on the Highlands are more interested in wars, leaders, and politics than in social structure.[6] So what I am saying about how people actually lived, particularly about the 1600s and earlier, is largely pieced together from bits and pieces.[7]

The king's sovereignty waned with distance from the territorial center—as did that of Wahunsonacock.[8] The king clearly did not have a monopoly on the use of force, and was unable to punish, at least in the Highlands, so a different strategy was needed. Feudal lords, both clan chiefs and barons, were gaining greater independence from the Crown in the 1200s, so, unable to stop this process, the king instead sanctioned it.[9] The Crown kept the appearance of control by rubber-stamping the new system, granting titles and feudal rights to clan lands to the chiefs who already held it and endorsing the hereditary passage of those feudal rights and titles to eldest sons.[10] The Crown gave charters to royally appointed justiciars and to many important clan chiefs, endowing them with the power to punish "with gallows and pit," that is, to execute and imprison. The pit was a dungeon of sorts—a deep hole with smooth unclimbable sides.[11] The lords and great chiefs during the thirteenth and fourteenth centuries were gradually appropriating the power to punish that the king held, at least theoretically. The already existing system of large kin-based clan groupings gained strength, developing during the 1300s into a more clearly defined clan organization. With the weakness of the Crown, particularly in the Highlands, clan leaders could resist the allegiance to the king that feudalism was supposed to entail, and shaped it for their own ends.

The Crown's sanctioning of the already existing power of clan chiefs made it appear that the power of life and death that the chiefs already wielded actually came from the king, the channel for the God-given right to rule. At the same time it meant a consolidation of power in fewer hands, taking away some of the right to kill that many local clan chiefs and clan judges had formerly exercised.[12] Under this system, clan chiefs were no longer simply trustees of the clan and its land as a whole.[13] Instead they were controllers of the lands that they now held as feudal lords, by hereditary right granted from the king. Gone was the old right of clanspeople to choose the chief's heir from among eligible clansmen. Perhaps acknowledging the role of the king in backing up their new powers, chiefs did begin aligning themselves with the Stuart monarchy.[14]

After Scotland became independent of England at the end of the 1300s, the power of local magnates, in the Lowlands as well as the Highlands, became so extensive that "the undue power of the nobles" made Scotland "an almost unmanageable country."[1] While the Crown's lack of power had been evident in the Lowlands, and to some extent still was, it was in the Highlands that punishing—and therefore sovereignty—was most severely tested, and for much longer. Without a large permanent military to provide backup force, "law and order" couldn't be securely placed in the hands of the king and functioned instead at the level of local magnates. So Highland chiefs, beyond the reach of the Scottish Crown, maintained their power to punish and continued to enforce the flow of wealth to themselves, frustrating the monarch, who couldn't punish there. Unable to punish, unable to govern, the Crown couldn't establish a convincing sovereignty.

The Lowland's developing clan system was far more feudal and more directly under the king's authority.[15] But in the Highlands, given the weakness of the Crown, there was no central authority to maintain order—that is, to punish transgressors effectively. Clan chiefs, responsible for the well-being of clan members, were free to punish them, to defend them against other clans, and to seek punishing revenge against aggressors—a very local exercise of the right to use force both externally and internally. The Highlands clan system gained strength and reached its height after the 1400s. Chiefs were able to ignore the king, and by the 1500s and 1600s clans had become warrior societies, constantly raiding, plundering, and feuding.[16] Highland clans saw themselves as separate entities more than as members of the same people, despite being nominally members of an overarching entity with the Scottish king at its head.[17]

In the Highlands, the clan system remained far less feudal than in the Lowlands. It was the organizing principle for access to land. Its foundation was based in kinship, alliance, and personal loyalty to the clan chief.[18] In some ways it overlapped with feudalism, though theoretically access to land depended on kinship in the clan among free men and women, rather than on serfdom and a king's grant of an estate's land and people to a lord. The whole system rested on the idea that land belonged to the clan as a whole, with the clan chief as manager, not owner, and that clan members all had a right to use it.

This was not unlike the Powhatan and Igbo system in its basic assumptions, both about access to land and the understanding that what constituted wealth was the ability to sustain large numbers of kin, followers, and retainers. It was abundance that counted, of people and of food and goods, not money (and coins were in short supply, in any case), and in the Highlands that abundance maintained the large fighting force that marked status. While this system was far more stratified than that of the Igbo or Powhatan, chiefs definitely had obligations for the welfare of clanspeople. The abundance was used for hospitality and generosity, providing land, charity for the unfortunate, feasting for huge numbers—massive conspicuous consumption, a display of wealth to guests. And raiding provided much of the wealth that made all this possible.[19] For both forms of abundance, food and people, the chief's control of the land was essential—land for farming and land for grazing the cattle (including those obtained in raids on rival clans) that provided the meat for feasting and thus marked status, wealth, and the clan's military prowess.[20]

The clan chief administered justice—he controlled punishing with the help of clan judges—and oversaw the distribution of clan lands to high-ranking clan members, including his close relatives, who eventually became a Highland gentry class referred to as tacksmen.[21] Tacksmen in turn oversaw the distribution of the land they administered to lower-ranking village people who did most of the actual farming, more or less communally. Tacksmen collected rent in kind, which, turned over to the chief, was meant to be available for redistribution to provide clans-people with security against bad harvests and to support the fighting force that was to protect them. This was an efficient system for main-taining as many people as possible, even though it was not necessarily the most efficient system for producing a surplus or profit.[22] An Earl of Cromartie (Cromartie is spelt with "ie," the place usually with "y"), writing in the 1970s, describes clan organization as it existed into the mid-1700s, listing numerous officials who served the chief in clan man-agement, all living within the castle household. His own family ranked high in a clan that in the 1400s could raise an army of well over two thousand, and Dingwall was within their territory.[23]

Making the clan system work obviously depended on a clan chief's control of land. Clans without adequate land or those driven out by war allied themselves with greater clans with land available. Kinship ties were then presumed by a "pretence of blude"—invented or created through marriage.[24] The Clan Davidson apparently did this, settling on Clan Chattan land at the end of the 1300s after their defeat at the hands of the Camerons, when the Davidson Clan chief and seven of his sons were killed.[25] War, then and now, is extraordinarily hard on everyone, on the survivors no less, perhaps more, than on those killed.

Clan chiefs were at first elected by high-ranking clansmen, who also acted as a council of advisers and war leaders.[26] Birth into the chiefly family mattered in selecting a leader—people believed that the blood of the chiefly lineage was purest, which was assumed to endow them with ability. There were numerous sons and nephews in the chiefly family, and all were eligible. Presumably, the actual selection was based on real ability, influenced a bit by wealth and undoubtedly by political maneu-vering.[27] Scottish kings also were chosen through this system. So the position of chief or king was not hereditary, but did tend to remain in the same family, broadly defined. It eventually became more clearly hereditary toward the end of the 1200s, though not without Highland

elites' resistance to their loss of control over the choice of, and opportunity to be, king. [28]

The chief theoretically had powers of life and death, and could
command allegiance in wars and other policy. In reality, the clan chief
depended on consent and on the support of a council.[29] Beyond that,
there was a somewhat diarchic division of power; the Church conducted its own courts, with jurisdiction over wills, economic affairs
that involved oaths, such as loans and contracts, as well as directly
spiritual matters.[30] In the Highlands, this meant formally the Catholic
Church up until the 1500s, although ordinary people were generally
only nominally Catholic and far more attached to ancient Culdee and
Norse pagan beliefs. After the Protestant Reformation of the 1500s,
it meant primarily Episcopalianism in the Highlands and mainly
Presbyterianism in the Lowlands.

When James VI became King of Scotland in 1567, at one year of
age, the independence of clan chiefs was still the norm, a situation he
regularly strove, unsuccessfully, to correct.[31] But in 1603, he became
king of England as well as Scotland and therefore had the power of
the English state behind him. Highlanders' resistance to a colonization attempt gave him the excuse he needed to demonstrate his ability
to punish, and thus, he hoped, to establish his sovereignty over the
Highlands. One chief was given a spectacular death; another's head
ended up on a spike over a gate in Edinburgh. The particularly recalcitrant MacGregor clan chief and five of his high-ranking relatives were
hung and beheaded. Others were incarcerated in Dingwall Castle's
notorious dungeons.[32] None of this actually did the job, however, as
the ensuing Jacobite uprisings demonstrated.

Indeed, it would take several kings, three Jacobite rebellions, and
the 1707 union of Scotland and England into one country under one
crown, not two countries who happened to have the same king, before
Scottish Highland regional chiefs lost their power to punish.[33] Highland
chiefs could ignore calls to appear before the Scottish Parliament, even
when indicted for treason.[34] This was still the case in the Highlands well
into the 1700s. John Mackenzie, 2nd Earl of Cromartie, for example,
the hereditary sheriff in the area around Dingwall, used his position to

avoid prosecution for debt in the 1720s, causing Lord Islay, the representative of the Crown in the Highlands, to write in disgust that "the difficultys [*sic*] that attends the execution of the Law in the Highlands seems to be the very essence of their barbarity."[35] The Crown's inability to punish in the Highlands, as in Powhatan Virginia, was, in the eyes of would-be rulers, the defining characteristic of a "savage" society—that is to say, one whose people were outside the Crown's sovereign control.[36]

WE CAN NOW RETURN TO ALEXANDER'S early life in the Highlands. Dingwall was a tiny trading town, with a population of four hundred and twenty in 1700, "inconsiderable" according to Richards and Clough, but nevertheless a Royal Burgh licensed to hold a market since 1226.[37] Whether the "inconsiderable" assessment is correct depends a bit on definition and on era. Dingwall was a port, or at least had once conducted a lot of foreign trade—in the 1200s it was one of the sixteen towns, along with Cromarty and Inverness, that was importing and exporting enough to require an official customs stamp to ensure that the Crown got its revenue.[38] Its burgesses (the official merchants and traders) made up a cosmopolitan enclave, largely composed of foreigners, as they were in other burghs: they were Flemish, French, Scandinavian, and English, not the Gaelic speakers of the countryside.[39] Dingwall Castle had been one of the most important forts in the Highlands, in territory held by Macbeth—the king of Shakespeare's play—some five centuries before the lives of X and Sarah.[40] By the 1720s, however, many independent fairs had sprung up, run by local lords, and Dingwall, its market bypassed, was nearly a ghost town.[41] So if Alexander really did grow up there, he would have lived in a town that was slowly dying.

All that now remains of the town as it was at the time of Alexander's birth is possibly the center tower of the Town House—once the Dingwall Tolbooth, the seat of burgh administration and the jail. In front of the Tolbooth was the Mercat Cross, indicating Dingwall's right to hold a market there. The cross itself, of now-eroded stone, is presently sheltered in the Dingwall Museum. Regardless of Dingwall's status, however, like other Scottish towns of the time its stench would have been impressive. It likely had open sewage gutters filled with rotting fish guts, and pig sties abounded, all contributing to a death rate higher than the birth rate. The Cromartie historian, perhaps with tongue in cheek, claims that the frequent house fires burned off filth and thus helped keep down infection. [42] Venis's people, with their carefully swept marketplaces and towns the first Europeans there described as beautiful, would have been shocked! [43]

FIGURING OUT WHAT SARAH McDAVID'S life might have been like has been a bit of a challenge. The telling of Scottish history, until very recently, seems to have been remarkably oblivious to the existence of women, as several editors of recent collections of articles about women in Scotland have pointed out.[44] For instance, historian Thomas Smout, in speaking of household furnishing and table settings, says, "each man in the Highlands kept a dirk in his sock to serve equally as a dagger and table knife." [45] Maybe women just didn't eat?[46] Women in this history rarely appear unless they are royalty, pawns in (or thwarters of) the marriage/property/title strategies of powerful men, or sacrificing themselves in service to royalty—like Flora MacDonald.

Held up as a heroine for saving the life of Bonnie Prince Charlie, the last Stuart claimant to the throne, as he fled from defeat after the 1745 Jacobite Rebellion, Flora rowed him, disguised as her servant woman, across stormy waters to safety. She is commemorated in a statue in front of the Sheriff Court at Inverness Castle. [47] She stands, shielding her eyes to gaze out to sea, awaiting, with the devotion illustrated by the dog sitting at her feet and gazing up at her face, the return of her prince. A not-so-subtle message to all about the proper role of women. And an inaccurate one at that; reality would have botched up the message. Among other things, Flora was not a Jacobite. Her family was part of the loyal gentry, and she was chosen for the job because she would not be questioned by the Crown's officers. A Jacobite would have been. The truth, says Maggie Craig, in her study of Jacobite women, is that while Flora did indeed save the Prince, she didn't do it voluntarily.

Getting her to do it took some pretty serious arm-twisting, and later she implicated some of those involved in the escape—and then headed to North Carolina with her husband. The "Flora Cult," part of the later romanticizing of Scottish resistance, disguises the role women actually played in the 1745 Rising, as Craig makes very clear. Some elite women actually raised regiments, for instance, and ordinary women were nursing and feeding soldiers, organizing supplies, and generally facilitating the army's ability to fight. It was those ordinary women who were imprisoned, many of them transported and sold as indentured servants in the colonies. These women were not mentioned by Victorian historians, or even some more recent ones—they didn't fit women's properly submissive role as it had gradually come to be interpreted after the Reformation. [48]

So locating women at all in Scottish history was a challenge, and once I did find the relatively small amount of research that has been done recently, good as it is, little of it deals with the Highlands.[49] What follows here is very much another case of collecting bits and weaving them together. Interestingly, it was far easier to locate women among the Igbo than in the Highlands or even in Scotland generally. And I think there is a clear reason for this. Igbo women were an independent political and economic force with whom the British had to reckon if they were to control colonial Nigeria. They couldn't just figure out the men and be done with it. In Scotland they could, or at least thought they could. So there are numerous accounts—accurate or not—by travelers, administrators, missionaries, and anthropologists that consider Igbo women worth mentioning. Not so for Scotland, and particularly not so for the Highlands, where the English and the Scottish Lowlanders generally assumed that men were barbarians who held "their" women in total subjection, as opposed to the more "civilized" treatment of women they attributed to themselves.

Although Highland women were not seen as equals, and didn't have the power of Igbo or Powhatan women, apparently they were not wrapped into as tight a patriarchal system as came later, nor in as tight a system as that of the Lowlands and especially of England.[50] Much of what is known of women in the Highlands in this era comes from court records, where women in towns appear surprisingly often in roles that mark them as independent economic actors—buyers and sellers, shop-keepers, printers, hawkers, entrepreneurs—and as effective managers of family businesses, essentially partners with husbands, sons, or fathers.

Class would have made an enormous difference in Sarah McDavid's life. In well-to-do families, daughters were married off to ensure the most advantageous passage of property and wealth.[51] So if Sarah came from such a family (which seems unlikely, considering the difficulty in locating anything about Alexander's parentage) guarding her reputa-tion, both before and after marriage, would have been crucial.[52] Too much—the passage of property from one man to another, one family to another—was at stake. Only as a widow would she have had con-trol of property.[53] If Sarah was from a lower-status family, however, she would have had far more freedom of choice in marriage, since little property would be at stake.[54] "Irregular marriages" and Gaelic mar-riage by handfasting, without a formal wedding service, continued in the Highlands until well after Alexander's birth, which may, of course, explain the difficulty in figuring out his background. [55]

Higher status would not mean a life of leisure for Sarah.[56] She would be training and supervising daughters and servants, she would be sewing and spinning, probably brewing ale, managing dairy, garden, and meat processing; she might be supervising the estate or business, particularly as elite men were frequently required to be at court in Edinburgh and later London, and left wives in charge. The more likely scenario, however, is that Sarah McDavid was of lower status. If she lived in or very close to Dingwall she may well have walked High Street with young Alexander in tow and bought goods in the weekly market in the Mercat Square in front of the Tolbooth.[57] Or she may have brought in goods from the countryside to sell, paying the market toll and setting up a booth. Or maybe she illegally hawked goods, avoiding paying the toll, or illegally bought more than her family needed and sold the rest in tiny amounts to people too poor to buy in market-sized quantities. The burgesses, who governed the market and made the laws, overlooked some of these activities because, though illegal, they actually provided a needed service in provisioning the poor.[58] Nevertheless, burgh records show women hauled into court over and over for violating laws about buying and selling. Sarah may have brewed ale—most women brewed some and bought some, for it was a basic component of the Scottish diet—and sold it from her home. If so, this was another opportunity to get in trouble with male courts, since both prices and quality were closely regulated. Again, Igbo women would have been shocked: like Igbo markets, Scottish markets "were very much women's places," but Igbo women controlled their markets.[59] They would never have tolerated men inventing laws that went against their interests—woe betide the man who tried!

But again, the more likely scenario is that Sarah grew up in an ordinary clan farm family; only a small percentage of the population lived in towns. With luck, the family held land from the local tacksman (a landholder of intermediate social status) or perhaps directly from the Earl of Cromartie. With less luck, they might have been cottars, and with even less, waged farm laborers. They would have lived in a farming hamlet called a *baile*.[60] They might have lived in a longhouse, a long, narrow building with few interior partitions, housing people, animals, equipment, even crops. For the better-off, these houses could be a hundred feet long. Others would have lived in a much smaller blackhouse, a single room with an attached cowshed.[61] In the Highlands these would be the cottars, who did much of the work on the lord's land, and had only the right to farm a very small plot and to graze a couple of cows on the common grazing land.[62]

Farming in the Highlands often involved wooden foot-ploughs, breaking ground by pushing a sharp shaft into the ground and then levering it up. Humans, not plough animals, provided the labor.[63] Much of the work was done communally. Several scattered strips of farmable land were allocated to each of the families of a village. The strips were rotated annually.[64] Women sheared sheep, loaded wagons, hauled peat, worked in harvesting crops, hauled water, spun, cooked porridge twice a day, helped with each other's birthings.[65] Unmarried young women often were servants and sometimes, having borne a baby, wet nurses, in order to pay the enormous fines the church imposed on unwed mothers.[66] Sarah, as a wife and mother in a farming family, would have been no delicate flower of feminine womanhood. Having described all this, Dumhnall Stiùbhart, historian of Gaelic culture, concludes that "the lower a family's position on the social scale, the more crucial the woman's role was to the household."[67]

During the earlier years of the Highland clan system, exploitation had been relatively mild. As time went on, however, Scotland, and particularly the Lowlands, came more and more under the influence of a gradually developing capitalism, and with it came the privatization of land. Although to some extent the Highland elites maintained their "wealth in people" approach to landholding well into the 1700s, they were at the same time more and more required to appear in London once the Scottish king moved the court there in 1603 when he became king of England as well Scotland. Having money became more important and landowners were turning rents in kind into money rather than using them to meet their obligations to clanspeople. That money allowed landowners to live in style in London, and to avoid appearing to be the barbarians Londoners assumed Highlanders to be. Demands on the peasantry increased—life got harder for people like Sarah and X.[68] They now had to consent to a lifetime of backbreaking labor, with, as time went on and exploitation increased, less and less to show for it. The wealth of the large landholders, however, showed clearly enough.

AS LIFE GOT HARDER, THE OLDER SYSTEM of diarchic control needed beefing up, and the Reformation, starting around the 1560s in Scotland, did just that—in two ways. First, it emphasized individual responsibility. Individuals, not the rituals of church and (distant) king or magnate, were responsible for the state of the community in God's eyes. Calamities came because individuals sinned, and thus communities needed to be cleansed of sinners; performance of church rituals by priests supported by local elites was no longer adequate. Ordinary people's behavior in that older system was more or less irrelevant to community well-being. In the new system, however, ordinary people did matter. Kings' power came from God by way of the church and Parliament, or, according to James VI and his supporters, directly from

God to King. So people (at least ordinary people) who resisted author-ity, either that of the king or local lord, were sinning against God and thus a threat to the community, ultimately to king and state, and needed to be purged.[69] Second, the Catholic ecclesiastical courts, which had authority over enormous areas, were abolished. Instead, local Protestant churches supervised a much smaller area, letting them pin-point their attention on the behavior of people who, in the old system, had largely been ignored.[70]

The Reformation version of diarchy, with its tighter system of sur-veillance, meant that church and magnate, sacred and secular, teamed up to enforce and legitimize the growing inequality that came with the changing emphasis from wealth in people to the profit motive.[71] With the Reformation, a life of hard work became a godly life, a life under "godly discipline," and transgressors of this ethos were punished. On the secular side, this power to punish, to kill, was retained by the great clan chiefs until 1747and the final defeat of the Jacobites.[72] They used it to protect their own interests, enforcing the payment of rents and the performance of what was essentially corvée labor, as well as punish-ing for damage to the landholder's property. In addition, the power to punish gave them clout in controlling intra-estate disputes that could have impeded the cooperation required by Scotland's various agricul-tural systems. They were micro-managing both farming and behavior.[73] Backing up the whole system were the Poor Laws, which required all able-bodied dispossessed people to "find themselves masters and to cease begging" on pain of imprisonment, losing an ear, branding, or banishment, with death for a second offense. Authorities who failed to follow through were to be replaced.[74] Traveling to change employ-ers could get you a vagrancy charge—no shopping around for a better situation. Unless you "truly" deserved charity, work or else was the rule behind the Poor Laws, ensuring a mostly "willing" labor force.

Much of the micro-managing of behavior was in the hands of the sacred side of the equation. The constant surveillance by the church was justified by the presumed need to ensure each individual's "moral" behavior, and people's sex lives were the ever-present target. Now justi-fied, that same surveillance enabled observation of other aspects of life:

someone was always breathing down your neck. So other failures were more easily caught—the failure to work hard, to obey your superiors, to observe the Sabbath—all visible. The surveillance that sexual conduct justified and the humiliating public punishment the Church inflicted for violations must have caused many people to internalize the Church-imposed discipline, a discipline that could then shape other areas of their lives.[75]

This system, needless to say, wasn't totally successful. The records of Dingwall kirk (church) sessions, for instance, like many others, frequently refer to the sinful propensity of the poor to work on Sunday. Dingwall's session records for March 1719 state, "It being represented that some of the poor people do profane the Lord's day by gathering kail in the fields, baking of bread and carrying in water to their houses on the said day, the Session ordered the elders in their several quarters to keep a strict eye o'er the people that the first who shall be found guilty of profaning the Sabbath in that manner may be prosecuted for a terror to others."[76] And the greatest proportion of Dingwall cases have to do with fornication, adultery, and illegitimate pregnancies, or with slander accusing people of such activities.[77]

So the discipline didn't necessarily work for everyone, but the punishments that could then be meted out must have made it clear to the more law-abiding that disciplining themselves was a good idea and that the behavior that got you punished by the authorities was truly ungodly. Much of the "intensity of control exercised by her [Scotland's] church courts" was directed at keeping the poor and dispossessed in line, for instance by enforcing the Poor Laws.[78] While this intense control wasn't phrased as control of women, it certainly had that effect, to the extent that Gordon DesBrisay says that the Reformation's "war on sin" was actually a "war on women," founded on the belief that they were "carriers of a socially corrosive sexuality."[79] Young, unmarried women were subjected to laws about where and how they could live that largely didn't apply to men, so they had little choice about being live-in domestics. Punishments that were meted out for sexual sins were often greater for women and in any case had a deeper effect because women generally had fewer resources. I would add that it was a war on poor women in particular—elites were largely exempt from public, humiliating punishment, thus gaining their cooperation in controlling everyone else, as Geoffrey Parker describes.[80]

So Sarah McDavid and X Davidson would know what awaited them if they transgressed church law. You could be required to attend church for weeks in a row sitting up front on the "stool of repentance" dressed in sackcloth, often with huge fines added.[81] Sarah might have seen Annie Bayne's humiliation after each of her two pregnancies, and she would have seen how it was generally the poor who were made to publicly repent and pay their fines. Annie was an unmarried servant in the household of Kenneth Bayne of Tulloch, the father of both her children. She took her punishment but the elite father, despite considerable pressure from the kirk, got away with it. And when he died, her children did not inherit, even though Kenneth had no other children.[82] Other laws said you could be "jouged" for quarreling—fastened with an iron ring around your neck to the Mercat Cross on market day. You could be fined, and if you couldn't pay what were sometimes massive fines, the kirk session could "poyne," confiscate, some of your property, with the caveat that they couldn't poyne tools or oxen that would prevent a farmer from doing the work needed to pay the rent—the landowner couldn't be deprived.

Rules such as this illustrate the collusion between kirk and landholders and burgesses—in fact, for the most part the church court was made up of the most powerful local men. Thus, obedience to church mostly meant obedience also to the secular power. This was certainly true in Dingwall, where even "imprications" against the magistrates could get people in trouble—as could failure to control a wife who "deforced" and "bled" an officer sent to "poyne" her husband.[83] Beyond all this were the still powerful secular courts, run by those same local landholders. Beyond even that, most people were dependent on the goodwill of the landholders to get access to the land that made life possible. Getting any kind of a new job or going to a new town required a letter from the kirk session.[84] In Dingwall, kirk, burgesses, and landowners together ran a tight system of control, and force, the power to punish, lay at its foundation. It wasn't slavery, though Scotland before the 1500s had

had a slave class. Slavery gradually disappeared as the developing clan system organized agricultural and military labor. It was actually reinvented in the mines and salt pits of Scotland between 1606 and 1660, where it hung on until 1775. So, no, the system of inequality in which Sarah McDavid and X Davidson lived, and into which Alexander I was born, wasn't slavery, but it certainly was enforcement of a system of unfree labor—a system that during their lives the controlling elites rendered increasingly exploitative. [85]

WITH THE REFORMATION CAME RENEWED attempts to tame Scotland—to coalesce it into a nation with a strong sovereign king, rather than a collection of warring clans and competing lords. [86] Taming Scotland, however, would require centralizing the power to punish, thus proving the Crown's sovereignty and enabling the king to bring rivals to heel. That was no easy task, and followed on several centuries of dispute over who had the right to punish. Who was sovereign, local magnates or the Crown?

The king needed something dramatic to make plain he had a necessary role as protector of the people and their communities, something to pull people together into a national identity that could override clan identity and loyalty. Wars can often perform this function, allowing the state to exert force externally, gaining legitimacy by protecting against enemies. But there was no war handy at the time. Instead, a good scare was needed, a crime wave that could be met only by the power of the state exerting force internally, one that would show people that they needed to acknowledge the Crown's sovereignty. The punishing had to be secular, not sacred, in the hands of the Crown, not the church. The balance of power between sacred and secular needed to tilt in favor of the Crown. As it was, treason was the only crime that belonged to Crown courts, thus requiring trial in Edinburgh, and the occasional case of treason was not sufficient to scare people into thinking they needed protecting.

Though there was no war, there was witchcraft, as historian and sociologist Christina Larner's important study of witchcraft panics explains.[87] The church normally handled accusations locally, and the emphasis was on repentance and restitution. Both elites and peasants believed witchcraft was real, but the peasants' conception of witches did not involve the devil—the elites' did. Their education made them far more conscious of the theology that posited a cosmic struggle between God and Devil. Witches for the peasantry were people who could and did use magic to harm people or livestock or to cure them. If, however, you bring in the devil, and a witch becomes someone who has made a pact with the devil, then the witch becomes an opponent of God. The king, as God's emissary on earth, was required to fight God's enemies. The witch was thus opposing the king, a crime on a par with treason.

Witchcraft suddenly becomes not just a sin, but also a crime against both state and community. Create a nationwide panic about the dangers posed by witches in your midst, who are part of a small, vulnerable group of people who are (usually) women, already under siege in the new Reformation surveillance system, (usually) older and poorer and cantankerous women, and punishment can be taken out of local hands. Finally there was a way to justify and gain consent to the centralization of the power to punish, not just the witches but the rest of the population. Since there is no constituency for witches, no significant block of witch supporters to be alienated by the prosecution of witches, there was no group to rise up and fight back as there might have been if there was a national panic about the dangers posed by the presence of a heretic community.[88] Going after witches was a pretty safe bet. I've been describing this shift as a purposeful cynical conspiracy—and to some extent it was. Although the elites who promoted it did sincerely believe in the witches' pact with the devil, they were also carrying out their own political agendas. But I am also trying to make obvious the parallels with our own lives today, where refugees, immigrants, and Muslims are likewise targeted to create a panic that justifies the shift of more power into the hands of the few. That panic is spearheaded by elites, at least some of whom probably sincerely believe in the dangers they describe.

Larner makes it clear that the panics were the work of the elites; witch-hunting was "an activity fostered by the ruling class." [89] Although, as she points out, peasants accused each other quite regularly; it was only in panics that those accusations received official recognition. Peasants didn't have the power to create a panic; once they made an accusation, the outcome was out of their hands. Handled locally by the church, the occasional convicted witch was dealt with and life went on.[90] Making a national panic, with hundreds of executions, requires elites writing laws. The Witchcraft Act of 1563, for instance, officially defined witchcraft as a crime to be dealt with by the Crown courts, removing jurisdiction over witchcraft accusations from the clergy and giving it to the Royal Court.[91] Making a panic also takes elites discussing among themselves the need to eradicate witches, so that local landholders, participating in or hearing about those conversations, take peasant accusations more seriously or make accusations themselves. It takes judges who get confessions of pacts with the devil, sometimes with the help of torturers and pin-pricking witch-detecting "professionals." Without all that, you just have communities where people go outside the church for healing and charms and sometimes accuse each other of malicious magic. That doesn't change. What does change is the behavior of elites who do or do not create a panic.

But for all this to work, the Protestant Reformation needed to have taken root, with its emphasis on individual choice and responsibility. You couldn't be accused of making a pact with the devil and making choices that damaged the community if your actions didn't particularly matter because community well-being was in the hands of the great lords and the church, not in the hands of ordinary individuals. The devil had to be diverted from the cosmic struggle with God to pursue individuals who were now believed free to choose him and disavow their baptism.[92] Otherwise why would the devil bother, and how could a person have the power to make such a pact or to repent of the pact?

Witchhunts were rare in the Highlands, perhaps because Presbyterianism had little grip there, but in the Lowlands they peaked several times between the Reformation and 1736, not long after the Union of Scotland and England.[93] As Larner describes it, witch hunting permitted a greater centralization of power in the Lowlands, and helped to legitimize the new regime.[94] The Lowlands became more governable and began to accept a Scottish as well as a clan identity—the nation-making project was to some extent successful there. Given that the seat of power had shifted to London, the protective punishing that supposedly lifted the scourge of witchcraft from Lowland communities came from there also. The connection with England must have seemed more palatable, or at least inevitable, to many. The project was far less successful in the Highlands, relatively unaffected as they were by the national panics. I'm tempted to speculate that the Highlands might not have been the backbone of the Jacobite rebellions—perhaps there would have been no rebellions—had witch-hunting panics successfully eroded clan chief power in the Highlands. Because it seems to me that hanging on to that chiefly power was largely what the Jacobite rebellions were really about—but we will get to that shortly.

SO LET'S SEE HOW ALL this affected the Dingwall that Alexander I would have known, growing up in the 1690s. This was a period of chaos, both economically and politically—a bad time to be born.[95] Indeed, during this decade an unusually small number of babies were born and survived to be baptized in Dingwall.[96] First of all, there was a war on, the first of the Jacobite rebellions that eventually sent Alexander to Virginia. But even worse than war were widespread crop failures in the Highlands, bringing desperate hunger, disease, and death. By the end of the decade, in 1700, some parts of the Highlands had lost over twenty percent of the population, perhaps over ten percent through death, and the rest either through a reduction in birth or emigration to Ulster. They joined the Scots already there as a result of James VI's attempt to conquer Ulster's Irish gentry by evicting them and giving the land to Scottish immigrants. [97] On top of this, British troops were quartered in Cromarty, and they commandeered animals and goods to such an extent that people were struggling to pay their rent.[98]

Even in the best of times those who actually worked the land made barely a subsistence living—a situation that might well have caused Igbo women to "sit" on those responsible, resorting to their dramatic method of changing men's behavior. People were particularly vulnerable to crop failure because dues to the landholder absorbed any surplus they might have held in reserve for bad times. If he was a proper clan chief, the landholder provided aid in time of need, but this was an obligation that George Mackenzie, as clan chief and later Earl of Cromartie in Alexander's time, appears to have neglected. He received rents twice a year, once paid with grain, once with animals. He exported about half of this from Dingwall port—Mackenzie was turning his in-kind rents into cash.[99] He was beginning to see his land-holdings with an "acquisitive attitude," all 345 square miles of them, not as the central foundation of the clan but as an economic resource for his personal use.[100] Capitalism was beginning to make its way into the Highlands, with its emphasis on personal profit off land and labor.

Mackenzie was much like other clan chiefs who were making this shift. They could raise armies, live in luxury, educate their sons, marry—and marry off their daughters—to enhance their position, and go nowhere without a large retinue.[101] In the 1690s Mackenzie (then Lord Tarbat) drove a coach-and-four in Cromarty "although the Scottish roads could barely carry them," had expensive clothes, wigs, a castle, a town villa, silverplate, fine books, elaborate furnishings, all an exhibition of the wealth built on the backs of the people who lived in those tiny houses he passed as he traveled through the countryside.[102] And to maintain that standard he shipped out grain even during famine years, when, if Cromarty was like the rest of the Highlands, one third to two fifths of the population needed some form of charity to survive, which churches and local towns and some lords struggled to provide.[103] Under Mackenzie, however, "the local population starved while food was exported." [104]

Mackenzie was rather early in making this move in the Highlands, "a precocious improving landlord," according to Richards and Clough, taking land out of cultivation by families to make additional pasture for his own cattle, a move seen by many elites as laudably progressive.[105] The state enabled such dispossession. Legislation starting in the mid-1600s, passed, of course, by the big landholders who made up Parliament, made it much easier to divide and enclose common land and to consolidate holdings, moving landholding to private landownership.[106] An export market for Scottish beef was developing and landholding elites could make more money this way than off the low rents of tenants.[107] While improvement may bring more money to landowners, history has shown it generally does not bode well for tenants and peasants, who either have to leave or, having lost access to land, are reduced to wages for agricultural labor. Those wages, as subsistence farmers are well aware, are almost always an inferior and less dependable basis for subsistence than growing their own food—but driven out, they had little choice.[108] In the fifty years ending in 1750, Dingwall's population doubled as people went there in hopes of wages, and continued to increase as a result.[109]

Tacksmen became the principal lease-holders, making up a newly formed middle class. They were still responsible for persuading, prodding, and, when necessary, threatening the men of the district into following the chief to battle, in feud, or in raiding, and were now also responsible for rents to the landowner, rents they acquired from their sub-tenants, cottars, servants, and landless laborers.[110] Ordinary clanspeople continued to believe in the more communal understanding of land and work—in Cromarty and the area around Dingwall they continued to farm communally until the early 1800s—and paid their rent jointly rather than individually.[111] They still saw themselves as kin to the chief and his tacksman and believed that they had a hereditary kinship right to use the land they farmed.[112] Nevertheless, regardless of their continuing communal ethics, they had little choice but to pay the much larger rents that more capitalist-oriented chiefs now required.[113]

The result of all this was that by 1698, there were by a contemporary estimate 200,000 beggars in Scotland. Even if this was an exaggeration, as Karen Cullen concludes in her study of the famine, improvement, capitalism, bad harvests, war, and famine had combined to make the decade of Alexander's childhood one of unmitigated misery for a tremendous number of Scots.[114] Nevertheless, through all of this, landowners saw themselves as benevolent patriarchs, not as oppressors, not as leading figures of a state and church through which they orchestrated their control and punished as needed. Instead, in public articles and private letters, they emphasized the affection and interdependence between themselves and their people, "glorying above all else in the paternal quality of their rule."[115]A twentieth-century descendant of the Earl of Cromartie who went into exile in Devonshire after his part in the 1745 Jacobite Rising speaks with apparent pride of the way the Earl was supported in exile. "Efforts were made," he wrote, "by the loyal and ever-generous clansmen—desperately poor themselves— to send money south, though it meant a double rent, the official one going to the government," which now owned the forfeited estate.[116] The landowners' attitude paralleled that of many powerful colonial slaveholders, whom Alexander would meet in Virginia and whom his son would eventually join in Kentucky.

SO NOW WE TURN TO THE ELITE struggles over sovereignty that led to the Jacobite rebellions that deposited Alexander, perhaps unwillingly, or perhaps choosing the lesser of two evils, on a dock somewhere in Virginia. Perhaps he even walked in the footsteps of Venis or her parents and those earlier Radfords.

We can start with a fast-forward through the rise and fall of Catholic, Presbyterian, and Episcopalian dominance and through the reign of Charles I, beheaded by Cromwell's administration.[117] On through the Restoration—the return of the House of Stuart with Charles II, son of Charles I—and finally we arrive at Charles II's brother, who became King James of both England and Scotland, as were all kings since James VI. As English king, he was James II and in the Scottish succession he was James VII. He was a Catholic who had been raised in France by his Catholic mother, Henrietta Maria of France.[118] While he didn't try to impose Catholicism, when his son James was born and christened a Catholic, the Protestant Parliament in England had had enough. He was deposed in1688, after a three-year reign, in the "Glorious and Bloodless Revolution." Parliament passed a Declaration of Rights establishing its power relative to the Crown, including its control over taxation and its right to choose monarchs (from among those considered eligible through bloodright), and permanently denying the monarchy to Catholics. Thus James's direct male Stuart line could no longer reign.

Instead, Parliament offered the Crown jointly to the Dutch William of Orange and his wife, Mary, who was James VII and II's daughter. William was Mary's cousin, and also rather distantly a Stuart, and both were Protestants, thus acceptable to Parliament. The offer was contingent on their signing the Declaration in 1689, which they did. The stage was now set for the first Jacobite uprising in 1690.[119]

The Highlands, and Jacobites more generally, were heavily but not exclusively Episcopalian. They were not as likely as Presbyterians to be deterred by the Catholic leanings of a king, and saw the line of the deposed James VII as the rightful, God-given succession to the throne. (The term Jacobite refers to *Jacobus*, the Latin for James.[120]) After his death, that succession was represented by his son, seen as James VIII by his supporters, and then finally with the third generation of exiled would-be monarchs, Charles III, Bonnie Prince Charlie. In the rebellions, many Scottish elites, particularly Highlanders, but also many Lowlanders along with some northern English Catholics, fought against some other, mainly Lowland elites and the English Crown to restore that succession. The Jacobites lost, but there were times when their belief in the possibility of a legitimate Stuart restoration didn't seem at all farfetched. When William of Orange was given the throne with Mary II, and when the very unpopular German Hanoverian George I became king in 1714, support for the Stuart succession in both England and Scotland was widespread.

In 1689, just before Alexander's birth, Jacobite Highland Scots, fighting in an early stage of the 1690 rebellion to bring back James VII, defeated William's army, but then lost at the battle of Dunkeld in 1690.[121] When Alexander was two years old, William's soldiers, with a regiment of Lowland Scots, conducted an infamous massacre in the Highland village at Glencoe, in the dead of winter when flight was impossible (ironically Glencoe is an incredibly beautiful spot high in the mountains). The village's MacDonald chief had been three days late in arriving to swear allegiance to William, giving the king the excuse he needed to deliver a punishing blow that was meant to teach the Highlanders proper obedience.[122] Though only thirty-eight people died, compared to much higher numbers in Virginia, I can't help but remember Opechancanough's punishing 1622 attack against the Virginia colony. The punishment William meted out for disloyalty—when he could get away with it—kept Jacobites relatively quiet for a generation, until Alexander was an adult and swept into the next eruption. [123]

By 1715, the situation had changed. England and Scotland were no longer separate kingdoms that happened to be ruled by the same king. They were a single kingdom, with a single Parliament, which met in London. Power was well consolidated, despite continued resistance, particularly from Episcopalian Scots. The nationalist cry for Scotland's independence joined the tangled web of religion and beliefs about righteous succession to the throne. [124] Together these became the excuse for drawing people into supporting their elites in the Jacobite rebellions in which Scottish chiefs—at the expense of their often very reluctant clanspeople—as well as some northern English lords--warred with the English Crown. And, as we have seen before, the sovereignty of the winner would be demonstrated in the power to punish.

About Alexander's participation in this next eruption, the 1715 uprising, the evidence is thin, but there is some. A history of the Kentucky church founded by Alexander II says his father was a "Jacobite exile" who went first to Ireland and then to Virginia as an indentured servant.[125] Since Alexander I was alive and well and fathering children in Virginia in 1744, I'm assuming that he was born during the first 1690 Jacobite uprising, probably participated in the second, in 1715, and was already in Virginia when the third and last occurred in 1745. Though I have no evidence of Alexander's family's involvement in that first rebellion, most Highlanders were Jacobites, including many Davidsons. So were the Mackenzie Earls of Cromartie.[126] And since Dingwall was heavily Episcopalian in 1716, the Davidson family probably was too.[127]

Alexander is not listed as one of the Jacobites captured in the second rebellion by the British and transported to the colonies, although there certainly are enough Davidsons in the list of transported rebels to make it clear that the Davidson clan was deeply involved. So I'm going to assume he did participate in the 1715 uprising, when he would have

been 25, perhaps not actually transported, but fleeing Scotland, as
many Jacobites did, to avoid capture, a Jacobite exile if the old history
of his son's Kentucky church is to be believed. Of course, the plain fact
of the matter is that the author of that church history could have been
wrong, and my Alexander could have been born in the colonies, the
son of an earlier Davidson, or maybe he somehow wasn't included in
the listings of transported Scots arriving in the colonies. [128]

The stage was set for Alexander's 1715 Jacobite Rebellion, assuming that he was part of it, when Lowland Scottish elites agreed to the
Act of Union with England in 1707, ending Scotland's even nominal
sovereignty. Scotland and England together made a new state called
Britain, but in reality England now ruled Scotland directly. Practically
everyone in Scotland opposed the Union except the more influential
Lowland merchants and entrepreneurs and a few of the "improving" Highland lords, all of whose ventures into capitalism had been
thwarted by restrictive English laws that treated Scots as foreigners for
purposes of trade. Outright bribery tipped the balance in the Scottish
Parliament; as a Jacobite song put it, "We are bought and sold for
English gold." [129]

In 1714, the English succession went to George of Hanover,
although the Pope had already recognized James VIII as king. This
was more than many Scots could stand, and there was briefly the possibility that the union would split, with James VIII returned from exile
to rule Scotland alone. Some northern English Catholics joined the
Jacobite Rebellion of 1715 in order to put him on the English throne
as well. They lost. King George found himself with 1,290 prisoners,
many of them Scottish Highlanders, while others fled. And for what
had they risked their lives as soldiers, and now risked a dreadful death
at the hands of executioners?

What strikes me about these rebellions is how different they were
from Bacon's Rebellion in Virginia, or rather from the poor people's
uprising that was part of that rebellion. There should have been a
poor people's uprising in Scotland. Conditions for ordinary people
were horrendous, yet nowhere in the histories of this rebellion is there
even a whiff of murmuring discontent with the extreme inequality that

was by now built into the clan system. Alexander would have been caught up in a rebellion of wannabe elites, similar to wannabe elites like Nathaniel Bacon, fighting to enhance their own power. But unlike Bacon's Rebellion, poor people did not latch on to it to demand freedom, land, or at least enough to eat. Had the Jacobites won, had their chosen monarchs gained the throne, there would have been no obvious improvement in the lives of the poor. And their lives did indeed need improving.

There should have been a revolt. There wasn't. Larner comments that "militant class consciousness" was "remarkably low," a situation she attributes to the utter insecurity elites had orchestrated through their hold on land, court, and church. [130] In fact, there was some resistance to exploitation in Scotland, even a "mob" raiding a Mackenzie grain shipment. [131] However, this resistance does not seem to have been part of a larger movement that could have influenced the Jacobite agenda. But might there have been a revolt of poor people if the Jacobite cause hadn't been available to distract people? An external enemy is always handy for elites bent on exploitation—as recent US experience demonstrates. Might the Jacobite and loyalist leaders both have known the advantages of a good war? Or were poor people blinded by an ideology of loyalty to the clan and its chief, an ideology that defined them as equal members of the clan, an entity bound together by kinship, of the same blood as their chiefs, a fiction to which the clan elites contributed by willingly chatting with one and all. [132] Despite their poverty, did clan "blood" act like whiteness, blinding people to their own interests by naturalizing an exploitative relationship, preventing them from recognizing the exploitation, or at least from feeling the moral right to act on that recognition? In contrast, the poor and the enslaved in Virginia were able to revolt—they weren't yet blinded by whiteness.

WARS THEN, AS TODAY, REQUIRE a justifying ideology. They are fought for elite benefit, but it is ordinary men, women, and children who do most of the suffering. It was the Jacobite elites who instigated the rebellions, though historians calculate that in the Highlands half of all families were directly involved, with close to a fifth of all adult men actually fighting, mostly on the Jacobite side. [133] On the surface, the wars were about both who should be king and religious doctrine—the justifying ideologies. In reality, it seems to me that at least the first two Jacobite uprisings, Alexander's uprisings, in 1690 and 1715, were largely about the struggle over sovereignty between territorial elites and a Crown bent on consolidating power in its own hands. The uprisings came at points when the Crown had taken a step toward centralized power, elevating the threat to clan elite independence. The 1690 rising came as William tried to shore up his power in Scotland, particularly in the Highlands, and the 1715 rising came shortly after Scotland's unification with England, depriving it of even the theoretical sovereignty it had had as a separate kingdom, though ruled by the same king as England.

So I think the elites who fomented the Jacobite risings fought to protect the relative sovereignty of the clan polities they ruled, not directly about which religion and which king gets to sit nominally at the top of a largely autonomous group of clan chiefs, though support for both the Stuarts and for Episcopalianism was certainly widespread. Neither religion nor Crown was something that was likely to seriously exercise ordinary clan families, struggling as they were with severe poverty and famine and the need to bring in the harvest. Much as with the witchcraft panics, it took an elite propaganda push to fan the flames, to get people to rise up.

Perhaps Alexander and many others did realize they had nothing to gain, and that all but the clan elites had much to lose. Tacksmen had to use persuasion backed by force, threats of hanging, and burning of homes to get the clans to rise up and follow their chiefs despite being honor-bound to do so, despite a long tradition of warrior manhood, and despite the clans' long history of ferocious warfare and raiding among themselves. [134] The Jacobite rebellions were not the old Highlander raiding, from which ordinary clan members could benefit, as well as the chief. Intense feeling, a passionate willingness to die, to "sacrifice for the nation" to "shed blood for the nation," to prove one's worth . . . all could be whipped up, but given the spectacular desertion rate, this was only temporarily successful. [135]

So my take on it is that there was something else going on, and that, like other wars that use religion to claim war is necessary, claims about God's choice of ruler were just another of the myriad excuses for getting ordinary people to "agree" to die for the benefit of an elite, be they bloodright aristocrats or wealth-right plutocrats. As I've stated, I believe the "something else" that was actually going on was, in terms of the themes of this book, the elites' desire to counter the threat posed by the increased power of the Crown in the ongoing contest between clan chief autonomy and kingly state sovereignty, or what cultural historian Murray Pittock calls the "nationalist freight" of the 1715 rebellion. That struggle played out particularly, Smout argues, over the Crown's increasingly forceful maintenance of law and order, as it established its monopoly on punishment. Scottish magnates fought each other, however, because some, such as the Campbell elites, believed they could parlay loyalty to the Crown into protection of their autonomy, while others, including most Highlanders and some Lowlanders, thought bringing back the Stuarts and Scottish national independence held more promise.[136]

AT THE END OF ALL THIS we have Alexander, probably not one of those captured. Nevertheless, as a rebel tainted with treason, he was potentially subject to the drawing and quartering that had caused Archibald Burnet's shrieks to be heard a mile away (surely I don't need to repeat the gruesome descriptions of spectacular deaths from the Introduction). Perhaps Alexander was one of the many who simply fled to avoid capture.[137]

How to punish such a huge number of Scottish prisoners without totally alienating the Scottish elites, who, even if they were themselves loyalists, all had close relatives and friends who were Jacobites, and who, given the close-knit nature of clan kinship and clan intermarriage, owed each other loyalty? As Charles II and his administration had found after Bacon's Rebellion, sovereignty can be demonstrated by deciding who may live, as well as who may die. And letting people live can be a much safer bet when you don't have the power to make them die—and when punishing would actually punish the whole population, not just those deemed guilty, because such a large percentage of the population either revolted or was sympathetic toward and tightly interconnected to those who did revolt. Charles II, in reversing Berkeley's punishing rampage after Bacon's Rebellion, had indeed demonstrated greater sovereignty. George I, in failing to punish, was acknowledging the power of the Scottish elite, without whom he could not govern Scotland.[138]

Those captured in Scotland in the 1715 rebellion were almost never executed or transported afterward—friends and relatives went to bat for them. As Margaret Sankey describes in her analysis of the aftermath of the rebellion, the great lords of Scotland were actually the ones who made the decisions of life and death, deciding for clemency, and pressuring the king to agree.[139] This sparing of rebel brothers and cousins was the price the king had to pay to get the support of the Scottish lords in regaining control of the rebel areas.[140] It also proved just about impossible to successfully confiscate rebel estates as required by a 1716 law designed to deprive the elite of the landed power base that made it possible for them to rebel in the first place.[141] In discussing the fate of the Jacobite prisoners, Sankey says that the "suppression of the rebellion and treatment of the rebels in its aftermath was the true test of the [Hanoverian] dynasty's legitimacy and sovereignty."[142] The king couldn't punish in Scotland after the 1715 uprising; a mere thirty years later the Jacobites rose again. And that time, they were finally and thoroughly quashed and sovereignty was established.

In England, however, the king could punish. The estates of the northern English Jacobite rebels were successfully seized, unlike in Scotland. However, even in England only thirty-three rebels were actually executed.[143] Although they were condemned to be drawn and quartered, most were "merely" hanged. They were taken to various Jacobite towns for execution—the public spectacle would demonstrate sovereignty, and a long-drawn-out execution gave the audience time to contemplate the power of the Crown—a contemplation extended by displaying the rebels' heads on pikes.

There were too many condemned to be able to execute them

within a reasonable time frame.[144] The threat of execution was meant not just to demonstrate sovereignty, but also to scare prisoners into agreeing to transportation to the West Indies. People couldn't be sentenced to transportation, but they could choose it as an alternative to hanging. In the end, 638 were transported, but only 143 of them to the West Indies, where conditions were so bad that indenture was the equivalent of a death sentence.[145] The profit motive thwarted the king's directive. The transportation was subcontracted, and captains actually delivered the prisoners as best suited their own pocket, going where prices for servants were best, or minimizing their costs by going to ports that were already on their itinerary, often in Virginia, Maryland, or South Carolina.[146]

Here, at the end of this story of Alexander's arrival, a bit of sober probability. He probably was a Jacobite, though the only proof is an unreliable church history. He may well have paid his passage to Virginia by indenturing himself, as family mythology claims. Although there is no record of his indenture, given the huge number of burned-out courthouses in Virginia, there is nothing surprising about that. So Alexander the rebel may well be fiction—but it does make a better story, and if it didn't happen to Alexander, it did happen to many others; that is not fiction.

THE GLORIOUS REVOLUTION OF 1688 had reverberated around the world with convulsions that likely spewed Venis and Alexander as well as thousands of others onto the shores of Virginia. Merchants, whose interests were paramount in a Parliament empowered through the Declaration of Rights, with leverage over the monarchy and control of the purse strings, were able to break the Royal African Company's monopoly on the slave trade. Ending the monopoly set off what historian Gerald Horne calls deregulation of the trade, or "free trade in Africans." The collapse of the monopoly came on the heels of Bacon's Rebellion, as Virginia elites were realizing that legislating white privilege, and thus solidifying whiteness, would control both their African and their English labor force. And at the same time Bacon's Rebellion made it clear that dependence on the increasingly long indentures and misery of English labor was problematic. Thus the demand for African labor rose exponentially, a demand slave merchants were now free to meet, making Venis and other Igbo likely targets. In addition, the Glorious Revolution was not so glorious for those who were soon to be caught up in the Jacobite Rebellions it helped to set off. In any case, Alexander did arrive in Virginia. And Alexander was one of those for whom the colonies eventually made good on the promise of a better future.

Venis, however, was given no such promise.

CHAPTER 5

Ancestor Tales of the Logic of a Slave Society

We return now to Virginia, backtracking a bit in time, to the early 1700s, to the world into which Sarah Ellis was born on a presumably cold day in November 1717, in Christ Church Parish, Middlesex County. This would have been around the time Alexander might have been fleeing from Scotland. It might also have been shortly before Venis was born. But these three lives that were eventually juxtaposed in marriage and servitude, Igbo, Highlands Scot, and colonial Virginian, bore no resemblance to each other. The friction, when they did come together, must have been enormous.

When Alexander and later Venis might have set foot in Virginia, Sarah was already there, a second-, and perhaps third-generation Virginian, the youngest of the nine children of Hezekiah and Mary Ellis.[1] Hezekiah shows up briefly in 1712 in Gloucester County, next door to Middlesex, witnessing a land sale, and then again right before his death, deeding a gift to one of his other daughters.[2] He died sometime between December 1726, when he wrote his will, and June 1727, when the will was proven in court. The will appears to indicate that he was not a slave or servant owner—or at least it says nothing about their disposal, or perhaps they were simply included in his "entire estate," which was to go to his wife, Mary, for use during her lifetime.[3]

That is it for the family Sarah was born into. So for Sarah's early life I have little to hang a story on. However, historians Darrett and Anita Rutman lay out the results of their massive study of the records of Middlesex County for this time period, and I can use that as the framework on which to hang a tale of a young girl who became one of my ancestors.[4] Her great-grandson, my great-great-grandfather, Thomas Davidson, married Elizabeth Ann Radford, my great-great-grandmother, thus bringing the two-family strands of this narrative together.

Sarah would almost certainly have grown up within a tight network of kin and longtime neighbor ties—similar to the nest of Radford connections a bit up the Rappahannock from Middlesex. The average household head had links to five other families in the county, an average of thirty-one such relatives, say the Rutmans.[5] Sarah's older siblings would have been starting to marry during her childhood, and may well have lived nearby. Beyond those kin were also friendships and client relationships, such as those between John Radford and Martin Cole, from whom John bought his first land. Friendships and kinships cemented one another, as siblings or cousins married neighbors and set up their own nearby households. [6]

The high death rate in colonial Virginia had not let up for Sarah's generation. Like fifty-seven percent of children born between 1710 and 1749 in Middlesex, she lost one parent before she was thirteen years old—Hezekiah died when she was nine.[7] There is nothing in the record to indicate when her mother might have died. A very common pattern, however, was that her mother, Mary, would have remarried shortly after his death, and that Sarah and the other children who were still at home would have lived with their mother and stepfather. Marrying landed widows was a major path to upward mobility for landless men. There is no record of Mary's remarriage, however, and perhaps her estate was too small to attract suitors. Since Hezekiah's will gave his widow a life interest in his estate, Mary could have become a widowed head of household, giving her considerably more rights to conduct her own affairs than if she remarried. Considering that she must have been in her late forties when Hezekiah died, this is a distinct possibility. But also, given her age and the extremely high death rate, she may well have died shortly after her husband, which would explain why she doesn't appear in the court record, either as a widowed head of household or as the "relict [widow] of Hezekiah Ellis, now wife of" a husband who had taken over her property. If she did die shortly after Hezekiah, she may have left instructions as to the care of her younger children, which the court was obliged to honor. Without instructions, the court, which had oversight of orphans, could have appointed a guardian for Sarah if there was an estate to manage or, if she was impoverished, would have her spend her childhood legally "bound out" to work for another family, who in return had to feed, clothe, and teach her until she grew up.[8] There is no evidence of either of these.

Perhaps an older brother and his wife had simply remained at home and taken over management of the land. Alternatively, if the family took responsibility for her, which was very common, then there is a good chance that she went to live with an older sibling, most likely with her brother William, with whom she was close until her death, and who took responsibility for her son, Alexander II.[9] William and his wife, Elizabeth, must have been married in approximately 1733, since their first child was born in 1734, followed most likely by another child every two years, like clockwork, judging by the number of children listed in William's will.[10] Just who Elizabeth was, however, remains a mystery. Much searching and tracking down of possibilities got me nowhere.[11]

But in any case, by marrying William, Elizabeth became part of the network of relatives in which Sarah grew up. Ties like these, being largely local, made it possible for women to visit and help one another; they were not as isolated in their own households as one might suppose from the fact that men had far more freedom and reason to travel about the countryside.[12] Those who controlled unfree labor, as the Rutmans document, spent a great deal of time visiting. But for those women without unfree labor, whether enslaved or indentured, work in English households was a heavy dawn-to-dusk proposition. They worked far harder than did Igbo women in Africa or Powhatan women in the time of Wahunsonacock. Sarah would have been participating in this work, either in her mother's household or in the home of a relative. If she lived with William, and if he already owned some enslaved

Africans—when he died some thirty years later he owned eighteen—she would have been spared the heaviest work.[13] He left directions in his will for the distribution of enslaved people to his children. The administrators were to purchase two more people, presumably so that each of his children could be given workers with comparable household talents, while his field hands remained under his wife's control until her death. Some of those eighteen might be the "increase" of people he had bought much earlier, or that came to him through marriage.

Though it is true that women were not thoroughly isolated, nevertheless their lives were vastly more constricted and legally far more dominated by men than the lives of either Igbo women or women of the remaining Native nations. Women could not stand for themselves in court; if they had to appear in court, a man had to represent them. Husbands were responsible for their wives' behavior. If a wife was fined by the court, for instance, the husband could either pay the fine or let the wife be punished by the ducking stool—his choice. And, as we saw in chapter 2, the church's moral codes were strict and backed by force that was administered by the court. Sarah would have been well aware of the consequences of premarital sex. That knowledge would be hard to avoid. Legally she had to attend church at least once a month. Failure to do so would have meant a fine for the head of her household. In church, she would have seen women accused of "bastardy" and hauled off to court for either a whipping or payment of a fine. She would have seen, or heard about, some of the great men of the county standing as surety for payment of an indentured servant's bastardy fine, though not claiming to be the father.[14] The whispers must have been rampant. She would have heard about women in labor, when supposedly they wouldn't be able to lie, being questioned by the attending women, who would report to the court about the identity of the father.

Sarah would also have been aware of women whose punishment was far worse than hers would be, should she become pregnant before marriage. She might be fined, and undergo the humiliation of being required to name the father, so that he, in turn, could be required to pay for the child's upkeep, but unlike indentured women, she would not be sentenced to an additional two and a half years in order to pay off the very hefty fine of 500 pounds of tobacco. [15] Nor would the court arrange her sale for the remainder of her servitude, along with the added time, to another owner if the court deemed her present owner to have purposely gotten her pregnant in order to lengthen her indenture.[16] Nor, like enslaved women, would her child be deemed "increase," a welcome addition to her owner's wealth and labor force. So yes, relative privilege, but once married she was under her husband's control.

Sarah would have been aware of her position within the increasingly hierarchical society that framed the 280-some white families of Middlesex, and indeed all of Tidewater Virginia, during the time she was growing up. [17] Her language and behavior in interacting with others would have reflected the position of everyone involved. She would address those above her with conscious deference and subservient behavior. Some she would address as Mistress, or occasionally Lady, others she would address by name; some would be esquire, gentleman, mister, or addressed by first name alone. It all depended on relative status in the larger community, as well as on your dependence on a particular patron for credit or for selling your tobacco. That hierarchy even prescribed who should attend whose deathbed. The Rutmans describe how, over the course of the century between 1650 and 1750, status differences increased dramatically, and thus the markers of status increasingly governed behavior.

Landownership was the most obvious criterion in establishing status, and during Sarah's youth and thereafter it was becoming harder and harder to find land available for sale, making class lines far more rigid than previously. Land was increasingly consolidated in fewer and fewer hands, bought up or patented by those with the wealth created by enslaved labor.[18] Smaller landowners often rented out the land they couldn't work themselves because they couldn't afford to buy even an indentured servant. But with fewer small landowners, the landless had fewer opportunities to rent as a first step toward landownership. Likewise, there were fewer relatively poor men inheriting land, selling a portion, and using the proceeds to develop the portion they kept. Thus buying small acreages was increasingly difficult. The result was that the transition out of landlessness was more and more blocked.

At the same time, there were fewer jobs available. Large landowners, now that enslaved Africans were far more plentiful as the African slave trade ramped up after Bacon's Rebellion, no longer had much need for free laborers. There were some jobs available as overseers, accountants, tutors, and ministers—not very helpful to the largely uneducated landless needing work. As towns developed, a few landless white people did succeed as tailors, blacksmiths, and tavern keepers— Alexander I, Sarah's future husband, might have been one of these. But beyond those jobs, there was little else. Big landowners had no need to pay independent artisans or laborers for plantation work—enslaved artisans were available for purchase or could be trained. An additional problem with hiring workers was that there was little cash available, and payment in tobacco was bulky. Eventually a tobacco warehouse and inspection system was established, under the governor's control. It provided tobacco certificates that circulated as money until they were redeemed when the tobacco sold—convenient, but also an increased centralization of state power. The tobacco economy was no longer totally in the hands of the local wealthy landowners with docks and warehouses, through which everyone else had, willy-nilly, to ship.[19] And this means we need to see what happened to poor whites.

MIDDLESEX HAD ALWAYS BEEN a hierarchical society, but something quite fundamental was changing. In the early days of the colony if you survived indenture (a big *if*, since back then half the workforce died within five years), then land was available, occasionally as freedom dues at the end of the indenture. Far more land was distributed through the headright system, which gave fifty acres to those who paid their own or someone else's passage to the colony. Thus, at least at first, it was relatively possible to "patent" land—to legally gain the use of Crown land.[20] Two interrelated conditions were at play in the changes that created a society in which opportunity was clearly blocked. One was the shift that made land—the means by which people were able to produce goods for sale and for sustenance—into private property, no longer available to patent. By this time the land to which the Crown laid claim in what became Middlesex had all been taken by patent, some by small new landowners, some by the wealthy abusing the head-right system. The Crown had made land relatively easy to get because it wanted people on the land producing tobacco—the primary Virginia source of revenue for the Crown, given that no gold had been found and the only lucrative item of trade with the local native polities was fur—a rapidly dwindling resource.[21] To patent land you paid a fee, and then an annual quit-rent to the Crown—basically, a real estate tax used to maintain the Crown's Virginia government. You had to develop the land—you had to build and plant or bring in people to do so. If you didn't fulfill this obligation, you had "escheated," and the land reverted to the Crown. In other words, it wasn't totally private property, and there had been a lot of it available early on.

But by the mid-1600s that was no longer true in the Tidewater counties—a fact that contributed to the anger that led to Bacon's Rebellion.[22] Land was now available only through purchase, at first from the original patentee, later from heirs or previous purchasers. Or land was available on the far fringes of the colony, land to which Native polities still laid claim, or which the Iroquois confederacy was eyeing—another factor in Bacon's Rebellion. Land that was safe, in other words, was now thoroughly subject to the dictates of capitalism. Middlesex had lost what vague resemblance it had had to the Igbo or Powhatan system that made land a communal resource available to all.

However, even when land had been relatively available, the need for labor formed a second blockage to opportunity. The goal of ownership of land is production, and ownership of more land than your family can work means you need an exploitable source of additional labor if you are to benefit from all the land you own. And how do you get people to turn their labor over to you, rather than putting it into production for themselves? Well, coercion, dispossession, and punishment, the specialty of the state, and a stately obligation. There need to be people who have no choice, or rather whose choice is between starvation and laboring for you in return for sustenance. In other words, you can't have a commons-like situation. People need to be dispossessed—denied the right to land or other means of making a living—and that requires force. It takes force, for instance, to back up the rules about trespassing and theft that protect your right to your property and to whatever was produced using that property. These rights were enforced in Middlesex by bringing suit in court and by the Church's oversight of boundaries, both backed by the force of the state—whipping, fining, executing if necessary. The state likewise enforced rules about contract and purchase, protecting owners' rights to control of people and labor—absconding from both indenture and slavery were crimes punished by the state.[23] The whipping post in front of the courthouse saw the blood of many a captured runaway. State coercion made it possible for Middlesex elites to hang on to thousands of acres and to the fruits of the labor of many workers, while at the same time there were people so poor that even when their indentures finished they had little choice but to continue working in return for room and board and nothing more. Many such men were unable to marry; indentured women were far more likely than free women to be brought up on bastardy charges and assigned further years of servitude, thus also not free to marry. Their children were declared orphans and bound out to work until adulthood. Those who didn't own land were considered failures unless they had a craft that allowed them to support a family.[24] Being able to play the role of patriarchal head of household was the bottom line for male status. Very few could do that without land, and achieving that status, if you weren't born to it, was becoming increasingly difficult.

The idea of continuing as Middlesex laborers was abhorrent to most men—how could they be real men, patriarchal heads of households under those conditions? The class structure was not sufficiently developed to cause English laborers to accept landlessness as normal and permanent wage labor as honorable.[25] And if the laborers were forced to accept permanent landlessness, the elites were quite sure there would be another, maybe even bloodier, rebellion. So after Bacon's Rebellion, as we have seen, the English, including indentured servants, were defined as white, free, or eligible for freedom, with the rights of Englishmen to private property. Those rights to property were a source of hope, even if they were a bit dubious—land was available only on the dangerous fringes, and human property was out of their price range. Nevertheless, by comparison with blacks, whites without property were definitely privileged, definitely different, and thus less likely to revolt.

Here we come to that fundamental shift in the nature of Middlesex's hierarchical society. The privatization of land and the shift to enslaved Africans as the primary workforce interacted with each other. Middlesex had been a society with slaves, where slavery was not basic to the social structure. But, as Ira Berlin describes, it shifted, along with the rest of Tidewater Virginia, and eventually the whole colony and much of the rest of the US South, into a slave society, where all institutions bowed to slavery. From marriage to inheritance to politics to economics, all had to enable slavery and avoid interference with its profits.[26]

SO, MIDDLESEX, AS SARAH CAME of age, was becoming a slave society with clear status markers. Middlesex had become safe enough and prosperous enough (for the already wealthy) that the purchase of a lifetime laborer now made economic sense, as opposed to buying a series of short-term indentured servants. The enslaved African you bought stood a reasonable chance of living long enough to justify their much higher purchase price compared to an indentured servant. An added incentive came in the form of babies: if you owned a woman who was enslaved your initial purchase might increase your wealth and your labor force through reproduction. Moreover, owning slaves carried status in itself, even if it made no economic sense, as the Rutmans maintain, for smaller owners who couldn't absorb the financial loss entailed in the death of an enslaved African on whose purchase they had spent all their available resources. Not only could they not recoup that loss, but without the labor they needed, they might lose their tobacco crop as well. Larger owners, like William Ellis, were not in this position—losing one-eighteenth of your investment and of your tobacco labor force is very different from losing 100 percent or even 50 percent. Buying a much cheaper indentured servant made more sense for those who were not wealthy. However, the fact that owning a slave conveyed status may explain why there are so many court records conveying one or two enslaved Africans from a father, usually of the bride, to a newly married couple. Or look at William's will, making sure each child was given an African.[27] That the gift was quite often a woman speaks to domestic help—but it also speaks to a woman's value as an investment. Like her, any children would be wealth—mortgage-able, lease-able, sale-able, all added security for the bride.

Sarah's family did own land and so was at least not among the landless poor; her father was able to be a proper patriarchal head of household. In terms of status, it appears that Hezekiah was some-where in the middle. He had enough property to justify writing a will, but was not among the upper third of men who were called to jury duty or to witness deeds.[28] So Sarah could see herself as above the landless poor as well as above the enslaved and the indentured. She would not be described as a "slut" or "promiscuous" as indentured women regularly were—or at least not without appearing to do some-thing to justify the term.[29]

These status distinctions were growing greater. When Hezekiah Ellis was born around 1680, the median estate as inventoried at death of the wealthiest fifth of the population was about 45 times that of the lowest fifth. By the time Sarah was born in 1717 that number was about 81 times, and when her son Alexander II was born around 1740, the distance had climbed to 117 times. Not only that, but the wealthiest were far wealthier in relation to the next group down than previously. The chasm between the elites who governed—burgesses, justices of the peace, clerks of the court, vestrymen, and church wardens—and everyone else had grown immensely, and rather unbridgeably.[30] By 1740, half of Middlesex households held at least one person enslaved, but owning only one or two did not bring anything like the prosper-ity of people like William Ellis. Owning one or two, however, could mean much needed household help for a woman like Sarah, or help in the fields, or assistance for a craftsman like Alexander—lessening the burden of heavy labor. But at the same time, as slavery spread, it also contributed to the growth of the status gap between small slaveholders and the other half of households without slaves, who were left even further behind. This growing chasm was one of the consequences of the shift to a slave society. Concomitantly, poverty rates rose, judging by the increased expenditures for welfare.[31]

It was those men at the top (sometimes dependent on women's testimony and undoubtedly sometimes influenced a bit by wives) who made the decisions about who was considered to deserve welfare—generally the provision of a small sum of money or a job such as cleaning the church for an elderly widow or payment to a householder for the "keep" of someone, male or female, too infirm or too young to be on their own. They decided also on building programs—in Middlesex this meant a grand new church and a courthouse with jail, pillory, and whipping post, the architectural symbols of the dyadic structure of sacred and secular authority, complete with reminders of the power to use force in punishing. Ordinary people deeply resented the court's decision to build that grand courthouse and church, a decision in which they had no say. Levies were doubled, going up to 76 pounds of tobacco per tithable person. Since a householder had to pay tithes for everyone under his authority—all men over sixteen, black women and unfree white women over sixteen—this could add up to a substantial sum. This was on top of the church tithes, which were generally larger.[32] And notice how huge this meant the five hundred pounds of tobacco bastardy fine was! By the mid-1740s, people were leaving Middlesex and neighboring Gloucester, heading out to the fringes of the colony where, at least for a while, land was still available.[33] Spotsylvania, north and a bit west of Jamestown and Middlesex, was a destination of choice, and that is where we go next.

AT THIS POINT, WE NEED to introduce Alexander Davidson back into the story, this time in Virginia as Sarah Ellis's husband, after having fled the Scottish Highlands in the aftermath of the 1715 Rebellion. Just how he got from wherever he had landed, perhaps in 1717 or so, to where he first shows up in the record in Spotsylvania in 1745, is a mystery. He may have been living in Gloucester County, next door to Middlesex, since that is where Alexander II was probably born in probably 1744, and where William Ellis, Sarah's brother, had been living. There is also the negative evidence that there is no mention of him or record of their marriage in Middlesex's far more complete records. However, William was already buying land in Spotsylvania, where he shortly moved and where Alexander first appears.[34]

So, here is a possible scenario. Alexander arrives and indentures himself. By the time he arrived, indentures were at least seven years, sometimes longer. Potentially he would be freed around 1725, at approximately age thirty-five. Like many others, it could have taken him a long time to build up enough capital to be able to afford marriage, and by the time he was ready to marry, it had gotten even harder.[35] Perhaps Alexander and Sarah met after William moved to Gloucester, perhaps with his own marriage, and Sarah moved in with her brother. Alexander and Sarah were likely to have lived fairly close to each other; the Rutmans' analysis for fifty years earlier in Middlesex shows that 95 percent of marriages were between families no more than five miles apart.[36] But in any case, Sarah and Alexander met. They must have married by at least 1743 when she was in her mid-twenties and he was in his late forties or early fifties. Men coming out of indenture did often marry late. By the time she married, the gender ratio among whites was no longer as imbalanced as it had been even fifty years earlier, when there was such a shortage of English women, so her choices might have been more limited than when there were three or four men of marrying age for every woman.[37] Given also that it was getting harder and harder for landless young men to establish themselves, maybe an older man didn't look so bad.

Alternatively, since we really do not know for sure when Alexander arrived, maybe he was not that old when they married. A letter written by one of Alexander II's granddaughters says he had two brothers, William and Philip. In 1751 William Ellis was ordered by the court to pay Bloomfield Long Jr. twenty shillings for "keeping and clothing of Alexander Davidson an orphan, out of the money in the hands of the sd Ellis that is due to the sd orphan." That orphan was Alexander II, the son of Alexander I and Sarah, who probably learned from the Longs the blacksmithing he later practiced in Kentucky, though I found no documents apprenticing or indenturing him. The next two entries in the court record order William Ellis to pay ten shillings to Thomas Smith for keeping William Davidson and Philip Davidson out of the money due them, verifying the granddaughter's letter.[38] Philip appears to have been younger than Alexander, born somewhere around 1745. According to his 1751 indenture as an apprentice to learn the "art and mystery" of making leather breeches, he was six years old.[39] But then why was only Alexander given a guardian, his uncle William Ellis, in 1752, with no mention of the other two boys?[40] I am totally puzzled![41] But in any case, if William Davidson was older, as the records appear to indicate, or if the occasional mention of 1740 for Alexander II's birth is correct, then Sarah and Alexander I would have been married before 1743, maybe as early as 1733, when she was sixteen and he was forty-three. But whatever their age at marriage, he was dead in 1748, Sarah was a widow, and Alexander left no will that might have provided some clues.[42]

But that is getting a little ahead of the tale. Alexander and Sarah may have moved to Spotsylvania to join Sarah's brother after William bought land there in 1743—moving in that common family cluster pattern. It was frequently new couples, as they were, who left the older counties such as Middlesex and Gloucester.[43] William became a resident of St. George Parish in Spotsylvania, which is centered on Fredericksburg.[44] Given the relationship between the two families, it is pretty safe to assume that the Davidsons lived there also. Alexander I's first appearance in the records is his appointment as constable in July 1745, after which he should have taken an oath before a county magistrate, but didn't. In November, the court ordered that he be "attached by the Sherrif [*sic*] to answer why he doth not take the Oath of a Constable." My guess?—1745 was the year of the final Jacobite uprising, and he was reluctant to swear to uphold the English king. But in December he apparently gave in—he was declared in contempt of court, but the case was dismissed. Presumably he gave the required oath, and the following December he was paid for work he had done as a constable. Two months later he was replaced. His next appearance is with William Ellis, and thereafter he and William appear together occasionally.[45] That Alexander was a constable, if briefly, and was on several

juries, would imply that, despite the lack of records, he did own property.[46] Very few landless people were called for juries, and it is even
more improbable that a landless man would have served as constable.

Alexander's estate inventory (the full inventory is in Appendix 1)
tells us he was a shoemaker: he owned shoemaking tools and leather.
As an artisan, he probably lived in or very close to Fredericksburg.[47]
The five horses, one a colt, and two cows with their last year's yearlings
and a steer from probably a previous year (given that it was February,
quite likely two more calves were due in the spring) all imply a noticeable degree of prosperity. Horses were still fairly uncommon, and with
two mares he would have been able to sell young horses, an additional
source of income. The cows meant milk and calves, and calves meant
either meat or income from their sale. The Rutmans use the purchase
of a butter pot as an example of luxury spending, and Sarah had two,
as well as a looking glass and other household goods, including a wash-
tub, a spice mortar and pestle, cooking utensils, a table and chairs.[48]
Then there were the three feather beds and bedsteads—feather beds
were important enough to be mentioned as legacies in wills. To even
have room for three bedsteads would imply that they lived in a type of
house that was still common in the 1730s in Middlesex, so likely also
in Spotsylvania. This would be a house with a foundation and wooden
floor, not a dirt floor, and a brick fireplace, stairs rather than a ladder
to a loft, or perhaps even two small downstairs rooms, making it a bit
larger than the most common kind of house, which was "not much
larger than a modern two-car garage." [49]

The Rutmans place leatherworkers below middle status in
Middlesex, especially if leatherworking was not combined with
planting.[50] By the 1740s, they say, it is very unlikely that friendships
would have crossed status lines; planters like William Ellis were rarely
friends with shoemakers.[51] Perhaps at the time of Sarah's marriage
the class difference was not so noticeable. William's status might have
risen over the years after the marriage, and certainly was quite high,
at least in terms of slave ownership, landowning, frequent jury duty,
and witnessing of transactions by the time he died in 1766. The value
of Alexander's estate on the other hand—about £89—places him in

middle status at his death.[52] His apparent lack of land, however, would likely have lowered his status. His estate is a bit over the median estate (in Middlesex) of £85 for those who served, like Alexander, on juries or held other low-level public service positions, although well below that of men who were constables, as Alexander briefly was. For comparison, the median in Middlesex for those who held colony-wide positions was £2,386.[53] Alexander was certainly out of William's league financially. His association with William can be explained by the brother-in-law relationship, and as William's status rose, perhaps the relationship between the two men included a bit of patronage. In any case, William seems at least to have been concerned with his sister and her children. Besides becoming Alexander II's guardian, he stood security for Sarah's administration of Alexander I's estate when he died.[54] And over half the value of the assets in the estate inventory was in two enslaved Africans, Venis and Adam.

I DON'T KNOW HOW OR WHEN or why Venis entered the lives of Sarah and Alexander. Certainly, it was not voluntarily. It is my theory that Venis, or perhaps both Venis and Adam, were gifts, probably from William, taking care of his little sister, playing the role fathers often played by providing her with enslaved help and status. It seems unlikely that Alexander could have bought two enslaved Africans—they would have cost more than the remainder of all his other assets. If Venis was closer to thirty than to twenty, Adam could possibly have been Venis's son, given his designation in the estate inventory as a "boy," a term that could be applied to any age from zero to twenty.[55] In that case, he could have been Alexander's son as well, or even William's, if my theory that they were gifts from William is correct. On the other hand, given his high valuation, he may have been too old to be the son of Venis, although he could still have been the son of William and one of the other women that William held enslaved. If he was, it was certainly not an unusual situation.

As William or Alexander's son, Adam would have been born enslaved, since a child took the mother's status. The child belonged to the mother's owner, exactly the way a foal belongs to the owner of the mare, regardless of the stallion or the stallion's owner. So men not infrequently owned their own children or grandchildren, or their overseer's or neighbor's children. White men, like both Alexander and the wealthy Thomas Jefferson, were thus protected from having to treat their black children as heirs; instead, they were saleable property. Only white children born in wedlock counted as heirs. So a man's property was inherited only by his white children whose mother was his legal wife, a status that gave her the right to inheritance for her children, and gave the husband the legal obligation to provide for her and her children—and the right to demand obedience and service from her. These laws were all part of the legal structure that transitioned Virginia from a society with slaves to a slave society. Without those laws, the distribution of property would have been very different, and as a consequence, the share of the country's wealth in black hands today would be far larger than it is.

But suppose the term "boy" didn't mean child but was instead the derogation of black manhood, as it certainly was later. This possibility is suggested by the fact that Adam is valued so highly. Historian Jennifer Morgan points out how common it was to purchase "pairs" in hopes of reproduction—maybe Venis and Adam were expected to be such a pair. [56] On the other hand, his value might have been relatively high for a youngster because he was well on his way to becoming a shoemaker, learning as Alexander's helper. Enslaved craftsmen were valuable. So there is no way to know what the relationship was between Adam and Venis. That she and Adam even existed at all is known only because of the public record showing that the biggest portion of Alexander I's estate was his human property, people identified as Venis and Adam. A bit more can be pieced together, as I will shortly describe.

BUT FIRST, THERE IS A PROBLEM, one that didn't even occur to me until I began doing the research for this chapter. I had never asked myself why slavery existed at all. Like most Americans, I took it for granted that slavery was a part of our history, and slavery itself seemed obvious. It was, I thought, because slavery was the cheapest way to get your tobacco grown or cotton picked. Why pay somebody when you can own somebody? And own their babies too—even if they are your own children? Then one day it hit me. I'd been working on understanding how states develop and how punishment connects to the concentration of power in the hands of an elite, and how it is the obligation of states to provide cheap labor for the benefit of the elite. What hit me was a question: has there ever been a state that formed without basing at least its early stages on some kind of coerced labor? I couldn't think of one, and as I soon found, other researchers said I was right.[57] Even the Powhatan, moving toward the more and more stratified society that is basic to the social organization of any state, had slaves who were war captives. Why does coerced labor seem to be so basic to state formation?

The answer seems to be that state formation is about concentrating wealth in a few hands, and the basic way to create wealth is by using human labor to transform resources into usable goods. So ultimately, if there is no class system to dispossess people who will choose to provide that labor rather than starve, then captives—people you can force—are the only answer to the labor problem. As society becomes a bit more stratified, with more and more wealth and resources concentrated in a few hands, and as those few hands gain control of the right to punish, then punishable people and debtors can be added to captives as part of the usable labor supply. Push the process a bit further, add in private property replacing communal rights, and you are making the shift to a state. But then we are left with the question of why the slavery Venis might have known in West Africa, before colonialism and the huge demand for slaves in the Americas, was so different from the slavery Africans encountered when they finally set foot on land after surviving the Middle Passage.

To make sense of slavery we need to look at forming or just-formed early states all over the world. Africa had its share of such polities, as did the Americas, Europe, and Asia. Looking globally, slavery is ubiquitous under certain conditions. One is that the society is sufficiently stratified that individuals can raise their status by exploiting another person's labor, concentrating wealth and power in their own hands and creating an elite. The other is that land is not monopolized as private property, so that people can farm for themselves, and thus only force, a system of unfree labor, will provide laborers for larger landowners.[58] Those with rights to use land in sufficient quantity to support themselves can perhaps be made to pay tribute or taxes, but only force or dispossession could cause people to turn the whole of their labor over to someone else. This means that slavery, the use of people, usually outsiders with no rights to land within the polity, is the tactic of choice for weak states, states that can't enforce dispossession of their own people. Slavery carries with it the inestimable advantage that much of the burden of supporting a lord and his court can be shifted from local communities to enslaved outsiders. Local peasants can be less pressed, thus less likely to revolt and more likely to regard the king or lord as a legitimate ruler.[59] Even now, most states around the world depend partially on outsiders who without full, or sometimes any, rights, can be exploited more thoroughly than can members of the polity, whose loyalty is needed to legitimize the state and who have therefore been able to gain the right to some limit on their exploitation.[60]

If Venis grew up in Igboland, she would have been familiar with what we now call "slavery." Alexander might have known about the enslavement of Scots in Scotland's mines and salt pits.[61] However, each would have had in mind a variety of quite different relationships between "slave" and "master," many of them very different from what slavery is generally taken to mean today. Only some of these relationships were violently coercive ones inflicted on outsiders whose entire lives were used by masters to create profit, and who could be sold to others. Using the single word *slave* to refer to all of these relationships obscures the role of coerced labor, as does using the term *free* to describe everyone else.[62] The terms we do have to differentiate people working under the control of others—indenture, apprentice, marriage, convict and prison labor, military conscript or volunteer, guest worker, illegal migrant, court-ordered community service—all obscure the coercion of people who supposedly are free, or once were, or will be soon. Their work, while not slavery, can be described as "unfree." Sarah, for instance, was under the control of Alexander. She was far from "free," and the value of the work she did legally belonged to Alexander, as did the value of the work Venis did. Indeed, both their bodies belonged to him as well, although with different limitations. Control through marriage and control through slavery were not the same—but in what ways? Like Powhatan women, Venis, if she had grown up in Igboland, must have been shocked by Sarah's servitude, as well as by her own.

The use of language—"free" versus "enslaved," "wife" versus "slave," "indentured" versus "slave" or, alternatively using the same word, "slavery," for both the "wealth in people" version that Venis would have known about in West Africa and the version she experienced in Virginia—can obscure the power to control. It can keep us from asking about the real similarities and differences between relationships of control, and thus about benefits to the controllers. We can't ask questions about variation and similarities of power and control, or about the way in which owners benefited from the purchase of a person, if we assume that they are apples and oranges because the words are different, or that they are the same because we use the same words.

So let's look at the purpose of the slavery Venis would have known about in West Africa, often called "domestic slavery." It was dramatically different from the "productive slavery" she would know in Virginia, where the point was not wealth in people, but wealth through the production of saleable goods. In domestic slavery, people who were enslaved produced crops, food, goods for the use of themselves, their owners, and their owner's retinue—for the use of the domestic household, not for sale. [63] Such systems often included ways to insert the children of enslaved women, and sometimes the women themselves, into the kin group as wives or junior members or loyal soldiers. "Wealth in people" was the object, and slavery as well as kinship contributed to creating that wealth. [64]

In those polities where an elite managed to concentrate power and wealth, excluding more and more people from an inner aristocratic circle as the polity became more and more state-like, increasing inequality raised the likelihood of peasant revolt. Slave armies and generals were particularly useful against peasants. [65] As outsiders, they

were disconnected from local people, which meant they had no conflicting loyalties, unlike local people who might hesitate to kill or extort
their own and related kin groups. Divided as they were in so many
ways, outsiders and local people were unlikely to join in revolt, even
when peasants were no better off materially than the agricultural slaves
supporting the court.

For a king wanting to consolidate power and therefore needing to
gain a monopoly on punishment, a governing bureaucracy and military consisting of slaves made perfect sense. Wrenching the command
of armies, soldiering, collecting taxes, and policing from the hands of
competing lineages or upstart kin was a form of consolidation in itself.
Equally, it was clearly safer to entrust these functions to well-trained
and loyal slaves whose rights to wives and to positions of prestige and
even luxury were dependent on a ruler accruing power, than to entrust
them to perhaps incompetent and self-serving blood-right aristocratic
relatives or lineage heads.[66]

To build wealth in people and the prestige that goes with it, slaves
are the logical choice—but only so long as it isn't too expensive to
obtain them. If large armies or raiding parties have to be sent long dis-
tances to bring back captives or if the polities being raided go on the
offensive, costs rise, and slaves become too expensive or even unavailable. Slavery becomes impractical and serfdom more practical. At the
same time, slaves may become available locally as slavery increases
the inequality between slaveholders and non-slaveholders. Debt and
poverty or the ravages of war can produce people willing to pawn or
sell themselves and their children in order to eat. Though slavery has
sometimes been glossed as charity, the fact that people need to sell
themselves in order to eat is clearly the result of elite unwillingness to
redistribute control of land and resources, thus maintaining dispossession, a far from benign attitude.[67]

Looking around the world, when the supply of enslaved outsiders
begins drying up, an intermediate step develops between slavery and
wage labor. In these systems the costs of reproduction, of producing
the next generation of labor, are placed squarely on the backs of the
laborers themselves. Instead of purchase or capture, labor is produced

locally, by families—peasant corvée, serfs in Europe, related systems in other parts of the world. Though in varying degrees tied to an estate, the workers are given access to farmland and to common grazing and limited use of an estate's open land and forests. They provide for themselves and their children, relieving the landholder of those costs. These rights to use of land and forest eventually become customary and are balanced—unequally, with the scales tipped in the estate-holder's favor—by the unfree labor the workers provide the estate-holder. Disagreements are common, as the numerous peasant wars and revolts to defend laborers' customary rights can testify. In Europe, the shift from the slavery of the Roman Empire to serfdom and feudalism accompanied the fall of the Empire, peaking in the 1200s. We saw such a shift in the Scottish Highland clan system, particularly as it became more exploitative and as slavery disappeared during the 1400s. Sharecropping in the United States would become a way of re-creating aspects of this system within a capitalist society, as we will see later.[68]

LOGICAL AS DOMESTIC SLAVERY WAS, however, even when slaves were abundantly available it carried with it a contradiction: slavery enabled greater inequality, and with it the need for more and more force to prevent a peasant revolt—requiring either a bigger and bigger slave population or heavier taxation of the peasantry. A tiger by the tail, clearly. From our perspective today, a solution seems obvious: pay workers so they can buy food, pay the army, pay for those luxury goods slaves had been producing for you. But that solution looks viable only in societies where most people are dispossessed. In societies like that of the Igbo or Powhatan or even Highland Scotland, land, the major resource, was either held communally or, as in Jamestown, was theoretically readily available. That means you don't automatically have people who need jobs—they can farm and provide for themselves. Why would they go to work for you instead? Especially if the pay is low and the work hard. Our perspective today is based on a very different situation from that of the Igbo or Powhatan. Ours, like that of most of the world, is a system of dispossession. We'll go more into how we got this way in the next few chapters, but here I just want to describe briefly our system of labor and dispossession to clarify the logic of slavery, particularly of the productive slavery of the United States.

We have a working class, people who are willing to sell their labor because their labor is all they have. Other options for supporting themselves and their families have been cut off by dispossession. I would argue that this is what state-formation is all about: cutting off options, one way or another—feudalism, capitalism, slavery all do this—so that resources are controlled by the few, leaving the many to supply the labor that creates wealth from those resources. Even indenture, as we saw, performed this function for limited periods. For those of us in countries like the United States, the dispossession that creates the class system associated with capitalism has been the situation for so long that most of us take it as normal, and see people without their own business or other means of support, but who don't or can't sell their labor, as immoral, at least lazy, or perhaps terribly unfortunate. We sell our labor because productive resources are privately owned. Coal mines, businesses, land, factories, sometimes even rights to water—all private property. Those productive resources are owned by a fairly small number of people, leaving the rest of us without the resources needed to produce what we need for ourselves or to sell. With options cut off, we sell our labor to the people with the resources. An enormous amount of morality is built around the idea that you should give employers an "honest day's work" and that private property is sacrosanct. There is no comparably powerful reciprocal morality that says employers must give an honest day's pay, or that the need for a full belly is sacrosanct.

Because of that system of morality, we tend to pay no attention to a huge advantage that would have accrued to slaveholders if they had shifted to wages. The advantage conveyed by wages is this, as anthropologist Claude Meillassoux explains: If you don't feed your slaves even when they have no work, they die.[69] You can't just lay them off until you need workers again; if you did, you would have to buy or capture replacements. You had paid upfront for a life's worth of labor when you bought the slave; if you let your slave die, you lose your investment.

Theoretically, you are still responsible for a slave who is too old or ill to work, although you can get around that by freeing the slave (making the use of the word *free* problematic again). The advantage to wages comes in here—you pay for an hour's worth of work or for the performance of a particular task, and you pay after the work is accomplished.[70] No lifetime investment there! And you can pay as little as it takes to induce people with few options to decide that crumbs are better than nothing. No obligation to provide food and shelter when there is no work or to pay enough to keep children healthy. Some abolitionists and economists in slave societies, as well as some scholars today, have argued that this very fact makes wage labor more efficient—people with the carrot of wages and the stick of starvation work harder and better. And without the upfront investment in the purchase of people, owners could invest in more efficient technologies.[71]

Many scholars claim that productivity per person did not rise during slavery; production increased purely by increasing the number of workers, largely because there was no incentive to improve technology in order to increase productivity.[72] But Edward Baptist documents an enormous increase in production of pounds of cotton picked per worker without any change in technology, unless you count the introduction of the bullwhip as an innovative technology. His compilation of statistics and testimonies shows that in cotton production, nobody on wages or shares picked faster and more efficiently than terrorized enslaved Africans. Owners did not invest in any other picking technology to increase production per person; the much-vaunted cotton gin was relevant only after the cotton was picked.[73]

There are also other arguments negating the advantages of wages. There is the fact that whether or not wage-work is more efficient, you can still take more away from slaves who are not expected to reproduce than you can from wage-workers.[74] That became the strategy of slave owners in the Deep South when cotton became the primary crop around the time of the Revolution. They were raising an extraordinarily labor-intensive crop in which women did much the same work as men, and they knew they could buy replacements from the Upper South, where owners were raising less labor-intensive crops and did encourage reproduction. The enslaved woman's value in the Deep South was in production, not reproduction. Those babies that were born did increase the wealth of the owner, but taking women out of heavy fieldwork in order to produce more babies, when workers were badly needed, didn't make financial sense to the owners. The result was a low birth rate and a high death rate. Workers wore out faster than they could be replaced by those babies, who would have to grow well into their teens before they could do the work of a valuable field-hand. In making sense of this, a comparison might be useful: many US employers don't pay enough to provide themselves with replacement workers either. They can get away with this because the US govern-ment provides them with a subsidy in the form of food stamps and other forms of welfare for the workers, and because immigrant work-ers are available.

An even more powerful negation of the advantage of wages is that, if you are to continue to have a local people to exploit—peasants, serfs, or a working class, those people do have to be able to reproduce to replace the labor force.[75] They can't be replaced by purchase. Super-exploitation isn't possible on a long-term basis unless there is a huge relatively unfree category, such as that provided by segregation or sharecropping. Which is why outsiders—immigrants, guest workers, contract laborers—continue to be highly valued by employers paying far less than a living wage. The costs of raising those outsider workers are borne elsewhere, and forcing their return or limiting their rights can place at least some of the costs of raising their children on the home society. Indenture in this sense is intermediate: you invest in only two to seven years of labor, but you do pay up front, so the early death that was so common for indentured servants in places like Virginia repre-sented a loss, but a much smaller one than the death of a slave. Plus, the king paid part of the costs of indenture: he gave the land the servant could claim (with luck) at the end of an indenture—a nice subsidy for people wanting laborers!

An additional problem for wage work: to hire workers you need cash—you need some way to pay them.[76] Without a highly devel-oped system in which some form of money can be used to pay for any commodity, you can't pay workers easily, and the workers may not be able to buy everything they need. Virginia for the first hundred or more years didn't have enough money—coins were in short supply, and tobacco or a tobacco warehouse certificate was used instead, a clumsy and undependable form of money, and not widely available. Yet another problem: to depend on buying food to support your army or retinue, there needs to be a well-developed market in food and other subsistence goods. Your hired workers will need to be able to spend their money for food. That requires people producing large quantities for the market.

If there is a well-developed market in food, as there was by X Radford's time in England, then there is also the option of shifting laborers from food-growing to long-term apprenticeships in craft production, since the needed food can be bought rather than grown. And in England, with the advent of gold and silver from Spanish mines in the Americas, far more money was available for purchases. So gradually a working class developed in England—people who could be paid wages and for whom employers had to take no further responsibility.[77] For many this meant poverty, and for some a trip to the colonies, where they provided coerced indentured labor.

WE CAN TURN NOW TO LOOKING at the plantation slavery—productive slavery—that Venis experienced when she arrived in Virginia.[78] Domestic slavery was certainly not benign. But it was nowhere near as exploitative as productive slavery.[79] Productive slavery involves production not for sustenance and use of household and retinue, as domestic slavery primarily does. Instead, it entails the production of commodities for exchange or sale: goods, products, or crops. Unlike production for use, there is no limit built into this production for profit. In production for use, once you have all you can use, there is no point in producing more. The potential for severe exploitation in productive slavery is thus obvious, its only built-in limit being the physical capacity of the workers, a limit that US plantation slavery, especially in the Deep South, sorely tested.

Productive slavery, particularly the extremely labor-intensive variety practiced in the Deep South, depended on a final advantage of slavery for owners, compared to dependence on serfs or peasants. Dying or worn-out slaves can be replaced by purchase. Serfs are tied to the land and additional serfs can't be bought elsewhere and brought in to work. Peasants also can't be bought. And this limits owners' ability to exploit them: severe exploitation means few births, dying children, and no next generation of workers—killing the goose that lays the golden eggs.[80] In contrast, the cost of raising replacement slaves, if they are raised in another polity and then captured, is borne by the people of that other polity. As tobacco land eventually wore out in the Upper South and landowners turned toward raising livestock and other crops in addition to some tobacco or hemp, work became lighter, and fewer workers were needed. It began making economic sense for owners to place greater value on reproduction both for their own replacements and for sale to the Deep South. In a sense the Upper South became the "other polity" from which the Deep South obtained its slaves after the close of the Atlantic slave trade in 1808.

Growing tobacco for market—or as money—was productive slavery. Productive slavery requires the presence of a market, mechanisms for transport, financial systems to fund investment, and capital to be invested directly in people and in producing crops or goods. In other words, productive slavery moves an economic system toward developing the infrastructure that enables capitalism. The financial and banking system of the United States was initially built around slavery.[81] Slaves were often bought on credit—and this meant that planters had to dig their way out of debt. The only way to do that was to get as much work out of each enslaved African as possible, so that the purchase cost was covered as quickly as possible—which meant a low birth rate and a high death rate, rising replacement costs, and continuing debt. Meanwhile, this human property could serve as collateral for further purchases on credit. A vicious circle, in all senses of the phrase. Productive slavery is by definition more exploitative than domestic slavery.

Virginia elites hung on to productive slavery despite the fact that Virginia had enough dispossessed people to make a small working class by the time of Bacon's Rebellion. But the other conditions that make wage labor feasible didn't exist. The colony had no adequate market in food—everyone was growing tobacco—and little cash. So long as land remained available by moving west and killing or dispossessing Indians, and cash wasn't easily available, slavery, indenture, and long apprenticeships remained the norm outside of bigger towns and cities. By the time that changed, it had become abundantly clear that the Deep South's version of productive slavery was far more profitable than wage labor, as Edward Baptist chillingly describes. The bullwhip got more work out of people than the incentive of wages could possibly induce. Under its influence, the advantage Meillassoux sees for wages disappeared, not just in the Deep South, but throughout the slaveholding regions. Landowners had no reason to switch to wage labor, despite their fear of slave revolts as the enslaved population grew larger and larger. Like slavers all over the world, they were caught in the contradictions of slavery—which is why constables like Alexander were frequently expected to catch and whip runaway slaves as part of their duties.[82] But we are getting ahead of the story here. Little of this was evident when Alexander acquired Venis and Adam, to whom we now return.

VENIS AND ADAM MAY HAVE been lucky—if anyone enslaved can be said to be lucky. They were owned by a man who apparently had little property and so probably was not growing tobacco. In Gloucester and Spotsylvania, they would have seen tobacco production all around, and been aware of its malignant effects on both enslaved Africans and indentured English. If Adam was assisting Alexander in shoemaking, he was learning a craft that would make him particularly valuable and might well save him from fieldwork after Alexander died. Venis might have done household drudge work, gardening, food processing, maybe some heavy outdoor work, like chopping firewood. This would have been closer to domestic slavery. It also would have marked status for Sarah, letting her avoid being seen doing the heavy outdoor work that might have been her lot otherwise. Or both Adam and Venis might have been hired out, a fairly common practice, for tobacco farming or other work, enmeshed in productive slavery as a source of income for the Davidsons, and therefore anything but lucky.[83]

What happened to Venis and Adam when Sarah died is unclear. As Alexander II's guardian, her brother William would have been in control of the child's estate, and apparently of the money due to his brothers, Philip and William Davidson, as well. This put Venis and Adam's fate in William Ellis's hands. In order to make the payments for Sarah's sons' keep, as the court directed in 1751, or perhaps to give them what was due them at maturity, William might have divided up the value of Alexander's estate. To do this, he might have kept Venis and Adam for himself and given his three nephews their value in money instead. When William died in 1766 his will specified that a slave named "Venus" was to remain with his wife as part of her life interest in his estate.[84] Spelling was not cast in concrete then, and so is no barrier to thinking Venis and Venus might be the same person. There was no mention of an Adam, however.

Some records hint at the possibility that Venis was sold to a William Grayham in North Carolina, a man with ties to Alexander II's brother-in-law, Moses Bridges. There was a Venus in Grayham's will in 1807 who was to be "freed from service and to have fifteen acres land."[85] When I first read that will I thought, "As an old lady she's finally been freed!" I imagined she might have been very much younger when Alexander I died than I had been assuming, putting her in her seventies in 1807. Maybe Alexander II had taken her along when he left Virginia around 1770 for the new frontier opening up in North Carolina.[86] Maybe he sold her to Grayham and used the money to buy land there. Or maybe he sold her when he moved on to Kentucky in 1797; she might have been too old to make the trip. And then I realized that even if this was the woman Alexander I had owned, my freedom scenario could not be the case. First of all, the law at that time specified that only meritorious service, as determined by the court, could be grounds for manumission, and the manumitting owner would have to post a huge bond—none of which was likely to have happened. Had she been manumitted a bit later, the situation would have been even worse: a freed Venis would have been required to leave the state, to leave family, friends, and home—to lose the sources of joy in her life—much as if she had been sold to someone leaving the state.[87] Secondly, there is no record of a free black woman named Venus (or anything else) owning fifteen acres of land at that time in that county. Third, freed from service didn't mean legally freed, I quickly realized. Far more likely that she was being put out to pasture. Still a slave, but no longer required to work as one, she was given the use of the fifteen acres and was to feed, house, and clothe herself, thus relieving her owners of one of the liabilities of slavery: the obligation to maintain unprofitable elderly people.

But there is an alternative possibility, one that isn't completely improbable, and that might mean a better old age for an elderly Venis. That allocation of land might represent not the unloading of a "useless" and unsaleable old lady, but an attempt to do right, within the limits of the law, for a Venus whom Grayham loved, or who had been, unwillingly, or maybe willingly, his faithful housekeeper and caretaker. Grayham was a widower, and Venus apparently was the only person he held enslaved at the time of his death, so it isn't totally improbable that he had bought Alexander's Venis (or some other Venis) when his wife died—which was perhaps cheaper and easier than finding a new wife. Under the directions in his will she would still be enslaved. But she was not required to leave his land. Her new owner, Grayham's heir, not she, was responsible for the tithes on black women, and, not owning that land, she was not required to pay tax on it. Still owned, she was not in danger of illegal capture, re-enslavement, and sale, as she would have been if she were free. And if she wasn't Venis, but someone else—a younger woman than Venis could have been, in 1807, merely middle-aged perhaps—she could have developed an independent living, raising a garden, selling produce, selling milk or eggs, and putting up food for herself. This may have been the best her owner could do for her, given the slave society in which she and Grayham lived. But I'm stretching the probabilities; Venis was most likely far too old for this scenario. Grayham's Venus almost certainly wasn't Venis, despite my wishful thinking.

Thus this story of Alexander I, Sarah, Venis and Adam, built mainly of perhapses and probabilities, ends here, in death for Alexander in his late fifties and for Sarah a few years later, in her mid-thirties, in continued servitude, perhaps in the tobacco fields of William Ellis for Venis, and perhaps after time on the auction block for Adam. Not good endings for any of them, but the bit of class privilege that together they transmitted to Alexander II, along with the male privilege that had existed since well before the earliest days of the colony and the white privilege that was now automatic, served him well through the turbulent state formation of 1776 and beyond.

CHAPTER 6

Ancestor Tales of the Birth of
a Slaving Republic

The turbulent state formation of 1776—civil war between colonists, war with and against allied Native nations, war against England, negotiations with still-potent Native arbitrators of the borders between Euro-American and Native settlement—marked the birth of the United States as a slaving republic. This chapter will take us there, by way of Alexander II and his wife, Anna Bridges, as they moved west following the moving frontier, and as they lived through the Revolution and beyond.

This part of the story needs to be set within three powerful frameworks that make it clear that there was nothing inevitable about the formation of the United States, nor about its present shape. It is only reading history backwards that makes it look inevitable, as a natural result of Euro-American actions that were automatically focused on independence.[1] In reality, the course of the United States was largely shaped by conflicting elite designs to enable slavery and corral wealth and power, making the Revolution a vicious civil war.[2] Those same designs intersected with enslaved African resistance and revolt, with poor white resistance and revolt, and with Native peoples' agency and resistance in defending their land against white encroachment, allying and warring variously with European states—England, France, Spain—and with one another. As Alexander II was growing up in Spotsylvania, probably in the rapidly growing town of Fredericksburg, where his father was probably a shoemaker, and where his uncle, William Ellis, became his guardian in 1752 when he was eight years old and both his parents were dead, and where he may have learned blacksmithing from Bloomfield Long, these forces were all around him, as they would continue to be throughout his adult life.[3]

SO, FIRST, NATIVE RESISTANCE as a framework. As Tidewater Virginia, including Middlesex, where Sarah Ellis grew up, increasingly came under the rule of wealthy planters, there was intense pressure to gain control of land to the west to make way for those whites who remained dispossessed. The land that eventually became Spotsylvania, north and upriver from Middlesex, however, had been held and defended against the English by the Manahoacs ever since they chased out John Smith in 1608.[4] Together with Monacans and then later Iroquois, they confined the English to the Tidewater for a century.[5] Spotsylvania was finally founded by the English in 1721 as a buffer against Native peoples and the French. The idea was to get poor people to settle there by tempting them with relatively cheap land and a ten-year tax moratorium, thus protecting the wealthy Tidewater elites from the dangers of the border.[6] By the 1720s, the Haudenosaunee (Iroquois) had become the fulcrum for the balance of power in Virginia as three at least partially realized empires—Haudenosaunee, English, and French—vied for control of the eastern side of the Appalachian Piedmont.[7] None of them could hold it on their own, which meant that the Haudenosaunee choice of one or the other as an ally could tip the scales toward either French or English. All three were making their choices based on their own interests in relation to one another and to other Native nations. Just as the French and English had no need to ally because they were all European, the Haudenosaunee had no need to ally with other Native nations because they all happened to live on the same continent. The Haudenosaunee carefully maneuvered this balancing act with some success through the French and Indian War and on into the Revolution.[8]

Some Shawnee leaders, rather than advocating alliance with Europeans, were playing a central role in the attempt to develop a pan-Indian confederacy, an effort that was gaining greater traction around the time Alexander II was born. Those involved in this pan-Indian effort—and not all Indians joined it—collaborated with similarly minded groups of Cherokee, Creek, Delaware, and at times even Haudenosaunee, despite long-standing conflict.[9] Its basis was religious. Messengers crisscrossed the eastern half of the continent carrying the words of prophets of various nations whose visions taught them that all Native peoples were one, all Indians, all created in a separate creation from whites, perhaps even by a different god, and that their land had been given to them at creation.[10] The problems they were encountering—loss of land, disappearance of game, sickness, war, drought—came because they had lost their spiritual power by allowing themselves to be polluted by white ways, ways not intended by the "Master of Life" for Indians.[11] To regain their lost spiritual power they needed to adopt new rituals or modify old ones and purify themselves, separating from whites, rejecting those white ways, like drinking alcohol and hunting for profit, which stood in the way of spiritual power and could not be adapted to Native independence.[12] In many of these prophetic visions, the dreamer followed a road that forked and saw people along the fork of impurity suffering horrible torments, while those on the fork of purity moved through flower-scented air to a land of peace.[13]

These ideas were widespread, but they didn't necessarily lead to the same political or military position. For some, accepting treaties that sold land and accommodated the flood of white settlers looked like the only possible route to a life in accordance with the Master of Life's plan for Indians. Otherwise, they faced what many saw as an unwinnable war of attrition. Having suffered the ravages of decades of war, sickness, burned-out crops and homes, white promises of annuities and supplies along with the promise that the rest of the land would be theirs forever, free of white encroachment, looked like the only way to avoid total dis-possession, for survival both as individuals and as a culture. It is only in hindsight that we know those promises would never be kept.

An alternative interpretation of the religious prophecies led instead to the developing idea of pan-Indian identity—the belief that Indians were all one people, to whom the Master of Life had given the land. And this in turn led to cross-nation, cross-clan, cross-enemy lines pan-Indian unity in resistance to white encroachment and to those groups within nations or clans who stood for accommodation instead of resistance. So those Shawnee, Cherokee, Delaware, and others who united in war against white encroachment could find themselves at the same time fighting, usually with words but sometimes militarily, other Shawnee, Cherokee, and Delaware.

The history we are taught sees Tecumseh, who came along much later, as a brilliant flash, the exception that proves the rule that Native people were too unorganized, too split by tribal antagonisms, to get together and resist whites who, yes, immorally but understandably, drove them off their land.[14]A comforting myth that makes it the fault of Shawnee, Cherokee, Powhatan, and all the rest that they didn't keep their land. However, both historian Gregory Dowd and anthropologist Sami Lakomäki make it clear that this is not the case. The religious basis for intertribal organizing was in full swing by at least the 1740s with organizing itself beginning in the 1750s, all long before Tecumseh was even born in (probably) 1768, but right around the time Alexander II and Anna Bridges got married.[15] Native Americans certainly did as good a job of connecting across their cultural and language barriers as Europeans did across theirs. It was these more widely organized efforts, along with the French and Indian War, that slowed movement into Piedmont North Carolina, where the newly married Alexander and Anna, with much of her family, moved sometime around 1768. By then white people were flooding into the Carolinas.

The second framework for Alexander and Anna's lives was slavery, which affected them on two levels. It was an institution that shaped the laws and economy within which whites lived.And it was the actions of enslaved people themselves, including resistance to slavery and efforts to establish family and community; their agency affected the daily lives of white people. Owners or not, all whites existed within the framework of slavery. Enslaved Africans were bitterly opposed to servitude, which was rapidly becoming harsher with the continued tightening of laws and with the continued spread of plantation agriculture—productive slavery. And as the numbers of the enslaved grew, so grew white fear of insurrection and of an enslaved alliance with Natives, French, or Spanish. What became of Venis and Adam during this time there is no way of knowing. There is no record of their presence, or of anyone owned by Alexander II until a bit later. Venis and Adam, undocumented but nevertheless just as real as Alexander and Anna, leave this story here. Slavery, however, does not.

For now, I am going to focus on the third framework, poor white discontent, and go with Alexander and Anna to North Carolina. As luck would have it, their move has introduced me to the revolt of the North Carolina Regulators, a piece of American history of which I, like most Americans, knew nothing.

ANNA AND ALEXANDER SEEM TO HAVE met in Virginia, probably in Prince William County. In 1767, Alexander, along with Anna's brother James and two others, committed himself to a £100 liability as security for the executor of a will—they were vouching for the integrity of the executor's work.[16] This fact would seem to indicate that Alexander had moved to Prince William, a considerable distance from Spotsylvania, had some kind of standing in the community, and was financially stable. I have found no record of their marriage, but there were many "lay" marriages, performed without clergy but nevertheless legal. Lay marriages let you avoid paying the marriage fee to the established Anglican Church, required of everyone getting married no matter their religion—a requirement that non-Anglicans found particularly galling. Let's assume it was a 1767 marriage, since their first child, James, was born in 1768.[17]

The new couple, along with Anna's brother Moses and perhaps other relatives, then moved on to Orange County, North Carolina, settling in the section that became Caswell County, midway along the long border with Virginia. They might have moved to North Carolina to escape Virginia's increasingly stratified society and to get land, practically unavailable in Spotsylvania.[18] They probably moved right after their marriage, since by 1771 Alexander appears to be already established there, having joined with a few of Anna's brothers and several hundred others in signing a petition for creating the new Caswell County. That he signed the petition probably indicates he was a landowner, and in 1772 he and Moses both bought more land.[19] At the time of their arrival, Orange County was a cauldron of white discontent with corrupt local elite rule that was enabled by the far more powerful colonial elites who controlled the Crown's government.[20] Orange County became the epicenter of what is known as the Regulator movement.

County officials were requiring people to pay extortionate taxes and often charged double or triple the designated fees that were mandated for all aspects of legal transactions. Merchants and landowners could call in debts at exorbitant interest, often at times in the crop cycle when farmers had no cash. When a farmer couldn't pay debts or legal fees or taxes, the sheriff was authorized to seize property to sell at auction. Because only the elites had sufficient ready money, there was little competition at auctions, and property went cheap, making it necessary to sell more to cover the debt. On top of that, far more than was necessary was often seized—a horse, for instance, to cover a minor debt—and the sheriff frequently kept the extra. The results were, on the one hand, dispossession for some farmers, turning them into wage laborers, while debt peonage reduced others to unfree labor.[21] On the other hand, property—land, slaves, horses—accumulated in fewer and fewer hands.[22] The Regulators wanted to "regulate" elite behavior, to make them follow the Crown's laws, and to pass new laws that would force the powerful to curb their greed. It was practically impossible to be unaware of the source of poverty and dispossession: the manipulating hands of the elites were far from invisible. One Regulator referred to them as "cursed hungry caterpillars."[23]

Alexander, like perhaps half the white men in Orange County, might have been a Regulator, although neither Alexander nor any of Anna's

Bridges relations are in the list of 883 known Regulators, the ones who signed petitions, led or hosted meetings, or were captured or killed.[24] He was a landowner by this time, and probably a slave owner, since the 1777 Caswell County tax list indicates that he was fairly wealthy, putting him outside the category of likely rank-and-file Regulators.[25] On the other hand, he was a Baptist. Though not all Baptists were Regulators, and not all Regulators were Baptists, there certainly was a significant connection between the two.[26] According to a letter written in 1901 by one of Alexander's granddaughters, Anna had converted, like hundreds of others, during the Great Awakening, a movement of intense evangelical revival meetings that had spread into North Carolina by the end of the 1750s. She was followed somewhat later by Alexander.[27] He took her to her baptism on their one horse. That he had only one horse would seem to indicate that Anna's conversion occurred well before Alexander had become the well-to-do man he was later. That they rode rather than using a wagon may indicate something about the undeveloped state of the roads. So their conversions may well have happened early in their marriage—and if so that ups the likelihood of Alexander's being a Regulator.

The Regulators, time and time again over the course of four years, petitioned, sued, and even got some of their own elected to the colonial North Carolina Assembly. They surrounded courthouses and prisons to protest imprisonment for what they felt was unjust confiscation of property, often for debts or loans called in by the elite. Farmers often needed those loans to pay fees only because actual money was so scarce that generally only the elite had any, and payment in kind was not legal. Regulators occasionally boycotted or threatened to boycott taxes. They made agreements to boycott the judicial system itself by refusing to take each other to court. Instead, they would refer their differences and debts to arbitration. Though generally nonviolent, they did haul judges out of the courthouse and they beat up the most hated official in Orange County and burned his house.

Tellingly, the focus of most of their efforts related to the county courts, which exercised enormous power. The courts had jurisdiction over the general running of the county as well as over legal matters.

Their control of punishing covered everything except the killing or dismemberment of a free person.[28] This, in other words, was where the state's control of punishment came to roost in local people's lives. What they wanted was a government that lived up to what they took to be its side of the social contract. They would give the state their obedience, their loyalty, and hand over the sovereignty that they believed inhered in "the people," to be exercised through a state, headed by the Crown. But the Crown was to use their taxes for the general white good, not that of the elite few. Indeed, the state was to protect them from the rapacious elite few, making it possible for them to prosper and grow their families as hardworking farmers.[29]

All those efforts to get relief from corruption failed. Even when they finally succeeded in getting petitions to the royal governor—whom Regulators mistakenly assumed would, as representative of the king they honored, move quickly to relieve his loyal subjects of the officials who abused their power without his knowledge—they were rebuffed. Even when all that failed, the Regulators still wouldn't quit, withdrawing their threat to march on the state capital only when a leader who had been arrested was freed. The state had just passed the Johnston Riot Act specifically to control the Regulators, essentially making gathering to protest an act of treason. The state could now call on its fallback position, the use of force, and would soon use it to beat down the protesters.[30]

In 1771, officials called the local militia for security at the upcoming trial of Regulator leaders. But the militia refused to oppose their neighbors. Instead, the Crown's governor, William Tryon, arrived at the head of 1,400 British troops. Confronted by over two thousand Regulators demanding that he hear their petition and negotiate, Tryon ordered them to disperse. When they refused, he used the state's fallback and opened fire, starting the brief Battle of Alamance, at Alamance Creek. Those who were armed—and many weren't, or only had enough ammunition for hunting, since no one had expected a battle—fought back, and lost. What followed was a demonstration of sovereignty—the ritual of public execution and public pardon, and, referring back to the Introduction, an exercise of the state's now reaffirmed monopoly on the use of force to punish and to determine, as Achille Mbembe said, "who shall live and who shall die," One captive was hanged the next day without trial, six others were later tried and hanged, with a blanket amnesty proclamation for 6,400 Regulators issued later, pardoning all but a few leaders.[31] Then followed a month-long devastating rampage through Regulator communities, burning, pillaging, and laying waste. A victory lap if there ever was one, and again, a proclamation of the monopoly on the use of force, an in-your-face declaration of sovereignty through punishment.[32]

The four years of Regulator struggle ended in disarray; state sovereignty was ensured, and Regulator proposals that had so horrified the elite were no longer a threat to the right to dispossess. The proposals put forth by the Regulators were, says historian Marjolene Kars, "extraordinary . . . [a] wide-ranging, radical, and concrete vision of agrarian reform . . . aimed at the heart of the system that allowed elites to fleece the free population."[33] The proposals included controls on corruption, legal provisions discouraging speculation in huge land grants, a more progressive tax system, a small claims court, and a warehouse certificate system to enable payment in kind rather than cash.[34] Radical? Yes, radical enough to justify gentry reluctance to let ordinary whites have a hand, or even a voice, in governing. Nevertheless, this is a *white* agenda, and largely a landed agenda.[35] There is little here to benefit the landless poor working for tiny wages or reduced to unfree labor. Not a word about slavery or debt peonage—the right to an exploitable labor force, black and white, goes unchallenged. Even if the state agreed to all these proposals (which it didn't), it would still perform its function, guaranteeing the provision of cheap or unfree labor. The right to use debt as an agent of dispossession—and thus of capitalism—goes unchallenged; those "cursed hungry caterpillars," are merely asked to take smaller bites.

The Regulators had passed up alliances with both the Cherokee and the enslaved labor force. The Cherokee were at least as opposed to elite white monopolization of land as the Regulators were, but, eager as the Regulators were for Cherokee land, such an alliance would have been improbable.[36] The enslaved were even more opposed to oppression by powerful whites than were the Regulators, whose leaders were in fact slave owners. When Alexander and Anna arrived, the majority of whites did have land, so few were sufficiently dispossessed to be forced into wage labor. Indenture, at least by the 1760s, had about disappeared in North Carolina.[37] Those whites who were landless still had the option of going a bit farther west rather than working for wages, so enslaved people were the primary source of labor beyond that of the family. Consequently, it appears that the Regulators never considered the black-white interracial cooperation that characterized Bacon's Rebellion. This was a revolt of the still-possessed, not of the dispossessed, and that is a vastly different proposition.

Had they allied with the elite's labor force or with the Cherokee, and had they played on the fear of slave rebellion or Indian uprising, the Regulators would have stood a far greater chance of bringing the elite to their knees, or at least to real negotiation. But, undoubtedly fearful of slave rebellion themselves, and hopeful of gaining for themselves the security slave labor could provide, that was an opportunity they passed up—it would have entailed loss of white privilege and brought into question the morality of treating allies as property. And the dispossession they feared wasn't just dispossession of land, tools, livestock. For the better-off slaveholders, the ones who led the Regulators, and for those with any slaves at all, it was also fear of being dispossessed of their enslaved labor force.[38] For those without enslaved people such an alliance would have meant forfeiting the eventual possibility of themselves owning a few enslaved workers.

That they didn't seek allies was a triumph of the logic of whiteness and of the ideologies of ethnic cleansing.[39] The failure by the Regulators to make either of these alliances was a testimony to the potency of the intersection of the elite interest in controlling white discontent with the frameworks of slavery as an institution and Native defense of their land. That intersection helped shape the course of U.S. history. Surely, had they made alliances they might have set a precedent for other revolts; black-white-Native cooperation might have made what became the United States a far different place. Divide and rule was working as it was meant to, preserving elite power to exploit.

Although the Regulators failed to get their more radical proposals accepted, the end result was no triumph for the local elites. In turning to the governor and the more powerful coastal elites to control the Regulators, local elites lost some of their former power to punish and were sucked more completely under the control of what in a few short years would become the centralized state government of the new state of North Carolina.

A BIT OF ANALYSIS IS CALLED FOR HERE. As Bacon's Rebellion demonstrates, using direct coercion against polity members in weak states, against people with some degree of rights in land and resources, is likely to provoke revolt that the state can't easily control. Dispossessing masses of people and accumulating wealth by taking their land and other property—which scholars these days call "accumulation by dispossession" and is a source of the "something from outside capitalism" that I discussed in the Introduction—is difficult.[40] But by the time Anna and Alexander arrived in North Carolina, plantation owners and merchant elites had had nearly a century of slavery in the context of developing capitalism, and the gap in wealth and power between them and ordinary farmers and entrepreneurs had widened enormously. As the elites' power increased, so did that of the colonial state they controlled in collusion and contention with the Crown. The less powerful backcountry elites, like those of Orange County, began flexing their muscles, counting on support from North Carolina's coastal elites— far wealthier planters and slave owners—who had far more power and more direct control of the colony's policies than did most of the Piedmont elites. Though the Piedmont elites didn't have colony-wide power, they did control the local county government. And, bottom line, they controlled the county militia, or so they thought. They thought they could prevent resistance or revolt. It turned out they couldn't.

A function of the state is to marshal the military, policing, and legal institutions that make dispossession possible on a large scale. To do so, the state draws on its taxing powers combined with the support of the elites who benefit from that dispossession. How strong the state needs to be depends on who is being seriously exploited. If they are imported outsiders, as we saw, the state can be quite weak and leave the use of force to control enslaved outsiders to their owners. The state needs to be much stronger, however, if the people being seriously exploited are defined as insiders to the polity—people like the Regulators, with some degree of rights and some degree of claim on land and resources. It takes a well-developed class system to create the poverty required to get insiders to "accept" super-exploitation while remaining loyal to the state. To create that poverty requires dispossessing people and keeping them that way, which in turn requires a strong state exercising its monopoly on the use of force to punish the resistant and thus caution the rest.

That strong state did not exist in the time of Bacon's Rebellion. But in backcountry North Carolina, which had a somewhat stronger state in the 1770s, there was the possibility that a white working class was about to become a reality. What the Regulators feared was a class-based dispossession that would reduce to permanent wage labor those who couldn't flee to recently "opened" land where they could repossess themselves.[41] This sort of dispossession of "insiders"—not of imported slaves and their children, like Venis or Adam, or even indentured servants, the super-exploitable "outsiders" discussed in chapter 5—is the basis of the class structure on which capitalism depends. This would mean that "insiders" could be treated almost as a kind of exploitable "outsider." The denial of standing this involved, the denial for landless and poor whites of full voice in local affairs and in government, was legitimized by the elite belief that backcountry North Carolina was "lubberland," that its inhabitants were "the vilest Scum of Mankind," slothful, squalid, ignorant wretches, as "ungovernable" as Indians.[42] Victim-blaming, promoted by such descriptions, made it possible for those not yet dispossessed to ignore the real causes of poverty: elite behavior could simply be dismissed as a valid explanation. And those victim-blaming images let those in power believe the use of force against insiders was justified.

Although the revolt was put down by force, it does show that the state in North Carolina was not yet strong enough to dispossess insiders without a revolt. Maintaining dispossession requires constant steps to keep the dispossessed at bay, and the state could not yet fully pull that off for white North Carolinians. Its system for creating insider poverty was not sufficiently developed; whites knew they had choices. They could risk revolt and go west if it failed. However, the state was strong enough to put down the revolt when it occurred, and it did not have to turn to some new strategy for control, as it did after Bacon's Rebellion.

The Regulators' revolt in the lead-up to the Revolution was often and mistakenly touted as a precursor of the American Revolution.[43] But the Regulators' goal was not independence from the king. They continued to believe in the benevolence of the king, who, they thought, would have acted to protect them had he known the true state of affairs. Rather than give up on the king, they eventually concluded that the Crown's governor did not reflect the king's intentions. Instead of independence from the king, they sought farmer independence from the rule of a corrupt and viciously extortionate local merchant and official elite allied with eastern planter elites and politicians. This history made backcountry North Carolinians particularly resistant to elite attempts to recruit them for military service during the Revolution.[44] The Battle of Alamance and the punishing that followed it brought an end to the Regulator movement. But as in the Jacobite's 1715 Rebellion and in Bacon's Rebellion, there were too many to punish without inciting further rebellion. Amnesty made good political sense when the colonial elite had a war with Britain looming and wanted backcountry loyalty. Even more, they could ideologically repurpose the Regulators' movement for the rest of the colonies as a rebellion, not against them, but against the king—after all, the Regulators had fought a battle against the king's governor. The fact that the uprising had been against the very elites who became North Carolina's leaders in the rebellion against the king was thus handily disguised, a well-designed face-saving device.[45]

IN 1777 OR 1778, THE DAVIDSONS and the Bridges moved farther west and south, to the recently formed Tryon County, North Carolina, on the South Carolina border, settling in the section that was then partitioned off in 1779 to become Rutherford County, and much later, after another partition, Cleveland County. Perhaps they headed west because so little land was left in what was now Caswell County. Perhaps instead they left because of debt and dispossession, as many did in the aftermath of Tryon's punishing rampage. If they were Regulators, whether or not they suffered Tryon's revenge, they may have left in disgust, as hundreds of families had done earlier, right after the Battle of Alamance, leaving many Baptist churches almost without a congregation.[46]

Whatever the reason for the move, it was sufficiently pressing to cause Moses Bridges and Alexander Davidson to leave the relative safety of Caswell County to join with relatives in Tryon County. A William Davidson, probably Alexander's brother, and Anna's probable brother, James Bridges, were already there, deacons in Buffalo Church, the church Alexander and Anna would join, just over the border in South Carolina.[47] Here they were much closer to a contested frontier than they had ever been before, on the edge of still active Cherokee communities in the mountains.[48] And this brings us back to pan-Indian organizing.

Shawnee and Cherokee were, for the most part, longtime enemies, but by the 1730s the Shawnee, far more than most Native nations, had split into numerous groups and joined other nations, including some Cherokee towns, in response to pressure from Haudenosaunee expansion.[49] As a result, most Shawnee had relatives who had married into or settled with other relatives in most of the southern nations. They retained their Shawnee identity, regardless of where they lived, creating a Shawnee network that spread from the Ohio Valley north and south, and even west of the Mississippi. When they began to travel to advocate a general peace among Native peoples, the existence of that network positioned them perfectly. It also probably made war between Cherokee and Shawnee seem unacceptable—too often it would mean fighting friends and relatives and people connected through them.[50] And indeed they did broker some unlikely peace agreements.

By the 1750s, building on that framework, many Shawnee were working to create a Native confederation with the goal of restraining white encroachment and protecting the general Native claim to land, thus connecting with the prophecies about the Master of Life's intentions. However, it wasn't until 1770, after the Treaty of Fort Stanwix, that militants among the Cherokee and Shawnee became actual allies against white settlement. The Treaty had involved the sale by Haudenosaunee of thousands of acres in the Ohio Valley, west of the 1763 Royal Proclamation line that had limited white settlement.[51] This was an altogether fraudulent deal. The colonial agents who bought the land disobeyed British instructions; they were not authorized to buy most of that land, nor was it the Haudenosaunee's to sell, as both parties well knew. It was, instead, land held by the Cherokee, Shawnee, Mingo, and Delaware, and was particularly important to the Cherokee and Shawnee as hunting grounds.[52] Finally united in opposition to this treaty, Cherokee and Shawnee militants fought together through the Revolution, allied with the British, who had at least wanted to limit white expansion—largely because of expense. The British simply couldn't collect enough taxes from the colonists to pay for the wars needed to enforce Native dispossession as colonists moved west, nor could they stop the westward expansion.[53]

So Alexander and Anna, moving to Tryon County in the midst of the Revolution, were close to contested territory. Alexander, as a private in the North Carolina militia, would have done little fighting, but what fighting the North Carolina militia did, was against Cherokee towns.[54] Twenty years later, when Alexander left for Kentucky, North Carolina Cherokee towns, except those deep in the mountains, were largely deserted, devastated by the destruction wreaked on them in the years after the Revolution. But the Cherokee, now concentrated in Georgia and southern Tennessee, had developed and were able for a while to defend a semi-sovereign Cherokee nation, with its own elites living much as did white elites, with a hierarchical order and a constitution, but still with land held in common, land that they refused to cede and was recognized as theirs by the United States.

Nevertheless, the Cherokee nation was only semi-sovereign. Colonial governments and then the US government claimed a degree of control over punishing. By treaty with England in 1730, the Cherokee right of punishment was limited: the English had jurisdiction over all murders except those involving only Cherokee, regardless of where the murders were committed.[55] Thus a Cherokee accused of killing a white person, even in Cherokee territory, would be turned over to the English courts, and a white person who killed a Cherokee, even in Cherokee territory, would not be subject to Cherokee justice. Indeed, North Carolina colonists, understanding the implications of punishing rights, objected to similar treatment when an act of Parliament took jurisdiction over treason out of their hands and required that they send the accused to England for trial.[56] Both marked limited sovereignty. The principle that control of punishment marks sovereignty has held, with modifications, throughout the history of the relationship between Native nations and colonial and US governments, and it is still a subject of dispute between Native reservations and states.[57]

This brings us back to the issue of sovereignty, and with that, we get into the very thorny question of the Revolution. Why did sovereignty seem so important that it was worth the massive dying it required—the equivalent of 2.5 million deaths in terms of today's US population, as historian Howard Zinn has pointed out?[58] The explanation lies in the interaction of the three frameworks I described earlier: slave agency and slavery as an institution, Native American resistance and agency, and roiling ordinary and poor white discontent, all conflicting with elite efforts to corral wealth and power.

STARTING FIRST WITH SLAVERY, we return to the construction of a slave society, as opposed to a society with slaves. In colonies that were slave societies, the framework of slavery as an institution was critical in getting ordinary colonists to believe sovereignty was worth dying for. That same framework was the bridge that allowed Northern and Southern elites to make common cause in the defense of property rights. Property ownership is what gave men the basis for independence and patriarchal manhood. Those who worked for others were "dependent," under the thumb of an employer, not full men, not worthy of the vote.[59] So private property was the basis of "liberty" as opposed to "slavery." And the ability to pass property to your sons then passed to the next generation your status as an independent man with voting rights.[60] Defense of private property was the defense of freedom, and thus the very essence of the role of government.[61] The freedom to own and to control what you owned became the freedom that counted— that is why taxation was such an issue. Your property was taken from you, forcibly if you resisted. Successful collection of taxes is proof of sovereignty. It can't be done without a firm grip on the power to punish as backup. However, if you have agreed to pay, through your vote and representatives, the "people" are still sovereign; tax collectors are doing your bidding, you are not a "slave," as many colonists put it, without seeing the irony.[62] The state still has the power to punish, but you can believe it does so only at the behest of the "people." The social contract appears to be intact.

Property owners, like Alexander was at the beginning of the Revolution, quite generally saw the right to make and administer the laws regarding property as critical. A slaveholding Regulator leader proclaimed, "Liberty! thou dearest name," and "Property! thou best of blessings."[63] For the elites, however, defense of property rights meant defending the right to monopolize land, to dispossess people, and to own and dispose of people without interference; all this, ironically again, was defined as "liberty." And administered by local elites, the court system would provide the necessary punishing for enforcement; courts could keep the dispossessed in line. Trading oppression by Parliament for oppression by powerful colonial elites is not precisely what many ordinary colonists had in mind when they fought for American sovereignty. Their aim was to protect the right of white men to make laws that would allow them to control their lives and defend their property, including against property-grabbing elites if necessary. As we shall see, former Regulators, and backcountry North Carolinians generally, living in what was not yet a full-fledged slave society, and mistrustful of elite intentions, were not exactly gung-ho supporters of the Revolution.

Making the shift to a slave society after Bacon's Rebellion, turning to enslaved outsiders for much of the coerced and dispossessed labor in the South's labor-intensive agriculture, had solved the problem of poor white revolt. Whiteness bought poor white loyalty to the colonial elites, who organized protection against revolt by the unfree section of the labor force, whom whites now feared. That fear, along with the racial identification of whiteness with rights, freedom, and property, led even poor whites to identify as white, not as oppressed labor with blacks. For a century that had pretty well worked—poor whites rarely joined blacks in resistance, and they didn't rise up in revolt again until just before the Revolution, when the backcountry people in North Carolina decided they had had enough and formed the all-white Regulators movement.[64] Those carefully constructed racial divides did their job.

BUT THE SOLUTION OF CREATING an unfree "Other" brought with it two inherent problems. One was the possibility of revolt by the growing enslaved population—black agency. Another was the threat posed to monarchy by the growing power of an enslaving elite. Both of these became issues for the Crown, as well as for people in the colonies. In England, this led to growing official support for abolition; in the colonies the elite response was the opposite, and both reactions need explanation. So, first, let's examine this from the Crown's perspective.

Why would the British Crown and governing elites suddenly begin listening to what principled abolitionists had long been saying about the moral dangers slavery held for slaveholders, for slave dealers, and for a society that allowed it? After all, the British Empire was built on the backs of people in various kinds of coerced labor—why the concern about it in the American colonies? Principled objection certainly contributed to the shift.[65] But, says Gerald Horne, it was fear of slave revolt that made the difference. Fear backed the abolitionists' arguments and eventually overcame officials' contradictory urge to keep profitable slavery going.[66]

Slavery, British abolitionists effectively argued, and British elites began to concur, weakened England's grip on its empire. Britain might lose the American colonies, maybe more, unless slavery was abolished. Slavery gave Spain and France an advantage: they could offer enslaved

Africans their freedom in return for military service, at one stroke enhancing their own armies and wreaking havoc with the English slave-based economy (despite their own slaveholding elsewhere).[67] A Spanish invasion that reached Savannah in 1742, for example, had included a regiment recruited in Africa and led by African officers; many runaway enslaved Africans from the English colonies joined in. London felt an arms-race pressure to beef up its armies with Africans, as Spain was doing, and in 1762 the British resorted to arming Africans in the war with Spain in Cuba, so that Africans fought on both sides.[68] People in the colonies were horrified at the very idea of armed Africans, but as the British elite saw it, if their plans for empire required arming Africans as soldiers in armies in both hemispheres, then slavery was an obstacle. It could jeopardize the willingness of African soldiers to fight for the empire in wars that defended enslavers.[69]

Equally frightening to the British were the rumors and reports of slave revolt. Rebels might ally themselves with Native polities or with Spain or France. Enslaved Africans were suspected of having allied with Spain in the 1739 Stono Revolt in South Carolina, in which twenty-nine whites were killed.[70] From the point of view of British abolitionists, the huge increase in the number of enslaved Africans made these scenarios even more likely, and more threatening to the British Empire, especially when there were many runaways, a few uprisings, and rumors of many more. British leaders were worried, and abolishing slavery would end all those worries. Slavery had to go to save the empire.

But I think there is another perspective to add to this explanation of British abolitionism, bringing us to the second of the inherent problems for the Crown in the shift to a slave society. Anthropological and historical studies of slavery around the world frequently note a historical incompatibility between slavery and a strong monarchy bent on centralizing power.[71] This wasn't an issue in those weak monarchies we looked at earlier that were based on "wealth in people," where the king did not have a real monopoly on the use of force.[72] But these studies of slavery suggest that "increasing political centralization invariably involved conflict between monarchy and aristocracy."[73] Historian

Joseph Miller, in his study of global slavery, says that commercialized slavery gave merchants unprecedented power, which created a "risk to monarchical and aristocratic interests."[74]And centralizing power is precisely what the British Crown, by the mid-1700s, was trying to do in the colonies, as it was in Scotland. In each American colony, the Crown worked to tighten control of the administration of justice with its power to punish and to collect taxes. Lastly, the Crown attempted to enhance the power of royal governors in order to prevent colonists from moving west and to punish them when they did. The state was too weak to pull off this last, however, and finally gave up, refusing to protect settlers who disobeyed. If settlers moving beyond the line were killed, the British would not retaliate. In essence, punishment for breaking English law was turned over to Native people for enforcement.[75]

We've seen this conflict between colonial elites and monarch at work already, in 1676 with Bacon's Rebellion. However, the elites of 1776—those revered Founding Fathers, many of them enriched directly or indirectly by slavery—now had a full century of the confluence of capitalism and slave labor behind them. They were far stronger, and their conflict with the Crown was intensifying. Colonial elites were creating wealth far more efficiently than had been possible for the elites of Bacon's Rebellion, when capitalism was just emerging.[76] Capitalism in the context of a slave society meant raising, selling, and investing in a valuable commodity such as tobacco, not just using enslaved labor to support a luxurious retinue. It meant also that planters could literally use the workforce as collateral in financing the loans they so regularly needed. It meant that every baby born to an enslaved woman increased the value of an owner's estate.[77]A powerful Southern slaveholding and Northern merchant elite developed, both dependent on the products and profits of slavery.[78]

The slaveholding planter class could now "command the region's resources, mobilize the power of the state, and vanquish competitors," and those planters held far more enslaved people than had been true a hundred years earlier.[79] With the financial elites who funded them, they posed a far greater threat to the monarchy's renewed attempt to consolidate power. Even, says historian Stephen Webb, "in 1676, royalists everywhere in the empire feared renewed republican uprisings," and by 1776 slave labor meant that the colonies were, as Horne puts it, "becoming formidable challengers to the metropolis."[80] Colonial elites were coming more and more to resent the power the Crown held, through Parliament, to govern the colonial economy and thus to set the conditions under which they would hold on to or lose their property. As colonial elites began seeing themselves as more independent of England, the possibility of Britain losing its colonies through a republican "independency" became ever more real. Some English actually feared the colonies would someday rule over England.[81]

Thus, when the Crown's administrators in England became concerned, their move toward abolitionism could have reflected not only the worries about slave revolt that Horne describes, but also a desire to remove slavery from the mix to stem the rising power of colonial slaveholders, financiers, and mercantile elites. Eliminating slavery would curtail the colonial elites' ability to amass wealth, giving the monarchy an edge: eliminate slavery and protect monarchy. Abolition would, in fact, affect more than just the labor supply; it would also, at one stroke, eliminate most of the wealth held by slave owners.[82] Think what freeing Venis and Adam, without compensation, would have done to the value of Alexander I's estate. Consequently, most abolitionist proposals, on both sides of the Atlantic, advocated either some form of compensation, or a very gradual form of abolition, or at least an end to the Atlantic slave trade, with labor supplied by semi-free blacks, along with a nod to free poor white labor.[83]

When the British mutterings about abolition grew louder, the contradiction became stark between powerful colonial elites bent on preserving their labor supply and wealth and the monarchical interests in controlling those same elites. This contradiction was most obvious in the South, but existed also in the North, where there were fewer people enslaved, but where much elite power rested on the business of slavery and the products of slave labor. So by 1776 the contradiction was intense. However, a worried monarch can't just say, "The elites are too powerful, so slavery is abolished." The Crown needed to get the British elites and general public opinion to concur that slavery was a bad idea. Emphasizing the danger slavery posed to Empire—and to relatives in the colonies—was a powerful way to get that agreement.

I NEED TO GIVE A BRIEF EXPLANATION of the language that I will be using to discuss the Revolution, chosen to reflect the fact that this was not just a war against Britain, but, as I have noted, also a vicious civil war fought among colonists themselves. Neither set of leaders, for the most part, had any intention of granting real power to ordinary colonists.[84] They had very little interest in democracy, and a big interest in their own continued growth in wealth and power—the general good was not their focus. This makes me reluctant to use the language that identifies these men and their followers as "patriots." Patriot is a term too loaded with positive emotional baggage, with heroism and the greater good, and with the unexamined assumption that those revolting against British rule were in the right, that "we" are all better off because of them. It also implies that only they "loved their country"; those who disagreed with them couldn't possibly hold that same love.

So, I'm changing the language to avoid that baggage, which is not to say that bravery, sacrifice, and heroism for the greater good did not exist. However, we need to look at the war without the *a priori* premise that the good guys were the ones who wanted to get rid of English rule and the bad guys were those who opposed them. Therefore, from here on out, I refer to those fighting to get rid of English rule as Separatists— they wanted to separate from England. Those who wanted to remain in the British Empire, I refer to as Royalists, rather than Loyalists. It is certainly true that many who took that position did it because they were loyal to the king. But there were many Separatists who felt loyalty to the king, although not to Parliament. And there were many who opposed Revolution, but not because they were particularly enamored of the king.

NOW I NEED TO TRY TO PLACE Alexander II and Anna during the Revolution. There are a few clues as to what Alexander's position

might have been. A compilation of taxpayers produced for genealogical purposes lists no slaves in the entry for Alexander in 1777 in
Caswell County. However, the introduction to that volume explains
that "in all cases taxpayers are listed by county of residence and date,
and in some cases additional information is supplied." In other words,
the lack of information does not mean he actually had no slaves, as I
thought at first. The original tax list itself gives only a total value for
each householder, with no information about the property on which
that value is based. But it is hard to imagine that the value of his taxable property could be as high as it was without the value slaves would
have added. In 1777, Alexander was listed twelfth out of 134 householders in his district of Caswell County, though the wealthiest were
valued at many times his property. His property was valued at a bit
over eight times the value of Moses Bridges', at a time when nearly
a third of the district's households had no taxable property at all.[85]
However, this is no rags-to-riches story. If he actually did own slaves,
his prosperity makes sense, given his family background. If my specu-
lations are correct, Alexander I had married well, and thus acquired
Venis and Adam, possibly as gifts from Sarah's brother William. That
gave the family a vaguely middle-class status and gave Alexander II
claim to an "estate," under William Ellis's guardianship, an estate that
may have included Venis and Adam. Venis's "increase" over several
generations could then have been the basis of what grew into significant wealth. If so, then Venis, without her consent, is the source of
the class privilege that my ancestors clearly acquired, and which has
certainly influenced my life.

In any case, a few years later in 1782, in what was now Rutherford
County, Alexander had five enslaved workers, whose work it must have
been to farm his 225 acres and care for his five horses and nineteen
cattle. The 1782 tax list placed the value of his taxable property in
the upper five percent of Rutherford County householders, while the
highest evaluation was over three times Alexander's. Moses lived next
door, and his property was valued at less than a quarter of Alexander's.
Alexander was a justice of the peace in 1783 in Rutherford County, a
position that after the Revolution continued to go to people of relatively

high standing.[86] In the 1790 census he still owned five people. In Piedmont North Carolina, a land where large slaveholders and large plantations were few and far between, and the majority of households owned no one, those five people now put him economically in the upper 3 percent in Rutherford County as a whole, and in the upper 20 percent among Rutherford slave owners. [87]

Since by the time of the 1790 census, his prosperity had been building for a bit, it would incline me to think that at the beginning of the Revolution, Alexander would have been among those who would equate liberty with the right to own property—including humans—to dispossess debtors, and to enforce both legally. However, that attitude was widespread, and doesn't do much to distinguish those who thought the Crown would do a better job of protecting rights from those who thought separation was the safer bet. Several factors might have been at play in his choice of sides. One is that the better-off, in Rutherford County at least, were more likely to be Royalists.[88] On the other hand, Alexander was a Separate Baptist, one of several Baptist sects, which, like the Quakers, were dissenters from the Anglican Church. Along with some other evangelical sects, they were subject to persecution in Virginia, as Alexander would have been aware growing up. They were refused license to preach and arrested if they did, assaulted at their outdoor meetings, and taxed to support the established Anglican Church. In North Carolina, there was considerably less persecution. Many Baptists, at least at the start of the Revolution, took a pacifist stance.[89] Alexander might well have been in sympathy with the Virginia Baptists and other dissenters who were refusing to fight for the Separatist cause unless and until religious freedom was guaranteed and persecution ended.[90]

If Alexander had been a Regulator, he was unlikely to feel loyalty to the colonial elites who became North Carolina's revolutionary leaders.[91] Those leaders were the very same people who were the rapacious local and coastal plantation elites the Regulators had tried to "regulate," who had refused to listen to the Regulators and eventually countenanced Governor Tryon's refusal to listen, his use of the military against them at the Battle of Alamance, and his punishing rampage afterward.[92] To backcountry people it was pretty clear that the elites had no interest in letting "peasants" and "bandits" rule.[93] The Committees of Safety, which governed North Carolina counties during the Revolution, consisted largely of local Separatist elites, and one of their primary functions was making sure that punishing continued to happen for failure to pay debts—wealth had to continue to flow in the right direction. The Regulators' best efforts a few years earlier had made no difference.[94]

Thus, judging by his social and economic position, Alexander could have swung either way. We know what he actually did, however. He was in the North Carolina militia, and thus a Separatist.[95] And whether or not Anna agreed with him. What about the decision to move in the middle of a war, with small children, and Anna most likely either pregnant or nursing, as she practically always was. Had she been in a Cherokee or Igbo home her opinion would have carried weight; women's voices were formally included in decision-making councils. But for Anna and most white women, that same patriarchal manhood that entitled Alexander dispossessed her of any formal voice in decision-making.

GIVEN THE LONG BUILDUP OF ANGER among backcountry North Carolinians it is not surprising that the backcountry largely supported the British and Royalists—at first. However, after the British failure to support the Royalists properly at Moore's Creek Bridge in 1776, where Separatist forces defeated them, any enthusiasm for the British waned.[96] But that shift did not translate into enthusiastic support for rebellion. Although North Carolinians became reluctant to join British forces, they were nearly as reluctant to join the Continental Army—North Carolina sent fewer recruits per capita than any other colony, many of them under duress, and had constant problems with desertion.[97] We can't know whether Alexander joined the militia with any enthusiasm. Maybe he was among the many North Carolinians who refused to leave the North Carolina volunteer militia to join the Continental Army.[98] Apparently many said "a pox on both your houses" and sat out the war insofar as possible, except when it came to fighting actual invasion, by either Cherokee or British/Royalist forces.[99] After 1776, neither Royalist nor British forces invaded again until 1780, close to the end of the war, when colonial Separatists fought against colonial Royalists at Kings Mountain, an example of the Revolution's civil war.[100]

Whether or not Alexander was present at any of the North Carolina battles, there is no way he and Anna were unaffected. Toward the end of the war, the area around their Buffalo Church was in the thick of the fighting. Both armies had become vicious by this time. Rape, pillage, burning, theft, torture—all were part of the devastation delivered by both Separatists and Royalists. Mary Ellis, Alexander's second wife, and perhaps connected with his mother's Ellis family, had been a child at the time of the Revolution, and told later of the country being "infested with Tories [Royalists]," who robbed her family and drove them out several times.[101] Even if not directly injured themselves, and judging by their prosperous condition in 1782, perhaps they weren't, though Alexander and Anna must have been close to people who were—church members, neighbors, friends. Maybe Alexander even participated in the violence—militias were definitely implicated.[102] He might also have participated in the attacks on Cherokees in 1780 and 1781.[103] Earlier he might well have been part of General Rutherford's 1776 North Carolina militia invasion of Cherokee territory, when fifty towns were demolished, men and women scalped, and children sold and enslaved; the survivors were forced to give up their claim to all land east of the Blue Ridge.[104]

But perhaps Alexander's support for the rebel cause was far more than lip service. He and Anna may well have been among those terrified by the prospect of abolition and of Africans earning their freedom by fighting for the British, armed and no longer under a master's control, out to get revenge with murder and mayhem, especially since they were probably slave owners themselves by that time. That fear is certainly what the Revolutionary leaders were promoting, hoping to bring recalcitrant colonists over to their cause. Conversely, as we saw, fear of slave revolt also brought the British to push for abolition.

HERE WE RETURN TO THOSE TWO problems inherent in the shift to a slave society, which we looked at from the Crown's perspective earlier in this chapter. There is the fear of revolt by the growing enslaved population, and there is the growing power of an enslaving elite. As we saw in the lead-up to the Revolution, England's elites played on fear about the possible loss of the American colonies brought on by slave revolt, making that fear a spur toward abolition in order to protect monarchy. In the colonies, Separatist elites promoted that same fear of slave revolt as a spur toward going to war to gain independence so that England couldn't enact abolition. Slavery as an institution, one of the frameworks I mentioned above, was certainly one of the roots of the Revolution. It brings us back to the manipulation of fear, this time by the Separatists, to manufacture consent and centralize power.[105]

Fear as a tool in centralizing power works by making people feel that they need more protection. Centralizing elites can then claim that to exercise protective force they need greater power, converting fear into consent to a stronger hand at the helm of state. That stronger hand can then enforce measures that would rouse resistance under ordinary conditions. Local elites, unable to exercise the force required to provide the protection needed in the face of danger, can be made to hand their powers over to elites further up the hierarchy.

To make this strategy work, people have to be afraid—you need people you can define as believable enemies. But what if there is no external threat, no armies massing on your borders, no war in progress to pull people together behind their leaders? Instead of external enemies, a category of people within the community can be framed as a dangerous cancer in the body politic, gnawing away at the health of the community from within. It takes special powers and the exercise of force within the community to detect and remove them. The polity is told that only state or church can exercise those special powers, to which they, ordinary people, must consent for their own safety, even if it means a loss of their own rights or of those of their local elites. This was the route taken, for instance, by elites who created the Scottish witch-hunting panics. It was the route taken by both British elites seeking abolition to grasp power from colonial elites and by Separatist colonial elites in their quest for sovereignty for themselves. Separatists, by maintaining that if the British abolished slavery, former enslaved people would be free to seek revenge, enflamed the already existing fear that the woman who cooked your meals, the butler who knew your most intimate family secrets, or the laborer in your or your neighbor's fields, might be plotting murderous revenge, someone you couldn't distinguish from those who didn't carry the cancer. Separation from England was the only way to protect you from dangerous British abolitionism.

Underlying all this was another deep-seated need to keep slavery. Without enslaved people to demarcate the value of being white and free, it would be hard to unite ordinary European colonists in support of the elites who governed them.[106] The elevated status that whiteness provided would disappear, and the inequalities of class would become far more relevant—a scenario that boded no good for elite interests. Such fears multiplied, North and South, in those cases where whites were also implicated in slave revolt conspiracies.[107] Whiteness, along with fear of Native Americans and of slave revolt, was critical in keeping the colonies cooperating during the Revolution, uniting Europeans across language, class, and religious divides in North and South.[108]

In fact, when war did come, Africans did revolt. Knowing where their interests lay, they largely sided with the British.[109] Historian Gary Nash says, "In reality, the American Revolution represents the largest slave uprising in our history."[110] Half of all those who were able, that is, mostly men between fifteen and forty-five years of age, without young children and without families left behind that could be subject to an owner's revenge, ran away to join the British whenever their troops were near. About 20,000 enslaved Africans joined the British army, along with many free blacks. They fought for abolition, against the society that had held them enslaved. In desperation, the Separatist army in the North eventually offered freedom, as did some owners who sent enslaved people to serve in their place; by the end of the war the Continental Army was one-tenth black.[111] But few of those who joined survived to realize the freedom each side had promised, and most of those who did got short shrift.[112]

In the context of all this fear, British abolition of slavery was looking more and more likely.[113] Even non-slaveholders, both Southern and Northern, feared the specter of their neighborhood's freed Africans, supposedly unwilling to work, bent on revenge, and perhaps allied with Cherokee and other Native nations.[114] On top of this was the edict by the Crown's Virginia governor, John Murray, Earl of Dunmore, that if the colonists did revolt, he would offer freedom to any Africans who joined the British army. There were also rumors that North Carolina's governor, Josiah Martin, might do the same.[115] I can imagine Alexander and Moses Bridges in worried discussions of the situation.

Some scholars emphasize the role of fear in uniting the South with the Northern colonies once shots had been fired at Lexington and Concord. Others emphasize that abolition would mean no market for surplus slaves and so a huge financial loss. Still others see the Revolution as an elite move to protect their massive property holdings against both the Crown and unruly common people such as the Regulators or the farmers of Massachusetts who drove their elite officials out and took over governing all but Boston.[116] Without British control, elites could make their own policies in regard to both slavery and rebellious whites. They would have control of force and its use in punishment. The Separatist leaders' goal was to set economic policy without interference or taxation by either the Crown or by ordinary colonists, and they used anger about British taxation—the equation of private property with liberty—as the kindling for revolt, particularly in New England.[117] Since those property rights included the right to hold people enslaved, all these arguments see slavery in one or another way as basic to inciting elites to rebel.[118] However, these arguments only explain what might have motivated the elites who felt confined by British rule to go to war against the Crown. Most people in the lead-up to war had little interest in either side. It took a lot of fear-mongering to convince them that war was worth it.

IN 1775, THE MAJORITY OF COLONISTS outside of New England were initially neutral, like backcountry North Carolinians soon became, with real support for revolution throughout the colonies peaking at around two-fifths, while about a fifth of white colonists were active in the Royalist cause.[119] Among elites, particularly in the South, there was a tendency for Separatist leaders to be among the seriously wealthy, but elite opinion was far from unanimous, even among the rich. In the backcountry, there were many farmers and smaller planters, even some local elites, who preferred to stick to the status quo, perhaps preferring the (hopefully) benevolent king to the rule of rapacious elites who held sway at a colony-wide level. Even Separatist leaders—including George Washington, who admitted as much in a moment of frustration—sometimes preferred a monarchy, and had no interest in real democracy.[120] As Noah Webster put it, "I would infinitely prefer a limited monarchy, for I would sooner be subject to the caprice of one man, than to the ignorance and passions of the multitude."[121] While most colonists would not appreciate his attitude toward themselves or the king, a majority of them, Royalist or not, shared his desire to remain subjects of the king, whom they largely revered. As the war was starting in 1775, representatives of Tryon County joined in an association that issued a statement leaning toward the Separatist side, but nevertheless continued to claim loyalty to the king. Although they proclaimed that anyone not subscribing to the association's agreement to oppose Britain with force was "inimical to the liberties of America," they expressed hope of a reconciliation between Great Britain and America on constitutional principles, "which we most ardently desire."[122] Like the Regulators, they saw the king as a benign protector—at least if they could get his ear. The majority wanted to remain in the British Empire, but out from under the thumb of the British Parliament, which passed the laws that they felt countered the king's natural benevolence.[123]

In what was, by the end of the war, Rutherford County, Royalists tended to be among the county's "most substantial citizens"—or at least they were among the most likely to later be accused of treason, that is, accused of providing some sort of support to the British or of refusing to take the required oath of allegiance to the state of North Carolina.[124] At the end of the war, 250 people were accused of treason. By my calculations, this was around 20 percent of Rutherford

County men, but in any case, those numbers bear witness to substantial resistance to Separatism, even at the end of the war, after years of pressure to change their position.[125] Rutherford's Committee of Safety, for instance, the local ruling body during the war once colonial officials and court were no longer functioning, "did not hesitate to put in jail, or to the whipping-post, all persons convicted of disrespectful language toward the cause of America."[126] Both during and after the war at least 60,000 white Royalists left the colonies as refugees dispossessed of land, but not dispossessed of the 15,000 enslaved people they took with them, and could keep enslaved when they arrived in other British colonies, particularly Canada, the West Indies, and Bahamas.[127] It is easy in the context of these internecine battles to see why many scholars consider that the Revolution was not just a war of independence from England but a civil war fought between colonists. Indeed, by 1780 there were "more Americans fighting for the British than for the Continental Army, including a number of formerly enslaved African Americans."[128]

So in joining the Separatist militia, Alexander may have been giving in to the pressure put on neutral or Royalist backcountry people, he might have been a Separatist out of conviction all along, or he might have succumbed to Separatist propaganda that flooded the colonies. Historian Robert Parkinson, in detailing the fear-mongering propaganda it took to bring backcountry colonists to the rebel cause, and Alan Taylor, in detailing class resentment, resistance to recruitment, desertion, even occasional mutiny, as well as the violence and humiliation used to suppress Royalists, make it clear that the colonists were no easy pushovers for conversion to the rebel cause.[129] Propaganda, as in all wars, was critical.

Starting in 1775 colonial leaders had begun carefully managing the news, including that of slave conspiracies. Reports were framed to blame the British, claiming they were trying to instigate black insurrection and Native attacks. The goal was to unite the colonies in revolt against the British. Much of the fear, as is often the case in such endeavors, appears to have been a reflection of people's perceptions, rather than reality. Although some scholars emphasize that African resistance and plots for revolts before the Revolution were without doubt very real, others maintain that actual uprisings such as the Stono Revolt were rare.[130] But fear was made to seem reasonable, regardless of whether slave revolts were actually imminent. "Unwittingly (perhaps)," writes Gerald Horne, "London had helped to construct a 'Black Scare' that propelled settlers toward secession."[131] As Parkinson puts it, "Precious little of this apocalypse had actually occurred," yet reason to fear Africans and therefore the British was kept constantly before the white public.[132] And, says Parkinson, that carefully managed fear succeeded in bringing colonists around to thinking separation from England was necessary; simply getting the Crown and Parliament to recognize colonists' rights and status as English subjects, under a king they revered, was not adequate protection.[133]

IF FEAR WAS SO IMPORTANT in setting the United States on the path toward becoming a slaving republic, then we need to look at the fear itself. Reports in both British and colonial newspapers often exaggerated an individual act of resistance into a harbinger of a much wider conspiracy and these reports were becoming increasingly common in the lead-up to Revolution.[134] North Carolina had its share of such scares, some of which may have involved real plots, but as elsewhere, rumors were more common than plots. Those rumors were given even greater substance when one of royal governor Josiah Martin's private letters was confiscated and published in newspapers throughout the colonies. "Nothing," he wrote, "but actual and declared rebellion of the King's subjects" could justify "giving encouragement to the Negroes."[135] By admitting that he could contemplate freeing slaves to go after whites, he contributed to the feeling of ordinary North Carolinians that remaining under the British was clearly dangerous.

Alexander and Anna could very well have been among those who panicked, for it was propaganda such as this that got ordinary whites to buy into the idea that sovereignty was worth dying for and that Separatist elites were worth following. This was an especially hard sell since colonial elites had joined the British in seeing ordinary colonists, the commoners who made up 95 percent of the white population, as incompetent, not leadership material, and when landless the object of real scorn.[136] Getting ordinary whites to follow the elites who scorned them into revolution was not easy. Manufacturing consent took serious and well-orchestrated news management, as well as violence against Royalists. Whether or not there was a real conspiracy to foment fear, or simply a group of men working together who shared the same views, nevertheless they managed the news to bring people around to support for an elite position that was largely contrary to both the wishes of ordinary white colonists and to their best interests.[137] Well-fed and carefully directed fear can be extremely useful in manipulating polities, as we know from witnessing the loss of civil liberties post-9/11, with the anti-Muslim and anti-immigrant fear-mongering that event enabled, and with Donald Trump's escalation of such fears as president.

Colonial elites had a carrot to hold out as well, the idea that getting rid of English control would bring what they called liberty, that is, the right to control their own affairs, in particular to prevent the British imposition of abolition and to reverse the British policies that refused to allow ordinary colonists to dispossess Native peoples west of the Appalachians and to protect them when they did. Important as that carrot was, it was insufficient by itself, especially since the elite leaders of the Revolution, some of the biggest slaveholders and biggest land speculators, were attempting to monopolize as much land as possible, legally or not.[138] Fear, as I have described, was the stick accompanying the carrot. Fear was equally available to both sides and thus became the excuse to get ordinary colonists to go against their own interests and die in a war to preserve slavery and the power it gave slaveholders over those ordinary colonists. And so they fought, an army of mostly poor men, whose sacrifice meant in the end that not the poor, but the better-off "might enjoy the fruits of victory."[139]

So the threat of war against external native enemies, the fear of internal black enemies, and manipulated conceptions of property and liberty finally got enough ordinary colonists to believe sovereignty was essential to their chances of future well-being. Joined with elites who wanted sovereignty in order to enhance their own power, they midwifed the birth of a new stage in state formation as the new country now exercised—or tried to—its own monopoly on the use of force. The colonies, now an independent country, became a "democracy of slavers," a "slaveholding republic." [140]

CHAPTER 7

Ancestor Tales of the Dispossession of Women, the Domination of Men, and the Definition of Liberty

D emocracy of slavers" . . . "slaveholding republic"— oxymorons, surely? Not really.

Those anthropological studies of slavery I discussed earlier suggest that, unlike strong monarchies, republics are not incompatible with slavery.[1] Greece and Rome, for instance, were both slaving republics.[2] Slavery meant that insiders of the republic—people with rights—could identify with the state and its elites because serious exploitation was reserved for outsiders. Republics allow elites, merchants, financiers, and planters, for instance, to write the laws; their power no longer challenges a monarch's sovereignty. Nor can exploited workers mount an effective political challenge since most are enslaved. They are legally property, not citizens. They are denied the vote and most other forms of voice, leaving revolt as their only option.[3] Republican constitutions can be designed, as was that of the United States, to limit the influence of free commoners. As James Madison put it, "to protect the minority of the opulent against the majority," that is, to protect property rights.[4] Elites can compete with one another, but they all have a joint vested interest in perpetuating the state, since it is the state that provides the force that protects their right to property in the face of those without, protects their right to slavery, and their right to the wealth that flows from enslaved labor.

IT IS INTERESTING TO SPECULATE about what might have happened if, instead of gaining independence from England, the will of the majority of colonists had prevailed. Don't start a war for independence but negotiate, boycott, and resist British and colonial officials, following the strategy of the Regulators in North Carolina and of Massachusetts farmers. Get full rights as British citizens with a colonial parliament, still part of the British Empire and still loyal to the King. The status of the United States today might be like that of Canada.[5] Slavery would probably have been abolished sooner, although the Atlantic slave trade might not have ended any earlier.[6] Without the additional generations of people born enslaved, there would have been significantly fewer people to free, and without the fear-mongering of the war, abolition might have been a little easier for whites to envision.[7] There would have been no Civil War. Perhaps there wouldn't be quite such virulent racism for politicians to build white supremacist appeals on today.

But perhaps Canada didn't join the Revolution precisely *because* it didn't have African slavery on anything like the scale the South did. Since nobody (with the probable exception of First Nations) was saying anything about ending the more clandestine Canadian enslavement of Native people, Canadians had no need to revolt in order to save slavery.[8] Or suppose the Revolution was fought, but the Separatists lost and the colonies remained colonies, as Canada was. Would we as a country—that is, the majority of us—be better off? As Howard Zinn has pointed out, working-class whites and those who owned small farms didn't benefit from the shift to a government run by US elites; enslaved people certainly didn't benefit; Native people didn't benefit.[9] It was elite men, and perhaps the women in elite families, who benefited—the people who fomented and led the Revolution and who suffered the least in it. My speculation doesn't get very far, but it does raise some uncomfortable questions.

BACK TO REALITY. THE MEN who signed the Constitution, most of them wealthy, many of them slaveholders, carefully crafted it to preserve slavery at the insistence of representatives of states where wealth was dependent on slavery. This included the Deep South states where slavery was a primary source of the labor that created wealth and the Upper South states where enslaved people themselves were the primary form of wealth, in addition to supplying labor. Representatives from Northern states, where there were fewer slaves, were often rather ambivalent. Much of the wealth of Northern states grew from slave trading as well as from commerce based on the products of slave labor. But at the same time there was significant abolitionist sentiment in elite circles, and black abolitionists were making their voices heard.[10] Abolitionist leanings in the South tended to be restricted to some poorer white workers and radical dissenting churches, like some of the Separate Baptists, and had little influence among most of the powerful elites who guided policy. Northern ambivalence brought with it a willingness to compromise by leaving slavery itself alone, but putting a cap on the Atlantic slave trade. The transatlantic traffic in slaves would continue until 1808—to the benefit of slave-trading Northerners and the Deep South states, which needed constant fresh supplies from Africa to replace their short-lived and non-reproducing workers. But after 1808, Congress could abolish importation of Africans. In other words, it was the political power that capitalists and capital have in republics that made the continuation of slavery possible.

So we are back to problems we have already met—this time in the context of slavery as it was developing in the United States as a slaveholding republic. If you can't purchase slaves from outside you can't exploit them as thoroughly as owners of cotton and sugarcane plantations think necessary. If you do, they won't be able to reproduce sufficiently to maintain your labor force.[11] Once the Atlantic slave trade ended (although there was a flourishing black market in illegally imported Africans, and enslavement of Native people flourished in what became the US Southwest), replacing non-reproducing laborers by importation was no longer possible and an alternative strategy became primary—producing enslaved people internally, within the US.[12] Ending the slave trade, in other words, was much to the benefit of the Upper South, which suddenly had a much bigger market in the Deep South for a growing surplus of enslaved laborers.[13]

And owners in the Upper South took advantage of that opportunity, as Ned and Constance Sublette chillingly and graphically describe in their history of US slave breeding.[14] The Upper South wasn't suited to cotton production, and raising tobacco didn't do nearly as much damage to the birth rate as did cotton, particularly for owners who no longer exclusively raised tobacco on their worn-out land.[15] Better fed, less exhausted mothers conceived more children, and more of them lived. The Upper South could replace Africa in supplying cotton and sugar laborers to the Deep South, especially as cotton production expanded westward.[16] Upper South slave owners could sell their extra enslaved people to Southern planters, satisfying the voracious cotton plantations' appetite for the consumption of black bodies. At least 875,000 were taken southward before the Civil War, most of them after the Atlantic slave trade ended, the majority by slave traders, the rest with their migrating owners.[17] Indeed, that is the storyline of Kentucky's state song, "My Old Kentucky Home." Slavery in the Upper South, in Kentucky, claims the unexpurgated version of the song, was benevolent, a place where enslaved children played happily and loving mistresses wept when enslaved favorites were sold downriver—a marvelous bit of propaganda!

Good plantation managers in the Upper South paid attention to reproduction, much as does a good dairy farmer. They allowed enslaved people time to work in their own gardens, perhaps keep a few chickens or pigs, allowed family formation, paid attention to pregnant women's workload and nutrition. Perhaps they saw this as the humane treatment required by God or conscience, but it was nevertheless a very practical encouragement of conception, successful and frequent births, and the survival of adequately nourished children—who could then be sold. Of course, since people don't multiply very fast and take a long time to grow to usefulness and saleability, the owner needed some way of making use of the adults in the meantime. That meant growing hemp and tobacco in Kentucky, where the Davidsons soon moved. Sale of children, who were, in effect, excess stock, was a bonus above the value of the labor the enslaved provided. Jennifer Morgan describes how even in the Deep South owners at least hoped for what they called "increase" and often directed that what might be considered matched pairs, male and female, be bought or given as dowry.[18]

But this scenario leads directly into a problem we have already encountered. How do you control all those enslaved people? How do you control all the thoroughly disenchanted insiders who object to the lack of jobs and land? Jobs were lacking because enslaved people did so much skilled work, not to mention manual labor. Land was unavailable because slave labor made possible the kind of wealth it took to own and profit from enormous estates. Even in states with few people enslaved, wealth grew out of Southern slavery through the buying and selling of people and Southern crops, and with it came increasing white inequality. The specter of white revolt was raised by Shays' Rebellion in 1786, when Massachusetts farmers joined in a Regulator-like strategy, blocking the courts that were enforcing extremely high taxes and reducing farmers to debt and dispossession. Coming right after the Revolution, it caused some Northern states to decide that a stronger federal government was needed, despite their reluctance to give over any of their sovereignty by signing on to the US Constitution.[19] For North Carolina, it was largely fear of Cherokee attacks that pushed them toward greater federal power; for Georgia and South Carolina, it was fear of Spanish invasion. Needless to say, all these fears joined and played off one another, along with the fear of slave rebellion. It would take a strong federal government to provide the protection that individual states were not strong enough to provide on their own. So the states signed on to the Constitution.

Planters' power in the new republic was ensured by the "three-fifths compromise," which allowed Southern states to count three-fifths of their enslaved population in determining the number of representatives they would have in the new Congress and enabled them to control the presidency.[20] As a result, planters' interests carried disproportionate influence in Congress, as well as within each slave state. Compared to the rest of the cotton-growing world, where "powerful indigenous rulers controlled the land, and deeply entrenched social groups struggled over its use," as Sven Beckert writes, the political power of US planters was "unparalleled."[21] This political power enabled planters to effectively promote the acquisition of the land of Native polities in a process that Anderson describes as ethnic cleansing.[22] Not only was the new republic free of the possibility of the Crown abolishing slavery, but also of the possibility that the Crown, in its dealings with other monarchies and with Native polities, would continue to forbid expansion, as it had done with the Proclamation of 1763, forbidding settlement beyond the Appalachians.[23]

Expansion was necessary if the cotton industry was to thrive; cotton wore out land rapidly and new land was constantly needed. Without expansion, without a profitable cotton industry, slavery would have made far less economic sense, and England would have gotten more of its cotton elsewhere.[24] In any case, without planter political power to take new lands, slavery might have diminished and the arguments of US abolitionists might have carried more weight. On the other hand, since enslaved people were already at work in, for instance, iron works in Baltimore, industrial slavery might have become the norm. Slavery and industry, despite claims to the contrary, were quite compatible.[25]

Unlinking from England enabled the increasing inhumanity that made possible the take-off in cotton production after the Revolution. The intense violence of the bullwhip, the system Edward Baptist calls "the whipping machine" enforced gang labor and an enormous work speed-up and helps explain the high death and low birth rates in the Deep South.[26] Since it was now planters and cotton merchants and financiers who controlled the political process, planters no longer had to worry about their cruelty inspiring British abolitionism; the Crown no longer made the rules. Planters could order the use of the bullwhip with impunity, and, as Baptist insists, the bullwhip and the utter violence directed against enslaved Africans made revolt practically impossible, despite moments such as Gabriel's Rebellion in 1800 and Nat Turner's much more effective rebellion in 1831.[27]

Slavery, though gradually abolished in the North, continued unabated in the South, despite Northern and Southern abolitionist efforts to remove Africans, free or enslaved, out of the then United States to the western territories or to Africa. Few abolitionists envisioned real equality between blacks and whites living as neighbors, although some thought about the possibility of intermarriage of white men and black women as a solution—leaving black men in the lurch, to be removed.[28] Most white abolitionists, however, thought that without slavery all blacks would have to live outside US borders.[29] But that is a tale for the next chapter.

THE FLIP SIDE OF OPENING UP new land farther west, in both North and South, was the ongoing dispossession of Native people, and with it the ongoing resistance to further dispossession.[30] For my story here, it is primarily the resistance of Cherokee and Shawnee that is most relevant. However, other Native peoples were engaged in similar battles. Comanche power, for instance, was sufficient to keep extensive white settlement at bay into the mid-1800s and the Mexican-American War.[31]

We have seen a bit of what happened to North Carolina Cherokee before and during the Revolution. The dispossession of people like the Cherokee was not easy, involving complex political and economic processes, as sociologist Wilma Dunaway makes clear.[32] They were still a force to be reckoned with, even after being pushed out of Piedmont North Carolina with the many deaths that entailed from malnutrition, illness, lack of shelter, as well as from the fighting.[33] They held on in the mountains and much of Georgia. The United States did not yet recognize Cherokee semi-sovereignty, but it was still clear that treaty rights said would-be land-grabbers would have to buy land, not simply barge in. How to get unwilling people to sell land? Debt was the obvious means, that tried and true tool of dispossession. But the Cherokee, and this was true of many other groups, held land in common.[34] It was not private property. Thus, no individual had the right to sell land, nor did chiefs. Whoever was actually using land had the right to keep on using it. Anyone could start farming on a bit of unused land. If land was no longer being used, it reverted to communal land, and someone else could begin farming there. This meant there were no dispossessed people; everyone had access to land and the means to support themselves and their families.

Incomprehensible as it was to whites, it was Cherokee women who did the farming, planting, hoeing, and harvesting, though men helped at planting and harvest.[35] To whites it looked like men lazed around most of the time, and the work they did do—hunting—whites saw as sport, not work. Cherokee men, thought whites, treated their wives like slaves, sending them off to do the demeaning drudgery of farming. Ironically, white women actually had to work far harder, since their farms had to produce a saleable surplus, while Cherokee farms did not.[36] For whites, a wife working full-time in the fields was a sign of failure, although of course she could occasionally "help out" without much loss of status, so long as she was still perceived not as labor, but as concerned only with house and garden, and maybe dairy. This is why white women had not been tithable in colonial Virginia and other colonies—they weren't "labor," as were black women and men and white men between sixteen and sixty. Had Venis somehow gotten her freedom and married, her husband would still have been tithed for her: being a wife did not trump being black.

But at the same time that whites thought Cherokee men treated their wives as slaves, they contradicted themselves by also chastising them for succumbing to a "petticoat" government. It was women who held the family's nominal right to the land and its produce.[37] Women, particularly older women, had a clear and recognized right to speak in decision-making councils, particularly on topics that related to land and community. Cherokee women, unlike white women, owned their possessions and controlled their crops. The system was matrilineal and matrilocal: a husband moved into his wife's family and gained no control over her or her property, although he still had a role to play as a member of his own family of origin.[38] This was dramatically different from English and then US patterns in which men took control of a wife's property. White behavior in trade negotiations left the Cherokee "incredulous." "Since the white man as well as the red was born of woman," asked Cherokee leader Attakullakulla of South Carolina's colonial governor in 1757, "did not the white man admit women to their council?"[39] That difference lay at the heart of the dispossession problem that whites had to solve if they were to get Cherokee land by any means other than outright, and expensive, war.

So half the problem boiled down to getting Cherokee women to back off on their claims to land and decision-making about land, which in white eyes was the only natural and moral thing to do.[40] If women took their proper role, dependent on and submissive to husbands, and husbands became proper household heads, individually responsible for the family's welfare and for farming their own plot of land, then men would no longer hunt and they wouldn't need all those hunting grounds. Whites could take up the land the Cherokee no longer needed. Then if you can get people to want your commodities, you can get them to spend too much, you can get them in debt, and full dispossession becomes possible. The primary commodities whites had for enticing Indian buyers were guns for use in the deerskin trade and alcohol, both products that appealed more to men than to women.[41] So men had to have the decision-making power, both over purchases and over land. Which meant Cherokee women had to be dispossessed— they had to become like white women.

And that was the point of the so-called civilization program that the US government adopted. George Washington, himself a land speculator, paved the way toward patriarchy for the Cherokee. [42] He spoke to Cherokee men as if they were the only representatives of the Cherokee, men who naturally held women, "their" women, in their grip. "Your wives and daughters," he said, "can soon learn to spin and to weave."[43] In other words, women were to become dependent on men who would provide them with food and shelter. They would no longer be the mainstays of family food production, partners with men who brought in meat. They would have no independent access to the means of production—land, livestock, farming tools, and the crops themselves would be under male control. "'Liberating' [Cherokee women] to be housewives," says Johnston, "was central to dispossessing Cherokees of their land."[44] Thomas Jefferson, another advocate of Cherokee patriarchy, was more explicit.[45] His plan? Divide Indian land into private property plots, offer powder and bullets and alcohol in exchange for deerskins, lower the price offered for those skins so more would be needed for purchases, offer credit, and debt would soon force dispossession. And overhunting would make deer scarce. A hunting way of life would be impractical, forcing men into farming.

Despite such pressures, the Cherokee were actually pretty resistant to this program, though huge class differences, including wealthy slaveholding among the Cherokee, did develop.[46] Women retained some voice; land was still communal. Gender roles began changing a bit in Oklahoma after the 1838 Trail of Tears forced relocation of most Cherokee.[47] But it was not until the late 1890s that communal landholding was forcibly ended with the allotment program. Cherokee land in Oklahoma was divided into privately owned plots that were allotted to each male head of household. Allotment made possible the triumph of patriarchy and the dispossession of women among the Cherokee.[48]

WOMEN LIKE ANNA, ALEXANDER'S WIFE, had been dispossessed generations earlier of the degree of control that European women had possessed during the Middle Ages over their own bodies, over rights to the use of land, over their work and tools, and over the products of their labor in relation to husbands and fathers. It was a degree that, though limited, seems surprising to us now. Though living in serfdom, the inequality they experienced was not dramatically more intense than that of the men of their families. They lacked the avenues to power that Igbo and Powhatan women had, but nevertheless were more independent of men than they became later. Federici, among others, says the shift happened in Europe during the sixteenth-century transition from feudalism to capitalism, and she takes us back to witch hunting to explain how and why. Which means we will eventually be going back briefly to the early Scottish witch hunts, and the incredible number of people, mostly women, killed throughout Europe. And I am going to add in the incredible number of people, mostly men, who were hanged in John Radford's day, mostly in cities like London.[49] But before we do that, we need to start with capitalism itself, and the transition to wage labor as it affected ordinary people's lives.

And that, in turn, comes down to the issue of dispossession—in this case the loss of rights to independent access to the means of production. Owners in the sixteenth and seventeenth centuries were making the moves that would eventually develop a true working class. By a true working class, I mean large numbers of people who are dispossessed, without access to land and resources with which to provide for themselves through their own labor. They work under the direction of someone who does own land or other resources, who needs labor if profits are to be extracted. The working class is made up of people who are entirely dependent on wages. This was not true of Scottish clanspeople, nor of serfs and peasants, nor even of men and women working at home in the putting-out system for a capitalist who provided the materials and paid, meagerly, by the piece. The pay supplemented what food they raised and sometimes sold. They were not entirely dependent on wages; they organized their own time and labor. They were not entirely dispossessed, although they had to be fairly close to full dispossession to be willing to labor late into the night to meet the capitalist's deadlines and quotas. Nor were urban workers entirely dispossessed. They had what are referred to as "customary rights," to take scraps and leftovers of the materials they worked with, for their own use or to run a small side business. And in many urban settings work crews organized their own labor; the owner had, surprisingly from today's vantage point, little say-so.[50]

In the early stages of the transition to wage labor, women continued to have recognized rights, which were gradually eroded. In the Scottish Highlands, for instance, women's rights to the tools such as spinning wheels, which they needed for their work, meant that women were not particularly dependent on husbands. Although her use of garden land might theoretically come from the estate holder by way

of a husband, a woman had control over it and over the food it produced. In some Scottish cottar systems, in fact, it was the wife's work
for the estateholder that gave the family rights to the use of land and
house. Her work was recognized as being as necessary to the family as
that of her husband. As we have seen, Scottish town women often ran
small businesses out of their houses, marketed produce, took over their
husband's business as widows, or worked as servants or wet nurses
independently. In England in X Radford's day, poor working women
also had considerably more independence than did better-off women.
And like men, they claimed their customary rights in addition to what
were usually minuscule wages paid at long intervals, tucking under
their skirts scraps of cloth or a loaf of bread from landholders, business
owners, and employers in household settings.

The creation of a true working class, replacing slavery and serfdom
as the primary source of labor, was a long-drawn-out and violent process, accompanying the gradual development of capitalist relations.
The process in England and Scotland included the gradual completion of the dispossession of women, marked by the witch hunts of the
1600s; the continuing dispossession through enclosure; the institution
of hierarchical work organization and the wage, achieved partly with
the hangman's noose of the 1700s; and finally, the institution of centrally organized policing in the late 1700s.

WHILE CAPITALISM CAN CERTAINLY flourish on slave labor—
anyone sufficiently dispossessed and thus relatively powerless and
exploitable will do—nevertheless, as we saw earlier, slavery has limitations: the problem of control, the problem of balancing production
and reproduction if the source of enslaved outsiders dries up, the
problem of insider discontent. Wage labor, as it developed in England,
provides a way around many of these problems. It is a solution many
societies have taken in the shift to capitalism, but that shift doesn't
happen overnight. Serfdom and other forms of unfree labor developed
as an intermediate step between slavery and agricultural wage labor.
Similar intermediate systems developed in cities—various forms of

indenture, apprenticeship, debt peonage, and long-term labor contracts in which workers weren't paid until the end of the year but had
customary rights. This was, to some extent, winked at by owners, so
long as the goods were taken clandestinely, so that both sides could
pretend nothing was happening. These rights had been developed
over the course of many years of struggle, and taking them was seen
by workers as a normal part of a job, though not always by employers.
Workers defended customary rights vehemently when challenged by
an employer who wanted to say they were stealing. These disagreements sometimes amounted to de facto negotiations about just how
much, and what, workers would take. And the system actually served
the employers' interests.[51] After all, it kept their workers alive, and the
fact that they had to wait months or sometimes a year for their very
inadequate pay kept them coming back to work. If they quit before the
end of the pay period, they forfeited pay for all the work done since
the last payday.[52]

TO SEE WHY ONE OF THE EARLY manifestations of the process
included a focus on women, we need to look at capitalism's dependence on what scholars now call "accumulation by dispossession."
Even when a class system is functioning successfully, it is never
enough. Social theorist Rosa Luxemburg pointed this out a long time
ago. Capitalism, she said, always requires something from outside capitalism.[53] That "something from outside" is what "primes the pump,"
the source that sets off the chain of accumulation. It involves labor and
resources that have not come by way of capitalist social relations—
acquiring them requires force, chicanery, dispossession, or all three.
This can give another perspective on slavery in a capitalist society.
"Insiders" can't be super-exploited, worked so long and hard for so
little that the capitalist wage relationship doesn't apply—at least not for
long. Nobody would work under those conditions voluntarily, and if
violently forced, they might revolt. An insiders' revolt could destroy the
whole system and delegitimize the elite who depend on the workers'
labor and loyalty to sustain their rule. So importing enslaved people

makes sense. So does the land-grabbing to which the Cherokee were subjected, as does war to take resources, ignoring the forces of supply and demand. Governed by neither the wage relationship nor market forces, both the stolen people and the stolen resources are expendable, depletable, and super-exploitable, the something extra from outside capitalism.

In the past, this non-market taking of people and resources has been called "primitive accumulation," the initial accumulation of wealth that made it possible for capitalism to take off—kind of like getting a loan might allow you to start a business that then takes off and needs no more loans, no further input from outside of the business itself. Calling it primitive accumulation implies it is needed only as capitalism establishes itself; thereafter capitalist accumulation ostensibly feeds off itself, making both profit and wages possible through normal market forces. However, it is now apparent that Rosa Luxemburg was right: capitalism requires a continuous stream of value from outside.[54] Thus, the term "accumulation by dispossession." This is the coercive, non-market taking that creates wealth for the takers, such as the dispossession of homes and savings that the sub-prime mortgage crisis permitted or the taking of resources by non-market means such as wars to gain control of oil or by enforcing structural adjustments to dispossess and privatize.[55]

And this is what Federici says was happening as women were dispossessed, partially through the enclosures that denied them the use of the commons, a right that had been particularly important for women's independence, and partially through laws that pushed them out of their productive labor. Women were, for instance, pushed out of bread baking in Aberdeen, Scotland, so that male bakers didn't have to contend with competition from women, and there were laws that kept women from working and living on their own.[56] Dispossessed women, when married, became adjuncts to their husbands' wage labor within the gradually developing male wage labor market as enclosures and "improving" landlords dispossessed men during the 1600s. Being outside capitalism, women's labor became the something that continuously supplied capitalism with an ongoing source of value. But, says Federici, it wasn't easy to pull this off; women resisted dispossession.

Those who most successfully resisted, particularly those who insisted on customary rights, and even more particularly those who were not under the control of a man, such as widows or single women, had to be eliminated. The witch panics in Scotland and England in the 1600s did just that. Terrorized, tortured, sometimes found innocent but more often guilty, burned at the stake, sometimes alive, sometimes "mercifully" strangled first—their ordeal served a double purpose. It eliminated troublemakers and its spectacular punishment of women sent a clear message, to men about how dangerous uncontrolled women were, and to women about the importance of subservience in the home and of keeping a low profile in public.

Women's gradual restructuring as a source of the something extra capitalism requires set the stage for a shift into capitalist relations. But another step was needed. Capitalism depends on the acceptance of the sanctity of private property, as does wage labor itself, on the redefinition of land and labor as property at all. And historian Peter Linebaugh argues, it took the public, spectacular, and remarkably numerous hangings in London as well as in other cities to gain that acceptance.[57] Like the witchcraft trials of mostly women, the hanging of mostly men disciplined the fringes of the new social order, solidifying the construction of a working class. The witchcraft trials peaked in 1662 and ended in the early 1700s, the hangings intensified a bit later, in the early 1700s, and slowed toward the end of the century.[58]

By the late 1600s, given dispossession and the massive poverty that accompanied it, instead of turning to wage labor, many men in cities simply exited the system—or were expelled from it—and turned to low-level burglary. This was a clear denial of the sanctity of private property and even of its identity, at a time when even the bits of wood left from carpentry were defined as an employer's property, rather than as a customary resource available for the taking. Burglary was a means of survival, and it brought with it independence and control of one's own labor. But it also carried a heavy price, in hangings. Burglary justified the replacement of earlier forms of patrolling with a centrally controlled police in the 1790s. Policing and less spectacular punishment replaced public hanging in disciplining workers trying to exercise their customary rights or rioting or protesting. By centralizing control over who was picked up and accused, by policing class itself, the state was tightening its monopoly on punishment, marking a strengthened sovereignty.[59]

So let us look at what the disciplining of men accomplished. Business owners and landowners both wanted greater control over the production process.[60] Like the Scottish improving landowners, they wanted to determine who did what, when, and how, so that they could institute new methods, which were touted as more efficient and more profitable, but that meant a reduction or elimination of customary rights. No more surreptitious taking of useful bits and pieces—that was now stealing. No more worker control of labor, no more job security—just a wage too small to live on, paid a bit more frequently. Labor and labor relations came to be governed by payment of carefully regulated wages rather than amorphously defined customary rights. Organization and supervision was taken out of the hands of master craftsmen and turned over to trained supervisors and managers. This shift, as Linebaugh describes, was all made possible through the increased mechanization and organization that was a precursor to the later development of factories. Mechanization de-skilled certain formerly highly skilled tasks, thus disempowering the skilled worker, and making it possible to require that work be performed in workshops on the employer's premises, under supervision, rather than as skilled piecework at home.[61]

So, how do you get the men, and it was mostly men, who worked in many of these industries—for example, shipbuilding and silk weaving—to agree to such treatment, other than by sheer force? Actually, sheer force was abundantly used as customary rights were criminalized, but once sheer force had done its job in forcing acceptance of wages, a bit of sugar-coating made acceptance a little easier. Male honor could be restored by redefining independence. A man could see himself as the proud breadwinner, king of his castle, deserving of obedience from wife and children. That ideological shift would not have been possible without the prior completion of the dispossession of women. Sheer force—witch hunting—had done its job with women as well as men. Well-disciplined, in effect women became servants of the king in his castle, subservient in their dependence on a husband's wage. Prevented legally and socially, as we saw with Scottish bread bakers and servants, from living and working on their own, their welfare became dependent on pleasing their husbands with obedience, making their labor his.

The wife is working out of duty, out of (we can hope) love, out of kinship obligations. The wife receives no wages, her labor is not for sale on the labor market, and she can't quit and find a different employer. So the fact that the husband's wages are too small to live on is disguised by pretending the wife's contribution, the food production, the manufacturing, all the work she does that makes it possible to survive on the man's inadequate wage—none of that is "work." It is just housekeeping. The man is to be seen as the sole breadwinner, honor restored, served by a wife who must obey him and whose labor belongs to him. Thus, the employer actually gets two workers for the price of one (inadequate) male wage.

The result of all this was the gradual construction of a true working class, with the something from outside capitalism that capitalism always requires draining out of wives by way of their husbands. Together the witchcraft trials and mass hangings paved the way to patriarchal capitalism; they facilitated a new social order in which women largely were dispossessed and thus dependent on men for their survival. In turn, men were dependent on employers, with masculinity no longer judged by access to the means of production, but instead by the size of a wage. Pride was assuaged by the right to the services and control of a wife, who, according to laws of "coverture," legally didn't even exist apart from the husband—a fact that mattered far more, to both of them, now that the wife was totally dependent on him. Coverture had primarily to do with property and with financial management. It would have had little relevance to peasants or serfs; it was largely a matter for aristocrats, merchants, and property owners, and some artisans. But as capitalist wage relations took hold, and money and private property affected far more people, the laws of coverture became more relevant. In a sense, working men were being extended upper-class privileges. Male privilege, like white privilege, was thus a tool of control, constructed in the interests of exploitation, based in the even greater exploitation of those without privilege.

THE LAWS OF COVERTURE CAME to the colonies with the English, although they were gradually modified in the Americas. Colonies, and later states, varied in their interpretations, but basically coverture meant that a wife was a "feme covert," legally hidden from the courts by her husband; the husband and wife were a single entity and he was the external manifestation of that entity. Thus it was the husband who conducted business, who was answerable in court, and who was legally responsible for representing his wife's property and financial interests, as well as his own, to the benefit of that single entity. Laws about property, inheritance, and marriage reflected this principle. Upon marriage, a wife lost the rights she had had as an adult single woman.[62] She could not keep control of her property. Any property she brought into the marriage or inherited during the marriage belonged to the entity—that is, was under her husband's control. She couldn't sell her property or even write her own will. However, he couldn't sell the property she brought with her without her permission.[63] Any money she might earn, any crops she might grow, any tools she might use, all belonged to him. This subordination was believed necessary to the smooth functioning of the family—no fights over decisions about property.[64] As a wife, she was under her husband's guardianship and was totally dispossessed. Patriarchy is the dispossession of women; but its flip side, particularly under capitalism, is a sop to the pride of men who, themselves partially or fully dispossessed, must submit to the control of other men.

However, there was more to this than first appears. Wives didn't truly disappear under the "cover" of their husbands; they weren't "things" rather than people, they did exist legally and the law couldn't ignore them.[65] Legally, a wife had the right to support from her husband as part of his possession of and responsibility for the household.[66] Legally, as well as culturally, family was the fundamental organizing principle of the social structure, and elites needed orderly families if they were going to keep control. Property, inheritance, and status all flowed through families. The distinction between landholders and the dispossessed, the basis of all wealth creation, thus depended on families. Clarity of ownership, smooth transfer of private property, and moral justification for the whole structure was needed to legitimize elite control. So if women were to be rendered legally powerless, they also needed protection or there would be constant fights, perhaps between the brother or father and the husband of a woman being violently abused. There would be wives running away, destroying families and the rights of heirs—chaos, and not good for elite interests.

Besides, as historian Hendrik Hartog points out, acknowledging that some husbands *were* abusive, and could terrorize their wives, and passing laws that, at least theoretically, would regulate men's behavior and punish those who nevertheless transgressed, allowed men to identify their own power over their wives as honorable. They were the good guys, and the law identified and punished the bad guys who didn't live up to the code of responsibility that coverture demanded of men. The law marked the line (often fuzzily) between honorable and dishonorable men, and in so doing coverture "rationalized and justified a structure of power," according to Hartog. "It existed for husbands as a ruling class, expressed a particular male vision of responsibility and duty and power" [67]

Despite its importance for controlling women and the family, coverture raised some problems for a smooth-running society. Although legally a wife was unable to act as her own person, there were practicalities to be dealt with. One of those practicalities is that husbands die, often leaving a wife and children. With no property, how is the wife to raise the children or even survive herself? She can, perhaps, remarry—but in that case, does the husband's estate go with her and become the property of the new husband, who may very well waste it or pass it on to his own children, not to those of the first husband? Alternatively, perhaps the property goes to the husband's heirs and the wife would be forced to go on the relief roles. That option was definitely not one that tithe- and tax-paying men preferred. Instead, it made more sense to protect these women's interests. Colonies and then states had different approaches, but all used the concept of dower rights—the rights of a wife to the use of at least a portion, usually the "widow's third," of a dead husband's estate during the remainder of her life, after which it would pass to his heirs, the children of the marriage. [68] But recognizing that men had coercive power over wives meant that wives needed to be protected against greedy or unwise husbands who might sell land, thus depriving a wife of her dower rights in the land sold. So, paternalistically, to protect wives who were held helpless by their own laws, men in most colonies and states decreed that property couldn't be sold without the court first conducting a private examination of the wife, without her husband present, to ascertain that she was not being coerced into agreeing to the sale.

When a man died, his estate was inventoried, not including the wife's personal possessions such as clothing. If he died without a will, as did Alexander I, the widow's one-third of the value of his estate would, in most jurisdictions, still go to his wife for use during her lifetime. It would be divided after her death, with the children receiving the remaining two-thirds in the meantime.[69] Things could work out quite differently if a man left a will. He could not leave a wife less than a third, but he could do as Sarah Ellis's father had done, and leave everything in the hands of his wife for use during her life, with the division of the estate waiting until after the wife died (or perhaps until she remarried).[70] Alexander II also left all his property, including the thirteen enslaved people he held by then, to Mary, his much younger second wife, for her use during her lifetime, with the exception of an ambiguously phrased legacy to go to each of their children as they came of age. The children he had had with Anna would receive nothing until Mary died, which didn't happen until 1849, five or six decades after they became adults—and even then, his estate had to be divided among all twenty children.[71] Anna's sons did, however, inherit white privilege, male privilege, and class privilege from Alexander, along with perhaps some financial help during their father's lifetime. The standing that came from him would make loans and credit available. It probably helped them make the transition to successful landowners or entrepreneurial artisans, small-scale capitalists, like Anna's son Hezekiah, a gunsmith and cotton-gin maker, from whom I am descended.[72] However, during the late 1700s dower rights were gradually eliminated or revised because they made land transfer so complicated and precarious—they were a "clog" in a capitalist land market.[73]

There was also another problem caused by the principle of coverture: there were women it didn't cover. Widows, like Sarah Ellis's mother, and like Sarah herself, who didn't remarry, for instance.[74] If they were to raise their children successfully, off the relief rolls, they needed to be able to manage their own affairs. They had to be able to sign contracts, make sales, and represent themselves in court. So while wives were "feme covert," a different status was needed for unmarried women: they were legally "feme sole," women on their own. How this all played out for Sarah when Alexander I died doesn't show up in court records, except that eventually her brother held Alexander II's inheritance in trust. As a "feme sole" she could act independently as executrix, and could later appear in court on her own to challenge a man, although there are no records to indicate what the case involved.[75] She could have conducted business on her own, taking over Alexander's business and land in trust for the children, as did Margaret Tennant Gordon and Susan Livingston, two well-documented women in Fredericksburg, both of whom were becoming important actors in the town's business community, back around the time Sarah Ellis Davidson was widowed.[76]

In addition, there were times when men needed their wives to be able to conduct business for them. With a husband's permission, a woman could be acknowledged as an "agent" for her husband or as a "feme sole trader," making it possible for her to manage an estate while he was away, perhaps at war or at sea, or simply to let her run a business of her own for the family's benefit. Moreover, there were, particularly in wealthy families, situations that parents tried to avoid in a daughter's marriage. They might, for instance, insist on a marriage settlement in which certain property was designated as her separate estate, that would never belong to her husband—a hedge against a husband who married an heiress with an eye to gaining her wealth. The wife's degree of control over this separate estate varied, as did state laws in the South that made separate estates easier to arrange. The wife's estate was often available for the husband's use during the marriage, even though he didn't own it. In other cases, the wife actually managed her own estate.[77]

However, most of this was irrelevant to most women for most of their lives. Many had husbands without property, so all the protections of dower rights or the possibility of separate estates meant little. Others, indentured, were not allowed to marry and thus had none of the protections that being "covert" provided; and none of it applied at all to enslaved women.[78] Venis couldn't marry, because legally marriage would give her husband, not Alexander I, the right to her body and labor and children.[79] Venis, looking at her own lack of protection, might well have envied Sarah's protected status, even while being well aware of how little power Sarah had compared to that of Igbo women.

For the rest, those who were married, as were most white women, became feme covert, and there was little they could do to counter a husband's control. Divorce, at least in the South, was not possible. Separation was possible, referred to as separation of bed and board, but it did not allow remarriage. Unless the woman could get a declaration of feme sole from her husband or from the courts, she was still a feme covert but with no husband available to conduct business for her, a really untenable situation.[80] In any case, getting a decree of separation required money for court expenses and the humiliation of trying to prove cruelty or desertion. Leaving a husband could also get you excluded from church.[81] Not an option for most women. So men had their obedient servants, wives were dispossessed, and that "something extra" from outside of capitalism was available. Patriarchy, capitalism, and dispossession working hand-in-hand—all with the help of the state and its power to punish.

This is what Anna lived with, and what Cherokee women were resisting.[82] Whether she also resisted I have no way of knowing. Her outlook, bearing eight children in approximately fifteen years, was bound to be different from Alexander II's. She died, probably in childbirth or shortly thereafter, in 1782 or 1783, after the birth of her son Elijah, and Alexander remarried shortly thereafter. Anna survived the Revolution, but had little time to enjoy the status Alexander had clearly acquired by then.[83] Alexander may have loved her, but as both the Sublettes and Gordon-Reed point out, love didn't stop Thomas Jefferson (or other men) from continually impregnating his wife, whose health had broken down under multiple pregnancies and miscarriages, resulting eventually in her death.[84] Alexander may have done the same. Anna had no right to deny him; he could not be accused of raping his wife—and if she, like many other women, died because she was so worn down, then it is hard to say that he was innocent of her death. There was certainly plenty for Anna to resist, should she be so inclined, and maybe she did. The fact that she joined a Baptist church before he did, and that it was the Separate Baptists she joined, does make me wonder.

I HAVE REFERRED TO BAPTISTS BEFORE, particularly about their anti-hierarchical theology and questioning of established authority—much to the annoyance of elites who believed that their wealth and education, if not their inherited status, obviously made them fit to rule over uneducated and uncouth peasants.[85] In North Carolina, many Orange County women certainly gave Anglican preachers little respect, audaciously heckling them, nursing babies under the preacher's nose, and, as one complained, coming to the service dressed to "shew the roundness of their Breasts, and slender Waists," with their hair greased and tied "in a Bunch like the Indians—being hardly one degree removed from them."[86] Those women were exhibiting clear disrespect for churchly patriarchy, subverting patriarchal gender relations, at least in church. Perhaps Anna had been one of those women?

Like the Regulators, Baptists, at least for a bit, seriously challenged elite rule. Baptist belief that individuals could directly experience God's word, and could interpret that experience for themselves, and were responsible for making choices, led them to see all people as equal in the sight of God, and closer to equal in the sight of men, than did any other group except the Quakers.[87] Wealth didn't matter in your ability to discern God's will, and neither did gender, nor race, nor condition of servitude. This didn't play out in real life as actual equality, but it certainly was closer than the norm for the time. And Separate Baptists took this further than other Baptists.[88]

Much to the dismay of most other churches, Separate Baptists allowed both women and blacks to speak to mixed audiences—black and white, male and female. Other Baptists and other evangelicals often allowed women to speak and take positions of leadership among other women, but generally they were to stay silent in the presence of men. Separate Baptists, however, allowed women to vote on church matters and to express their opinions in meetings.[89] Some actually preached, that is, they claimed the authority to interpret scripture to others. Others were "exhorters," people who described their own sinfulness and their experiences of God, conversion, and forgiveness, hoping to get others to see the light. As sociologist Jennifer McKinney puts it, "Baptist women in the mid- to late eighteenth century served along with men in unprecedented access to Baptist governance and authority. Women participated in all major decisions, including election and dismissal of ministers, admitting and excluding of members, and vociferous theological debates."[90]

So when Anna told Alexander that she wanted to be baptized, he could well have been nonplussed. Her request meant that she had gone through what felt to her like a life-changing experience of God's presence. Perhaps her conversion happened very dramatically at one of the rural revival meetings in Orange County, a hotbed of Separate Baptists spearheaded by the Sandy Creek Baptist Association. She would then have described that experience to church leaders, who would have been convinced she had experienced a true conversion. With their approval, she would be baptized by immersion and admitted to the church.[91] Alexander could well have felt such a powerful experience would challenge his authority and Anna's loyalty to him. He did have the power to forbid her. Women were expected to take the religion of their husbands, and she had no right to leave him if he forbade her to act according to her beliefs. Nevertheless, if he forbade her to follow her conscience, people might well think that his behavior was immoral, and that he had "earned her disobedience."[92] Laura Davidson Baird spent much of her childhood living with her grandmother, Alexander's second wife, Mary, after they moved to Kentucky and Alexander died. One of the pieces of family history that she passed on in a letter to a cousin concerns Anna's baptism. "Grandfather's first wife [Anna]," she says, "was a very pious lady, and she finally wished to unite with the Baptist Church. It was with reluctance that Grandfather gave his consent for her baptism. (At that time he was opposed to religion.) He owned only one horse, so he took his wife riding behind him to the baptismal waters, and as he rode home he said he felt like she was not his wife anymore.... Not a great while after this, he was convicted [convinced, convicted by his own mind and heart] of his sinfulness and sought mercy at God's throne of grace."[93]

So that vaguely egalitarian Baptist world was the one in which Anna and Alexander lived. But by the time Alexander remarried after Anna's death that world was changing, as Baptists became more mainstream. The Baptist world his second wife experienced for all but perhaps the first decade of their marriage was far less egalitarian. Anna and Alexander had become Separate Baptists during a rather brief window of time when women, while not on an equal footing with men, certainly had a real voice, with some acting independently of husbands as preachers, exhorters, deaconesses, and leaders of women's religious gatherings.[94] That world was coming to an end.

WE SHIFT NOW TO MARY ELLIS JONES, often identified only by her maiden name, who married Alexander II in 1783, perhaps only a couple of months after Anna died. She was a widow with a little girl named Rachel. She was still a young woman of twenty-one when she took on responsibility for Anna's eight children, who ranged in age from fifteen-year-old James to the infant Elijah. Mary and Alexander had probably known each other when she was a child; she was probably the much younger sister of Alexander II's brother William's wife, and probably also related to Alexander I's wife, Sarah Ellis. Just to further complicate matters, two of Anna's sons were married to two more of the sisters in Mary's family! Two sisters married to men of one generation, two more to men of the second generation.[95] By 1782, Alexander II had joined Sandy Run Church, in Mooresboro, North Carolina, through a letter from Buffalo Baptist Church. Sandy Run was just close enough that moving would have been unnecessary. Joining by letter meant that Buffalo Church certified that Alexander was baptized and in good standing as a member of the Buffalo church, and that his leaving the church to go to Sandy Run was acceptable. It meant he didn't have to go again through the process of proving that his was a genuine religious experience that led to his conversion. Anna is not listed on the 1782 church roll; Mary Ellis is. Alexander and Mary married in April of the following year. If in fact Anna died in 1782, perhaps Alexander joined Sandy Run to court Mary.[96]

Little did Mary know when she married that thirteen years later Alexander would feel called to preach, and that in 1796 he would be ordained and she would acquire all the responsibilities, and gravitas, of a minister's wife. So in addition to running a household that included the six or eight children she and Alexander had had by then, along with Anna's younger children, she would be expected to lead women's prayer groups and to give counsel and comfort to the women of the congregation.[97] All while continuing to have frequent pregnancies up to somewhere around 1801, a total of eleven children with Alexander, plus her daughter from her first marriage. Then there was the move to Kentucky in 1797, where, under difficult and recently extremely bloody frontier conditions, she would be expected to contribute her bit to starting a new church.[98]

The move came right after Alexander II's ordination, and within a year he was founding Mt. Tabor Church near Glasgow, Kentucky, the first Baptist church in the area. So probably it was not wanderlust that took Alexander to Kentucky, but the call to take Separate Baptist religion to the outer edges of white settlement, like many other newly ordained ministers. Anna's brother, Moses Bridges, and his wife and family, went too, and bought land on Sinking Creek, very close to Alexander's farm on Skaggs Beaver Creek in the section of what was to become Barren County.[99] Other members of the Sandy Run congregation may have come too. Their presence on the journey and in establishing a home must have been a comfort to Alexander and, we can hope, to Mary.[100] He did wait to move until 1797, when the hodge-podge land-granting system south of the Green River had finally been worked out, and landownership was more secure.[101] We can only wonder how Mary felt about all this.

By the time of Alexander's ordination things were beginning to change for Baptist women, and these changes would have affected Mary as a minister's wife. By the early 1800s, women had begun losing their authority in the church, although they could still use the church courts to push men to act honorably in relation to legal disputes, payments for their produce, and as husbands and fathers.[102] What historians now call the Cult of True Womanhood or the Cult of Domesticity was beginning to take over throughout the country. This was a set of beliefs about gender, and the social structure built around them, that described white women as emotional, fragile, and spiritually superior to men. They were to exercise their talents within the home.[103] There, sheltered from the corruption of the outer world, they could maintain their purity and raise boys who would eventually govern well as men, and girls who, as wives, would be properly submissive and spiritually gifted for child-rearing and maintaining a well-ordered home. If indeed it was Anna who had convinced Alexander to become a Baptist, she had taken on the role of spiritual guide for the family. Mary, a couple of decades later, if she hadn't been a minister's wife, would have been restricted to that role alone. And even as a minister's wife, she would have been far more restricted than similar wives thirty or so years earlier.

This Cult of True Womanhood was the model being held up for Cherokee women to emulate, not just Mary.[104] It played a part in legitimizing dispossession and an increasingly rigid class structure, and helped ensure that the something from outside capitalism that Rosa Luxemburg said is always needed, would be available. It legitimized the structure already put in place by raw violence—the dispossession accomplished by burnings and hangings and elite monopolization of land could be sugar-coated to create a kinder, gentler, less noticeable form of control.

And it spoke directly to class issues. Artisans and entrepreneurs were becoming increasingly important and wealthy, and they chafed at the landed gentry's power and privilege. They strove to emulate the gentry's marks of status. They bought luxury items from the East Coast; they built impressive houses; they dressed to impress.[105] It was women's work to manage most of this status marking. Which meant a wife couldn't be spending her time at moneymaking or laboring occupations. Her work was to be in the home, aimed solely at enhancing the family. To do this successfully meant she needed either servants or enslaved people. Having the help that allowed a wife to devote most of her time to household management, to guiding and educating children, to church, and to entertaining was a status marker in itself, pointing to an at least minimally successful man. That the wife was dispossessed was, under these conditions, irrelevant to fulfilling the requirements that would mark her as a good wife. This mattered: men judged each other partially by their wives—and surely women judged each other.[106] A man's status could rise or fall depending on how successfully his wife enacted gentility.

That a man could be an honorable householder and still be dispossessed of land—of the means of production—was a fairly new idea in a society where landownership had been a prerequisite for patriarchal manhood. It reflected the increasingly differentiated class structure that the development of capitalist market relations was creating. An intermediate class was gaining strength, between the powerful local elites who hobnobbed with the even more powerful state and national elites who ran both state and national government, and ordinary farmers and laborers. This was a class of well-to-do artisans, merchants, entrepreneurs, and professionals like lawyers and doctors and well-paid business and financial managers.[107] Instead of land, which had long been the critical marker, you could now, with the help of a proper wife, document your status as a successful owner of possessions. You might even have to work for other men, or provide them with services, but, though dispossessed of land, you could accumulate goods to mark status. This would be more important in towns, where most men by then didn't own land that could make them either a successful farmer or a member of the landed gentry, but was where this new class of well-to-do lived. So having a wife who lived up to the Cult of True Womanhood, who accepted her moral and spiritual superiority over men in exchange for dispossession and coverture, who was adept at the display of class markers, was a matter of pride among men who were themselves dispossessed, a class between the powerful elites and ordinary farmers and poorer people.

On the one hand the Cult of True Womanhood helped control a rising, landless but ambitious middle class. On the other hand, and perhaps more important, it legitimized using women married to lower-wage workers as a source of the something extra from outside capitalism that primes the pump of accumulation in the hands of the few. It was the job of those wives to make it possible to survive on the low wages that enabled a capitalist to increase profits. If the employer had to pay the wages it would take to allow a family to live and reproduce successfully without a wife's work, if instead of all that cooking, cleaning, food processing, preserving, and storing for winter, cheese and butter-making, and clothes sewing, if all these necessities had to be paid for out of the husband's wage, the employer's profit might well evaporate. Or else the working class would die off, thus again running into the problem of killing the goose that lays the golden eggs.

This was what the shift to wage work meant, starting with the earlier shift to the dispossession of women and men that had required burning witches in Scotland and hanging thieves in London to enforce. But now, long after the fact, the Cult of True Womanhood could make all this seem good and natural. Women in poor families, striving to survive, could see their striving as living up to the norms for women, norms based on the resources available to women in wealthier families. Those beliefs could keep poor women believing that they were living up to God's intentions for women and that the more successfully they did this, the more respectable was their family. That their unpaid work contributed to an employer's profits would seem natural and unremarkable if noticed at all.

AS WE HAVE SEEN, ALL OF THIS functioned in the interests of white property-owning men. In the colonies and later the States, everything, from the Constitution itself to laws about coverture, about slavery, about inheritance, was based on the nearly religious faith that liberty meant the freedom to accumulate. The state was to provide only the minimal interference required to keep business running smoothly, to protect the sanctity of private property, and to keep people from revolting. Freedom meant the right to dispossess, to accumulate possessions, to accumulate capital, to accumulate people, to accumulate the value produced using other people's labor. This was the liberty envisioned by the Founding Fathers that was successfully enshrined in the Constitution and ensuing laws, and upheld by church and state and policed by both, a vaguely diarchic system. That conception of liberty continued to frame the lives of Mary and Alexander II as they moved to Kentucky, accompanied by the people they believed they "owned." Slaveholding democracy is indeed no oxymoron, not if "Life, Liberty, and the Pursuit of Happiness" is carefully defined and "religion," as we will see, is carefully separated from "politics."[108] My family mythology says, "We were abolitionists in Kentucky." But were we? And who is "we"?

CHAPTER 8

Ancestor Tales of Life in a Capitalist
Slaving Republic

So, were "we," that is, my ancestors, Alexander Davidson and his
family, actually "abolitionists in Kentucky," as my family mythology claimed? Abolitionist slaveholders? Of course not, I thought.
There is no such thing. After all, Alexander II was a pretty good-sized
slaveholder, his holdings having benefited by a good deal of "increase"
in Kentucky, growing from the five people he held enslaved in 1782 to
thirteen by the time he died in 1817.[1] So I am starting another chapter with an oxymoron. And surely it is, but whether my family were
abolitionists depends on what you mean by "abolition." There were,
in fact, a number of "antislavery" slave owners throughout the United
States, who thought slavery was wrong but saw no way to abolish slavery without consequences they could not abide, for themselves or for
the nation. But they were not abolitionists, people who believed slavery could and should be abolished, and acted on that belief. And the
question of whether my ancestors were abolitionists also depends on
whom you are including in the "we." But on the face of it, from today's
perspective, the answer is clearly no, we were not abolitionists, with
one possible exception, Elijah, Anna and Alexander II's youngest son.

Alexander, as the delegate from Warren County to the 1799 Second Kentucky Constitutional Convention, was one of 55 out of 58 delegates who signed the document that tightened up any possible misunderstanding left in the earlier 1792 Kentucky constitution about the rights of enslaved people, free blacks, and Indians.[2] In signing, he reaffirmed the protection of property rights, including those of huge landholders, thus enforcing dispossession for much of the rest of the population as well as enforcing the slavery that robbed people of the right to their own bodies. The document he signed seeks to secure to all citizens of Kentucky "the enjoyment of the right of life, liberty and property, and of pursuing happiness," equating the importance of property rights, including the rights to enslaved property, with those of life and liberty. And it declares that "all free men, when they form a social compact, are equal." In the 1792 constitution, it had been "all men" who are equal when they form a social compact. But the 1799 constitution immediately contradicts the equality it appeared to grant to free men: free Indians, free blacks, and free mulattos couldn't vote. Nor could anyone who couldn't meet residency requirements of a year in the county where he would vote or two years in the state, effectively disenfranchising the mostly poor white men who, without land, had to move frequently as tenants or laborers.[3] Both constitutions allowed the legislature to make laws permitting owners to emancipate enslaved people, so long as creditors were not going to lose money as a result, and so long as the former owner made sure the newly freed person did not end up depending on the county's tax money—meant to be spent only on the "deserving" poor. The 1799 constitution also reaffirmed the prohibition on making laws that would emancipate someone without the owner's consent or without first paying an owner the full market value of their enslaved property.[4]

The constitution's support of slavery obscures a reality to which Coward points in discussing the lead-up to the convention. "During the 1790s," she says, "the institution of slavery in Kentucky underwent perhaps the sharpest challenge that it faced anywhere in the South. Kentucky appeared to offer emancipators a good chance of success . . . there was a good deal of antislavery sympathy." This "surprising amount of support" included some slaveholders, even some with large holdings.[5] Slavery was the primary issue at play among politicians before both conventions.[6] In fact, the vote on the inclusion of the clause protecting slavery in the 1792 convention was surprisingly close: 26 to 16. However, three antislavery delegates chose to vote to keep the clause. In other words, there were actually 19 delegates who opposed slavery. Had those three voted otherwise, the pro-slavery votes would have won by a margin of only four.[7]

But in reality, the raucous debate about slavery had ended before the conventions were ever held, with the election of primarily pro-slavery representatives to write the two constitutions, particularly the second one. The clincher seems to have been the argument that slaves were property, and if the state could confiscate them, the road would be paved for the confiscation of other property: dispossession was around the corner. Even if you didn't own slaves your land and livelihood were at stake.[8] Even many of the relatively poor voted for wealthy candidates, as leaders had hoped. In organizing the convention, they had gambled successfully that if they removed property requirements for voting they would soothe the increasingly restive poor white population, whose "fears that the wealthy intended to deprive them of their rights would be proved groundless, and they would not 'always oppose the better kind of people, those who are best qualified to serve the public.'"[9] By 1799, only one delegate was not a slaveholder.[10] So despite the facts that three-quarters of Kentuckians didn't own slaves, that most of those who did owned very few—big plantation slavery was not the norm in Kentucky—and that barely half even owned land, they voted for delegates who would preserve the very institution that underlay their dispossession.[11] The state that emancipationists had once thought might be the first of the Southern states to abolish slavery turned out instead to be the last holdout after the Civil War.[12]

Where Alexander stood on slavery during the convention is not at all obvious, and there is no record of the vote on the slavery clause in the state constitution—apparently, unlike a number of other measures, no one felt the need for a roll call; seven years earlier slavery had been the only issue that did require a roll call.[13] So we don't know how he voted. But when there were roll calls on other issues, his votes indicate at least an antislavery leaning, despite the fact that he did sign the constitution.[14] He was one of three ministers at the convention, all Baptist, one of whom was adamantly pro-slavery. Alexander didn't vote with that minister and the big slaveholders from the wealthy Bluegrass section of central Kentucky. Instead, he seems to have been one of several outliers, voting primarily with four other loners, one of whom was the third minister, John Bailey, who was an "emancipator."[15] Despite being one of his county's bigger slaveholders, Alexander must have felt very much out of place among delegates like John Breckinridge, an influential and wealthy Bluegrass landowner, lawyer, slaveholder, and investor, who said the barrens of the Green River district, where Alexander lived, were "filled with nothing but hunters, horse-thieves & savages . . . where wretchedness, poverty & sickness will always reign."[16] Coward describes Alexander as a "little known Baptist preacher from the south country" (a comment my father would surely have enjoyed, right along with his enjoyment of the claim that the Davidson clan in Scotland didn't amount to much after the Battle of Invernahavon). [17]

So, were we abolitionists in Kentucky? There are some clues, even if their meaning can be hard to discern. There is the fact that Alexander was a Separate Baptist. Like many other Protestant denominations, the Baptists were seriously divided, church by church, on the issues of slavery and of racial equality, though Separate Baptists were more likely than others to grant at least theoretical equality to blacks. Nevertheless, the great majority of Baptists were either silent on the issue of slavery or actually approved of it, despite the stand against it taken by the Baptist General Committee of Virginia in 1788.[18] According to a contemporary analysis, of the 17,511 Baptists in Kentucky in 1811 "only 300 members, twelve ministers, and twelve churches" were openly antislavery.[19] But Alexander hung out, at least in his early days in Kentucky, with three people who might well have been counted among those twelve ministers. He organized Mt. Tabor Church, the first church in Barren County, outside the town of Glasgow, in association with Carter Tarrant, William Hickman, and John Murphy, all actively antislavery. [20]

Carter Tarrant was an "enthusiastic emancipationist" and became minister of Mt. Tabor when Alexander left to organize and become the pastor of nearby Sinking Creek Church.[21] Tarrant lasted only a year, but during that year he apparently caused quite a ruckus with his abolitionist preaching, staying "long enough for him to sow the seeds of discord in the church, which afterwards produced an abundant crop of confusion."[22] He left the church early in 1802 because of its attitude toward slavery, and, driven out by what he called "a kind of crusading inquisition," went on to help form New Hope Church in Woodford County, which a Baptist historian in 1823 called the "first emancipating church in this part of the world."[23]

John Murphy, the first clerk of Mt. Tabor, was later ordained, and Tarrant described him as "the first minister of Green River [an area that included Barren County], who publicly opposed slavery."[24] Last of the three was William Hickman, "the famous old pioneer," who had made a visit to Mt. Tabor from Elkhorn Baptist Church, near Frankfort, several counties away, to join in providing the ministerial authority that formally established new Separate Baptist churches.[25] He later left Elkhorn "on account of the practice of slavery as being tolerated," but returned in 1809, two years later.[26] Further linking Alexander to at least two of the three is that Elijah, Anna and Alexander's youngest child, married John Murphy's daughter Margaret in 1802. Carter Tarrant officiated, and the couple named their first child after him.[27]

Alexander was the pastor of Sinking Creek Church in what became Barren County until his death in 1817, and helped in the formation of many other churches.[28] He was a close associate of Jacob Lock, who replaced Carter Tarrant as pastor of Mt. Tabor, for whom there are no indications of abolitionism.[29] Lock's long tenure of forty years at Mt. Tabor implies an ability to ride out storms, including ones about slavery. It was under Lock's leadership that Mt. Tabor later refused to take a stand against slavery.[30] And, for the record, I need to point out that the Baptist Church's support of antislavery, ambiguous as it was, largely disappeared in the later antebellum period, as the church became more mainstream and leaders became wealthier.[31]

None of this leaves us with a clear picture of where Alexander stood in relation to slavery, except that he was unlikely to be either an "enthusiastic emancipator," that is, a true abolitionist, or a strong pro-slavery advocate. Quite likely he lived with ambiguity, considering slavery an "evil necessity," wrong, perhaps immoral, the "national vice," as David Rice, Kentucky's famous antislavery preacher, described it, but not to be tampered with until God saw fit to bring about change, acting through Congress or through the Kentucky state legislature.[32] Until that happened there was no call to feel guilty or complicit—and meanwhile the "increase" of the people Alexander held in perpetual bondage gradually increased the value of his estate. I'll come back to the contradiction between thinking slavery was an evil and yet owning slaves, but first let me finish the Mt. Tabor story.

John Murphy had continued attending Mt. Tabor for another six years after Carter Tarrant left; he was an important man, frequently sent to other churches and association meetings, often with his son-in-law Elijah. Their respected position lasted until 1808, at which point Murphy and Elijah caused a ruckus.[33] In March of that year, the church formally addressed the query, "Is abject, unmerited, and hereditary slavery a moral evil?" The church refused to answer.[34] At the next monthly business meeting Murphy and Elijah, neither of whom owned slaves, both said they "declare nonfellowship with the Church" on account of slavery and are "no more of us."[35] As a result, says Carter Tarrant, John "received but little thanks, but some threatenings."[36] Elijah's wife, Margaret, and John's wife, Rachel, declared nonfellowship a few months later.[37] Did the women do this voluntarily, on principle, as the men had? Were they pressured? Or was it perhaps Margaret, sharing her father's abolitionism, who pressured Elijah into leaving? In any case, two years later Elijah and Margaret were received back into the church "by recantation."[38] Their return came shortly after the church decided that someone who had withdrawn from the church couldn't preach there, followed by an inquiry by Elijah's brother William about whether someone who wasn't a member and hadn't produced a letter from another church could "sit and act with them."[39] Perhaps he was asking on Elijah's behalf, and the negative answer produced the recantation. The family tensions during those years must have been intense.

Elijah returned immediately to the position of trust he had previously held, appointed treasurer of the church, and later a deacon.[40] There was apparently some effort at reconciliation in 1812 when the "emancipating brethren" invited delegates to attend a conference with them, at John Murphy's house. Elijah, his older brother Hezekiah, who had joined the church in 1810, and their brother William were among those sent, along with Jacob Lock, to attend and to "make report of the proposition" at the next business meeting. Which they did. The terse church minutes make no mention of what the proposition was, but "the church decided that they had nothing to do with that business."[41] Nobody left the church as a result.

At that point, weighing all these clues, I thought, there goes the possibility that we were abolitionists in Kentucky. And yet, later on, I came upon an early Baptist historian's comment on ministers who openly opposed slavery. Elijah was included, along with John Murphy, Carter Tarrant, and a few others, as being among the "ablest ministers of the denomination . . . all men of piety and influence" during the period from 1788 to 1820, when "slavery was by far the most fruitful of mischief of all the questions that agitated the Baptist churches of Kentucky." [42] However, despite the implication of this quote, Elijah wasn't actually a minister when he first became outspoken in 1808: he wasn't ordained until 1824, although he had been a deacon since 1812.[43] But still, you don't get a whole lot more definitive than that list.

HERE I RETURN TO THE CONTRADICTION of the "slaveholding abolitionist"—an oxymoron, surely? Yes, if by abolitionist you mean people who want to end slavery immediately, as opposed to those who take an antislavery position, simply believing slavery was wrong—even if they held slaves themselves.[44] This is a distinction people made at the time, but is no longer regularly recognized, except by scholars dealing with the issue—and it helps to explain why my ancestors might now be, mostly inaccurately, described as abolitionists. In the decades around the turn of the century there were a few true abolitionists. Most of them supported colonization in Liberia or elsewhere as the only acceptable means of responsibly freeing adults at once. Theirs was a very different attitude from the more common one that said blacks were biologically inferior or even a different species from whites. Instead, they believed that any difference between blacks and whites was due to the effects of white racism and enslavement. Nevertheless, even this group believed it was biologically impossible for two races to live together as equals. That had never happened anywhere in the world, they said; one race always subjugated the other. Nothing to be done about that except separate.[45]

Even Carter Tarrant, strongly opposed to slavery as he undoubtedly was, may have had no clear plan for emancipation, other than convincing as many as possible that slavery was a sin. Preaching at the meeting that formally organized the antislavery Friends of Humanity Association of Churches, of which his New Hope Church was one, he said, "As to the question, What shall be done with these [enslaved] people? We answer, That when we as a people are willing to do our duty, we shall obtain a suitable answer to this question, and not before."[46] Winney, a woman enslaved and owned by a member of the Elkhorn Church, where William Hickman was minister, had a much clearer picture of the future of whites who did not end slavery. "Thousands of white people," she said, "are Wallowing in Hell for their treatment to Negroes." She was excluded from the church.[47]

So if abolition is taken to mean the immediate end of slavery, did people think that could happen without sending freed slaves to some place like Liberia? During the 1790s and well into the 1820s there were few people in Kentucky—or anywhere else in the South, who believed it could.[48] Even Kentucky's David Rice, a famous antislavery preacher, did not free his own slaves. He advocated gradual emancipation—stopping the importation of enslaved people, and recognizing children born after a specified date as free at birth.[49] Slavery in this system would gradually fade away as the parents died. But freed children would have to be educated to be good citizens, because their supposed incompetence would introduce disorder into Kentucky's emerging society. Disorder was anathema to conservatives, both to those who felt slavery was wrong but nevertheless a necessary evil, and to those who actively supported slavery.[50] And it certainly made a good excuse for continuing to profit from slave labor and sale: a good third of babies born enslaved in Kentucky in 1820 ended up not just sold, but sold out of state.[51]

Carter Tarrant may have been an exception, a true "emancipator." And like his New Hope Church, there were other churches that refused to admit slaveholders and stated that it was improper to take communion with them. There were also people who, though financially able, refused, on principle, to own slaves. It is possible Elijah was one such person; at least he seems never to have owned anyone. Hezekiah, my direct ancestor and Elijah's older brother, may have had similar sentiments. He briefly owned a boy under fourteen, listed in the 1820 census, who does not appear in the preceding or following census.[52] True, Hezekiah could have sold him, but he might also have freed him when he became old enough. One of the exceptions in which emancipators in Carter Tarrant's church could hold slaves was that of a person "holding young slaves, and recording a deed of their emancipation at such an age as the church to which they offer, may agree to."[53] That there is no record of Hezekiah having done so proves nothing: by that time his part of Barren County had become part of the newly formed Hart County, and the Hart County Court House and most of its records were destroyed by fire in 1927. Beyond that, there is the fact that Hezekiah helped a free black man named Sampson (sometimes referred to as "Free Samuel") obtain land, held the land in his own name for Sampson for safekeeping, and acted as his agent in business dealings. Legally free blacks could own land, but the laws were also full of pitfalls. As a free black you could not lift a hand in your own defense if a white person attacked you. Your freedom certificate could be stolen, or your former owner might fail to post bond for emancipation. A white sponsor with some clout was invaluable insurance. Sampson named Hezekiah as the executor of his will, calling him "my friend Hezekiah Davidson," perhaps hoping Hezekiah would go on to protect his wife, Rose, who had a life interest in Sampson's estate.[54]

ALTOGETHER IT SEEMS MOST LIKELY that Alexander would have been one of those conservatives, vaguely antislavery, the ones historian Harold Tallant says adhered to the theory that slavery was a "necessary evil," not the ones who thought slavery was a positive good, but also not an active abolitionist.[55] But, as Tallant points out, there were slaveholders who said "necessary evil" with emphasis on the *necessary* and others whose emphasis was on the *evil*.[56] I don't think we can know which Alexander was. And, as Tallant also points out, either version kept people from having to act.[57]

You were, however, as a good church member, expected to treat the people you owned "humanely."[58] Baptist churches (and some other evangelical churches) policed their members' behavior, and blacks and whites were both hauled in for discipline if they got too far out of line. Rape, adultery, and unmarried sex were forbidden. However, while white men were called to task for "fornication" with white women, there were no white men brought before Mt. Tabor Church for sex with a woman of color, free or enslaved, despite the fact there were undoubtedly men who could have been accused. You weren't supposed to whip slaves "too hard." Selling slaves was seen as a moral failing, though it happened frequently, and breaking up families could get you looked down on.

Whites were occasionally called to answer for their treatment of blacks, and if they refused to accept the church's judgment, were very occasionally excluded from the church, although they were much more likely to be acquitted.[59] Mt. Tabor minutes include only two such examples and both involved a member being violent toward someone else's property. In the first, a member struck someone else's "servant .. . in very warm blood," in the churchyard and excused his behavior by citing the anger that the servant's "insolence" had aroused. The church decided he had "gone too far." At the next meeting the member agreed that his behavior was wrong, and was acquitted.[60]

The issue in the second, however, appears not to be the violence itself, but whether you could "correct" someone you didn't own, but who was a church member over whom you had authority. Such a situation could arise if, for instance, you were renting an enslaved church member from the member's owner.[61] Would you first have to go to the church for mediation to try to settle the issue before resorting to correction? One member accused another of "whipping a black sister" who was a member of the church and the property of another member. This led to the church's first addressing the query "whither [*sic*] any case could arise that would justify a member of this church to correct or chastise a servant or person under their authority which is a member of said church without first dealing with them in the church in gospel order." The answer was yes. This appears to assume that whipping your own enslaved worker without going through the church was perfectly acceptable, and the church's decision merely clarifies that this privilege extends to non-owners. The case was then heard; the whipper was acquitted, and the whipped sister admitted her fault and was also acquitted.[62] Thus whites' belief in their own honor was upheld; they were adhering to rules about being "kind" while waiting for God to fix the "necessary evil."

In some early Baptist and other evangelical churches, unlike more mainstream churches, there was also an acknowledgment of black personhood, sometimes with the right to vote and help determine church policy to exhort, and occasionally even to preach. There is some evidence in the Mt. Tabor minutes that implies some degree of equality. An enslaved man was included on a committee that inquired into an accusation of intoxication made against a white woman; the committee found her guilty.[63] Mt. Tabor minutes only occasionally refer to enslaved people by the terms Brother and Sister, which they use scrupulously for whites.[64] Instead they are identified in terms such as "Smith's Jenny," or "Jenny, Bro Smith's servant." But the church seems to have followed the exact same procedure with accusations made against slaves as with accusations against whites. For instance, Mt. Tabor minutes include accusations of adultery made against both enslaved and white women. In 1811, for instance, two enslaved women were accused of adultery; although marriages between the enslaved had no legal standing, the church itself did recognize them. Both were summoned to a church hearing; one was acquitted for lack of evidence, the other excluded.[65]

Several years later another enslaved woman was accused of adultery, which apparently prompted the query "is there any case that could occur, which would justify blacks to marry again, while their companions are alive? Answered in the affirmative." Presumably the question is whether the sale or removal of your spouse to some distant region functions, for slaves, as a death and therefore allows remarriage. Apparently, the woman didn't meet that standard, and the decision didn't save her from exclusion.[66] Several years after that, however, the same decision enabled a different woman to marry a second time, having been separated "beyond the hope of reunion" from her first husband, who remained in Virginia. Of course, it gave her owner the hope of children and greater wealth. And apparently the church granted black women the same right of self-defense as white women, even though legally blacks could not lift a hand against a white person; in one case, charges of immorality were dropped for a woman who pled self-defense, although there was no mention of who her attacker was. Perhaps not coincidentally, she was accused of theft two months later—and again exonerated, there being "no proof of her guilt, but much of her honest character."[67]

On the other hand, the church enforced property rights in human beings, summoning a woman who kept running away to appear before the church.[68] And when black members requested the appointment of a black elder, perhaps so they could meet separately, or perhaps simply to have representation in the church leadership—the minutes do not explain—the request was refused. They were to continue "in the Church as heretofore."[69] Regardless of the actual degree of equality, however, church membership may have helped somewhat. With luck, white members' belief that being humane justified slavery, along with the policing conducted by the church, prevented some families from being broken by sale, made some whippings less intense, and protected some women and girls from sexual abuse by white owners and neighbors.

The church's stand on what constituted "respectable" white behavior in no way mitigated slavery and the violence that was inherent in and underwrote the whole system. Whether individual slaveholders worked to maintain a facade of respectability, whether they beat the people the state allowed them to say they owned, whether they forced marriages or matings between enslaved people, whether they required or forced sexual services from enslaved women, whether or not they did any of this as individuals, didn't much matter to the overall system. The fact that they could make those choices and the fact of the constant, unceasing threat of random violence, of directed violence, of sale down the river, of separation, of death, all enabled by the state, made it possible for some slaveholders to define themselves, by using less violence, as kindly, paternalistic guardians of "their child-like people."[70]

THERE IS SOME EVIDENCE THAT Alexander, and later his second wife, Mary, paid attention to the church's injunctions and probably regarded themselves as kindly guardians of enslaved people. The 1818 inventory made after Alexander's death and the inventory made when Mary died thirty-one years later both include names of the enslaved.[71] All but one of the people who were listed as boys and girls in 1818, a girl named Mariah, are still there in 1849. Two of the girls of 1818, Rose and Malinda, have infants in 1849, while the third, Nancy, who was given a very high evaluation in 1818, and therefore was probably close to childbearing age, has no infant in 1849, and a fairly low valuation, and so was probably past childbearing age. Of the five adults in 1818—two women, Judah and Depha (her name is unclear in the handwritten inventory), and two of the men, Adam (valued too highly to be Venis's Adam, who would have been at least seventy by then) and Sam—are gone in Mary's inventory. Comparing inventory names, tax lists, census numbers, sexes, and ages between the 1782 tax list and the 1849 inventory, it appears that shortly before the 1810 census two men were sold or died, and two women were bought. By 1818 there were eight children. Maybe Alexander made the purchases of the women with "increase" in mind, perhaps he agreed to buy the women because they were the wives of men he already owned, or perhaps Mary had lobbied for help in managing her large household. We will never know. But it does appear that children were kept, as were their mothers.

The resulting wealth is clear. Comparison with other Barren County estate inventories made in 1818 and 1849 shows that Alexander had gradually increased his wealth over his lifetime, and that Mary, when she died in 1849, with twenty-nine people enslaved, had become one of the richest people in Barren County. For comparison, in 1850, about a quarter of Kentucky households owned slaves, and of those slave owners, a quarter owned only one. Just five had more than a hundred slaves. Alexander and Mary's wealth reflected the growth of inequality in an area that had once been a bit more egalitarian in its distribution of land than the rest of Kentucky. Alexander owned 700 acres—the value of which is not counted in his inventories, since inventories count only movable property.[72] When he died, the majority of his wealth was in the people he owned, as had been the case with his father. Sixty-four percent of the value of Alexander's inventory was the thirteen people he owned, and in the years immediately before and after his death there was only one Barren County inventory valued higher than his. There was quite a shift during the years after his death; by the time of Mary's death, 96 percent of the value of the estate was in the twenty-nine people listed in her inventory. Twelve of the sixteen additional people since the 1818 inventory were clearly children of three of the women; the other four could well have been adult children—all "increase." The remaining 4 percent of the inventory, all the rest of the goods, livestock, machinery, and furniture, was still worth more than the vast majority of inventories that listed no enslaved people. I have found no record of what eventually happened after Mary's death, except that each of the three mothers she owned, with their children, were placed with a land-owner who had to pay the estate nothing for the hire of the mother and older children, but instead took on the cost of providing clothes and food for the non-working little children.[73] This certainly appears to have been an attempt to keep mother and child together. Legally, Mary could certainly have freed them all instead, assuming she could afford to post the required security bonds without selling someone, but that would have been no guarantee that families could remain together. The state could seize children of poor parents and essentially re-enslave them as apprentices.[74]

Under Alexander, judging by his 1818 inventory, work on his seven hundred acres could easily absorb the labor of his enslaved workforce, men and women. As was common in central Kentucky, farming produced both food for use on the homestead and a range of goods and crops for sale. The inventory included a large herd of cattle, a large flock of sheep, hogs, a few mares and foals, and a wide range of crops—wheat, corn, hay, oats, and apparently an orchard producing apples for cider and vinegar and, judging by the copper still, something alcoholic, perhaps Kentucky's famed cider brandy.[75] Alexander, according to his granddaughter Laura Davidson Baird's letter, did blacksmithing for his own use and for others, and blacksmithing tools are listed in the inventory. In addition, Laura says, the household produced practically all its clothing, including shoe leather. The hair from the tanned skins was "mixed with cotton, carded, spun, and woven into blankets for the colored family."[76] The 1818 inventory includes a loom, five cotton and two flax wheels, plus kitchen utensils—evidence of the work of the women.

Under Mary, however, there were far fewer cattle, horses, and sheep, which decreased the proportion of the value of the estate's livestock compared to 1818. Hogs remain, and there is a sizable amount of bacon and lard in the inventory. Farming implements, corn, and oats are listed. A loom, cotton and flax wheels remain. But, though the sale records accompanying the inventory are ambiguous, with far more people and some decrease in farming, Mary may have shifted to hiring "surplus" people out by the year—apparently thirteen of them at the time of her death, ten men and the three women without young children, leaving one man, three women, and a lot of children of all ages on the farm. Above and beyond the potential sale value of her vastly increased group of enslaved people, the value of her holdings reflects the long-term buildup of material possessions that slavery enabled.

So it appears that the best I can do for the family mythology that we were abolitionists in Kentucky is to hold up people who aren't my direct ancestors, my great-great-great-great-uncle, and perhaps his wife, Elijah and Margaret Davidson, who were certainly antislavery, and may have been "enthusiastic emancipators," abolitionists acting to make change in the present, as were Carter Tarrant and John Murphy. I can point to my direct ancestor Hezekiah as someone who may have been antislavery; he helped Sampson, a free black man, hold on to property and may have freed the one boy he did briefly own. But to include in "we" my great-great-great-great-grandparents, Alexander II and Anna, or Alexander's second wife Mary, as abolitionists? That doesn't fly. Even claiming they were antislavery is a stretch, though it is possible to interpret the facts in that direction. They may have believed slavery was a necessary evil; they may have avoided what they believed was the immoral breaking up of families at a time when many wills and estate sales in Barren County sold enslaved workers or parceled them out to each of the heirs of an estate.[77] But having antislavery attitudes, thinking slavery is wrong but necessary, believing that being nice to your slaves fulfills your moral obligations to God and society and justifies your continued profit from slavery—that is not being an abolitionist, not even an abolitionist working for gradual emancipation.

SO FAR WHAT I'VE SAID ABOUT antislavery in order to contextualize family mythology and the Davidsons in early Kentucky focuses on their likely beliefs about the morality of slavery, given their very solid Baptist orientation. However, there is a whole other dimension to the antislavery position, which I doubt was foremost in their minds. That dimension is important in bringing us back to my recurring theme of sovereignty, punishment, dispossession: the need to create the labor supply capitalism requires and the "something extra" from outside of capitalism that primes the pump.

First, there was a strong antislavery argument in Kentucky that rested on economics, particularly on the purchasing power of whites, on whom local merchants, artisans, and manufacturers depended for an income.[78] Elites did some local purchasing, but they often imported their luxury items, bypassing Kentucky merchants and free artisans. This was particularly true after the War of 1812.[79] Skilled enslaved workers provided most of the rest of elite needs, an entire workforce that did very little purchasing. Local artisans and manufacturers, already in competition with slave labor, were being driven out of business as larger merchant-manufacturers began taking over, using machinery and an enslaved workforce to produce, for instance, rope, yarn, cloth, and hemp bagging.[80] So without the prospect of either wages or a market for their wares, ordinary whites had little money to spend, further depressing local businesses. Whites had begun leaving the state in droves for states north of the Ohio, where they wouldn't have to compete with enslaved labor.[81]

None of this was good for townspeople, who were more likely to resent slavery than rural farmers who depended on enslaved agricultural labor. Those who needed jobs saw slavery as the system that made jobs scarce. Those with businesses were likely to see slavery as "a withering blight," denying them consumers and retarding the economic development that would benefit them.[82] So there was a bit of an urban-rural split on the issue.[83] However, those who might like to see slavery disappear couldn't see a practical way to shift to free labor, since white labor was in short supply. They saw it as a vicious circle: you can't get rid of slavery because there isn't enough white labor, and whites won't stick around to become labor because of slavery. The obvious solution, to have free black laborers working along with whites, was unthinkable to most whites.[84]

There was also the argument that whites refused to work at jobs involving heavy manual labor because such work was associated with slavery and they found it demeaning. White men, for instance, refused to work in ropewalks, part of the grueling labor of turning hemp into rope.[85] Needless to say, employers found this attitude annoying and claimed that slavery made whites lazy (ignoring that ropewalking and similar jobs were ones no one would voluntarily undertake, especially for minuscule wages). Capitalists and would-be capitalists often saw slavery as an impediment to the industrialization they sought as the route to Kentucky's development and their own enrichment. Slavery blocked the development of the "free" labor they believed was cheaper, as they claimed it was in Indiana and Ohio, and more efficient.[86] The argument was essentially that as the free population grew, labor would no longer be scarce, and therefore wages would drop, and whites would work harder. Although not put quite this way, the logic was that wage workers, dispossessed, could be incentivized by the threat of starvation around the corner if they refused low wages, and being in competition with one another, would work faster both to get and keep what jobs there were and to feed their families. Slave owners, on the other hand, couldn't stop feeding their workforce, even during off-seasons.[87]

The more ardent abolitionists added that owning slaves also made slaveholders lazy, not just poor whites. Even worse, it made them tyrannical, expecting every whim to be indulged, growing up with aristocratic attitudes inappropriate for the leaders of a republic.[88] Added to this was the argument that there were not enough whites in Kentucky compared to blacks, seen as a dangerous situation because it increased the likelihood of slave revolt and depressed the economy, causing the state to fall behind Northern free labor states.[89] This all added up to a considerable degree of sympathy for the antislavery position based on economics and demographics.

NOW, IF YOU BELIEVE IN COINCIDENCES, here is an interesting one. Just as the economic arguments about lack of white labor were heating up as a prelude to the 1792 and 1799 state constitutional conventions where the question of slavery would be addressed, some Kentucky and Virginia elites began toying with the possibility of changing the penal code. Twenty-seven crimes were punishable with death under the Kentucky laws inherited from Virginia.[90] Between constitutions, however, there was growing dissatisfaction. Even if "an eye for an eye" seemed an acceptable approach to justice, death for a petty crime was hardly that. John Breckinridge, a prominent member of Kentucky's General Assembly, called the existing laws "sanguinary, cruel, and unjust."[91] Just before the 1799 constitution came into effect the Kentucky legislature passed a bill to make punishment proportionate to the crime.[92] Only first-degree murder would now get you killed by the state.[93] Instead of dying, criminals were to pay for their crimes by being trained to be useful members of society. That is to say, they were to be put to work, and their work was to profit the state.

Jails up to that point, like the one for which Hezekiah made a new lock, had simply acted as holding pens where people briefly awaited trial, whipping, or execution.[94] But in 1798 the legislature mandated the construction of a penitentiary.[95] Convicted criminals would live for years in a massive building surrounded by a walled yard enclosing workshops where convicts made fetters and clothing for use in the prison, and barrels, cloth, shingles, nails, shoes, and dressed stone for sale, the profits being income for the state.[96] The first penitentiary opened its doors in 1800. While it took a couple of decades to get the kinks worked out, the penitentiary was eventually privatized, giving the state some income and making fortunes for the leaseholder/managers. Kentucky's penitentiary system, says historian Paul Knepper, became a model for other states and was the beginning of American convict leasing.[97]

But here is where it gets interesting. The prisoners were all white. Enslaved people were mostly punished by their owners, although when accused by someone not their owner, the case might go to court and be tried by a jury; they sometimes were even acquitted.[98] While conditions were bad and hours of work long and arduous for whites in the early penitentiaries, it wasn't until after the Civil War, when blacks became citizens and thus targets for criminal and vagrancy charges, that convict leasing became the truly vicious substitute for slavery that it eventually became. So the people whose lives were being saved by the penitentiary and the change in the penal code were white. The people who were to be turned into a labor force for the state and leaseholders were white. And these were the people that there were too few of in the Kentucky labor force, whose percentage in the population needed to be increased. Don't waste whites; don't, as Breckinridge put it in the preamble to the new law, "weaken the State" by killing them.[99] Instead, keep them alive, put them to work, and let them be "living and long continued examples to deter others."[100] In other words, the object was to discipline the entire free workforce, not just those who were imprisoned. Work—obedient, hard, honest work—was the way to deal with dispossession. Theft was not. While there weren't a lot of prisoners, their labor was outside the wage relationship, another source of that "something from outside" of capitalism, a source that grew much bigger after the Civil War.

This system of punishment required a far more powerful and organized state than the previous one: hanging someone is comparatively cheap and quick. Holding people for years in massive buildings with a major industrial infrastructure to enable profitable manufacturing is not. Nor, as slaveholders well knew, is it easy to force people to work hard and efficiently against their will. A state that could pull this off against insiders— people with some rights, people on whom, in a democratic (slaveholding) republic, elites depended for the legitimation of their rule—was, on one hand, centralizing control of punishment. Punishment became a state function, not a local one. On the other hand, it was making a statement about sovereignty by exhibiting that it was powerful enough to add unfree life for insiders to its options in determining who should live and who should die. It advertised its power by building massive awe-inspiring buildings that imitated at first forts and later castles.[101]

To me this looks like laying the groundwork for disciplining a growing and permanently dispossessed white labor force, much of which was already desperate. On top of that desperation, scientific managers had begun to envision subjecting employees to workplace regimens that treated them as machines, "denying the humanity of the labor force."[102] But many could vote, and all could see, if they looked, the wealth held by the few, and could, if push came to shove, decide to revolt. How was that working class to be disciplined? As the gap between rich and poor grew ever wider, and as class resentments continued to make elite rule difficult (elites had had to give in and allow direct popular election of the Kentucky state senate, for instance), a more efficient control system was needed.[103] As Breckinridge and others may have recognized, you couldn't just go on hanging people right and left if more and more people were being pushed down into the class most eligible for hanging. Too many people would be angry, and they were insiders; they needed to give at least a modicum of consent to continued elite rule. The new system would need to adhere to the avowed principles of a democratic republic, a state where sovereignty lay with the people, a state that was to foster "the pursuit of happiness," where all free white men were created equal. The laws would have to appear to be just; punishment would have to appear to be deserved, so that the principle of equality among all whites could appear to be upheld, and insiders could feel their rights as insiders were being respected. And so the penal code was changed and the first penitentiary built.

Thus, under the legitimizing rubric of the protection of private property for all, the state was now prepared to maintain dispossession, enabling the wage relationship of Kentucky's developing capitalist system. The dispossessed were left to face the penitentiary or become a labor force for those who, protected by the law, possessed more than one person or one family could productively exploit. Trying to do this by direct force would have been impractical. Force is expensive, both in the sense of expenditure of money—maintaining and equipping an army, the police, a prison system—and in the sense of expenditure of good will and trust, ultimately of legitimacy. Pre-revolutionary North Carolina elites, for instance, had paid that price in putting down the Regulators, and as a result had a very hard time convincing Piedmont North Carolinians to follow them into the Separatist cause.

Far better if a legitimizing ideology can make much of the force required appear natural, unremarkable, not even force but "the law" or "God's will." But more important, once internalized such ideologies can keep people from challenging the system, making the blatant exercise of force unnecessary. That need for legitimacy takes us full circle, back to diarchy and the legitimacy it lends to a regime of exploitation, and into a tug of war between church and state, over sovereignty and over primacy in the diarchic partnership of sacred and secular.

We will be going back to Mt. Tabor. We'll end up eventually with the role the church and its doctrines played, quite likely unintentionally, in enabling state sovereignty for a state that still had a rather weak, though growing, monopoly on the use of force.

RELIGION, SAYS TREVOR STACK, can "authorize all sorts of practices and institutions that government is unable to control directly."[104]

Religion in a modern state thus becomes "a part of the technology of statecraft."[105] This interpretation resonates with diarchic implications, with religion under capitalism left with circumscribed authority, a vestige of the sovereignty it formerly shared in sacred/secular diarchy, but still functioning to justify and legitimize state power and the violence the state monopolizes. A state is required to manage dispossession but can't admit to doing so without provoking revolt. If "relationships that involve extraction, exploitation, and domination are among the most important that are cloaked behind the mask of the state," then religion can serve as "a category of governance," contributing to the management of dispossession.[106]

Religion can produce people who are governable in a class system where, unlike in Scottish clans, bloodright, with God's blessing, does not determine possession or dispossession and where, unlike slavery, force is not the obvious instrument in getting the dispossessed to turn their labor over to others. Keeping invisible the force that is actually there, behind the scenes, requires some serious legerdemain, a feat that can be performed by a church complicit, whether consciously or not, with governing elites. For early Kentucky, as we have seen, the problem was managing dispossession and defining an honorable manhood that included neither landownership nor control of one's own labor. The church could provide yet another means of coping with that problem. The church provided white men with significant opportunity for positions of respect and responsibility, far more than were available in the economy or court system for anyone other than the wealthy. This was particularly true of small churches, such as William Hickman's Elkhorn Church, with only twenty-five white men as members.[107] The resulting sense of self-worth must have helped men to accept the idea of wage labor and to become governable citizens in a capitalist class system. Like women and blacks, some men may have found comfort in the intense experience of membership in a church that, unlike the hierarchal organization of other denominations, affirmed an individual's worth within the church, despite inequality outside it. There is some evidence that the evangelical revivalism of the Second Great Awakening, which led to numerous Baptist conversions, was strongest in those parts of Kentucky where inequality was greatest.[108]

This manipulation of people's attitudes was something the governing elite power structure couldn't do directly, and certainly couldn't accomplish by exerting force. But it needed to be done or the whole facade of a democratic republic, where blatant exploitation was glossed over, would crumble. Religion could help produce changed attitudes that would allow the state to be sovereign in the form of a democratic republic. It could induce men to accept permanent wage labor, permanent lack of the means of production, and the permanent dispossession that required them to give up any hope of the independent self-governing manhood that previous generations had defined as liberty. Bowing to another man's will, doing as you were bid, accepting as a wage only part of the value you produced, and watching your work enrich someone else—all that had been considered acceptable only as a temporary phenomenon for white men, as apprenticeship, indenture, or tenant farming. Many never made it past that point, but the expectation and the hope was there. In 1800 in the United States as a whole, working for wages was rare. Most white men were tenant farmers, in debt peonage, bound out for long indentures or apprenticeships—or they were independent craftsmen, businessmen, or farmers. By 1860, however, about 40 percent of men worked for wages in the North, and the numbers in wage work were rising in Kentucky.[109] This was an enormous transition, and it required an enormous shift in attitude.

We saw earlier how the Cult of Domesticity contributed to making this new version of manhood acceptable to men—and to women. The church played a critical part in convincing women that their God-given role was to accept their own dispossession so that their labor, itself outside of capitalism, could provide part of the something extra that capitalism needs, although of course it was not framed that way. Women were to help keep a husband willing to continue bowing to another man's commands in order to provide for his dependents, to maintain the little castle where, when he returned each day, he became king, where others had to bow to him. Significantly, as we have seen, the definition of women as naturally more spiritual than men also laid on women the obligation to bring men to the church. There they were exposed to considerable pressure to live the orderly and productive lives that made capitalism's dispossession of insiders and the exploitation of wage labor possible. Making religion a matter of choice—freedom of religion—and for evangelicals, a choice you made in the heat of intense emotion, gave your submission to the church's code an intensity it might well have lacked otherwise.

The individualism that had formerly defined people as able to make personal choices and thus able to choose to reject their baptism, making them vulnerable to the Devil—the stuff of witchcraft panics—had now morphed into "possessive individualism."[110] If you were "free" then you as an individual had the ability to act independently because you owned your own property and your own body (and thus your own labor, which you could choose to sell to an employer). If you had that ability, then you were vulnerable to yourself, God, and the church: you, and you alone, were responsible for responding to God's gift of grace and forgiveness. Likewise, you were responsible for your own fate, although just how you were to be responsible depended on gender.

The Cult of Domesticity set the parameters for women: raise well-behaved children and keep your man functioning and hopefully rising in the class structure. Doing so, doing your duty to family and church, was your personal responsibility, and failure left you vulnerable to your conscience and the church.[111] If you were a dispossessed man, it was your job to do something about that condition; a class-based society did not require that you remain dispossessed forever, and striving became part of the American ethos. But even if you remained dispossessed, you could now be an honorable householder through wages and correct behavior (especially with a well-chosen wife). That the landless in Baptist churches had an equal vote with people of far greater wealth, called them Brother and Sister, and could occasionally sit in judgment on them, was one of those apparent equalizers that helped disguise inequality and upheld honor.[112] So also was the Baptist rejection of horseracing, gambling, and conspicuous consumption such as fancy dress and holding balls, as well as their queasiness about slaveholding—these were all planter class markers, and saying they were immoral meant rejecting the behaviors that marked class inequality.[113]

Under those conditions, moments of revolt, of white class-based uprising, like that of the Regulators, could be kept to a minimum. The elites the Regulators opposed, those "cursed hungry caterpillars," had perhaps learned their lesson: in a republic, even a slaveholding one, the forcible hand of the elite had to be invisible even as it manipulated the state. Churches, when functioning "properly," helped make this possible. This production of a governable people was a role the state couldn't easily undertake without letting the cat out of the bag. The state's role in keeping dispossessed people dispossessed, backed by the naked force that would be required to keep them that way if they objected, would become obvious. That force had to be reserved for people who were seen to be a threat by the general public, and they could now be placed in the penitentiary and productively punished. This was a diarchic partnership of church and state in, ironically, a republic that had explicitly rejected a state religion.

The church thus became, in diarchic fashion, a flipside of the new penal system. Jointly, the two labored to produce a governable white class system of dispossession. The latter punished physically by exerting the force of the state as the bottom-line backup system. The other punished those who were recalcitrant emotionally and rewarded emotionally—with lives enriched with a sense of purpose, hope, and community—those who abided by its dictates, who accepted the class hierarchy and the rules about mobility within it.

SO, LET'S LOOK AT HOW THIS ALL played out at Mt. Tabor. First, the tug of war between diarchic partners.[114] Kentucky Baptists in the early 1800s were in competition with the fledgling state for control of punishment in south central Kentucky. Baptist churches claimed the right to adjudicate disputes between members. The behavior being enforced was that of honorable white manhood within the bounds of the morality of capitalism, in which truthfulness, decent treatment of family, sobriety, and responsible handling of money and debt were paramount.

It is worth noting that most of the prohibited behaviors, other than sexual ones, were likely to be male behaviors. Men, both black and white, could be called before the church for wife beating, and excluded for refusing to listen to the church. Gambling was likewise grounds for exclusion, as was rough language and lying. For example, there was the case of a member lying about who had killed another member's "choice sow." One memorable dispute, which dragged on for a year, involved killing a hog, arguments about who owned it, and several bags of corn. Men were not to play fast and loose with money by drinking or fighting. Like gambling, that behavior raised the specter of poverty-stricken women and children ending up on the county relief rolls. [115] Even more emphatically, men were to pay their debts and respect property rights.

At Mt. Tabor, for instance, a church business meeting decided it could not "justify a member, who covers his property [hides possessions] so as to keep just creditors from getting their right ansr [sic]." They then sent for a member they suspected of having done just that, which had "made the minds of the church uneasy." Apparently, he failed to appear. The following month the church agreed that you couldn't accept property from someone who was trying to evade the creditors' just claims. Three months later the suspect member was "accused of having a ball in his house, etc, and having been regularly dealt with according to gospel direction and refusing to attend the church[,] proceeded to excommunicate him."[116] The failure to abide by the morality of capitalism—pay your debts honestly, don't waste your money—came together with the flouting of church morality, and together got him punished. How much he minded is, of course, a different question.

The church set up a committee, to which Elijah Davidson was appointed, to deal with disputes between members having to do with temporal matters. Decisions, however, could not be enforced, even when appealed and brought before the church.[117] The church's only power was that of religion and of public opinion. It did not have a monopoly on the use of force—it could not use force at all—except that of dismissal from the church, which of course brought with it the likelihood of a punishing afterlife spent in hell. Those were powerful incentives for correct behavior, and the Church was not shy about wielding them. Most of Mt. Tabor's monthly meetings included some effort to exercise the church's authority over behavior, but without the use of force the church was limited in the control it could exert.[118] When the church decided, after hearing a case between members over money owed, that the accused actually had to pay up, with interest, he was ultimately excluded because he "utterly denies to submit to or hear the church." [119] If taken to the county court, however, force could be applied.

The church thus, in its apparently contradictory roles, was both complicit with and competitive with the state in a diarchic partnership in which the church claimed primacy but couldn't really exercise it. Nevertheless, it did much of the policing required to maintain the orderly family structure and property structure on which the passage of wealth within the landed class and between classes—that is, between the dispossessed and the possessed—depended.

IN THE COMPETITION FOR PRIMACY, however, the state legal system was winning. It is true that church members were not to take each other to court and could be excluded for doing so.[120] It is also true that the church did settle numerous disputes. But many others, particularly concerning money or property, ended unsuccessfully with the exclusion of one of the parties who refused to accept the church's judgment. The county court was then the only option.[121] Many of the functions the church had played in colonial Virginia had gradually shifted to the state, whose legal jurisdiction over people's lives kept expanding. Churches and their courts no longer had legal control of family, inheritance, and surveillance of property. It was now the county court, for instance, that ordered the processioning that clarified boundaries. It was to the county court, not the church, that Hezekiah and his neighbor turned when a boundary dispute arose.[122] churches still did the marrying, but the state licensed ministers like Alexander to do so. Alexander's license appears in the Barren County Court Order book as one of the early actions that body undertook when the county was formed.[123]

And it was now the county court, not the church, that determined who were the deserving poor who should receive help from the county. A 1793 law directed the court to take children from land-poor families to be bound out. The justices decided which unwed mothers would have their "bastards" taken from them at age two and indentured to "learn" housekeeping or farm work until age twenty-one, and which orphans—that is to say, children whose father had died, even if the mother was alive—should be likewise bound out, rather than made wards of relatives.[124] The state, in other words, was supplying children as more cheap labor—and sometimes meeting resistance from the women involved. Two such resisting mothers, each with four children, were called in to court to "shew cause if any they can why their children shall not be bound out agreeably to law."[125] Another woman, whose orphan daughter had been bound out, successfully petitioned to get her back on the strength, apparently, of having remarried.[126]

With the new penal code and the shift to penitentiaries, punishing was becoming a more effective instrument for patrolling the margins of capitalism.[127] In many local towns the first building to be built had been a jail—the declaration of intent to punish—but the penitentiary was a far more powerful expression of that intent. To a large extent those the local authorities disapproved of were those who were perceived as not working and propertyless; vagrancy laws provided the legal justification to punish anyone who was not producing value for the benefit of the elite. This was one of the services provided by the state as part of legitimizing itself in the eyes of people like Alexander. Another was the legal right of a man to punish both enslaved people and "dependents"—in Alexander's case, Anna, then Mary, and their children. This meant, of course, that the state did not have a total monopoly on the use of force. And this means we need to take another look at slavery.

THERE IS AN ABSOLUTE BOTTOM LINE in understanding slavery, and thus in understanding slavery within households. It would not exist without violence; nor would any other system of unfree or viciously exploitative labor. And the household during the late eighteenth and early nineteenth century was a worksite, a production site, not a private site of domesticity.[128] This applies just as much to Mary and Alexander, regardless of whether they were kind or not, as it does to the most vicious slaveholder, for instance, the woman who "uster box my ears, stick pins in me and tie me ter de cedar chest and whoop me as long as she wanter," as one former Kentucky slave described. [129] These are points that historian Thavolia Glymph emphasizes in her analysis of the slaveholding household and the relations it fostered between the white and black women within them. She concludes that "violence on the part of white women was integral to the making of slavery, crucial to shaping black and white women's understanding of what it meant to be female. . . . At the same time, white women's violence contradicted prevailing conceptions of white womanhood—and still does." Women discussed their violence in letters and diaries. Slave narratives, Glymph says, indict women more frequently than men with unprovoked, vicious, mean, and frighteningly random violence. Men's violence was apparently more predictable. Women's violence was very much part of the essential violence that enabled slavery, part of a culture that excused that violence as a "natural" reaction to "provoking" black behavior.[130]

Glymph points out a difference between the experience of slaveholding for men and for women.[131] Men were often not in constant direct contact with the men they owned; women were. Alexander, for instance, was frequently away from home on church business. Owners of much land and many slaves, like Alexander, with thirteen people enslaved and seven hundred acres, frequently hired white overseers.[132] And even if he didn't have an overseer as a buffer, at least part of the time Alexander would have been giving directions to someone else, maybe a son, maybe Mary, maybe one of those enslaved. At least some of the time the enslaved might have been working at a distance, out from under the gaze of a potential punisher.

Life for Mary, her older daughters, the enslaved women Depha and Judah, and the older enslaved children, would have been quite different.

They were in constant and direct contact. There was no buffer between them, and very little time away from one another. The amount of work to be done was enormous. Basic housekeeping was the least of it, for the household was a worksite, just as much as was Alexander's blacksmith shop and the farm. The goods women made supplied the household itself and also entered the local economy, where they were bartered to merchants for imported goods and were "central to the merchants' success" and to Kentucky's economy generally. [133] The domestic worksite produced hams, soap, cider and vinegar, yarn, cloth, clothes, blankets, butter, cheese, jam, bread, fresh vegetables, and stocked root cellars. Women without enslaved help, of whom there were many in Barren County, did all this themselves; women like Mary, however, did more supervising and less physical labor. [134]

Mary's status—and to some extent Alexander's—depended on her successful performance of domestic order, efficiency, prosperity, and hospitality, all of which depended on her daily control of a productive enslaved labor force. [135] All of this, according to the dictates of the increasingly important Cult of Domesticity, was to be performed with serenity, elevated spiritual awareness, and submission to Alexander's decisions. But within the household worksite she was, as Glymph insists, no mere representative of her husband's power to enforce obedience of the enslaved. She was, in her own right, the source of the power to punish. [136] And if she was like the majority of slaveholding women whose views are expressed in letters and diaries, she saw Judah and Depha as "obstinate, self-willed, cross, and dirty," a constant irritant to a minister's wife expecting to be held to the highest standards of domestic perfection. [137]

Adding to the potentially explosive household dynamic is the fact that enslaved women could be forced to "breed." Judah and Depha might or might not have consented to sex with whomever fathered their children; they might or might not have consented to a church-sanctioned marriage that carried no weight in law; they might or might not have been in love. They might have been sent off for breeding, as one sends a mare, to a chosen stud. [138] Or Alexander, or his sons, or a white neighbor might be the father of their children. The enslaved woman might or might not have resisted, but lack of resistance cannot be presumed to be consent. Either way, Mary might have overtly blamed the woman for sex with her husband or sons or she might carefully appear unaware, while her anger simmered below the surface, as might Judah's or Depha's at being used in such a way. Slavery, wrote former fugitive slave Harriet Jacobs in her autobiography, is "terrible for men; but it is far more terrible for women. Superadded to the burden common to all, they have wrongs, and sufferings, and mortifications peculiarly their own."[139]

The Radford descendents of John and Bruen Radford had moved to Kentucky in 1814, to Christian County, well to the west of the Davidsons, and, like the older generation of Davidsons, the older Radfords were slave owners. There was then a Davidson and Radford younger generation exodus from Kentucky in the early 1830s. Perhaps it was the desire to leave either the competition of slave labor or the discomfort it caused their consciences, or perhaps it was the draw of land, but in any case, Hezekiah and Elijah Davidson moved to Illinois with their entire families. Elijah and part of his family eventually joined a wagon train for Oregon.[140] Benjamin Radford II moved to Illinois with his family at about the same time as the Davidsons, where they met. He, along with Caleb Davidson, William's son and Hezekiah's nephew, was a founder of Eureka College (which Ronald Reagan attended many years later). His granddaughter, Elizabeth Radford, married Hezekiah's son, Thomas Davidson. It was her brother, Benjamin J. Radford III, who was my father's great-uncle Ben, who, according to family mythology, watched Lincoln playing horseshoes—only he didn't. It was Ben's father-in-law, sent to summon Lincoln into the courtroom.[141]

MEANWHILE, THOUGH MY ANCESTORS were probably not conscious of it, Native people were strategizing to exploit the tensions between international powers in the lead-up to the War of 1812, as they had done off and on for years. Indian prophets, particularly Shawnee, had continued their quest for a pan-Indian unity that they hoped, through an alliance with the British during the War of 1812, would allow them to create a separate Indian state in the Old Northwest, the area north of the Ohio and west of the Appalachians. But perhaps that possibility had already been lost, with the Native defeat at Fallen Timbers in 1794, when their British allies failed to come to their support against a US army under Anthony Wayne, and the alliance of Native nations began to fall apart. Some see that battle as having been "[i]n hindsight, the Indians' last best chance to stem the tide of American expansionism."[142] But had things worked out just a little differently in 1812, this country could have been a very different place—indeed, not *this* country at all. North America would today contain four countries instead of three, had the Native strategy succeeded.

Throughout the late 1700s and early 1800s a pair of Shawnee brothers, Tecumseh, a talented organizer, speaker, and military strategist, and Tenskwatawa, a charismatic prophet, continued to insist, along with other prophets, that the Master of Life had given the land to Indians, not whites. Activists and emissaries went to and fro through Kentucky on trips between the Shawnee towns north of the Ohio and Chickasaw, Creek, Choctaw, and Cherokee towns south of Kentucky, as well as contacting Indians west of the Mississippi. My guess is that my ancestors were pretty oblivious to their passage through the state, since the travelers did not advertise their presence. They probably did, however, know of the rising tensions that led to renewed war with England, the War of 1812. And they certainly knew some aspects of the war itself—Elijah was one of the soldiers.[143]

As we saw back in chapter 6, there had been many years of pan-Indian organizing and many Native prophets had spoken powerfully about the need for purification by rejecting white culture, or the most damaging parts of it, and adopting new rituals. So there was nothing particularly original about Tenskwatawa's message, nor about his brother Tecumseh's agenda of unification. Nor was their partnership particularly unusual: one was the prophet, the sacred power; the other was the active, secular power. Diarchy again. Though their ideas were far from new, it is also true that Tecumseh was an extraordinarily charismatic and energetic organizer.[144] And he completely rejected the idea that negotiation and concessions would win anything permanent for

Indians. The trail of broken treaties was much too obvious. He also rejected the idea that certain tribes had claim on a particular territory. In his view, the Old Northwest should be a polity belonging to all Indians. And the only way to accomplish that was by force. Indians were seriously divided. Should they grant whites more concessions and hope cooperation would bring peace and secure territory? Or should they go to war, with all the risk and heartbreak that entailed, and suffer the inevitable white reprisals that would follow when Indians killed whites? Unable to bridge this divide, says Gregory Dowd, Tenskwatawa and Tecumseh never achieved the degree of pan-Indian unity of the late 1700s.[145]

Nevertheless, during the War of 1812, the British in Canada required Native allies to hold off the United States, that land-grabbing republic on their southern border, just as they needed black allies in their naval attack on the East Coast. Blacks, free and enslaved, hoped to manipulate war into freedom. Many along the coast escaped to British ships and joined in the British assault on the American coastline, both as fighters and as guides. According to Alan Taylor, their "expertise enabled the British to outfight Virginians on what they had once considered their own terrain."[146] Others may have considered another potential route to freedom: there were mutterings toward the end of the war about the US military hiring enslaved men from owners who would receive the recruit's wages and enlistment bounty. Those recruits who survived would be given freedom and land in the West.[147]

The inland aspect of the War of 1812 presented the perfect opportunity for Tecumseh's strategizing. Allied with the British, he pulled together enough fighters to tip the scales and protect Canada from US incursions.[148] To keep Britain's Native allies, and in acknowledgment of their importance, the British general supported Tecumseh's plan for the Old Northwest's Native buffer state between Canada and the United States, whose territory could not be alienated by Indians or anyone else. Indians were to be included in the peace negotiations at the end of the war, where details would be worked out. The British prime minister agreed, as did the governor-general of Canada, the foreign secretary, and the secretary of war and the colonies. Since a buffer state suited British interests, this was not an unrealistic dream. Had the British won a decisive victory, such a state might have become reality.[149] There was also some support among US officials for an Indian state within US borders.[150] But there was no decisive victory by either side. Tecumseh was killed at the Battle of Thames (in which many Kentuckians fought), and the Treaty of Ghent simply restored the status quo ante, with no buffer state, no improvement of land rights, but without punishment for having fought against the United States.

Native nations would never again play a decisive role in international relations, says Tecumseh biographer John Sugden.[151] The pan-Indian movement fell apart, and never again was the United States seriously threatened by the Native people it dispossessed, says Dowd, in concluding his history of pan-Indian organizing.[152] And its disappearance, I would add, meant that a black bid for freedom was also suppressed. This view of the end of Indian power describes what happened to the tribes in what was then the United States, but it fails to take into account the Comanche Empire that, well into the 1800s, historian Pekka Hämäläinen describes as the controlling influence in what was to become the US Southwest. He documents that "as Spanish, French, British, and US empires vied with one another over land, commerce, and raw materials, Comanches continued to expand their realm, profoundly frustrating European fantasies of superiority."[153]

Nevertheless, Tecumseh's defeat and the fragmenting of pan-Indian organizing meant that within US-controlled territory, US elites were now free to pursue their agenda with little regard for Native resistance. "Manifest Destiny" was free to shape the country; land-hungry whites could continue to hope they could hold off dispossession—whiteness still offered the dream of owning land. Opening land to white settlement relieved the building pressure of growing inequality among whites. Revolt against elite rule was staved off yet again.

But Native revolt was not staved off, as the nineteen-month takeover of Alcatraz in 1970–71 and the American Indian Movement's 1973 stand at Wounded Knee demonstrate. Nor was Native resistance overcome by the state's violent reaction at Wounded Knee and other protests, nor by the punishing regime inflicted by the state's imprisonment of Native leaders and disproportionate imprisonment of young people. Instead Native women have led resistance to rape and murder by whites. The Lakota Nation has declared its independence from the United States. Native people have organized with indigenous people around the world to bring human rights abuses before the UN, leading to the adoption by the UN in 2007 of the Declaration on the Rights of Indigenous Peoples. Working worldwide with other indigenous people and within the United States, Natives have frustrated elite projects by leading the fight against environmental degradation in places such as the winter encampment at Standing Rock, followed by suing the Trump administration over the construction of the Keystone XL pipeline.[154] Manifest Destiny has not had as smooth a ride as the defeat of Tecumseh seemed to predict.

AND HERE WE LEAVE THE ANCESTORS, on the cusp of this story of state formation, punishment, dispossession, and family. The United States by 1815 or so is about to be recognizably the country in which we now live. The punishing discipline, the mechanics of state violence needed to manage a permanently dispossessed large-scale wage-earning "free" white working class, are in order. So is the accompanying ideology that made the violence behind the whole system invisible and the dispossession acceptable. And capitalism continues to need that something extra from outside capitalism, and it still comes primarily from people of color. The stage this tale of ancestors has set is a platform from which I will move on to illuminate the present—which is perhaps the only reason this story matters.

CHAPTER 9

Tales of the Present

I f we are going to illuminate the present, we need to fast-forward through history from the early 1820s, where I abandon the ances-tor tales, as the United States was making the shift to primary dependence on wage labor for whites, relying on the backing of a state strong enough to enforce the dispossession of insiders. But that shift didn't mean the end of unfree labor or of the punishment required to enforce it and to discipline class boundaries. So we need to go through the next two centuries and the processes that connect unfree labor past to unfree labor present. Unfree labor—indenture, slavery—was where we started these ancestor tales: it was foundational to the formation of the United States. It is critical in the present as well, although people often don't recognize it as such, since it goes by different names and is driven by different mechanisms. Nevertheless, it still provides a bit of that "something from outside" the capitalist system itself. It still requires punishing to sustain it.

AFTER THE CIVIL WAR, EMANCIPATION meant that the state took over control of the black labor force, adding it to its existing con-trol of the white working class, as we have seen with institutions like

Kentucky's new penitentiary. Without slavery, and with landowners' desire for workers as cheap as slave labor had been, a new system of dispossession was needed for the black labor force. And it needed to be one that would keep blacks and whites divided. The biracial organizing of the Farmers' Alliance and People's Party of the 1880s and 1890s made the need for separation of blacks and whites glaringly obvious. Those organizations challenged the monopolistic system of the banking and manufacturing elites that together kept the prices farmers received for their products disastrously low. It took the violence of the Ku Klux Klan and propaganda about the dangers black men posed to white women to get blacks and whites irretrievably separated.[1] What W. E. B. Du Bois called "the psychological wage of whiteness" came to join white privilege, working to keep discontented whites from joining blacks in revolt.[2]

This "psychological wage" was a new twist in the meaning of the whiteness that had been so powerful in keeping blacks and whites divided ever since Bacon's Rebellion. Many politicians, local elites, ministers, and newspaper editors began promoting the belief that whiteness in and of itself made you superior to all blacks, even if they were better off than you and just as free as you. So long as slavery had marked the difference between black and white, white superiority had seemed self-evident. Now that the difference between slavery and freedom no longer marked the difference between blacks and poor whites, and both were being exploited, something was needed to keep poor whites from identifying by class rather than race, and allying with blacks. Hence the propaganda about whites' innate superiority, natural ability, and capacity to rise. The psychological wage was the boost given to white egos, a "payment" from people with power and money or authority to poor whites, a pat on the back, an endorsement of your racial kinship and thus worth. Even if you were poor and powerless, you could still get a psychological boost from thinking, "At least I'm white." And that boost was badly needed, because poor whites as well as blacks were drawn into the trap of sharecropping.

Sharecropping was organized to replace slavery right after the Civil War.[3] The state was thus continuing to perform its state obligations, enforcing dispossession, making cheap labor available, and enabling forms of something extra from outside capitalism. Right after the war, during Reconstruction, the Union Army and Republican Party provided some protection for blacks from enraged and fearful whites. Until about 1877 when Union Army support was withdrawn and white elites regained control of Southern state legislatures, black men's right to vote was enforced. Voting rates were high, and blacks were elected to state legislatures. Consequently, blacks were able to resist a return to the plantation gang labor that landowning whites wanted. Though hopes for forty acres and a mule as restitution for generations of unpaid labor were thwarted, blacks could, and some did, buy land. However, most could not. Though technically free, they were still dispossessed.

Legal recognition of black marriages meant that black husbands had authority over wives and children, and husbands and wives alike were insistent on home and work lives that they, not owners, controlled. With Union Army backing, they gained this right, at least technically, through sharecropping. Sharecropping was, and in some cases still is, a system whereby the farm laboring family bears all the risks of farming and all the costs of raising the next generation of labor. They manage their own provisioning with some combination of gardening, purchase, and barter, as well as with minimal provisions furnished on credit by the landlord throughout the year. They live in a dwelling and farm on a section of land allotted to each sharecropping family by a landowner. When the crop is sold the landlord gives them half the money—minus the cost of the supplies the landlord has furnished during the year, which generally leaves them with nearly nothing, or frequently in debt to the landowner. Debtors provided landlords with unfree labor: debt peonage laws made it illegal to leave an employer until the debt was paid. The sharecropping contracts—legal contracts backed by state force, which the husband would sign, up until the early twentieth century—would have given him very limited rights, while providing to the landowner very broad rights over the labor and behavior of the whole family. Wives and children alike were expected to work under the direction of the husband, as required by the landowner, who much preferred families with lots of kids. This was not slavery, but it certainly was not freedom either. Poor farm-laboring and tenant-farming whites were also drawn in, so that former slaves and former free workers came more and more to resemble each other. White privilege, however, continued to provide some protection to white sharecroppers.

Blacks could have been brought into the class system as wage workers, and some were. But the abolitionists' claim that free waged labor would become cheaper than slavery wasn't working out. Waged work would not provide what landowners wanted: people who would work for nothing except a (frequently inadequate) roof over their heads and barely enough to stay alive from one harvest to the next, little more than in slavery. Sharecroppers provided labor that was outside the wage relationship; their meager share of the crop and the conditions under which sharecropping was undertaken did not amount to freely contracted work for wages. The system took violence to maintain, administered legally by the state and illegally by white Christian terrorists, often framed as the protection of white womanhood from a supposed black rapist. This "Southern rape complex" contributed mightily to the fear and hatred that kept blacks and poor whites divided. And it meant that blacks who challenged their exploitation risked their own lives as well as retaliation in the form of rape or whippings for their families.

While white sharecropping grew rapidly—after all, available land was still scarce in the South because the big landowners who had led the rebellion against the US government were allowed to keep their land after the war—it was only against blacks that the real violence that accompanied sharecropping was directed.[4] However, that violence was organized more centrally than it had been in slavery. The state claimed, although rather ineffectively, something much closer to a monopoly on the use of force, a move toward centralizing the right to punish.

But the state's control included turning a blind eye to the illegal exercise of force. In the new system, former slave owners lost the legal right to punish. Instead, the local white community took over punishing blacks. Led by local elites, a wide range of whites used force illegally, and with impunity. With compensation no longer demanded by owners for the destruction of their human property, lynch mobs punished by killing.[5]

This in itself was something of a centralization of punishing—out of the hands of individual slave owners and into the fewer hands of community elites, but not effectively into the hands of the state. The state, obviously, was still relatively weak—it didn't stop lynching, nor did it try very hard to establish a monopoly on punishing violence.

Illegal violence was accompanied by perfectly legal violence.[6] For quite a while the state gave landowners the legal right to use violence against sharecroppers for a variety of so-called offenses. And the debt peonage and vagrancy laws, state-sanctioned and enforced, provided debtors as unfree labor. Technically these laws were color-blind; in reality, they were invoked far more often against blacks than against whites. Courts imposed heavy fines and legal fees. Unable to pay, thousands of black men, generally unjustly accused of trivial offenses, had to work off the debt with unfree labor for whoever paid the fees for them, keeping them out of prison, but unfree. Or they could go to prison and work off the debt. This system of debt peonage, combined with illegal lynching, produced a punishing terrorist regime in the South. By promoting white fear of blacks with claims about the dangers blacks supposedly posed to white womanhood, it kept poor whites as well as blacks under control and dispossessed. Whites, since Bacon's Rebellion, had largely identified with their whiteness, but that identification was now additionally marked by their participation in the violence that had formerly been exercised mainly by slave owners and patrollers and by serving on the juries that enacted legal violence. Their participation encouraged a sense of being one people with the elites who supposedly kept them safe from blacks, despite huge class differences. That identification went a long way toward keeping them from joining with blacks in revolting against the sharecropping system that actually damaged both. Even more viciously, it was white violence, legal and illegal, that kept blacks largely dispossessed and caught in a sharecropping system that provided, in many cases, a standard of living little better and with little more freedom than many had experienced in slavery. And it provided a similar level of profit for landowners.[7] Almost certainly sharecropping was the fate of most of the enslaved youngsters listed in Mary Davidson's 1849 estate evaluation.

LOOKING THROUGH THE LENS OF THE PAST, we can see the importance of reproduction in this shift from slavery to sharecropping. Through that lens, the shift is a rather accelerated case of the shift to serfdom that tends to occur when the supply of slaves dries up or becomes prohibitively expensive (a situation discussed in chapter 7). With emancipation, workers could no longer be replaced by purchase; they had to be produced locally. Freed blacks refused to return to gang labor as if nothing had changed, and with federal backing they demanded access to land and houses during Reconstruction.[8] Sharecropping, the resulting compromise with landowners, bears a distinct resemblance to serfdom, although it did not tie people so tightly to a particular estate. But it did create unfree labor outside the wage relationship. Just as serfs had to be permitted some way to raise children, both to prevent revolution and to ensure access to a new generation of labor, so did sharecroppers, despite the noticeably higher death rate in their families than in the landowners' families.[9] With legal marriage for blacks, a semblance of patriarchal manhood was now possible—a man was now the head of his household, the king of his castle, with some degree of control over the family workforce. The husband had the patriarchal right to protect, punish, and control his family—a right that was often usurped by landowners if the sharecroppers were black.

While sharecroppers were technically free to leave at the end of the annual contract, debt peonage and terrorism often made that right irrelevant, increasing the resemblance to serfdom, particularly for blacks. As is also typical in the shift to serfdom, people who formerly had greater independence—in the United States poor farm-laboring or tenant-farming whites—were also drawn in, so that unfree labor spread into a wider portion of the population.

Kentucky passed an anti-lynching law in 1897, though a federal anti-lynching law was voted down over and over—until its passage, finally, in 2018. With Kentucky's anti-lynching law, the state took a further step toward gaining control of the use of force and the exclusive right to punish. This was a further centralization of the power to punish, removing it from the control of community mobs. But what it meant in practice was that while public lynching diminished, execution of blacks by the courts increased. The evidence presented to juries was just as flimsy or fraudulent as that used to justify lynching. Death by this "legal lynching" was accompanied by impunity for whites who murdered blacks. They were rarely even indicted and never convicted by all-white male juries. The system was now more clearly state-sponsored terrorism.[10]

The civil rights movement, still later, sought to shift punishment further into national control, away from the local elites who ran county and state governments and toward a centralized monopoly on the use of force, allowing the federal government to assert its sovereignty over the Southern states. In the South, however, the idea of state's rights—of a degree of sovereignty for autonomous members of a federation—still contests a national state monopoly on the use of force. In the presidential election of 2016, these ideas joined with the belief that the state was failing to exercise sovereignty properly, leaving borders undefended against a wave of supposedly dangerous terrorists and job-stealing immigrants. That belief, played on by racist and alarmist propaganda, led many to vote for Donald Trump and his Wall and thus for the federal use of force, despite its impingement on state's rights autonomy. Fear, well-managed, once again helped bring allegiance while disguising an elite agenda.

THERE WAS ANOTHER EVEN MORE blatant system than sharecropping for bringing in that extra something from outside the wage relations of capitalism. The penitentiary was repurposed to provide a new form of unfree labor, partially replacing slavery, a shift which Knepper says was led by Kentucky.[11] After the Civil War, the usual story goes, slavery was abolished with the Thirteenth Amendment to the Constitution. In fact, it was not. Instead it was pointedly preserved.[12] Slavery was abolished "except as a punishment for crime whereof the party shall have been duly convicted." Historically, slavery has been a common tactic as punishment for crime. For example, we saw it at work with the Aro and their shrine in Igboland. While the Thirteenth Amendment did limit slavery's scope, one could argue that the convict-leasing system that developed after its passage made enslaved labor available at a considerably lower price. Slaves—convicts—could now be rented, not bought, as Douglas Blackmon describes.[13]

The convicts were now mostly black, not white, as they had been in the early 1800s when Kentucky established its first penitentiary and put whites to work. And there were many more of them than had been the case before emancipation. The state, performing its function of providing cheap labor, had already written the necessary laws to make this form of unfree labor available—laws about petty theft, vagrancy, and debt peonage requiring fines far beyond the financial ability of many of those accused, leaving them with the legal alternative of imprisonment. Convict leases could be bought and sold. Industrialists, for instance mine owners, would buy up the rights to all the convicts from a particular jurisdiction, saving the state or county the costs of housing, feeding, and guarding them. There was no incentive to keep convicts alive and descriptions of conditions are reminiscent of Nazi labor camps. The shift in many Southern states to state-run chain gangs in the early 1900s was no improvement. Literally chained together, dressed in stripes, prisoners were subjected to grueling labor and whipping, and were housed together in nine-by-nine-foot cages, provided with inadequate or rotten food, and little medical care.[14]

Between the Civil War and the Second World War, thousands of people, mostly black men, but a few white men, were caught in the clutches of this system. While far fewer black women than men were convicted, they worked alongside the men. Sarah Haley, scholar in gender and African American studies, uses Georgia to illustrate the raced and gendered workings of the legal system. White women, rarely convicted, were almost never put on chain gangs as black women were, and their appeals for clemency were frequently granted. With the institutionalization of the chain gang came a system of probation for black women. After serving the minimum that their sentence specified, they could be paroled for at least a year, during which time they were placed as domestics in white homes, under the control of their "employer" and under the threat of a return to the chain gang for disobedience or work that did not meet the housewife's standards. White women, living their privilege, as Haley describes, were thus made into agents of the state and white homes into sites of incarceration.[15]

This system of punishment served multiple purposes, and therein lay its power. It provided a massive labor force for industrialists, arguably undergirding the rapid industrialization of the United States before the First World War, as slavery had done for the Industrial Revolution of the 1800s. For instance, the Tennessee Coal and Railroad Company leased convicts for mining and working coke ovens for one dollar a day, per prisoner, under a law known as the Zebra Law, thanks to the convicts' black-and-white striped uniforms.[16] With the shift to state-run chain gangs the state moved from directly subsidizing industrialists to an indirect subsidy: chain gangs built infrastructure needed for industrial development, most notably roads.[17] Second, with the Thirteenth Amendment, the criminal justice system joined the KKK and lynch mobs in a terrorist system that prevented rebellion, thus underwriting the injustices of unfree sharecropping. The state was, once again, supplying the coercion needed to provide a dispossessed labor supply. Third, convict leasing gave real substance to white privilege. Poor whites, even if they were convicted, were rarely leased; they would not be enslaved and for many there was little else, except freedom from the threat of lynching, that distinguished their poverty from that of blacks. This benefit of whiteness, created through the workings of the legal system, was being added to the psychological wage of whiteness.

Looking through the lens of racialized gender, Sarah Haley vividly describes the ways in which the imprisonment of black women differentiated them from white women.[18] Black women, in white eyes, might be female, but they were not women. Women were white, fragile, pure, innocent, and vulnerable to rape by black men; black females were anything but. So, in an era when white women were beginning to get jobs, to frequent theaters and dance halls, demand the vote, and generally shake up patriarchy a bit, the differentiation between black and white females assuaged men's fears about their own increased absorption into the dependent status of wage laborer. White women needed protecting, and that protecting was the foundation of white patriarchal supremacy. Thus, upholding the elite right to use convict slave labor elided with upholding white supremacy, buying poor white consent to their own exploitation.

But it should be clear that various forms of unfree labor have never applied to blacks alone. Slavery before the Civil War and its modification after emancipation into convict-leasing took place in a broader context of unfree labor. Native Americans were massively enslaved and shipped to the Caribbean. In the Southwest, Spanish colonial grants of land and the labor of people living on it, provided a feudal-like system of unfree labor, the encomienda and hacienda systems, followed under US rule by intensive debt peonage that amounted to slavery. And poor white Southerners joined blacks in sharecropping debt peonage.[19] Nor did it apply to men alone—women who worked as sharecropping wives or as domestics or in industry were often very far from free, even when they were not convicts.

IT MIGHT SEEM THAT, HAVING fast-forwarded to the present, the discussion of unfree labor should end, that the nation is now free of it. Unfortunately, that isn't the case. And it is still true that capitalism requires something extra from outside capitalist relations to prime the pump of wealth creation. Prison labor still provides some of that extra something.

Use of convict labor was kept briefly in check from the 1940s until the 1980s by labor unions' objections to job competition from unpaid labor. Organized labor has lost strength since the 1980s, however, so convict labor is again becoming a source of profit. There has been a sevenfold increase in incarceration since 1980, peaking in 2007 at 1.6 million in prison, but when jails are included the number is more like 2.2 million, and if all those under court supervision are included it is an estimated eight million.[20] Though overall prison incarceration has declined slightly, at this rate of decline it would take until 2166 to return to 1970 levels, and in places like Kentucky it is rising so rapidly that if the present rate continued, everyone in the state would be in jail by 2131.[21] The United States has the highest incarceration rate in the world, many times that of comparable countries, for instance about 5.5 times that of Canada.[22] Much of the rise has been due to the "War on Drugs," but Marie Gottschalk points out that even without counting those with drug charges, the US rate is higher than other countries, and also higher for whites than in other white majority countries.[23]

In 2010 convict labor was justified yet again in a federal court ruling, using the Thirteenth Amendment's provision for slavery.[24] It is now backed by legal requirements that all prisoners work if they are medically able, as certified by prison medical staff.[25] Federal and state prison industries function as corporations run by the prison and produce for sale an incredible range of products, ranging from sunglasses to electronic components for the military to deboned chicken to furniture, with pay in state prisons averaging in 2017 between $0.33 and $1.41 an hour. Profits are fed back into the prison system. Prisoners also work directly for the prison in service sector jobs such as cooking and cleaning, so that their labor subsidizes the prison. Pay in federal service sector prison jobs is between $0.12 and $0.40 an hour. In state prisons, such jobs, with a few exceptions, have a much wider range, from $0.12 to $2.00 an hour, although some states pay nothing at all.[26] People in Daviess County, Kentucky, clear roadside trash forty hours a week for $12.50 a month, of which half is taken for jail and county debts.[27]

Prison labor provides a controlled and extraordinarily cheap labor force for a wide range of industries, which now operate in state prisons or subcontract work to prisons. This is a labor force not only supplied by the state at great expense, but underwritten by tax write-offs and other subsidies for the corporations. For instance, companies can receive a write-off for hiring "risky" workers or keeping jobs in the United States rather than moving them to Mexico.[28] The Kentucky state government is now soliciting industries to set up operations in prisons. The state says prisoners would receive "near private sector wages," how near, and how much would be withheld, appears to be an open question.[29] Supposedly, corporations and private industries, as opposed to federal and state employers of prisoners, have to pay the prevailing wage for prison labor, as Kentucky says it will do. Reality is different. In Seattle, for instance, Boeing replaced people earning $30 an hour with inmates paid $7—most of which, in most states, would be confiscated by the state to pay for room and board, and by charging exorbitant prices for things like toothpaste, as well as for victim restitution.[30] Health and safety regulations are at best lax, and in some cases expose inmates to toxic conditions, such as when recycling electronic waste, or to dangerous ones, such as when they are put on firefighting teams.[31] By 2010 approximately 1.1 million prisoners were working full-time, either directly for the state in service sector jobs such as cooking and cleaning and in prison industries, or for private corporations inside or outside the prison.[32] Beyond even the federal and state prison numbers, are those of people in the rapidly expanding private for-profit prisons, which also operate their own industries or team up with a private business.[33] The organizers of the 2018 nationwide prison strike denounced all of this as "modern day slavery."[34] And, of course, prison slavery continues to be perfectly legal under the aegis of the Thirteenth Amendment.

Not only is prison labor profitable, but incarceration in itself is profitable. In choosing to privatize jails, prisons, and detention centers, the state also provides capitalists, most of whom are white, with the opportunity for immensely profitable investment. Punishing in private prisons is made even more profitable because their administrators assign added time for extremely minor conduct violations, thus keeping the prison operating at capacity and causing inmates to serve approximately 90 days more than they do in public prisons.[35] Punishing is, in fact, so profitable that, as journalist Aviva Shen writes, "The private prison industry spent millions seeking to increase sentences and incarcerate more people in order to increase the industry's profits" and to "sway the political process toward detention-focused policies."[36]

Just as the state enforced the sharecropping system for those outside of prison through force, it now enforces extremely cheap or even "volunteer" labor. People outside the prison on probation or parole are threatened with a return if they violate the terms of their release, and those terms frequently require getting and keeping a job—any job, regardless of pay, thus enabling a rush to the bottom.[37] Even imprisonment for debt for fines and costs has returned. The massive protests following the police shooting of Michael Brown, an unarmed young black man in Ferguson, Missouri, in August 2014, sparked a federal investigation into local policing and courts. That report revealed that the county government effectively supported itself on the backs of poor and mostly black citizens. Fees are often charged for failing to make a court date, or for court-mandated "services," such as probation supervision or providing and monitoring electronic ankle tags. These services are now operated by corporations for profit, which pay the county government for the right to make money off people who are arrested. Those sentenced to use these services but can't afford them are fined or jailed. Thus, both the county and service-providers have a major source of income in arresting and convicting people of color disproportionately—as in the days of convict leasing and debt peonage.[38]

Ferguson's system is merely a particularly egregious example of what sociologist Katherine Beckett and political scientist Naomi Murakawa describe as the "shadow carceral state," operating at the edges of the criminal justice system more generally. Its proceedings, defined as civil and administrative rather than penal, are not subject to due process rights, enabling the "ensnaring [of] an ever-larger share of the population through civil injunctions, legal financial obligations, and violations of administrative law." [39] Decreases in formal incarceration are being offset by these shadowy methods, and by intense supervision—for instance with electronic ankle tags—of those released or diverted from incarceration.[40]

Although the percentage of the total white population imprisoned is far lower than that of blacks, Native Americans, or Latinos, the majority of prisoners, both those in prison and those caught under the shadow of the carceral state, are white and generally poor.[41] Nevertheless, political rhetoric and media portrayals of criminals and prisoners focus on people of color, so that in the public imagination whites are not associated with prisons. Thus corporations, with a few modifications, are again able to take advantage of the Thirteenth Amendment and its provision for slavery without seriously threatening white privilege. Racism, token wages, the claim that such labor is voluntary and claims of job-training provide the cover needed in the post–civil rights era to deflect the public eye.

And, since the state has chosen an intense punishment regime, it needs lots of people to do the catching, processing, and warehousing of the people to be punished. Punishment, in other words, can provide a huge number of jobs—well over a million in the United States.[42] Most of the people who benefit from the jobs and the investment opportunities are white, particularly in the many prisons being placed in rural areas where prison employees are drawn from a largely white local population—another piece of white privilege. But this is a fraught privilege, as privilege generally is, bringing with it PTSD and rising rates of domestic violence.[43]

THERE IS YET ANOTHER SOURCE of seriously exploitable labor, again enabled by the state's laws and policies that limit people's rights so that they are close to unfree. And, of course, the state employs violence as needed for enforcement. The United States has a long history of dependence on "unfree waged labor," that is, labor performed at below-market wages under coercive conditions that make quitting or changing employers difficult or illegal. In other words, this is not a true capitalist wage relationship.[44] Immigrant workers, denied rights, are particularly vulnerable to such conditions. By the early 1900s, thousands of people were crossing the Southern border into the United States on labor contracts—enforced by vagrancy laws and a discriminatory justice system—that kept them virtual prisoners. This was followed by the Bracero Program, from the Second World War until 1964, which brought millions of Mexican workers to the United States under contracts that enforced their return to Mexico when no longer needed. While the program formally protected rights and guaranteed wages and decent working conditions, those rights were not enforced, making it impossible to strike, negotiate wages, or change employers, leaving the workers vulnerable to employers who cheated or abused them. Working in agriculture and on railroads, they, like other immigrant workers, joined convict laborers in underwriting the increasing industrialization of the United States.

Under recent presidents, enhanced border enforcement has made possible a new incarnation of "unfree wage workers," undocumented workers who are kept (mostly) under control by the threat of detention and deportation. Their work supplements the increased immigrant contract labor in the United States, which is nominally legal.[45] And if they're not able to disappear into the "shadow economy," where there are paid illegally low wages and receive no benefits, they are ever more likely to be arrested and housed in privately owned detention centers, which have been reaping huge rewards for housing detainees in abysmal conditions. Detention of undocumented workers has risen dramatically, going from a daily average of fifty-four people in 1981 to 32,095 in 2011, with the Trump administration announcing plans at one point to increase the number of slots (euphemistically called "beds") for detainees from the present 34,000 to 80,000. Criminal immigration prosecutions increased tenfold between 1986 and 2012, most involving minor crimes and even misdemeanors. Nevertheless, they carried with them the threat of severe punishment—exile from family and community through deportation.[46] The threat of ICE raids on homes and worksites, followed by detention and deportation, produces an exploitable immigrant population to replace the low-wage black labor that was expelled once the civil rights movement made ignoring black workers' rights a bit more difficult.[47] All of this enforces class, underwrites whiteness, and provides a pool of low-wage "voluntary" workers. These threats have become even more specifically racial with the advent of the Trump presidency, through both the president's rhetoric and the legitimizing of the racially oriented political and social movements that led to his election.

The laws criminalizing border crossings have been used to create yet another source of essentially enslaved labor, much to the benefit of the corporations that depend on them. On average, every day 5,500 immigrants in detention centers work for a dollar a day or less, which they need to buy necessities, such as soap and adequate food, which many detention centers fail to provide. These immigrants provide the labor required to keep private detention facilities operating—a cozy arrangement in which the state pays the corporation and inmates provide the labor needed to facilitate their own detention.[48] In 2017, this system was challenged in a class action lawsuit, claiming it violates the Trafficking Victims Protection Act, an outgrowth of the Thirteenth Amendment: detained immigrants have not been convicted of a crime and therefore are not constitutionally subject to forced or slave labor.[49]

While this incarnation of unfree labor applies to people who are not citizens, its presence may discipline citizens who will be more and more vulnerable to super-exploitation as the remnants of the social safety net are further shredded.[50] Serious exploitation can thus move a bit further up the class ladder, justified by racialized designations such as white trash, or by wars on terror or drugs, all designed to make certain insiders appear to be like outsiders, undeserving of full rights.

RACIAL IDEAS ARE STILL USED TO justify super-exploitation of both blacks and immigrants.[51] Racialization is a form of "Othering," claiming that certain groups are not part of "us," not part of the people, and therefore not deserving. It is generally used both to justify extreme exploitation and to legitimize sovereignty by punishing these Others and defending the nation from them—think of the Scottish witchcraft panics.[52] In the United States the claim is that those Others are not the real citizens (even if legally they are), not the birthright ones, whose ancestors fought and died for this country, the founders of the nation, who made it grow. Nor are they the ones who raise dynamic, intelligent, creative leaders, scientists, inventors, business magnates, the people who once "made America great," and, says President Trump, will "Make America Great Again." Again? Does he mean the America of indenture, of slavery, of land-grabbing, of elite corruption, of the Trail of Tears? Or the America of sharecropping, of convict leasing, of Jim Crow segregation, of women denied rights and voice, of cotton mill workers dying of brown lung and miners of black lung, of wars in which ordinary people gain nothing, but die to protect elite interests? Or does he mean the white middle- and upper-class America that thrived on the value drained out of all those people? I can imagine a vast multitude of voices from the past wondering exactly which era of American history he is referring to as "great."

So let's look at immigrant exploitation through the lens of the past. Though not actually enslaved, immigrants can provide some of the benefits of slavery that have been discussed in this book.[53] Like the people who have been captured, enslaved, and brought into a polity, the costs of bringing immigrants through childhood to the age of usefulness are borne by some other country. They are, in this sense, a cheap source of labor. Like the enslaved, they can be denied adequate resources for dependably successful child rearing and educating. In the United States this has meant poor healthcare, early deaths, high infant mortality, underfunded schools, and high poverty rates.

But none of that matters much in terms of capitalism and the state because immigrants are easily replaceable through laws about borders and the conditions under which they can be crossed. Immigrants can be chased out of the country if political or economic conditions make that desirable for elite interests, unlike blacks, who, though also racialized, are citizens. And that gives blacks the dubious right to be imprisoned instead—when not needed they are likely to be defined as criminals and expensively warehoused in prisons. Immigrants don't need to be placated, unlike the "true insiders" on whom elites depend, whose support they need to legitimize their rule, who can vote, and who can't be kicked back across a border if they revolt. They are not legally defined as members of the polity, who, in order to prevent revolt, do need, unless imprisoned, to have at least minimally adequate access to resources for raising families and caring for themselves. Members need also to have at least a mildly reasonable belief in the likelihood of joining or continuing in the less exploited labor force. The black-white racial divide is thus reinforced by that of immigrant versus native-born. Together these divisions provide those who profit from the current system with the attitudes they need to divide and conquer. In the case of healthcare, for instance, universal care can be denied by playing on the racially loaded idea that some people don't deserve healthcare because they are too lazy or stupid to make a living and get insurance for themselves.

We have seen how laws in the past were written to provide criminals who could be turned into cheap or unfree labor—all the way from

England's vagrancy laws to Jim Crow. That process is ongoing, and without it white privilege would collapse, and so would racialized cheap labor. Criminalizing certain drugs has laid the groundwork for producing a reliable supply of prisoners—users, sellers, and people engaged in the violence of drug-related business competition. Requiring the right piece of paper when crossing the border produces more people defined as criminal, enhanced now by the intensified surveillance of the War on Terror. Beckett and Herbert have pointed out that "nearly all of the increase in incarceration rates is a consequence of policy shifts rather than an increase in crime rates."[54]

The work of scholars in a variety of social science disciplines, including Aviva Chomsky, Joseph Nevins, and Nicolas De Genova, on the creation of the Mexico-US boundary demonstrates that, in relation to the criminalization of immigrants, "the state has not so much responded to a 'crisis of illegality' as created it" through laws and policies enforcing that boundary.[55] Nevins documents the role of state actors in creating a panic about immigration; Otto Santa Ana shows that the media reflects the views of political elites, shaping the attitudes of the general public.[56] Sang Hea Kil and Cecilia Menjivar point out that the militarization of the border has created criminals.[57] Without such laws there simply wouldn't be enough people defined as dangerous to provoke the fear needed to demonstrate sovereignty through protection. When internal enemies were needed, as several other scholars document, politicians and the media—under elite control—worked hard to create them. For example, Wajahat Ali, with a group of journalists and scholars, documents the production of Islamophobia by think tanks, foundations, and politicians to frighten the US public into acceptance of Homeland Security's attack on civil rights while claiming to protect them.[58] Those agents of the state involved in panic production, allied with some news corporations and aided by the reproduction of false information on social media, are the primary source of fear of illegals. Through the lens of the past, this looks like the propaganda that used fear to bring resistant colonists to the Separatist cause, against their own interests.

That the state organizes the production of criminals, race, and fear is mainly invisible to the majority of those not targeted as dangerous. Their belief in the legitimacy of their privilege comes from not seeing the fact that a massive amount of punishment upholds their privilege and feeds the capitalism of which they, higher on the food chain, are comparative beneficiaries. One of the privileges that goes with whiteness, particularly when combined with at least a little class privilege, and to some extent with middle-class status regardless of race, is that ability to deny, to not know, to let the hidden remain hidden. [59]

SO FAR, I HAVE BEEN TALKING PRIMARILY about the continuing existence of unfree labor. But that unfree labor today exists in coordination with apparently voluntary waged labor organized by dispossession, and that is what most readers have probably experienced directly. So, at this point we turn to wage labor to see how it looks through the lens of the past. I am going to argue that American lives are more conditioned by the existence of unfree labor and punishment—the force that creates it—than many might think.

As we have seen over and over, providing labor for wealth extraction is an essential function of the state, dependent on the state's monopoly on the use of force—to punish the disobedient and noncompliant and put down revolts. A strong state with a solid monopoly on the use of force and a well-developed class system can keep insiders dispossessed, despite their actual rights of citizenship. Dispossessed, they apparently voluntarily turn to wage labor, at whatever wage they can extract from the employer. And that is basically what class is—a system of dispossession without direct coercion that is only possible in a state that enables ownership of the means of production for the few, patrols the dispossession of the rest, manages the uneven distribution of income and status among the dispossessed, and perhaps provides moderators for disputes among competing elites.

This system is backed by ideologies, beliefs such as "the poor will always be with us." Such beliefs make the class system, with the poverty it inevitably creates, seem natural, not the result of choices made by people with power.[60] It is reinforced by racial beliefs, by continued faith in the American Dream and American exceptionalism, and by the belief that wealth is a result of individual brilliance and hard work. It keeps many from noticing that poverty is useful, just as it was for the English elites who said, back in John Radford's day, "Only the poor can make wealth." And as it was for the American elites who said slavery would die out because there would be so many poor white people that wages would drop to the point that hired labor would be cheaper than slave labor. Without the threat of poverty would people be willing to indenture themselves to the military, risking disability, post-traumatic stress disorder, and their lives? All this in return for an education or job training, forfeiting many civil rights, including the right to quit or to disobey, thus putting themselves outside the capitalist wage relationship? And without the poverty that produces people who can be criminalized, where would the prison industry be? Those incarcerated bodies are a source of profit from outside of capitalism. And who would clean hotel rooms, do back-breaking work in nursing homes or in agriculture, even work at daycare centers? It is poverty that supplies people "willing" to do the underpaid and low-paid work that is the basis of wealth creation.

All of this depends at base on dispossession, a situation most Americans take so for granted as the backdrop to their lives that it barely rises to conscious awareness. This appears to be just the way things are. It is getting a job and accepting wages, it is the law, it is contracts, it is the sacred concept of private ownership of the means of production. That ownership of the means of production, supported legally by the state, enables the owners, not workers, to take total possession of the value employees produce. In return, workers receive in compensation only as much as worker resistance and occasional revolt have made necessary to convince them to remain on the job.

We've seen how dispossession was fought, but nonetheless was created for many. Native people are still fighting, both for enforcement of their treaty rights and to protect the environment—frustrating capitalist exploitation of resources. Most people in the United States have ancestors who were dispossessed, perhaps several generations ago, perhaps more recently. That condition of dispossession can be made to continue, passed on through generations, only because active steps are constantly taken by elites to keep the dispossessed at bay.[61] Laws about property, about trespassing, about labor contracts and labor relations, about border crossing, often blatantly lobbied for by those with the money to promote their own interests, and all backed by the power to punish, help to police dispossession.[62] But with time this secondary coercion—the coercion that follows the initial dispossession—becomes invisible and class begins to seem natural, accompanied by what seems a natural and necessary protection of citizens' rights to private property. That invisible coercion is accompanied by raced and gendered ideologies that appear to substantiate the naturalness of class. That powerful combination can make it appear inevitable that those Others are the ones at the bottom of the pile, the ones who provide that something extra from outside capitalism itself, and who are the primary target for punishment.[63] Should all else fail, there is the deployment of the military or militarized police, as we saw in Ferguson, Missouri, in 2014.

So today in the United States there are those who have been selected as Other, as targets for the state's demonstration of sovereignty. Those who have not been so selected, like myself, are somewhat protected by the construction of race and class that was ongoing through these tales, and continues to morph today. Because those not targeted are less likely to experience directly the violence of the state (exercised either legally, though often with racial and class bias, through the courts, or illegally, such as through police murders) and because their loyalty is courted by the state with legitimizing ideologies, they are likely to take for granted that the state punishes. They see its right to do so as legitimate—but punishment is seen as far from legitimate by many of those who are targeted.[64] And though it is obvious that state agents exercise force in order to punish, many of the protected are only rarely actively aware of that fact.

Most of those in the United States who have not been Othered, unless their loved ones or community are directly subjected to it, are barely conscious of the ways in which a state's ruling elite maintains its monopoly on the use of punishing force, both internally within the borders of the territory they rule and externally against designated out-siders. That those living within that territory are not allowed, except under specific, state-permitted conditions, to use force seems natural to many of those who have some protection, even though some argue about what those state-permitted conditions should be. For most, it seems perfectly natural that state-designated individuals and institu-tions act with force in the name of the state.

Schools, much of the media, and many churches work to contain thoughts about the state's use of force within the framework of the social contract—the belief that citizens have made a contract with the state for their own benefit. The contract allows the state to use force to punish, supposedly for the benefit of all—to maintain order and safety, to allow business to proceed, to make "civilized" life possible. In return for this security, the citizens allow a small number of power-holders to govern, to extract wealth from workers, and to punish those who are believed to threaten or violate that contract. Few, regardless of their position, see that this system of dependence on wages in return for labor results from a dispossession that the state itself carefully enforces.

Dispossession is masked by the protection of private property. That protection guards your ownership of your home if you are a home-owner. But at the same time it protects and coercively enforces the distinction between owning and not owning the means of production. Capitalism can't exist without it. The condition of not-owning the means of production feels natural to those raised that way. Thus class itself feels natural. Working for wages feels natural, as does the fact that some people's wages are astronomically higher than those of others. This system has become naturalized, so ingrained that most people, unless they or their community directly experience the coercion involved, rarely question dispossession or recognize it as an ongoing process. Thus there is little consideration of alternatives, such as a more communal ownership of the resources on which we all depend. Dependence on wages isn't recognized as being on a continuum of dis-possession at whose bottom is slavery. Nor is there much recognition of the continued maneuvering on the part of the state and the capitalist class to keep in place the system of accumulation by dispossession.

BUT THERE IS A CAN OF WORMS HERE: insiders, as citizens, have rights. The state needs to balance between providing adequate force to control a labor supply and providing enough care, protection, and access to resources to keep people accepting the state as legitimate.

Creating the poverty that gets insiders to allow themselves to be super-exploited in preference to actual starvation requires violation of what would seem to be the state's duty to protect. This means the state has a conflict. On the one hand, it needs to appear to provide care and protection to maintain its legitimacy in the eyes of the people who do the work of wealth production. But on the other, as the tool of the elites who benefit from that wealth, the state must produce a cheap and docile workforce or lose its legitimacy in the eyes of the people with the power to determine its sovereignty. It must, in other words, get people to agree that they have but limited rights to the fruits of their labor. Their sweat, skill, and knowledge go to make wealth for others, and they must put up with the consequences, which for many means a life of serious struggle and potentially early death. So there are two requirements: first, the need to at least appear to provide care and protection, and to actually provide enough of the real thing to keep most people from noticing the coercion, doubting the reality of care, and then perhaps revolting. Second, the need to provide cheap labor. But providing cheap labor *causes* the suffering that needs to be disguised by care; creating a cheap labor force can itself lead to the doubting that could topple the whole system. So how to handle two requirements that are in direct conflict with each other? [65]

Part of the answer lies in the administration of care and coercion differentially according to a person's placement in the graded hierarchies of race, class, and gender.[66] Larger "doses" of care go to those higher in those hierarchies, larger doses of coercion go to those lower in the hierarchy and to those who fail to live up to the standards of behavior that are said to mark compliant individuals. Larger doses of care and protection are administered to two major groups. One is the members of a social control class—police, social workers, managers, teachers, judges—buffering the capitalist class from direct contact with the more exploited members of the working class.[67] The other group that receives greater care and protection is composed of people whose skills are critical in the technologies, planning, and engineering that make labor more profitable.

The usefulness of these two groups depends on their active consent and cooperation; alienating them is therefore a risky proposition. The coercion they experience must be well disguised with care that is in some degree real. In addition, to make it possible for the social control group to administer coercion with a clear conscience to those who have been Othered through various combinations of poverty, race, and gender, this too must be at least minimally framed as care. Justice Studies scholar Judah Schept shows how juvenile detention, for instance, becomes not coercion but treatment and rehabilitation, thus manufacturing consent and avoiding alienating those who might otherwise be inclined to question the very basis of punitive coercion.[68] Naomi Murakawa documents how promoting the belief that safety is the primary civil right has manufactured consent for increasing surveillance and coercion, described as fulfilling the state's obligation to protect—to care.[69]

However, gaining the active consent of those whose low-wage labor is the basis for wealth creation can be a bit impractical, given their likely degree of suffering. Too much care, by state or by employer, and the flow of wealth up the class structure will be seriously impeded. But too little care could, as they used to say, produce a communist under every bed. So how to get people, particularly those at the bottom of the system who are paid literally too little to live on, to be compliant?

We can use anthropologist Maggie Dickinson's work on food stamps and the need for them as an example of this problem.[70] The 1996 Personal Responsibility and Work Opportunity Act, meant to end welfare as we know it, forced people into low-wage jobs in a pretty blatant exercise of coercion, carrying the risk of greater unrest. There was too little care and too much coercion—the dosages had to be adjusted. The cure was a dramatic increase in the provision of food stamps going to people coerced into jobs that paid too little to keep food reliably on the table. In essence the state provides welfare not to workers but to employers, who don't have to pay wages sufficient to keep their employees and their families alive. Coercion for the workers, welfare for the employers—and it gets described as care, and is experienced as care by some food stamp recipients, but also by the administrators themselves. More important, that appearance of care can assuage the potential guilt of the better-off who might be concerned about those on low wages. Coercion, the iron fist, is disguised by the velvet glove of rhetoric about care. When such velvet glove strategies are successful, people with their low wages keep working, perhaps aware of the coercion, but also kept from revolt by the state's provision of at least a little care and protection (in this case protection from employers whose wages would starve them).

But what about those who have "failed" in their obligation to serve the processes of wealth production, or have done so in criminalized enterprises, or who don't meet carefully standardized modes of "appropriate" behavior? They also receive graded amounts of coercion and care, but the iron fist is far more in evidence than the velvet glove. Children, for instance, are coercively removed from homes in the name of care, often for reasons that have to do with poverty, such as nonstandard childcare arrangements. The child could have stayed at home rather than be shipped off to foster care if the state provided quality daycare for all (as it does in many countries).[71] People are sent to prison for being mentally ill; for sleeping while homeless; for standing on the wrong street corner.[72] Or they sell sexual labor, or sell their labor in criminalized enterprises (many of which, if legal, would cause far less harm than many legal enterprises, such as manufacturing tobacco products and alcohol). Many of these enterprises, such as drug dealing, are violent simply because they are illegal, as liquor dealing was during Prohibition.

So the state creates criminals and it creates the consequences of poverty, all at far greater expense than providing either the social services or eliminating the poverty and inequality that result in people being placed in the hands of the state.[73] Anthropologist Faye Harrison has argued that such structural violence, as well as the direct state violence that accompanies the enforcement of the inequalities on which neoliberalism and globalization depend, in the United States and elsewhere, is a human rights issue. Thus, for resisting these policies, "at their most effective, human rights are a moral and legal device for constraining the flow of unreasonable and illegitimate state power."[74] In a scathing indictment of the United States' poverty level and of the human rights abuses that flow from it, the Special Rapporteur to the UN Human Rights Council wrote in 2018, "The existence of extreme poverty is a political choice made by those in power. With political will, it could readily be eliminated."[75] Instead, the United States incarcerates.

The coercion of incarceration is seen by most as the state fulfilling its side of the social contract, bringing law and order to protect the compliant from criminals and other dangerous types. Those dangerous types are never the far more deadly corporate elites who, for instance, have ignored safety regulations so extensively that one chicken processing plant's machinery has amputated the limbs of 750 workers over the course of seven years—all made possible by loopholes, weak enforcement, and falsified records.[76] The apparent protection from those the state has defined as dangerous is part of the care that states are obligated to provide, helping to create a degree of consent among the more privileged. At the same time the combination of care and coercion can induce behavior deemed appropriate, that is, appropriately in service to the capitalist system, among some of the less privileged. Failure can get you defined as legally negligent or criminal; following the rules leaves you with only the option of accepting whatever degree of care the state is willing to provide—that is, whatever degree of care the state can be pushed into providing.

These graded hierarchies define those who are to be well protected as deserving and identify them as different from the undeserving Others who are to be coerced. And since, as I've noted, those who are protected are likely to feel that the coercion has nothing to do with them, they can ignore it: a classic tactic of divide and rule. Graded hierarchies are part of how the state deals with the contradiction of policies that damage the very people the state is supposed to protect. If you give more protection to some, their actual coerced dispossession is nearly always unrecognized and unacknowledged, ensuring allegiance and legitimation for elite rule. And you give more coercion—punishment—to those who won't or can't be compliant. That brings us to the second part of the answer to how the state can exist with the contradictions inherent in capitalism: In reality, prisons and punishment have a great deal to do with *all* Americans.

PRISONS HAVE BECOME A CORE institution of society, "generative hubs of state sanctioned means of governance" in the world's most punishing state.[77] They are not marginal or extreme, they are central to the functioning of society in the United States. And that means that they affect all Americans, every day, no matter how far those without loved ones in prison may think themselves from prison walls.

Most obviously, prisons are the site of state power coming to rest directly in people's lives, within the prisons themselves and in the communities from which prisoners come—largely poor communities, white, black, and Latinx, that is, the communities of the most exploited citizens. Within prisons, state power is directed at creating submissive, self-governing citizens who take full responsibility for their criminally defined actions and ignore the inequalities of the context in which their actions took place. This pressure is both gendered and racialized.[78] Women are to conform to a white middle-class updated version of the old Cult of Domesticity that now entails working outside the home while providing "appropriate" care and guidance to children. The pressure to conform to these expectations is intense. Men are to perform an emasculated submission to a male power structure, a submission that, for blacks, reverberates with the proper, in white eyes, behavior for black men under Jim Crow. This training is meant to produce self-surveillance, individuals who will accept authority, who will be productive workers unlikely to cause trouble about labor conditions or wages outside of prison. They will blame themselves, their mistakes, their poor decisions, or their lack of effort if they find themselves in oppressive and exploitative situations. They will accept capitalist, racialized patriarchy.

But regardless of whether individual prisoners actually buy into the model that is being pushed on them, when they leave prison they carry with them the knowledge of that model, bringing it into the larger community. So do the corrections officers, the job counselors, the social workers, and the probation officers—everyone even remotely connected to the justice system. And that means pretty much everyone in the United States—your aunt who is a social worker, your classmate who ended up in juvenile detention, your encounter with a traffic cop, your friend who had jury duty. With even those distant connections comes the hegemonic discourse that says if you are good and work hard you will succeed, so if you don't succeed, especially if you end up in jail, it is no one's fault but your own, and it certainly has nothing to do with a rigged justice system, racial oppression, or a seriously tilted playing field.[79]

This narrative of individual full responsibility, of fault and redemption, has permeated communities and serves as a challenge to those who point out the otherwise obvious alternative way of looking at the problems of communities of color and of poor whites.[80] This narrative—that the justice system works and that those caught in its net can use only their own bad choices as explanation—plays a critical ideological role in governance. Although this has been threatened somewhat by a heightened awareness of injustice and inequality in the wake of Trump's presidency, talk about capitalism's dependence on inequality and the carceral state's enforcement of that inequality continues to look silly to many. Tolerance of such talk, at least if the speaker is not poor, appears to be spreading in what may prove to be a window of opportunity for change. Nevertheless, the narrative of personal responsibility still allows a wide swath of the public to dismiss those who bring up such issues. It means that when those who suffer talk about inequality, about injustice, about the far from level playing field, they can be framed as whiners who evade responsibility.

This narrative also functions ideologically to justify laws that, when unevenly enforced, target particular populations to be removed from the streets and warehoused, with civil rights denied. It allows those whose work involves the enforcement of inequality, from judges to prison guards, to believe in the righteousness of their work.[81] Without that belief, the prison as a system of governance could be in jeopardy, and with it the whole system of punishment on which the state

depends. That overall system is actually far more important in producing the docile workforce capitalism requires than the redesigning of
individuals in prison.

The prison produces governability throughout the nation, not just
among those who have gone through the prison system. It is foundational to a capitalist system in which class, not direct force, is used to
create a labor force. Those laws that enforce dispossession and the
apparent necessity of prison for those who challenge or opt out or take
inadmissible routes to sustain themselves, make all the punishing seem
reasonable. Perhaps it even provides the sacrificial victims that magi-
cally justify state sovereignty by cleansing the nation of the "pollution"
that can cause gods and spirits to withdraw their favor—all reminiscent of Powhatan sacrificing and Scottish witch hunting.[82] After all, if
you are among those who are in the more protected category, the laws
and the punishing are what supposedly keep you and your possessions
safe. Those outside that category may see things quite differently. But if
you buy into the idea that you are protected, not recognizing that those
same laws and punishments also dispossess you, it is almost impossible
for you to even consider challenging your own dispossession. Thus
at least the white middle class is kept compliant—a compliance that
is today shaken by capitalism's blatant favoring of the rich in the face
of economic insecurity for everyone else, with consequences for state
legitimacy and punishment.

Prison, the punishing it inflicts, and the hegemonic discourse about
personal responsibility it enables, is thus central to the state's fulfillment
of its function in governance, that of providing a labor supply. Prison
maintains class itself, as well as the racialized and race-like divides that
make class appear natural. None of this would be possible without the
state's power to punish in order to enforce the laws that make people
vulnerable. This hegemony of these racial, sexist, and classist ideologies and fears contributes to keeping those outside of prison from
protesting their own dispossession. Prisons do indeed matter, deeply.

AND IF THE PRISON IS CENTRAL TO THE US state then we need

to look again at the concept of the state, going back to the introduction for these tales. Throughout the book I have been using the term "the state," probably without raising questions about what I mean specifically—but it *should* raise questions. It is a term we take for granted. It's the government, it's the land and people within our borders, it's our defense against enemies. But if you push a bit, the idea of a "state" is problematic. You can't touch it, you can't see it. So what is it that does all this punishing?[83] There is a considerable literature, both inside anthropology and in other disciplines, concerned with pinning down just what a state is.[84] Is punishment carried out by a "state" or, as some have suggested, by a bureaucracy posing as a state, or by a regime using the "state" as an ideological fiction, or maybe by a "protection racket"?[85] Regardless of how states are defined, however, punishing is critical to "stateness" and to carrying out the will of the elite of the nation. But in our daily lives we simply know that punishment awaits, or should await, those who "transgress."

My take on the arguments is to see the use of "the state" as an abstraction, or maybe more accurately as a euphemism. Saying "the state" lets us refer to a set of social relations that constitute elite rule—the control of the few over the lives, fortunes, and futures of the rest of us—without actually mentioning those rulers, as if the power they exercise is somehow distinct from them. The "state" becomes an almost supernatural presence, which helps justify, a bit as religion can, the power of the individuals who happen to be wielding the tools of governing. If, as Abrams maintains, the ideological function of the state is "legitimating the illegitimate," masking "the pretensions of regimes to be states," then reference to the state acts as a "master metaphor of legitimacy."[86] It invokes the authority of that supernatural entity to "manufacture consent" to actions we might well question without that authority.[87]

If the state is actually a regime, the implication in a republic is that a governing class acts, using economic and political power, to create a framework that operates to extract wealth. As a class, they have a vested interest in maintaining that framework, despite their often-conflicting individual interests. With the authority and cover conveyed by the state the regime can orchestrate a state bureaucracy to perform its primary duties. It must provide—and mask—the force necessary to shift value from the people who do the work into the hands of the elites who control the means of production. And it must protect, with force if necessary, the elites' rights to their control of the means of production. We have encountered that process over and over throughout these ancestor tales. Much scholarship on states and state formation examines the role of coercive force in creating and maintaining the inequality and status differences that enable expropriation and maintain stratification. As I've argued, the power to punish is the essential tool that makes this possible.[88] Without such a system, the severe stratification that defines a state would be impossible. Those who are exploited, being the vast majority of the population, would simply repossess themselves of the means of production.

But as we also have seen, the state's legitimacy depends on the effectiveness with which it maintains an orderly society, providing its citizens the local peace needed to raise families and to fulfill the state's requirement of taxes and the elites' requirement of labor without fearing that even more is going to be taken from them by marauding neighbors or outsiders. That is to say, the structure of the state depends on maintaining public order. This is a service of enormous value to those citizens who get to live their lives in comparative security. But public order also enhances the orderly flow of value to the owners of the means of production, and is thus of far less value to those subjected to the poverty or punishment on which that flow depends. The more intense the inequality that the state is sheltering in the interests of its elites, the more intense the accompanying punishment regime. But what happens when the legitimacy of that control is threatened?

When questions of legitimacy arise, as they have been, especially since the 2008 recession, when it appears that the state is failing to uphold its side of the social contract, that it is failing to protect, then the state takes steps to refurbish its mask of legitimacy. So, for instance, let's look at the United States when its defeat in Vietnam caused that mask to slip at the same time that the continued viability of the social structure appeared to be under threat. There was the civil rights movement, the antiwar movement, women talking back to patriarchy. There were riots sparked by police violence but propelled by intense black resistance to the declining value of the civil rights so recently procured and to the dire poverty that followed as blacks were expelled from the formal labor market. The state's response was increased punishment—the wars on drugs and on crime, justified by claims of black criminality and rampant drug use and enabled by changing laws to create more criminals.[89] Blacks were clearly targeted, as numerous researchers have demonstrated in painstaking detail.[90]

Propaganda played on fear among economically and racially insecure whites, and the cry became ever louder for a punishing national cleansing to restore the "greatest nation on earth"—that is, to give more material basis to white privilege through the punishment and deportation or incarceration of those scapegoated for the decline of the nation.[91] Thus punishment rapidly escalated for two groups in particular: blacks and immigrants, both racially defined providers of cheap labor, both defined as deleterious to the nation unless they were working in the formal economy, both historically defined as the usual suspects.[92] But the wars on drugs and crime, the incarceration, amounting to mass incarceration, didn't seem to make most citizens feel much safer. Worries that the United States was slipping from its position of world domination added to the mix, particularly after 9/11.

In recent years, the state has responded by dramatically increasing the militarization of the border with Mexico, providing apparent proof that protection is real, that the state is still sovereign despite globalization and the emergence of competition for the position of global hegemon.[93] If the state had failed to protect against real external enemies in airplanes, and was unable to win against imagined enemies such as Afghans, it could at least demonstrate its ability to punish by appearing to protect its citizens from imagined enemies crossing the US border—a tactic Trump has played to the hilt, along with his international sabre rattling. Maintaining a border is, after all, a major component of sovereignty and a major component of the protection states are supposed to provide. Militarizing it appears to do just that.[94] So long as enough people buy into these tactics, the emphasis on law and order, homeland security, and illegal aliens keeps immigrant labor and incarcerated labor cheap; it maintains white privilege, it legitimizes the state, and it nourishes capitalism.

ALL OF THIS HAS BEEN NEEDED because a regime, particularly one in a democratic republic, needs to be accepted as reasonably benign, working for the general good. Otherwise the right of rulers to rule can be questioned; they don't have birthright or the church or the divine right of kings to fall back on for legitimation. So all the violence that maintains the inequality capitalism depends on needs to be masked, and when unmasked it needs to appear justified. As we've seen throughout this book, racial ideologies have been used throughout US history to make that justification easier.

This explains, for instance, the media emphasis on the violence of some of the black protesters at the time of the Ferguson revolt and on the possibility that Michael Brown had done a bit of shoplifting, framing him as a person unworthy of the presumption of innocence in his encounter with the officer who killed him. The mainstream media paid some attention to the viciousness of the militarized policing that followed the extrajudicial murder of Michael Brown by an agent of the state, but much less to the viciousness of the local racial regime, where the roots of the protest lay. This reporting was underwritten by the unacknowledged and often unrecognized white assumption that black men are inherently dangerous and that black men and women are inclined to criminal behavior. The public perception of the events in Ferguson was being shaped by reporters who may or may not have been aware of their own biases, by media owners and managers who chose which reports to air, and by politicians who chose which reports to emphasize. The devastating criticisms of the white regime in Ferguson that were detailed in the report of the nonpartisan Ferguson Commission and in the Department of Justice investigation of the Ferguson justice system that should have corrected those perceptions received very little mainstream attention.[95]

Thus the manufacture of consent is the safest route to legitimation, the route of an ideology, of beliefs that act as a lens through which policies of the elite and the actions of their agents appear benign. If this works, people learn to be comfortably ignorant. Most Americans do know something of the obvious acts of violence backing injustice and inequality in US history—but only as isolated factoids. They aren't seen as part of a larger pattern, a pattern of continuous violence that is ongoing today: the forced dispossession of the Native peoples of this land, the enslavement of Africans, the forced indenture of English convicts and children, the lynching and executions of Jim Crow. Some know about the enforced servitude of Indians of the Southwest under Spanish and then American rule, the confinement and dispossession of Japanese and Japanese Americans during the Second World War, the near enslavement of Chinese railroad workers. But most people don't see the violence involved today in mass incarceration and immigrant deportation as a continuation of that pattern, as is the state's failure to protect people of color, and some poor whites, from unauthorized murder by its own agents.[96] Even people who are uncomfortably aware of the way vagrancy laws and debt peonage replaced slavery with convict labor and sharecropping bondage may remain comfortably ignorant about the reincarnation of coerced labor in prisons and in the gross mistreatment of immigrant labor.

But beyond the clear use of obvious force there is also a masked violence, a daily violence that accompanies the status quo, a violence that is critical in maintaining the privilege that accompanies whiteness, a privilege that only partially coincides with middle class status, and that occasionally crosses racial lines.[97] It is the violence created by inequality itself—structural violence—the continuous low-level violence required to maintain inequality: incarceration, low wages, violence against women, social service confiscation of children rather than provision of resources, deaths from poverty and discrimination, the maintenance of a school-to-prison pipeline, the daily struggle to survive without attracting the dangerous attention of the state. But it is largely hidden violence, hidden, that is, from those with a bit of privilege. It is presented instead as "law and order," or as the unfortunate collateral damage that accompanies a benevolent, or at least inevitable, capitalism, or as the fault of the individuals involved. It isn't seen as part and parcel of the Trail of Tears and the Middle Passage. With consent successfully manufactured, people can't see the violence required to provide elites with cheap labor and cheap resources, and the somewhat privileged with some degree of comfort.

But the people in these tales can bear witness to the foundations of the present; this is not new, nor should it be hard to see. Venis, or perhaps her ancestors, wrenched from their homeland, and Adam, with Judah and Depha, born enslaved and kept enslaved, dispossessed of the right to even their own bodies—they can all bear witness to the violence it takes to provide elites with the labor they want. Maybe X Radford, indentured, would join them. The Powhatan, the Cherokee, Tecumseh and the Shawnee—all can tell of the violence it takes to dispossess people of land on which that labor will be used. Sarah McDavid, subject to the daily low-level violence of inequality imposed by the clan system, might talk of the violence of witch hunting as it enabled the dispossession of women and the eventual domination of male laborers in capitalism's wage relationship. X Radford and John Radford might tell of the hangings of men that were part of that process. Sarah McDavid and X Davidson, her husband, might talk of the futile wars that drove their son, Alexander I, to sell himself in order to flee a punishing state. Little did they know that he would, himself, eventually join the punishers. Nor that their grandson, Alexander II, would become part of an American elite that, under the influence of a developing capitalism, was bent on maintaining the rights of private property and the rights to the labor of the dispossessed—much as was happening in the Highlands with clan chiefs like George Mackenzie.

Alexander II might have opposed the power of those elites as a Regulator, but he was himself quite probably involved in dispossessing Cherokees, and certainly in keeping Judah, Depha, and eleven others enslaved. Venis and Adam might have heard tales of that early revolt when Africans and dispossessed English joined together. John Radford might tell of Bacon's Rebellion too, but not from the perspective of the dispossessed. He and his progeny, like Alexander I's, would experience the whiteness and white privilege that developed afterward, which gave protection and prevented further revolt, and helped the elite maintain control of both blacks and whites. Alexander II, like his father in Scotland, was caught in the midst of a war for elite benefit, this one made possible, at least partially, by manipulation of the flipside of whiteness—the fear of blacks. And then there is Sarah Ellis, marrying Alexander I, and Anna Bridges and Mary Ellis, marrying Alexander II. What might they say, or carefully not say, about the exploitation of women by husbands? Venis might tell them another way is possible, as it was in Igboland. What might those slaveholding women say about their own exploitation of other women? And all of them involved in the violence of the state, both the direct coercive violence and the daily, less obvious violence of the status quo, which they all, except perhaps the enslaved, must have seen as at least partially legitimate. Much violence had gone into manufacturing their consent.

IT IS WHEN THIS DAILY VIOLENCE FAILS, when the ideology that masks it loses legitimacy even in the eyes of the more privileged, that the tanks begin to roll, most generally first against racialized Others. Violence, like that in Ferguson, is not new. It punished, but it also sent a message to the more privileged, as it did after the attack on the Boston Marathon in 2013, when tanks rolled through the streets of Watertown, Massachusetts: the state has your back, it will protect you and your property from thugs, looters, and terrorists; it will protect your privilege. But should you cease to be compliant, the state is sovereign; it can decide who shall live and who shall die; the tanks could come for you. It is seeing that larger pattern that could make a better world possible, for what we can't see, we can't change. Making visible the pattern of dispossession and of the violence and punishing required to create and maintain it, seeing the forces that were at work throughout the stories of my ancestors—of all Americans' ancestors—morphed, yes, but still very much alive and well today, that is why these tales of the past matter.

INVENTORY OF THE ESTATE OF ALEXANDER DAVIDSON
Spotsylvania County, Virginia, Will Book A, 487

February 13, 1748 then appraised ye Estate of Alexander Davidson

As follows: Negro Woman named Venis	£30.0.0
One Negro Boy named Adam	25.0.0
Two Cows two yearlings & a Young Steare	4.10.0
One Sorrel horse Flaxen mare & tack.	3.0.0
One Bay horse & mare & horse colt	5.0.0
One Feather bed and Furniture	4.0.0
One Do & Do [ditto & ditto]	3.0.0
One Do & Do	2.0.0
Six Sides of Sole Leather & 8 sides of Curried Leather	3.10.0
Two raw hides	0.8.0
A parcel of old Pewter	0.16.0
Two old Chests & Small Box	0.8.0
Two Stone Butter pottes two small Stone Bottles	0.6.0
One Doz. Glass Bottles & some old Earthenware	0.3.6
One old Gun & [?] sword	1.0.0
One old Spice Mortar & Pestle & one Small Looking Glass	0.2.3
Two & 1/2 Shoelasts 15/ [?] a Doubblersott? of Shoemaking	
Tools £5.0. [?] . . .	2.0.0
One handsaw Auger & hatchet	0.6.0
One Box Iron & heel [?] 3/ and old Warming Pan 0/6	0.6.6
A parcel of old Books	0.16.0
Half a Doz. Knives & ? & one small Gimblett	0.3.0
Half a Doz. Flagg [?] Bottomed Chairs & a table	0.7.6[?]
Two Iron Pottes & [?] hooks one frying pan & fleshing(?)	
Fork one Ladle & an Iron Skillett	0.12.0
One Cubbard or safe	0.13.0
Three piggins a washing tub & an old Spinning wheel	0.7.6
One old saddle Bridle & horse Bell	0.8.6
	£89.17.9

SARAH DAVIDSON ADM   EDWD HERNDON
                         THOS BLASSINGAM
                          THOS BURBRIDGE

NOTE: The paper in this section of the Will Book was in bad condition and the handwriting particularly cramped. This and other court records had been buried before the courthouse burned during the Civil War, though most survived in much better shape.

INVENTORY OF THE ESTATE OF ALEXANDER DAVIDSON
Barren County, Kentucky, Will Book 1, 529–30

Inventory of the personal Estate and Slaves of Alexander Davidson,
Decd Taken this 12th day of November 1818

1 Negro Man by the name of Hercules	$400
1 do [ditto] Adam	700
1 do Sam	600
1 do Woman Depha	500
1 do Judah	550
1 ___ Boy Ned	500
1 do George	400
1 do Jim	350
1 do Anderson	250
1 Girl Mariah	100
1 do Nancy	400
1 do Rose	200
1 do Malinda	90
	$5,040

1 Bay Mare	50–
1 Black do	50–
1 Sorrel Colt	30–
One Bay Mare (paymaster)	25–
1 Colt do	35–
1 old bay Mare	20–
1 Wagon and Team Gear [?]	300–
21 Head of Sheep	40–
Stock Hogs supposed to 118	508–
Stock of Cattle 45 in number	340–
1 Lott of Black Smith Tools	90–
Plantation Tools $49.50 Grindstone $2	51.50
1 Loom and Gear	20–
Kitchen Furniture $32.50 Pewter & tin ware $14.50	47–
1 pr Stelyards 9/ [?] Irons 7/6 Rifle Gun $18.20	20.25
Candle Sticks 3/ Cupboard Furniture $25.50	26–
1 Press $25 two Tables $10 One Doz Chairs $4	39–
1 Watch $8 Lott Book $5 four Saddles $36	49–
5 Cotton Wheels and 2 Flax Wheels	12–
1 Copper Still $100 Bar Iron $4	104–

7 Feather Beds and Furniture complete 210–
3 do $60 Trunnel ? $10 70–
1 [?] of wheat about 15 Bushels, old 5.50
1 [?] flax Hackle 18/ Leather $16 21–
1 Cow Hide 12/ 2–
Crop Corn about 250 Bu .400–
11 Stacks Fodder $30 2 do Oat 33 63–
Wheat in Straw 7.50
7 Stacks Hay Supposed 16000lb 120–
1 Sorrel Mare (Adams) 20–
14 Empty Casks 7–
12 Tubs $6 Cyder $7.50 Vinegar 37/6 . . . . 19.75

$7,844.50

BENJAMIN DAVIDSON   EX
MARY DAVIDSON   EXIX

[*appraised by*]
SAML MURREL
G BLAIN
THOS WIRREN[?]

APPENDIX 3

INVENTORY OF THE ESTATE OF ALEXANDER DAVIDSON
Barren County, Kentucky, Inventories and C #6, 40–46
April 27, 1849

Cash on hand.	2.00
Three Beds, Bedsteads, & Bed Covers	20.00
11 old chairs	1.50
2 Spinning Wheels	1.00
1 Bed Stead	.50
Coffee & Coffee Mill	1.00
1 Box? Of Lumber	.75
Spun Cotton & Flax	2.50
Old Press & Table Furniture	7.00
1 Chest of Dried Fruit	1.00
2 Tables & 4 Books	3.00
Crockery Ware	1.00
Tin & Pewter Ware	1.50
Hackle &Seive [?]	1.25
1 Box & 3 Sacks	.50
2 Cotton wheels & Reel	1.00
2 Barrels & Basket of Beans	37.50
2 Wedges Coulter & Caroy [?] Plough	4.75
Old plows & Singletrees	6.00
2 Grindstones 1 Scythe & Drawing Knife	2.00
6 Axes & 3 Hoes	4.00
1 Lot of Castings & Hooks & Pot Rack	5.00
Coopers ware & Baskets	2.00
Corn in two Cribs	80.00
Loom & its appurtenances	4.00
4 Raw Hides	5.00
Unbroke Flax & doz Fowls	1.75
Bacon Lard & Salt	25.00
Black Smith Tools	10.00
Stock of Cattle	65.00
do of Hogs	45.00
Wagon Gear & Log Chain	20.00
4 Head of Horses	130.00
Sheaf & Threshed Oats & fodder	12.00
Stock of Sheep	22.00
Broad ax & Wheat Fan	10.00
Bee Hive	1.50

Note for hire of Anderson on John Button
for $45 Due 25 Dec. 1849 with credit of $18.20 . . . . 34.80

$535.67½

List of Slaves

Isham 550	Alfred 325
Haydon 600	Hercules 300
Hubbard 550	William (Malindas) 150
Henry 550	Dick 180
Ned 400	Felix 150
Anderson 150	Nancy 300
James 350	Rose & her child Dorham . . . 400
Little Jim 500	Malinda & her child Josephine . 300
William 450	Eliza & her child Nancy Jane . . 400
George 400	Mary 400
Andy 400	Eyalina or Elaline [?] 450
Edmond 300	Sylvia 200
Green 300	Delphia 250

$9,305.00

Hire of Negroes during balance of year 1849
[Excerpt from the record of the estate sale following the inventory]

Henry 45.00	William 17.00
Jim 35.00	George 13.00
Isham 40.00	Andy 8.50
Andersen 2.00	Evaline 11.50
Hubbard 40.00	Mary 8.78
Haydon 45.00	Nancy 27.00
Little Lim 35.00	

AMT OF NEGRO HIRE $327.75

Malinda & her 5 children & feed & clothe them the estate to pay all their
    doctors bills

Rose & 3 children & feed & clothe them the estate to pay doctors' bills

Eliza & 4 children & feed them, their clothing and doctors' bills to be paid from
    the estate & the estate to pay all charges except feeding.

Genealogy of Ancestors Mentioned in *The Punishment Monopoly*

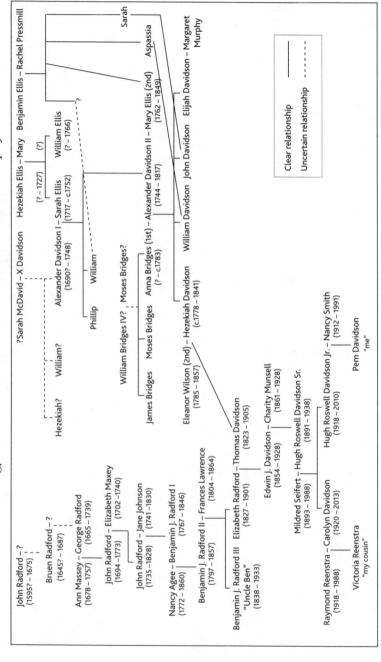

Notes

INTRODUCTION: ANCESTOR TALES

1. Benjamin Woolley, *Savage Kingdom: The True Story of Jamestown, 1607, and the Settlement of America* (New York: HarperCollins, 2007), 34; Karen Kupperman, *The Jamestown Project* (Cambridge, MA: Belknap Press of Harvard University Press, 2007), 13, 215.

2. Benjamin Radford, *The Autobiography of Benjamin Johnson Radford* (Eureka, IL: n.p., 1928), 14. Another piece of family mythology said we had among our Davidson relatives a general in the Revolutionary War. Although there certainly was a general, after whom Davidson College is named, he wasn't a relative.

3. Pem Davidson Buck, *Worked to the Bone: Race, Class, Power, and Privilege in Kentucky* (New York: Monthly Review Press, 2001).

4. Eric Williams, *Capitalism and Slavery* (Chapel Hill: University of North Carolina Press, 1994 [1944]), 13–14. For a description of conditions on board see Philip Bruce, *Economic History of Virginia in the Seventeenth Century,* vol 1. (New York: Peter Smith, 1935), 625–28. Conditions were so bad that Bennett refers to the transport of indentured servants as the "white Middle Passage." See Lerone Bennett, *The Shaping of Black America: The Struggles and Triumphs of African-Americans, 1619–the 1990s* (New York: Penguin Books, 1993 [1969]), 45.

5. Frederic Gleach, *Powhatan's World and Colonial Virginia* (Lincoln: University of Nebraska Press, 1997), 76; Kupperman, *Jamestown Project,* 242–43.

6. Max Weber, "Politics as a Vocation," in Weber, *Rationalism and Modern Society,* trans. and ed. Tony Waters and Dagmar Waters (New York:

Palgrave Books, 2015 [1919]), 129–98. For various approaches to the state's relationship to the control of force, see, for example, Achille Mbembe, "Necropolitics," *Public Culture* 15/1: 11–40, 2003; Charles Tilly, *Coercion, Capital, and European States, AD 990–1992* (Malden, MA: Blackwell Publishers, 1992); Charles Tilly, "War Making and State Making as Organized Crime," in Peter Evans, Dietrich Rueschemeyer, and Theda Skocpol, *Bringing the State Back In* (New York: Cambridge University Press, 1985),169–91. See also these edited volumes: Aradhana Sharma and Akhil Gupta, eds., *The Anthropology of the State: A Reader* (Malden MA: Blackwell Publishing, 2006); Jonathan Friedman, ed., *Globalization, the State, and Violence* (Walnut Creek, CA: AltaMira Press 2003); Nicolas De Genova and Nathalie Peutz, eds., *The Deportation Regime: Sovereignty, Space, and the Freedom of Movement* (Durham, NC: Duke University Press, 2010); Bruce Kapferer, ed., *State, Sovereignty, War: Civil Violence in Emerging Global Realities* (New York: Berghahn Books, 2004).

7.   For the defining characteristics of a state see Thomas Patterson, *Archaeology: The Historical Development of Civilizations,* 2nd ed. (Englewood Cliffs, NJ: Prentice Hall, 1993), 100–104; Brian Fagan, *World Prehistory: A Brief Introduction,* 8th ed. (Upper Saddle River, NJ: Prentice Hall, 2011), 218; Patrick Kirch, *A Shark Going Inland Is My Chief: The Island Civilization of Ancient Hawai'i* (Berkeley: University of California Press, 2012), 6–7. In addition, all discuss the process of state formation. However, none of these discuss the topic on which I focus: how an elite goes about concentrating enough power to be able to do the punishing that is foundational in gaining and maintaining the control needed to develop a state.

8.   For example, David Theo Goldberg, *The Racial State* (Malden, MA: Blackwell Publishing, 2002); Jacqueline Stevens, *Reproducing the State* (Princeton: Princeton University Press, 1999); Pem Davidson Buck,"Whither Whiteness? Empire, State, and the Re-Ordering of Whiteness," *Transforming Anthropology* 20/2 (2012):105–17; Pem Davidson Buck, "Stating Punishment: The Struggle over the Right to Punish," *North American Dialogue* 17/1 (2014): 31–43; Anthony Giddens, *The Nation-State and Violence,* vol. 2: *A Contemporary Critique of Historical Materialism* (Berkeley: University of California Press, 1987); Judith Skhlar, *American Citizenship: The Quest for Inclusion* (Cambridge: Harvard University Press, 1991). Faye Harrison points out that the state's "role in social control and security, with the political will and technologies to repress and to inflict lethal regimes of violence, has clearly not [declined]." For her analysis of the role anthropologists have played in the understanding of state, power, and politics, see Faye Harrison, "Anthropology Interrogating Power and Politics," in *Ethnology, Ethnography and Cultural Anthropology, Encyclopedia of Life Support Systems,* ed. Paolo Barbaro

(Oxford: UNESCO/EOLSS Publishers, 2016), http://greenplanet.eolss. net/EolssLogn/mss/C04/E6-20D/E6-20D-68/E6-20d-68-17/E6-20D-68-17-TXT-04.aspx#citation.

9. See Buck, "Whither Whiteness?"; Benedict Anderson, *Imagined Communities: Reflections on the Origin and Spread of Nationalism,* rev. ed. (New York: Verso, 1991 [1983]).

10. Tilly, "War Making."

11. Edward Herman and Noam Chomsky, *Manufacturing Consent: The Political Economy of the Mass Media* (New York: Random House/Vintage, 1995).

12. David Nugent makes a parallel argument that "state processes inevitably conjure into being powerful phantoms that are said to provoke the disorder that state activities themselves generate (or encourage), and, in the process, threaten the common good. . . . It is these imagined entities—brought into being through the process of displacement—that become the focus of official efforts at surveillance and control, and on which the coherence of the state depends." See Nugent, "Appearances to the Contrary: Fantasy, Fear, and Displacement in Twentieth-Century Peruvian State Formation," in Christopher Krupa and Nugent, *State Theory and Andean Politics: New Approaches to the Study of Rule* (Philadelphia: University of Pennsylvania Press, 2015), 186–209, at 209.

13. Michael Tonry, *Thinking About Crime: Sense and Sensibility in American Penal Cultures* (New York: Oxford University Press, 2004), 14. See also Ruth Gilmore, *Golden Gulag: Prisons, Surplus, Crisis, and Opposition in Globalizing California* (Berkeley: University of California Press, 2007); Marie Gottschalk, *Caught: The Prison State and the Lockdown of American Politics* (Princeton: Princeton University Press, 2015); Elizabeth Hinton, *From the War on Poverty to the War on Crime: The Making of Mass Incarceration in America* (Cambridge: Harvard University Press, 2016); Jordan Camp, *Incarcerating the Crisis: Freedom Struggles and the Rise of the Neoliberal State* (Oakland: University of California Press, 2016); Naomi Murakawa, *The First Civil Right: How Liberals Built Prison America* (New York: Oxford University Press, 2014); Loïc Wacquant, *Punishing the Poor: The Neoliberal Government of Social Insecurity* (Durham, NC: Duke University Press, 2009).

14. Giorgio Agamben, *State of Exception,* trans. Kevin Attell (Chicago: University of Chicago Press, 2005). See also Buck, "Stating Punishment" and "Whither Whiteness."

15. Mbembe, "Necropolitics," 11.

16. Steve Martinot, *The Rule of Racialization* (Philadelphia: Temple University Press, 2003), 114.

17. Agamben, *State of Exception.*

18. Margaret Sankey, *Jacobite Prisoners of the 1715 Rebellion: Preventing and Punishing Insurrection in Early Hanoverian Britain* (Burlington, VT: Ashgate, 2005), 52.

19. Helen Rountree, *The Powhatan Indians of Virginia: Their Traditional Culture* (Norman: University of Oklahoma Press, 1989), 117, 84.

20. Michel Foucault, *Discipline and Punish: The Birth of the Prison*, trans. Alan Sheridan (New York: Vintage Books, 1995 [1975]), 3–6.

21. Foucault, 116.

22. Foucault, 106.

23. Nor was it inevitable that the Southwest would be part of the United States, or that English, not Spanish, would be the legally recognized language, as pointed out by De Genova, *Working the Boundaries*, 97–106.

24. See Rosa Luxemburg, *The Accumulation of Capital*, trans. Agnes Schwarzschild (Mansfield Center, CT: Martino Publishing, 2015 [1913]), 348–67 in particular. For examples see Morton Wenger and Pem Davidson Buck, "Farms, Families, and Super-Exploitation: An Integrative Reappraisal," *Rural Sociology* 53/4 (1988):460–72; Pem Davidson Buck, "Colonized Anthropology: Cargo-Cult Discourse," in Faye Harrison, *Decolonizing Anthropology*, 24–41 (Washington, DC: American Anthropological Association, 1991).

25. Colin Calloway, *The World Turned Upside Down: Indian Voices from Early America* (New York: Bedford/St. Martin's, 1994).

1: TALES OF A MYTHICAL ANCESTOR, PUNISHMENT, AND DIARCHY

1.   Charles Meacham, *A History of Christian County, Kentucky: From Oxcart to Airplane* (Markham, VA: Apple Manor Press, 2016 [1930]), 610.

2.   William Kelso, *Jamestown: The Buried Truth* (Charlottesville: University of Virginia Press, 2006), 28–34; *Jamestown Rediscovery, Original Settlers* (Association for the Preservation of Virginia Antiquities, 2000), http://www.apva.org/history/orig.html.

3.   On the interpretive process see Margaret Williamson, *Powhatan Lords of Life and Death: Command and Consent in Seventeenth Century Virginia* (Lincoln: University of Nebraska Press, 2003), 2–15; Karen Kupperman, *Indians and English: Facing Off in Early America* (Ithaca, NY: Cornell University Press, 2000), 10–15; Matthew Jennings, *New Worlds of Violence: Cultures and Conquests in the Early American Southeast* (Knoxville: University of Tennessee Press, 2011), xx–xxxi; Donald Fixico, ed., *Rethinking American Indian History* (Albuquerque: University of New Mexico Press, 1997).

4.   Karen Kupperman, *The Jamestown Project* (Cambridge, MA: Belknap Press of Harvard University Press, 2007), 6, 73–108, 184, 192; Jace Weaver, *The Red Atlantic: American Indigenes and the Making of the Modern World, 1000–1927*, 136–52 (Chapel Hill: University of North Carolina Press, 2014).

J. Leitch Wright, *The Only Land They Knew: American Indians in the Old South* (Lincoln: University of Nebraska Press,1999 [1981]), 41–43; Stephen Potter, *Commoners, Tribute, and Chiefs: The Development of Algonquian Culture in the Potomac Valley* (Charlottesville: University Press of Virginia, 1993), 161–66; Don Jordan and Michael Walsh, *White Cargo: The Forgotten History of Britain's White Slaves in America* (New York: New York University Press, 2008), 82, 87; Charlotte Gradie, "The Powhatans in the Context of the Spanish Empire," in Helen Rountree, *Powhatan Foreign Relations 1500–1722* (Charlottesville: University Press of Virginia, 1993), 154–72.

5. Potter, *Commoners, Tribute, and Chiefs,* 163.

6. Frederic Gleach, *Powhatan's World and Colonial Virginia* (Lincoln: University of Nebraska Press, 1997), 56–57, 119–21; Jeffrey Hantman, "Powhatan's Relations with the Piedmont Monacans," in Rountree, *Powhatan Foreign Relations 1500–1722,* 94–111, at 109–10; Kupperman, *Jamestown Project,* 228–30; Helen Rountree, "The Powhatans and the English: A Case of Multiple Conflicting Agendas," in Rountree, *Powhatan Foreign Relations1500–1722,* 173–205, at 178.

7. Quoted in Kupperman, *Indians and English,* 216; Gleach, *Powhatan's World,* 75; James Horn, *Adapting to a New World: English Society in the Seventeenth-Century Chesapeake* (Chapel Hill: University of North Carolina Press,1994), 64.

8. On diarchy generally see Rodney Needham, *Reconnaissances* (Toronto: University of Toronto Press, 1980), 63–105; Ananda Coomaraswamy, *Spiritual Authority and Temporal Power in the Indian Theory of Government* (New Haven: American Oriental Society, 1942). For Powhatan diarchy see Williamson, *Powhatan Lords,* 202–55; Gleach, *Powhatan's World,* 35, 142. For an interesting Greek take on the role of religion in enforcing laws, see Sextus Empiricus, "Critias Fragment" from *Adversus Mathematicos,* trans. R. G. Bury, rev. by J. Garrett, 2009 [n.d], ix, 54, https://people.wku.edu/jan.garrett/302/critias.htm.

9. For a brief discussion of egalitarian societies and of the role religion can play in both egalitarian and stratified societies see Pem Davidson Buck, *In/Equality: An Alternative Anthropology,* 4th ed. (Palo Cedro, CA: CAT Publishing, 2016).

10. Kupperman, *Indians and English,* 110.

11. Ernst Kantorowicz, *The King's Two Bodies: A Study in Mediaeval Political Theology* (Princeton: Princeton University Press, 1957), 44–48, 60–61.

12. Rodney Needham, *Reconnaissances,* 64; Kantorowicz, *The King's Two Bodies,* 43. For a discussion of the political/theological arguments in England about whether a king's authority came directly from God or by way of the pope, see Kantorowicz, *The King's Two Bodies,* 320–29. On the interconnection of religion and the authorization of power see Quentin Skinner,

The Foundations of Modern Political Thought, vols 1 and 2 (Cambridge: Cambridge University Press, 1978).

13. Allen Feldman, *Formations of Violence: The Narrative of the Body and Political Terror in Northern Ireland* (Chicago: University of Chicago Press, 1991), 38; Georges Balandier, *Political Anthropology,* trans. A. M. Sheridan Smith (New York: Pantheon Books, 1970), 120–21. Feldman's discussion of violence of Northern Ireland and Balandier's discussion of religious strategies in political power struggles in early African states both suggest a connection between weak states and strong religious institutions.

14. Immanuel Wallerstein, *The Modern World System II: Mercantilism and the Consolidation of the European World Economy 1600–1750* (Berkeley: University of California Press, 2011), xxi. See also Charles Tilly, *Coercion, Capital, and European States, AD 990–1992* (Malden, MA: Blackwell Publishers, 1992), 75– 76.

15. For a discussion of the philosophical/theological positions taken on both sides of the argument about the power of the church relative to the state see Skinner, *The Foundations of Modern Political Thought,* 12, 127–30; 144–48; 189–238; 302. For the specifically religious arguments about the relationship between king, God, and people see Kantorowicz, *The King's Two Bodies.*

16. Alexander Grant, "Crown and Nobility in Late Medieval Britain," in Roger Mason, *Scotland and England 1286–1815,* 34–59 (Edinburgh: John Donald Publishers, 1987), 48–49; John Bellamy, *Crime and Public Order in England in the Later Middle Ages* (Toronto: University of Toronto Press/ Routledge & Kegan Paul, 1973), 1, 2.

17. Kupperman, *Indians and English,* 92.

18. Bellamy, *Crime and Public Order,* 47. Like Wahunsonacock's, his power diminished in proportion to distance from his capital. On the outer reaches of the territory, he only theoretically ruled territorial elites who had long before wrested punishing from local groups and still retained for themselves the right to use force for punishing. See Skinner, *The Foundations of Modern Political Thought,* 211. On the importance of borders in state–ness see Pem Davidson Buck, "Whither Whiteness? Empire, State, and the Re–Ordering of Whiteness," *Transforming Anthropology* 20/2(2012): 105–17.

19. Quoted respectively in Williamson, *Powhatan Lords,* 140, and in Kupperman, *Indians and English,* 92, see also 103.

20. Kupperman, *Indians and English,* 37–38; Potter, *Commoners, Tribute, and Chiefs,* 164.

21. Kupperman, *Indians and English* 38; Potter, *Commoners, Tribute, and Chiefs,* 165.

22. Williamson, *Powhatan Lords,* 47, 59. Turner and Potter both specify the East Coast, but by 1600 many of the comparably complex polities in the rest of what is now the United States, such as Mississippian kingdoms and

Chaco Canyon, were already gone or in decline. See E. Randolph Turner, "Native American Protohistoric Interactions in the Powhatan Core Area," in Helen Rountree, *Powhatan Foreign Relations 1500–1722* (Charlottesville: University Press of Virginia, 1993), 76–93, at 92; Potter, *Commoners, Tribute, and Chiefs*, 1.

23. Kupperman, *Indians and English*, 38; Kathleen Brown, *Good Wives, Nasty Wenches, and Anxious Patriarchs: Gender, Race, and Power in Colonial Virginia* (Chapel Hill: University of North Carolina Press, 1996), 50–53. See also Pem Davidson Buck, "Stating Punishment: The Struggle over the Right to Punish," *North American Dialogue* 17/1 (2014): 31–43.

24. On wealth and class structure see Potter, *Commoners, Tribute, and Chiefs*, 16–17; Williamson, *Powhatan Lords*, 129, 153–60, 221; Helen Rountree, *The Powhatan Indians of Virginia: Their Traditional Culture* (University of Oklahoma Press, 1989), 100–103, 143, 85. While Rountree says that there was no aristocratic class between rulers and ruled, her description of the relationship between ordinary people and the "better sort" appears to indicate an uncrossable line between them. Kupperman and Williamson both describe what appears to be a separate elite class. See Kupperman, *Indians and English*, 38, 64–109; Williamson, *Powhatan Lords*, esp. 129.

25. Helen Rountree, "Introduction: Who Were the Powhatans, and Did They Have a Unified 'Foreign Policy'?," in Rountree, *Powhatan Foreign Relations 1500–1722*, 1–19, at 11; Rountree, *The Powhatan Indians*, 85, 115–17, 145–47; Potter, *Commoners, Tribute, and Chiefs*, 16–17; Williamson, *Powhatan Lords*, 138.

26. Alex Barker, "Powhatan's Pursestrings: On the Meaning of Surplus in a Seventeenth-Century Algonquin Chiefdom," in Barker and Timothy Pauketat, *Lords of the Southeast: Social Inequality and Native Elites of Southeastern North America*, Archaeological Papers of the American Anthropological Association (Hoboken, NJ: WileyBlackwell, 1992), 61–80, at 68; see Gleach, *Powhatan's World*, 29–31; Williamson, *Powhatan Lords*, 202–6; Rountree, *The Powhatan Indians*, 145.

27. Georges Balandier, *Political Anthropology*, 99, 101.

28. Rountree, *The Powhatan Indians*, 110–11, 144–47. Tribute was also paid in labor, growing corn in Wahunsonacock's fields; in return beads, a valuable, were given; these beads however, were themselves acquired by him through tribute.

29. On the relationship between priests and chiefs see Kupperman, *Indians and English*, 123, 125; Rountree, *The Powhatan Indians*, 116–17, 145; Williamson, *Powhatan Lords*, 189, 202–6, 236–39; Gleach, *Powhatan's World*, 51.

30. Kupperman, *Indians and English*, 124, 138–39. On theft see Williamson, *Powhatan Lords*, 139–40.

31. Brown, *Good Wives*, 53; Potter, *Commoners, Tribute, and Chiefs*, 40. Potter speculates that the demand for corn might have become oppressively heavy. There are significant disagreements about what portion of people's production was actually given in tribute. See Rountree, *The Powhatan Indians*, 85, 109–10,144; Kupperman, *Indians and English*, 97.

32. Rountree, *The Powhatan Indians*, 79, 85, 87; Brown, *Good Wives*, 51; see Barker, "Powhatan's Pursestrings," 69.

33. Charles Tilly, "War Making and State Making as Organized Crime," in Peter Evans, Dietrich Rueschemeyer, and Theda Skocpol, *Bringing the State Back In* (New York: Cambridge University Press, 1985), 169–91; Charles Tilly, *Coercion, Capital, and European State.*

34. Rountree, *The Powhatan Indians*, 122; Williamson, *Powhatan Lords*, 52.

35. Williamson, *Powhatan Lords*, 64, 72, 228; Rountree, "Introduction", 3–4; Rountree, *The Powhatan Indians*, 119, 121. Gledhill brings up the distinction between borders, with a clear and defended line of demarcation in a state strong enough to maintain that distinction, and frontiers, where sovereignty gradually fades away and sovereignty of another polity gradually picks up, a condition found in weaker states. See John Gledhill, *Power and Its Disguises: Anthropological Perspectives on Politics*, 2nd ed. (London: Pluto Press, 2000), 15.

36. Rountree, *The Powhatan Indians*, 114–15, 119–20; Williamson, *Powhatan Lords*, 202–4; Kupperman, *Indians and English*, 103; Potter, *Commoners, Tribute, and Chiefs*, 16.

37. Williamson, *Powhatan Lords*, 171.

38. Williamson, 52–53; see Rountree, *The Powhatan Indians*, 109–11, 122; see also Tilly, "War Making."

39. See Potter, *Commoners, Tribute, and Chiefs*, 16.

40. Kupperman, *Indians and English*, 16–34, esp. 23, 91–92.

41. Kupperman, 174; Williamson, *Powhatan Lords*, 144; Gleach, *Powhatan's World*, 35; Kupperman, *The Jamestown Project*, 228–29; Weaver, *The Red Atlantic*, 144–47.

42. See Brown, *Good Wives*, 51–52; Kupperman, *Indians and English*, 77; Benjamin Woolley, *Savage Kingdom: The True Story of Jamestown, 1607, and the Settlement of America* (New York: HarperCollins, 2007), 311; Gleach, *Powhatan's World*, 116–22.

43. Horn, *Adapting to a New World*, 51.

44. Horn, 51, 49–53, 62–64.

45. Horn, 76. Lengths of indenture varied considerably, both over time and with age and skill. See Horn, 65–67; Philip Bruce, *Economic History of Virginia in the Seventeenth Century*, vol. 1 (New York: Peter Smith, 1935), 578–83.

46. Eric Williams, *Capitalism and Slavery* (Chapel Hill: University of North

Carolina Press, 1994 [1944]), lvi. See Wright, *The Only Land They Knew*, 76; Horn, *Adapting to a New World*, 69.

47. Horn, *Adapting to a New World*, 69; Williams, *Capitalism and Slavery*, xlix; Jordan and Walsh, *White Cargo*, 14, 89–90. The institution of the headright system in 1618 meant that there were more "voluntary" indentured servants, but it was largely the poor who saw this as a reasonable thing to do. On demographics and social position of those who went, see Horn *Adapting to a New World*, 19–77.

48. Horn, *Adapting to a New World*, 5, 49, 62–69; Nancy Isenberg, *White Trash: The 400-Year Untold History of Class in America* (New York: Viking, 2016), 17–28.

49. Kupperman, *Indians and English*, 218; Jordan and Walsh, *White Cargo*, 64–65. On political choices to remove poor people see Horn, *Adapting to a New World*, 63–64; Isenberg, *White Trash*, 20–28; Bruce, *Economic History*, vol. 1, 583–84; Woolley, *Savage Kingdom*, 100.

50. Peter Linebaugh, *The London Hanged: Crime and Civil Society in the Eighteenth Century* (New York: Cambridge University Press, 1992), xxi; Bruce, *Economic History*, vol. 1, 603.

51. Bruce, *Economic History*, vol.1, 603–4; Lerone Bennett, *The Shaping of Black America: The Struggles and Triumphs of African-Americans, 1619–1990s* (New York: Penguin Books, 1993 [1969]), 39–45. For details of British policy, indenture, and criminalizing laws see Jordan and Walsh, *White Cargo*, 21–125; Bruce, *Economic History*, vol. 1, 603–4.

52. Jordan and Walsh, *White Cargo*, 85.

53. See Kupperman, *The Jamestown Project*, 241, 255–59; Woolley, *Savage Kingdom*, 99–118; Kelso, *Jamestown*, 76–77; see Williams, *Capitalism and Slavery*, xxvi–xxviii. On failure to work and the punishing required to enforce working, see Jordan and Walsh, *White Cargo*, 62–64.

54. For an explanation of the way religion differs from ritual and spirituality, and develops as part of the same process that creates elites and inequality, "usurping" ritual's power to connect people and thus establishing a source of social control, my thanks to Derrick Hodge, personal communication, October 2018.

55. Jordan and Walsh, *White Cargo*, 64.

56. Barker, "Powhatan's Pursestrings," 68. See also Brown, *Good Wives*, 62–63; Wright, *The Only Land They Knew*, 73; Jordan and Walsh, *White Cargo*, 63–64; Woolley, *Savage Kingdom*, 95.

57. Brown, *Good Wives*, 66–73. For continuing prohibition on trading see Gleach, *Powhatan's World*, 163.

58. Kupperman, *Indians and English*, 218.

59. Woolley, *Savage Kingdom*, 99–104; Horn, *Adapting to a New World*, 137–39.

60. Jordan and Walsh, *White Cargo*, 71, 105–6.

61. Jordan and Walsh, 108–109; Horn, *Adapting to a New World,* 268–69.

62. Jordan and Walsh, *White Cargo,* 69.

63. Williams, *Capitalism and Slavery,* xlii–xlv; Jordan and Walsh, *White Cargo,* 89–90; Kupperman, *The Jamestown Project,* 284–88; Bruce, *Economic History,* vol. 1, 504–20.

64. For analysis of the role of women in the early colony I am particularly indebted to Brown, *Good Wives,* 80–104.

65. Brown, 80–89, 91.

66. Rountree, "The Powhatans and the English," 175. See also Rountree, *The Powhatan Indians,* 88–94; Brown, *Good Wives,* 45–59.

67. Jordan and Walsh, *White Cargo,* 84–85; Brown, *Good Wives,* 81–82.

68. Rountree, "The Powhatans and the English," 197.

69. Jordan and Walsh, *White Cargo,* 94.

70. Gleach, *Powhatan's World,* 158, 175. For a history of the 1622 coup see Gleach, *Powhatan's World,* 148–58; Woolley, *Savage Kingdom,* 380–85. For background on Mississippian concepts of war and violence see Jennings, *New Worlds of Violence,* 1–28.

71. Wright, *The Only Land They Knew,* 64, 78; Gleach, *Powhatan's World,* 164.

72. Wright, *The Only Land They Knew,* 70, 67; Kupperman, *The Jamestown Project,* 59, 304.

73. Gleach, *Powhatan's World,* 148–49; Kupperman, *The Jamestown Project,* 59, 306.

74. Brown, *Good Wives,* 108; Gleach, *Powhatan's World,* 163, 169.

75. On changed attitude after 1622 see Wright, *The Only Land They Knew,* 75; Gleach, *Powhatan's World,* 159–64. On Powhatan servitude see Wright, *The Only Land They Knew,* 131–34, 227–28, 282–83.

76. Wright, *The Only Land They Knew,* 84, 227–28; Gleach, *Powhatan's World,* 183, 188–89.

77. Wright, 84, 98, 133; Gleach, 184–85. Rountree points out that as the Powhatan weakened, punishing theft and murder returned to local hands and individuals. See Rountree, *The Powhatan Indians,* 115.

78. Gleach, *Powhatan's World,* 175.

79. Michael Oberg, *Native America: A History* (Malden, MA: Wiley-Blackwell, 2010), 327, 333–34.

80. Horn, *Adapting to a New World,* 384. The General Assembly consisted of the House of Burgesses, first assembled in 1619, plus the governor, who was directed by the Virginia Company, and the Governor's Council.

81. Brown, *Good Wives,* 97–98, 145–49.

82. Brown, 148.

2: ANCESTOR TALES OF DISPOSSESSION AND A REVOLT OF THE UNFREE

1. *Records of Colonial Gloucester County, Virginia, October 1652*, ed. Polly Cary Mason (Baltimore: Genealogical Publishing Co., 2003 [1946]), 74. John was born about 1595, thus age fifty-seven in 1652. He died around 1657. See *Virginia Colonial Abstracts*, vol. 2, August 1655, November 1657, ed. Beverly Fleet (Baltimore: Genealogical Publishing Co., 1988), Northumberland Co., 32, 149.

2. *Virginia Colonial Abstracts*, Northumberland Co., July 1654, 355, 395–96.

3. Anthony Parent, *Foul Means: The Formation of a Slave Society in Virginia, 1660–1740* (Chapel Hill: Omohundro Institute and University of North Carolina Press, 2003), 28–29.

4. Eric Wolf, *Europe and the People Without History* (Berkeley: University of California Press, 1982), 202.

5. There is little clear evidence on Bruen's parentage or birth and death, or for his being the father of George Radford. For the sake of the story I am simply accepting family researchers' statements. However, that Bruen did exist is clear.

6. *Virginia Colonial Abstracts*, Northumberland Co., July 1654, 356–57.

7. Philip Bruce, *Economic History of Virginia in the Seventeenth Century*, vol. 2 (New York: Peter Smith, 1935), 13.

8. Bruce, 2:518–27; Darrett Rutman and Anita Rutman, *A Place in Time: Middlesex County, Virginia 1650–1750* (New York: W. W. Norton, 1984), 75.

9. James Horn, *Adapting to a New World: English Society in the Seventeenth-Century Chesapeake* (Chapel Hill: University of North Carolina Press, 1994) 206; Rutman and Rutman, *A Place in Time*, 113. This was also a result of the lack of women—men who were landless couldn't compete for wives with those who were landed.

10. Kathleen Brown, *Good Wives, Nasty Wenches, and Anxious Patriarchs: Gender, Race, and Power in Colonial Virginia* (Chapel Hill: University of North Carolina Press, 1996), 154.

11. Rutman and Rutman, *A Place in Time*, 114, 95.

12. John Nelson, *A Blessed Company: Parishes, Parsons, and Parishioners in Anglican Virginia 1690–1776* (Chapel Hill: University of North Carolina Press, 2014), 13–16.

13. Nelson, 15–16.

14. Nelson, 74–76.

15. Nelson, 30–31, 128; Rutman and Rutman, *A Place in Time*, 52. On church building see Nelson, *A Blessed Company*, 60–61.

16. Rutman and Rutman, *A Place in Time*, 103.

17. Rutman and Rutman, 57; Nelson, *A Blessed Company*, 14, 21–23.

18. Rutman and Rutman, *A Place in Time*, 87, 208; *Virginia County Court Records, Order Book Abstracts of Middlesex County, VA, 1680–1686,* February 7, 1680/81, ed. Ruth and Sam Spartico (McLean, VA: Antient Press, 1994), 4. Note: Dates for this time period are recorded in transcriptions as 1680/81 because at that time the calendar year started in March, so that for part of the year what is now called 1681 was called 1680.

19. Rutman and Rutman, *A Place in Time*, 107; *Virginia County Court Records, Order Book Abstracts of Middlesex County, VA, 1680–1686,* 4; *Virginia County Court Records, Deed Abstracts of Middlesex County, VA, 1679–1688, Deed Book 2, Part 1,* June 1680/81, ed. Ruth and Sam Spartico (McLean, VA: Antient Press, 1989), 8–9,.

20. For example, *Virginia Colonial Abstracts,* Northumberland Co., September 1653, 347. See Brown, *Good Wives,* 323, 361–62; Allan Kulikoff, *Tobacco and Slaves: The Development of Southern Culture in the Chesapeake 1680–1800* (Chapel Hill: University of North Carolina Press, 1986), 9–12, 262–63. However, for a fuller picture of Virginia politics see John Kolp, *Gentlemen and Freeholders: Electoral Politics in Colonial Virginia* (Baltimore: Johns Hopkins University Press, 1998).

21. See Edmund Morgan, *American Slavery American Freedom: The Ordeal of Colonial Virginia* (New York: W. W. Norton, 1975), 223–24, 204–11.

22. *Virginia Colonial Abstracts,* Northumberland Co, July 1654, 395–396; *Virginia Colonial Abstracts,* Northumberland Co., September 1653, 347.

23. Stephen Webb, *1676: The End of American Independence* (Syracuse, NY: Syracuse University Press, 1995 [1984]), 251–54, 290; James Rice, *Tales from a Revolution: Bacon's Rebellion and the Transformation of Early America* (New York: Oxford University Press, 2012), 9–10; Michael Oberg, *Native America: A History* (Malden, MA: Wiley–Blackwell, 2010), 102, 66.

24. On Bacon's Rebellion see particularly Rice, *Tales from a Revolution;* Webb, *1676;* Brown, *Good Wives,* 137–86.

25. For instance, Alan Gallay, *The Indian Slave Trade: The Rise of the English Empire in the American South 1670–1717* (New Haven: Yale University Press, 2002); Peter Silver, *Our Savage Neighbors: How Indian War Transformed America* (New York: W. W. Norton, 2008); Gary Anderson, *Ethnic Cleansing and the Indian: The Crime That Should Haunt America* (Norman: University of Oklahoma Press, 2014); Daniel Usner, *Indians, Settlers, and Slaves in a Frontier Exchange Economy: The Lower Mississippi Valley Before 1783* (Chapel Hill: University of North Carolina Press, 1992); Sami Lakomäki, *Gathering Together: The Shawnee People Through Diaspora and Nationhood, 1600–1870* (New Haven: Yale University Press, 2014); Pekka Hämäläinen, *The Comanche Empire* (New Haven: Yale University

Press, 2008); David Silverman, *Thundersticks: Firearms and the Violent Transformation of Native America* (Cambridge, MA: Harvard University Press, 2016); Oberg, *Native America.*

26. Gallay, *The Indian Slave Trade,* 181–82.

27. Gallay, , 2, 4–6, 96–98, 156, 241–42, 350; Oberg, *Native America,* 2–3.

28. Webb, *1676,* 251–54; 355–59. See also Alan Taylor, *American Revolutions: A Continental History, 1750–1804* (New York: W. W. Norton, 2016), 251–57; Sami Lakomäki, *Gathering Together.*

29. Bruce, *Economic History,* 1:618; Don Jordan and Michael Walsh, *White Cargo: The Forgotten History of Britain's White Slaves in America* (New York: New York University Press, 2008), 127–136.

30. Brown, *Good Wives,* 150–151; Jordan and Walsh, *White Cargo,* 103–106, 194, 206–207; James Horn, *Adapting to a New World,* 252, 269–276; Bruce, *Economic History,* 2:30–31, although he is inclined to discount reasons servants might have for discontent.

31. Karen Kupperman, *The Jamestown Project* (Cambridge MA: The Belknap Press of Harvard University Press, 2007), 61, 3; Karen Kupperman, *Indians and English: Facing Off in Early America* (Ithaca, NY: Cornell University Press, 2000), 17; Tim Hashaw, *The Birth of Black America: The First African Americans and the Pursuit of Freedom at Jamestown* (New York: Carroll & Graf, 2007), 101; Immanuel Wallerstein, *The Modern World System II: Mercantilism and the Consolidation of the European World Economy 1600–1750* (Berkeley: University of California Press, 2011), 36, 64–71. Wallerstein describes Dutch hegemony during this period, with England and Spain still contesting, unsuccessfully, for position.

32. Jace Weaver, *The Red Atlantic: American Indigenes and the Making of the Modern World, 1000–1927* (Chapel Hill: University of North Carolina Press, 2014), 191,194.

33. Kupperman, *Indians and English,* 18; Wallerstein, *The Modern World System II,* 31, 92–93; Horn, *Adapting to a New World,* 253, 261.

34. Ernst Kantorowicz, *The King's Two Bodies: A Study in Mediaeval Political Theology* (Princeton: Princeton University Press, 1957); Quentin Skinner, *The Foundations of Modern Political Thought,* vols. 1 and 2 (Cambridge: Cambridge University Press, 1978), esp. 148–73.

35. Thomas Warner, *History of Old Rappahannock Co VA 1656–1692, Including Present Counties of Essex and Richmond and Parts of Westmoreland, King George, Stafford, Caroline, and Spotsylvania* (Tappahannock, VA: Pauline Pearce Warner, Publisher, ca. 1965), 16.

36. Williamson discusses whether Wahunsunacock was in fact a monarch in this sense, and concludes he was not. See Margaret Williamson, *Powhatan Lords of Life and Death: Command and Consent in Seventeenth-Century Virginia* (Lincoln: University of Nebraska Press, 2003), 204. Kantorowicz

discusses how the conception of the King's Two Bodies: the body politic (which never dies and passes to the king's successor) and the body natural (the king as mortal), corresponded with the development of absolute monarchies, making the king "pontifical." See Kantorowicz, *The King's Two Bodies*, 441–50, 7–33. Put in the language of dual sovereignty, Kantorowicz's description of the King's Two Bodies represents a permutation of the priest or judge—the spiritual authority—and the secular power, who are now combined in one person, with the body politic being the principal (the source of authority, the "mover") and the body natural being the actor, instrumental in making things happen. Investing both in the person of the king would diminish the authority of the Church and concentrate power in the hands of the king. Foucault discusses the shift in France from religious control of regulating and punishing social transgression to state control through disciplinary policing and surveillance; religious control lasted longer in England than in France; "By means of a wise police, the sovereign accustoms the people to order and obedience." See Michel Foucault, *Discipline and Punish: The Birth of the Prison*, trans. Alan Sheridan (New York: Vintage Books, 1995 [1975]), 213, 215.

37. Charles Tilly, *Coercion, Capital, and European States, AD 990–1992* (Malden, MA: Blackwell Publishers, 1992), 156.

38. Kupperman, *Indians and English*, 95.

39. J. Leitch Wright, *The Only Land They Knew: American Indians in the Old South* (Lincoln: University of Nebraska Press, 1999 [1981]), 65.

40. Brown, *Good Wives*, 84, 92, 139.

41. Brown, 193–94; Horn, *Adapting to a New World*, 211–212; Bruce, *Economic History*, 2:38.

42. Brown, *Good Wives*, 92–96. 133–34, 188–94; Bruce, *Economic History*, 2:34–38. For example, *Virginia County Court Records, Order Book Abstracts of Middlesex County, VA, 1673–1677*, May 1677, ed. Ruth and Sam Spartico (McLean, VA: The Antient Press, 1989), 59.

43. Interracial marriage was legal until 1691 and did occur. Brown, *Good Wives*, 126; Kirsten Fischer, *Suspect Relations: Sex, Race, and Resistance in Colonial North Carolina* (Ithaca: Cornell University Press, 2001), 29; On the position of interracial children in matrilineal societies see Fischer, 73, 90.

44. *Westmoreland County, Virginia, Order Book, 1675/6–1688/9*, August 1684, ed. John Dorman (Washington DC: J. F. Dorman, 1988), 67–68; *Virginia County Court Records Book: (Old) Rappahannock County, Virginia, 1682–1687*, March 1684/85, ed. Ruth and Sam Sparico (McLean, VA: Antient Press, 1990), 47; *Virginia County Court Records, Deed Abstracts of (Old) Rappahannock County, Virginia, 1686–1688*, December 1686, May 1687, ed. Ruth and Sam Sparico, eds. (McLean, VA: The Antient Press, 1990), 25, 52, 56.

45. Rutman and Rutman, *A Place in Time*, 145.

46. Warner, *History of Old Rappahannock*, 70.

47. Webb, *1676*, 10–11, 16, 30.

48. Brown, *Good Wives*, 149.

49. Rutman and Rutman, *A Place in Time*, 180; Edmond Morgan, *American Slavery American Freedom: The Ordeal of Colonial Virginia* (New York: W. W. Norton, 1975), 297–98.

50. Rice, *Tales from a Revolution*, 163; Gallay, *The Indian Slave Trade*, 46–47, 299–311, see 290–91 for an example; Wright, *The Only Land They Knew*, 132–34; Silverman, *Thundersticks*, 56–76. On the concept of "just war," see Matthew Jennings, *New Worlds of Violence: Cultures and Conquests in the Early American Southeast* (Knoxville: University of Tennessee Press, 2011), 59–61.

51. For Jamestown and the 1600s in Virginia see for instance Brown, *Good Wives;* Horn, *Adapting to a New World;* Rutman and Rutman, *A Place in Time;* Parent, *Foul Means;* Kupperman, *Indians and English;* Ira Berlin, *Many Thousands Gone: The First Two Centuries of Slavery in North America* (Cambridge, MA: Harvard University Press, 1998).

52. For example, *Virginia County Court Records, Order Book Abstracts of Middlesex County, VA, 1673–1677*, February 2, 1673/74, September 6, 1675, 6, 38.

53. Gray, *History of Agriculture*, 386–88.

54. Rutman and Rutman, *A Place in Time*, 73–75.

55. On access to land and its engrossment by the 1660s see Parent, *Foul Means*, 25–29, 39; Lewis Gray, *History of Agriculture in the Southern United States to 1860*, vols 1 and 2 (Gloucester, MA: Peter Smith, 1958), 387, 394–97, 399–406; Bruce, *Economic History*, 1:487–571. On revenue to the Crown see Morgan, *American Slavery American Freedom*, 196–98.

56. See Robert Miles, *Capitalism and Unfree Labor: Anomaly or Necessity* (New York: Tavistock, 1987), 198–222.

57. Brown, *Good Wives*, 137–86; Rice, *Tales from a Revolution*, 220.

58. Webb, *1676*, 121–22; Philip Morgan, "British Encounters with Africans and African Americans," in Bernard Bailyn and Morgan, *Strangers within the Realm* (Chapel Hill: University of North Carolina Press, 1991), 157–219, at 195; Brown, *Good Wives*, 168.

59. Parent, *Foul Means*, 141–143; Brown, *Good Wives*, 150.

60. Brown, 156.

61. Warner, *History of Old Rappahannock*, 52, 53; Webb, *1676*, 19.

62. Warner, *History of Old Rappahannock*, 61.

63. Quoted in Brown, *Good Wives*, 170. See Warner, *History of Old Rappahannock*, 56.

64. Webb, *1676*, 16, 21–25. For a focus on Indian strategies see Rice, *Tales from a Revolution*.

65. Webb, *1676*, 7.
66. The English Crown before 1676 had no real monopoly on the use of force in Virginia. So long as tobacco taxes arrived in the Crown's coffers, the Crown's governors were given a relatively free hand. See Morgan, *American Slavery American Freedom*, 254, 271, 275. Berkeley, with his cronies, ruled Virginia for years, not like part of an empire, but as an almost independent polity under indirect rule. See Webb, *1676*, 12, 67, 129, 131; see Brown, *Good Wives*, 154–59, 173. For a summary of various theories regarding the rebellion see Jane Carson, *Bacon's Rebellion: 1676–1976* (Jamestown, VA: Jamestown Foundation, 1976).
67. Brown, *Good Wives*, 158–61; Webb, *1676*, 42–43, 84, 129.
68. Webb, *1676*, 94–96. For a chronology of the events surrounding the rebellion see Carson, *Bacon's Rebellion*, 1–11. For detailed accounts see Webb, *1676*; Rice, *Tales from a Revolution*; Morgan, *American Slavery American Freedom*, 250–82.
69. Quoted in Webb, *1676*, 16, 34. Berkeley offered freedom to servants of rebels if they joined him, but few did; Bacon offered freedom to slaves as well if they belonged to Berkeley loyalists, and got many takers. See Morgan, *American Slavery American Freedom*, 268.
70. Rice, *Tales from a Revolution*, 114.
71. On land redistribution and political voice for ordinary people see Webb, *1676*, 34, 39–40; Brown, *Good Wives*, 156, 168–69; Parent, *Foul Means*, 39. The Royal Commission investigating the causes of the rebellion cited the lack of land and consolidation of land ownership as a chief cause. See Nancy Isenberg, *White Trash: The 400-Year Untold History of Class in America* (New York: Viking, 2016), 37–41. On the lack of real legislative change that resulted from Bacon's Rebellion, see Brown, *Good Wives*, 173–74; Morgan, *American Slavery American Freedom*, 277–79.
72. Brown, *Good Wives*, 158.
73. Morgan, "British Encounters," 195; Webb, *1676*, 121; Rice, *Tales from a Revolution*, 114. See Pem Davidson Buck, *Worked to the Bone: Race, Class, Power, and Privilege in Kentucky* (New York: Monthly Review Press, 2001), 19–27.
74. On the ungovernability of Virginia due to Berkeley's mismanagement, as seen by the royal commissioners sent to restore order and reform Virginia's government, see Webb, *1676*, 134–62.
75. Brown, *Good Wives*, 164.
76. Rutman and Rutman, *A Place in Time*, 81.
77. Rutman and Rutman, 85–86; Morgan, *American Slavery American Freedom*, 272, Webb, *1676*, 130.
78. Warner, *History of Old Rappahannock*, 77. For a different version of the statement, with the same intent, delivered not by the king but by the royal

commissioners, see Morgan, *American Slavery American Freedom,* 273.

79. Achille Mbembe, "Necropolitics," *Public Culture* 15/1 (2003):11–40, at 11. See also Steve Martinot, *The Rule of Racialization* (Philadelphia: Temple University Press, 2003), 114.

80. Webb, *1676,* 130.

81. Webb, 135.

82. Kolp, 41, 43.

83. Brown, *Good Wives,* 173–74; Webb, *1676,* 158–62.

84. Webb, *1676,* 127, 137; Morgan, *American Slavery American Freedom,* 279, 281, 292–315.

85. See Buck, *Worked to the Bone,* 23–33.

86. Morgan, "British Encounters," 163. For a detailed account of the difference see Berlin, *Many Thousands Gone,* 7–10.

87. Parent, *Foul Means,* 59; see Horn, *Adapting to a New World,* 50; Gerald Horne, *The Counter-Revolution of 1776: Slave Resistance and the Origins of the United States of America* (New York: New York University Press, 2014), 44; Peter Linebaugh, *The London Hanged: Crime and Civil Society in the Eighteenth Century* (New York: Cambridge University Press, 1992), 428–29.

88. Karen and Barbara Fields, *Racecraft: The Soul of Inequality in American Life* (New York: Verso, 2014), 123–25.

89. Lerone Bennett, *The Shaping of Black America: The Struggles and Triumphs of African-Americans, 1619–1990s,* rev. ed. (New York: Penguin Books, 1991), 73–74.

90. For emphasis on the control of the entire labor force, white as well as black, see Buck, *Worked to the Bone*; Bennett, *The Shaping of Black America*; Theodore Allen, *Invention of the White Race,* vol. 2: *The Origin of Racial Oppression in Anglo America* (New York: Verso. 1997). For a more detailed account of the creation of a racial divide see, among others, Berlin, *Many Thousands Gone*; Parent, *Foul Means.*

91. Brown, *Good Wives,* 127, 181–84.

92. Brown, 181, 194–201; Paul Finkelman, "Crimes of Love, Misdemeanors of Passion: The Regulation of Race and Sex in Colonial Virginia," in Clinton and Gillespie, *The Devil's Lane,* 124–35. Previously servants in this situation were sold for an additional five years. See Bruce, *Economic History,* 2:37.

93. See Tilly, *Coercion, Capital, and European States,* 14–15.

94. On increased Crown control see Webb, *1676,* 102, 127–32, 149–63, 212–13; Brown, *Good Wives,* 168, 173–74; Morgan, *American Slavery American Freedom,* 281–85, 289–90. For the strengthening of local elites' control of punishment of slaves accused of crimes such as murder, assault, and theft, see Brown, *Good Wives,* 180–81.

95. Quoted in Nelson, *A Blessed Company*, 261.

96. Parent, *Foul Means*, 136; Morgan, "British Encounters," xxii.

3: ANCESTOR TALES OF SLAVERY, SLAVING, AND WOMEN WITH VOICE

1. Epigraph: From the estate inventory of Alexander Davidson I, *Spotsylvania Will Book A*, February 13, 1748, 487. For the full inventory see Appendix 1.

2. On "just war," see Matthew Jennings, *New Worlds of Violence: Cultures and Conquests in the Early American Southeast* (Knoxville: University of Tennessee Press, 2011), 59–61; Alan Gallay, *The Indian Slave Trade: The Rise of the English Empire in the American South 1670–1717* (New Haven: Yale University Press, 2002), 46; Paul Lovejoy, *Transformations in Slavery: A History of Slavery in Africa*, 3rd ed. (Cambridge University Press, 2012), 82–83.

3. "White" refers to people of English and Scottish ancestry in Virginia, taking the place of "English" and "Christian" more solidly after Bacon's Rebellion. It was a term that continually morphed to include more and more people of European ancestry, particularly during the American Revolution. "Black" likewise solidified after Bacon's Rebellion, designating anyone identified by their African ancestry, replacing "African" and various origin designations such as Igbo. However, it also morphed, including terms such as "mulatto" and sometimes expanding to include Native Americans.

4. Darrett Rutman and Anita Rutman, *A Place in Time: Middlesex County, Virginia 1650–1750* (New York: W. W. Norton, 1984), 173–74, 180.

5. Herbert Klein, *The Atlantic Slave Trade* (New York: Cambridge University Press, 1999), 209. Estimates vary, however, going up to over 11 million. See Jennifer Morgan, *Laboring Women: Reproduction and Gender in New World Slavery* (Philadelphia: University of Pennsylvania Press, 2004), 56; Mazi Ojiaku, *Yesteryear in Umu-Akha: History and Evolution of an Igbo Community (1665–1999)* (North Charleston, SC: Booksurge Publishing, 2008), 58.

6. What is now called Igboland was at that time made up of a large number of closely related societies that all later came under the heading of Igbo. Consequently the term Igbo as used by slave traders and owners is not terribly precise. The Aro at the time were peripheral to this culture but are now seen as an Igbo subgroup. See G. Ugo Nwokeji, *The Slave Trade and Culture in the Bight of Biafra: An African Society in the Atlantic World* (New York: Cambridge University Press, 2010), xvi–xvii.

7. On the likelihood of women and girls being sold into the Atlantic slave trade see Nwokeji, *The Slave Trade and Culture*, 5, 118, 121–25, 144–77; Morgan, *Laboring Women*, 60.

8. John Thornton, *Africa and Africans in the Making of the Atlantic World*,

1400–1800, 2nd ed. (Cambridge: Cambridge University Press, 1998), 321; Nwokeji, *The Slave Trade and Culture*, 1–2, 42.

9. Nwokeji, *The Slave Trade and Culture*, 5; Morgan, *Laboring Women*, 57.

10. Nwokeji, *The Slave Trade and Culture*, xiv, 6; Thornton, *Africa and Africans*, 304, 310.

11. Thornton, *Africa and Africans*, 318; Morgan, *Laboring Women*, 104, 108. Also see Ira Berlin, *Many Thousands Gone: The First Two Centuries of Slavery in North America* (Cambridge, MA: Harvard University Press, 1998), 112.

12. Thornton, *Africa and Africans*, 319.

13. Anthony Parent, *Foul Means: The Formation of a Slave Society in Virginia, 1660–1740* (Chapel Hill: Omohundro Institute and University of North Carolina Press, 2003), 227–28, 281; Rutman and Rutman, *A Place in Time*, 97–103; Berlin, *Many Thousands Gone*, 95–96.

14. Parent, *Foul Means*, 87.

15. David Northrup, *Trade without Rulers: Pre-Colonial Economic Development in South-Eastern Nigeria* (Oxford: Clarendon Press, 1978), 54.

16. On the relationship between capitalism and slavery, see Sven Beckert and Seth Rockman, eds., *Slavery's Capitalism: A New History of American Economic Development* (Philadelphia: University of Pennsylvania Press, 2016); Edward Baptist, *The Half Has Never Been Told: Slavery and the Making of American Capitalism* (New York: Basic Books, 2014); Eric Williams, *Capitalism and Slavery* (Chapel Hill: University of North Carolina Press, 1994 [1944]); Sven Beckert, *Empire of Cotton: A Global History* (New York: Alfred A. Knopf, 2015). See also Eric Wolf, *Europe and the People Without History* (Berkeley: University of California Press, 1982), 199–200; Gerald Horne, *The Counter-Revolution of 1776: Slave Resistance and the Origins of the United States of America* (New York: New York University Press, 2014), vii–ix.

17. St. Clair Drake, *Black Folk Here and There*, vol. 2 (Los Angeles: Center for Afro-American Studies, University of California, 1990), 227–29.

18. Ojiaku, *Yesteryear in Umu-Akha*, 58.

19. See James Scott, *Against the Grain: A Deep History of the Earliest States* (New Haven: Yale University Press, 2017), 150–82.

20. For example. see Peter Boomgaard, "Human Capital, Slavery and Low Rates of Economic and Population Growth in Indonesia, 1600–1910," in Gwyn Campbell, *The Structure of Slavery in Indian Ocean Africa and Asia*, 83–96 (Portland, OR: Frank Cass, 2004), 89; Gwyn Campbell, "Introduction: Slavery and Other Forms of Unfree Labour in the Indian Ocean World," in Campbell, *The Structure of Slavery in Indian Ocean Africa and Asia*, vii–xxxii (London: Frank Cass, 2004), at xiii. See also the articles collected

in Indrani Chatterjee and Richard Eaton, eds., *Slavery and South Asian History* (Bloomington: Indiana University Press, 2006).

21. For example Northrup, *Trade without Rulers*, 116; Simon Ottenberg, *Leadership and Authority in an Africa Society: The Afikpo Village-Group* (Seattle: University of Washington Press, 1971), 25.

22. Joseph Miller, "A Theme in Variations: A Historical Schema of Slaving in the Atlantic and Indian Ocean Regions," in Campbell, *The Structure of Slavery in Indian Ocean Africa and Asia*, 169–94 , at 185. Others also provide examples of this sort of organization where the goal is "wealth in people." See Nwokeji, *The Slave Trade and Culture*, 71, 157–58; Lovejoy, *Transformations in Slavery*, 8–14; Thornton, *Africa and Africans*, 72–97; Claude Meillassoux, *The Anthropology of Slavery: The Womb of Iron and Gold*, trans. Alide Dasnois (Chicago: University of Chicago Press, 1991 [1986]), 18, as well as the edited volumes by Chatterjee and Eaton, *Slavery and South Asian History*; Campbell, *The Structure of Slavery in Indian Ocean Africa and Asia*; and Martin Klein, *Breaking the Chains: Slavery, Bondage, and Emancipation in Modern Africa and Asia* (Madison: University of Wisconsin Press, 1993).

23. For descriptions of various forms of slavery in northern Igboland at a later time period see Nwando Achebe, *Farmers, Traders, Warriors, and Kings: Female Power and Authority in Northern Igboland 1900–1960* (Portsmouth, NH: Heinemann, 2005), 72–75.

24. For the shift in Biafra see Lovejoy, *Transformations in Slavery*, 177–84. For contending interpretations of the relationship between slavery in Africa before the Atlantic slave trade and the far more extensive use of slavery in Africa after the ending of the legal Atlantic trade, see Thornton, *Africa and Africans*; Lovejoy, *Transformations in Slavery*. See also Nwokeji, *The Slave Trade and Culture*, 24–26; Yaw Bredwa–Mensah, "Slavery and Resistance on Nineteenth Century Danish Plantations in Southeaster Gold Coast, Ghana," *African Study Monographs* 29/3 (September 2008), 133–45.

25. Catherine Coquery-Vidrovitch, *The History of African Cities South of the Sahara: From the Origins to Colonization*, trans. Mary Baker (Princeton: Marcus Wiener Publications, 2005 [1993]), 142–43; Thornton, *Africa and Africans*, 66–71.

26. Nwokeji, *The Slave Trade and Culture*, 49, 51–52; Lovejoy, *Transformations in Slavery*, 7.

27. Achebe, *Farmers, Traders, Warriors, and Kings*, 34; Elizabeth Isichei, *The Ibo People and the Europeans: The Genesis of a Relationship—to 1906* (New York: St. Martin's Press, 1973), 18.

28. For examples see Nehemia Levtzion and Jay Spaulding, eds., *Medieval West Africa: Views from Arab Scholars and Merchants* (Princeton: Marcus Wiener Publications, 2003).

29. Nwokeji, *The Slave Trade and Culture*, 165.

30. Thornton, *Africa and Africans*, 310; Nwokeji, *The Slave Trade and Culture*, 25; Olaudah Equiano, "The Early Travels of Olaudah Equiano," in Philip Curtin, *Africa Remembered: Narratives of West Africans from the Era of the Slave Trade* (Prospect Heights, IL: Waveland Press, 1997 [1967]), 69–98.

31. For example, see Margaret Green, *Ibo Village Affairs* (New York: Frederick Praeger, 1964 [1947]). On rioting see Judith Van Allen, "'Aba Riots' or Igbo 'Women's War'? Ideology, Stratification, and the Invisibility of Women," in Nancy Hafkin and Edna Bay, eds., *Women in Africa: Studies in Social and Economic Change*, 59–85 (Stanford, CA: Stanford University Press, 1976); Judith Van Allen, "'Sitting on a Man': Colonialism and the Lost Political Institutions of Igbo Women," *Canadian Journal of African Studies* 6/2 (1972):165–81.

32. Wolf, *Europe and the People Without History*, 1982.

33. G. I. Jones, "Olaudah Equiano of the Niger Ibo: Introduction," in Curtin, *Africa Remembered: Narratives of West Africans from the Era of the Slave Trade*, 60–69; Nwokeji, *The Slave Trade and Culture*, 25.

34. For Igbo ethnographies see Nwando Achebe, *The Female King of Colonial Nigeria: Ahebi Ugbabe* (Bloomington: Indiana University Press, 2011); Achebe, *Farmers, Traders, Warriors, and Kings*; Ifi Amadiume, *Male Daughters, Female Husbands: Gender and Sex in an African Society* (London: Zed Books, 1987); Green, *Ibo Village Affairs*; Northrup, *Trade without Rulers*; Ojiaku, *Yesteryear in Umu-Akha*; Ottenberg, *Leadership and Authority*. For more general analysis see among others Beth Greene, "The Institution of Woman-Marriage in Africa: A Cross-Cultural Analysis," *Ethnology* 37/4 (1998): 395–413; Jones, "Olaudah Equiano"; Lovejoy, *Transformations in Slavery*; Nwokeji, *The Slave Trade and Culture*; Thornton, *Africa and Africans*.

35. Nwokeji, *The Slave Trade and Culture*, xv–xvii. For influences of specific cultures see Isichei, *The Ibo People and the Europeans*, 29–43, Coquery-Vidrovitch, *The History of African Cities*, 168–69; Achebe, *Farmers, Traders, Warriors, and Kings*, 31. The ancient kingdom of Benin existed from the 1100s to the end of the 1800s.

36. Green, *Ibo Village Affairs*, 137.

37. Northrup, *Trade without Rulers*, 92–93. There is some dispute over the distribution of actual authority. See Nwokeji, *The Slave Trade and Culture*, 14. Most ethnographies seem to tend toward a rather diffuse/democratic model, rather than a powerful eze model. Given the variance in Igbo village-groups in different areas of Igboland, both interpretations may apply. See Achebe, *The Female King of Colonial Nigeria.*

38. Amadiume, *Male Daughters, Female Husbands*, 30.

39. For the following descriptions of family structure and compound

organization, patrilineage, and village and village-group organization see Green, *Ibo Village Affairs*; Ojiaku, *Yesteryear in Umu-Akha;* Amadiume, *Male Daughters, Female Husbands*; Ottenberg, *Leadership and Authority.*

40. Victor Uchendo, "Ezi Na Ulo: The Extended Family in Igbo Civilization," *Dialectical Anthropology* 31 (2007): 167–219, at 181; Amadiume, *Male Daughters, Female Husbands*, 32, 35.

41. Ottenberg, *Leadership and Authority*, 308; Green, *Ibo Village Affairs*, 137.

42. Northrup, for instance, in discussing village governance, totally misses the role of women and, despite writing a book about trade, never mentions that women controlled the local markets and were the principle local traders. Long-distance trade was largely male; local was female. See Northrup, *Trade without Rulers*, 92–93.

43. For analysis of women's positions as biological women and as women gendered as male, see Greene, "The Institution of Woman-Marriage;" Achebe, *The Female King of Colonial Nigeria*; Achebe, *Farmers, Traders, Warriors, and Kings*; Amadiume, *Male Daughters, Female Husbands*; Kamene Okonjo, "The Dual-Sex System in Operation: Igbo Women and Community Politics in Midwestern Nigeria," in Nancy Hafkin and Edna Bay, *Women in Africa: Studies in Social and Economic Change* (Stanford, CA: Stanford University Press, 1976), 45–58. Green, in *Ibo Village Affairs*, while making no mention of gender flexibility, is very clear on the power of women as women.

44. Achebe, *Farmers, Traders, Warriors, and Kings*, 144; Amadiume, *Male Daughters, Female Husbands*, 66.

45. Van Allen, "'Sitting on a Man.'"

46. Achebe, *Farmers, Traders, Warriors, and Kings*, 165. Names for this position varied.

47. Amadiume, *Male Daughters, Female Husbands*, 55.

48. Amadiume, 53–56. For description of a somewhat similar system in a different area of Igboland see Achebe, *Farmers, Traders, Warriors, and Kings*, 165.

49. Okonjo, "The Dual-Sex System;" Achebe, *Farmers, Traders, Warriors, and Kings*, 162–77; Achebe, *The Female King of Colonial Nigeria*, 106, 162.

50. Ottenberg, *Leadership and Authority*, 52–68, 157, 160. Green, in *Ibo Village Affairs* refers frequently to the role of age grades in recounting village doings.

51. Amadiume, *Male Daughters, Female Husbands*, 34–40; Van Allen, "'Sitting on a Man,'" 168.

52. For discussion of women as men, of woman-woman marriage, of male daughters, and of women in male positions see Amadiume, *Male Daughters, Female Husbands*; Greene, "The Institution of Woman-Marriage"; Achebe, *Farmers, Traders, Warriors, and Kings*; Achebe, *The Female King of Colonial Nigeria.*

53. Achebe, *The Female King of Colonial Nigeria*, 24–25, 174–77.
54. Achebe, *Farmers, Traders, Warriors, and Kings*, 121; Achebe, *The Female King of Colonial Nigeria*, 39–42; Amadiume, *Male Daughters, Female Husbands*, 71.
55. Achebe, *The Female King of Colonial Nigeria*, 55, 58–60.
56. Amadiume, *Male Daughters, Female Husbands*, 31–33; Greene, "The Institution of Woman–Marriage."
57. Nwokeji, *The Slave Trade and Culture*, 158. On the roles of female husbands see particularly Amadiume, *Male Daughters, Female Husbands*.
58. Amadiume, *Male Daughters, Female Husbands*, 185.
59. On the Aro see particularly Nwokeji, *The Slave Trade and Culture*; Northrup, *Trade without Rulers*; Lovejoy, *Transformations in Slavery*, 81–83.
60. Nwokeji, *The Slave Trade and Culture*, 17–19.
61. Nwokeji, 3.
62. Lovejoy, *Transformations in Slavery*, 56, 58, 93–95, 98–100; Isichei, *The Ibo People and the Europeans*, 47–48.
63. Northrup says that they used the already existing trading system; they were just much more single-minded about it. They combined all the existing marketing networks into a single marketing grid in which they and others participated as equals—they didn't control it, they just were the center pin of it. They used kinship to make alliances with other Aro. He maintains that they made not a state but a nation, and this common identity enabled them to work together when necessary. That identity was maintained partly by insisting on their elite status in the towns where they lived. Northrup, *Trade without Rulers*, 141–44.
64. Nwokeji, *The Slave Trade and Culture*, 12, 65, 69–70; Ottenberg, *Leadership and Authority*, 25; Isichei, *The Ibo People and the Europeans*, 55. On the various means used to enslave see also Northrup, *Trade without Rulers*, 65–80.
65. Lovejoy, *Transformations in Slavery*, 13. For differing interpretations of pawns' ability to redeem themselves see Achebe, *Farmers, Traders, Warriors, and Kings*, 73.
66. Nwokeji, *The Slave Trade and Culture*, 80; 95; Isichei, *The Ibo People and the Europeans*, 36–37, 49.
67. Nwokeji, *The Slave Trade and Culture*, 141–42.
68. Achebe, *Farmers, Traders, Warriors, and Kings*, 54–55. See also Achebe, *The Female King of Colonial Nigeria*, 97–135.
69. Ottenberg's description of Afikpo particularly lends itself to the interpretation of dual sovereignty. See Ottenberg, *Leadership and Authority*, 157–60, 187. See also Achebe, *The Female King of Colonial Nigeria*, 54–55, 77–78, 106, 121; Achebe, *Farmers, Traders, Warriors, and Kings*, 54–55; 162–66 .

70. Ottenberg, *Leadership and Authority*, 187–88, 308–09.

71. Green, *Ibo Village Affairs*, 100–101.

72. Achebe, *The Female King of Colonial Nigeria*, 121.

73. This description depends on Green, *Ibo Village Affairs*, 99–115.

74. Green, *Ibo Village Affairs*, 113, 198. For example, Ottenberg, *Leadership and Authority*, 126; Amadiume, *Male Daughters, Female Husbands*, 51–68.

75. Achebe, *Farmers, Traders, Warriors, and Kings*, 28.

76. For contrasting views see Lovejoy, *Transformations in Slavery*, 183; Uchendo, "Ezi Na Ulo," 193; Isichei, *The Ibo People and the Europeans*, 58–59.

77. Ojiaku, *Yesteryear in Umu-Akha*, 55–57. See also Achebe, *The Female King of Colonial Nigeria*, 60.

78. Ojiaku, *Yesteryear in Umu-Akha*, 60–61; Isichei, *The Ibo People and the Europeans*, 58–59. See also Bredwa-Mensah, "Slavery and Resistance," 139–40.

79. Northrup, *Trade without Rulers*, 71, also 69–73; Nwokeji, *The Slave Trade and Culture*, 77–80.

80. Nwokeji, *The Slave Trade and Culture*, 76, 114.

81. Northrup, *Trade without Rulers*, 143–44; Nwokeji, *The Slave Trade and Culture*, 55.

82. Nwokeji, *The Slave Trade and Culture*, 55; Northrup, *Trade without Rulers*, 115–19, 138, 143–45.

83. Nwokeji, *The Slave Trade and Culture*, 77.

84. Nwokeji, 6, 45, 77–78.

85. Nwokeji, 77; Northrup, *Trade without Rulers*, 71–72, 137–38; Ottenberg, *Leadership and Authority*, 25; Lovejoy, *Transformations in Slavery*, 83.

86. Green, *Ibo Village Affairs*, 100–102, 114–15; Northrup, *Trade without Rulers*, 72–73; Achebe, *The Female King of Colonial Nigeria*, 55–58.

87. Northrup, *Trade without Rulers*, 72; Isichei, *The Ibo People and the Europeans*, 48; Nwokeji, *The Slave Trade and Culture*, 132–140.

88. For example Northrup, *Trade without Rulers*, 69, 72, 76, 138; Isichei, *The Ibo People and the Europeans*, 48; Nwokeji, *The Slave Trade and Culture*, 129; Lovejoy, *Transformations in Slavery*, 83.

89. Green, *Ibo Village Affairs*, 138; Amadiume, *Male Daughters, Female Husbands*, 21; Van Allen, "'Sitting on a Man,'" 166. However, for a less egalitarian interpretation see Nwokeji, *The Slave Trade and Culture*, 11–19. See also Northrup, *Trade without Rulers*, 118, 139, 141, 145. For an interesting 1920s twist on the question of state, sovereignty, and punishment, see Van Allen, "'Aba Riots' or Igbo 'Women's War'?; Achebe, *Farmers, Traders, Warriors, and Kings*, 176–77.

90. For pointing out the way in which a whole economy could be involved in the production of materials and services required by the slave trade I am

indebted to Yvonne Jones, April 2014. For a similar analysis, specifically of the production of guns both for use in and as trade goods for colonial America and in Africa, see Priya Satia, *Empire of Guns: The Violent Making of the Industrial Revolution* (New York: Penguin Press, 2018).

91. Beckert, *Empire of Cotton*, xvi, 29–55; see also Coquery-Vidrovitch, *The History of African Cities*, 149–150; Nwokeji, *The Slave Trade and Culture*, 14.

92. For contrasting views see Northrup, *Trade without Rulers*, 118, 141–42; Nwokeji, *The Slave Trade and Culture*, xiv, 16, 64.

93. Northrup, *Trade without Rulers*, 140; Nwokeji, *The Slave Trade and Culture*, 15.

94. Nwokeji, *The Slave Trade and Culture*, 15, 64, 65, 71.

95. Klein, *The Atlantic Slave Trade*, 79–80; Horne, *The Counter-Revolution*, 5, 45–49, 82.

4: ANCESTOR TALES OF THE REVOLT THAT HAPPENED, AND ONE THAT DIDN'T

1. My assumption was based on a variety of sources. The first were Ancestry. com sources, some more serious than others. More reliably, I thought, there was a Clan Davidson Tour website which has since been updated and no longer puts an Alexander Davidson in Dingwall, but in another nearby town. See Clan Davidson touring information, http://www.ancestralscotland. com/plan/ itineraries/davidson. There is also a DNA site and a manuscript by a careful family researcher. See *Davidson/Davison/Davisson Research DNA Study Project*, Family 8, kit 21985, http://www.tqsi.com/davidsongenes2/results.php; Landon Chambliss, *Baird–Davidson–Rogers–Wood and Allied History*, typed ms., Davidson file, Hart County Historical Society, Munfordville, KY, 1989.

2. Earl of Cromartie, *A Highland History* (Berkhamsted, Hertfordshire: Gavin Press, 1979); Norman Macrae, *The Romance of a Royal Burgh: Dingwall's Story of a Thousand Years* (Dingwall: The North Star Proprietors, 1923; repr. EP Publishing Ltd., East Ardsley, Wakefield, Yorkshire, 1974); Eric Richards and Monica Clough, *Cromartie: Highland Life 1650–1914* (Aberdeen: Aberdeen University Press, 1989). For additional frequent references see Karen Cullen, *Famine in Scotland: The 'Ill Years' of the 1690s* (Edinburgh: Edinburgh University Press, 2010).

3. Macrae, *The Romance of a Royal Burgh*; Mt. Tabor Book Committee, *The History of Mt. Tabor Baptist Church: The Oldest Church in Barren County, Kentucky* (Glasgow, KY: South Central Kentucky Historical and Genealogical Society, 1988), 23.

4. There is another obvious possibility. There was an Alexander Davidson transported to Maryland in 1747, after the third Jacobite Uprising, a

shoemaker, and my Alexander I was a shoemaker in Virginia. The shift from Maryland to Virginia is not particularly problematic, but Alexander's first appearance in the records is in 1745, and if his son Alexander II really was born in 1744, then Alexander II can't be the son of the Alexander transported in 1747. Or Alexander I could have been one of the Alexanders who arrived at any time between 1715 and about 1740. See David Dobson, *Directory of Scots Banished to the American Plantations* (Baltimore: Genealogical Publishing Company, 1983), 36–37; David Dobson, *The Original Scots Colonists of Early America, 1612–1783* (Baltimore: Genealogical Publishing Company, 1995), 70–71.

5. Alan McNie, *Clan Davidson*, rev. ed. (Jedburgh, Scotland: Cascade Publishing Company, 1989), 14.

6. For example John Macleod, *Highlanders: A History of the Gaels* (London: Hodder and Stoughton, 1996); Allistar Moffat, *The Highland Clans* (New York: Thames and Hudson, 2010).

7. For a fairly brief description of this period see T. C. Smout, *A History of the Scottish People 1560–1830* (Glasgow, Scotland: Fontana/Collins, 1969), 17–46.

8. Smout, *A History*, 33–34.

9. Cynthia Neville, however, sees this instead as a sharing of power that allowed for the importance of kin groups, not as an inability of the Crown to govern. See Cynthia Neville, *Land, Law, and People in Medieval Scotland* (Edinburgh: Edinburgh University Press, 2010), 13–14. For the changing justice system and its variations see Neville, *Land, Law, and People,* 1–35. See Moffat, *The Highland Clans,* 35; Macleod, *Highlanders*, 113; Christopher Whatley, "Order and Disorder," in Whatley and Elizabeth Foyster, *A History of Everyday Life in Scotland: 1600–1800* (Edinburgh: Edinburgh University Press, 2010), 191–216, at 198–199; John Bannerman, "MacDuff of Fife," in Alexander Grant and Keith Stringer, *Medieval Scotland: Crown, Lordship and Community* (Edinburgh: Edinburgh University Press, 1998), 20–38 at 23–24; Ian Whyte, *Agriculture and Society in Seventeenth-Century Scotland* (Edinburgh: John Donald Publishers Ltd, 1979), 44–51.

10. See Michael Brown and Steve Boardman, "Survival and Revival: Late Medieval Scotland," in Jenny Wormald, *Scotland: A History,* 69–92 (New York: Oxford University Press, 2005), 91; I. F. Grant, *The Social and Economic Development of Scotland Before 1603* (Edinburgh: Oliver and Boyd, 1930), 24–31; Smout, *A History*, 34.

11. On justiciars, see Alan Young, "The Earls and Earldom of Buchan in the Thirteenth Century," in Alexander Grant and Keith Stringer, *Medieval Scotland: Crown, Lordship and Community,* 174–202 (Edinburgh: Edinburgh University Press, 1998), 178; A. D. M. Barrell, *Medieval Scotland* (Cambridge: Cambridge University Press, 2000), 35–36; Macleod,

Highlanders, 113. See also Moffat, *The Highland Clans*, 46. More generally on the power of lords see Grant, *The Social and Economic Development of Scotland*, 138, 174–86; Daniel Szechi, *1715: The Great Jacobite Rebellion* (New Haven: Yale University Press, 2006), 22. For the pit see Sheila Livingstone, *Confess and Be Hanged: Scottish Crime and Punishment Through the Ages* (Edinburgh: Birlinn, 2000), 21.

12. See Barrell, *Medieval Scotland*, 35–36; Smout, *A History*, 34.

13. See Cromartie, *A Highland History*, 71–72; Robert Dodgshon, "'Pretense of Blude' and 'Place of Thair Duelling': The Nature of Scottish Clans, 1500–1745," in Robert Houston and Ian Whyte, *Scottish Society 1500–1800* (New York: Cambridge University Press,1989), 169–98, at180–81.

14. Macleod, *Highlanders*, 126–27; Ian Whyte, *Scotland Before the Industrial Revolution, c.1500–c.1750* (New York: Longman, 1995), 268.

15. Whyte, *Scotland Before the Industrial Revolution*, 253.

16. Whyte, 253; Grant, *The Social and Economic Development of Scotland*, 506, 528–30; Livingstone, *Confess and Be Hanged*, 53–64; Smout, *A History*, 39–40, Moffat, *The Highland Clans*, 46. For a word of caution about the prevalence of feuding, however, see Alexander Grant, "Crown and Nobility in Late Medieval Britain," in Roger Mason, *Scotland and England 1286–1815* (Edinburgh: John Donald Publishers, 1987), 34–59.

17. Grant, *The Social and Economic Development of Scotland*, 481; A.D.M. Barrell,135–36; Moffat, *The Highland Clans*, 46, 49–50, 65; Macleod, *Highlanders*, 98–99. See also John Bellamy, *Crime and Public Order in England in the Later Middle Ages* (Toronto: University of Toronto Press/ Routledge & Kegan Paul, 1973), 47; Smout, *A History*, 41–43, 313–21.

18. My description of clan structure is based particularly on Dodgshon, "'Pretense of Blude'; Whyte, *Agriculture and Society*, 29–56; Whyte, *Scotland Before the Industrial Revolution*, 251–59; Smout, *A History*, 35, 41–44, 313–20; Margaret Sanderson, *A Kindly Place? Living in Sixteenth-Century Scotland* (East Linton, UK: Tuckwell Press, 2002), 1–31; Grant, *The Social and Economic Development of Scotland*, 16–26, 42–43, 51–52, 64–65, 154–57, 478–524. Biases toward both the romantic view of clans and toward the primitive savage view are evident in several of these references, often resembling what Pittock calls the myth of the Highland clans. See Murray Pittock, *The Myth of the Jacobite Clans: The Jacobite Army in 1745*, 2nd rev. ed. (Edinburgh: Edinburgh University Press, 2009).

19. Dodgshon, "'Pretense of Blude,'" 189; Smout, *A History*, 132–33.

20. Macrae, *The Romance of a Royal Burgh*, 185; Macleod, *Highlanders*, 101; Whyte, *Scotland Before the Industrial Revolution*, 261; Dodgshon, "'Pretense of Blude,'" 188; Moffat, *The Highland Clans*, 44–46.

21. Smout, *A History*, 129, 131; Whyte, *Scotland Before the Industrial Revolution*, 254; Whyte, *Agriculture and Society*, 157. See also Grant, *The*

Social and Economic Development of Scotland, 98, 294, 519; Macrae, The Romance of a Royal Burgh, 185–86; Macleod, Highlanders, 144; Cromartie, A Highland History, 75; Moffat, The Highland Clans, 35, 46.

22. Whyte, Agriculture and Society, 138; 117; Smout, A History, 39.

23. Cromartie, A Highland History, xiv, 72–77, 99, 114–23; Grant, The Social and Economic Development of Scotland, 495, 498; Archie McKerracher, Davidson (Newtongrange, Midlothian: LangSyne Publishing, n.d.), 12.

24. Dodgshon, "'Pretense of Blude.'" See Grant, The Social and Economic Development of Scotland, 501–5.

25. McKerracher, Davidson, 16; Matthew Dawson, "Battles of Invernhaven and Perth–1300s," Clan Davidson Society of North America, https://clandavidson.org/the-clan/history-of-clan-davidson/battles-of-invernhaven-and-perth-1300s/2/.

26. Whyte, Scotland Before the Industrial Revolution, 254; Macleod, Highlanders, 82.

27. Moffat, The Highland Clans, 46. See also Cromartie, A Highland History, 37–38; Grant, The Social and Economic Development of Scotland, 520.

28. Cromartie, A Highland History, 57, 66–67; Moffat, The Highland Clans, 50; Macleod, Highlanders, 112.

29. Grant, The Social and Economic Development of Scotland, 95, 520; Moffat, The Highland Clans, 46.

30. Jane Dawson, Scotland Re-Formed 1488–1587 (Edinburgh: Edinburgh University Press, 2007), 18; Christopher Whatley, "Order and Disorder," 194.

31. Moffat, The Highland Clans, 46–52; Grant, The Social and Economic Development of Scotland, 535–42; Whatley, "Order and Disorder," 210; Smout, A History, 103–6.

32. Moffat, The Highland Clans, 52–55; Grant, The Social and Economic Development of Scotland, 540–42; Macrae, The Romance of a Royal Burgh, 78, 80.

33. Smout, A History, 212.

34. Moffat, The Highland Clans, 48; P. G. Maxwell-Stuart, An Abundance of Witches: The Great Scottish Witch-Hunt (Stroud, Gloucestershire: Tempus Publishing, 2005), 106, 178, 206–7.

35. Quoted in Richards and Clough, Cromartie, 54. See also Cromartie, A Highland History, 306; Grant, The Social and Economic Development of Scotland, 536.

36. On the concept of barbarians, see James Scott, Against the Grain: A Deep History of the Earliest States (New Haven: Yale University Press, 2017), 219–56.

37. Macrae, The Romance of a Royal Burgh, 85, 88, 181; Richards and Clough, Cromartie, 7. For discussion of burghs and the class structure within them

in the 1500 and 1600s see Smout, *A History*, 28, 146–70.
38. Grant, *The Social and Economic Development of Scotland*, 117, 119; Cromartie, *A Highland History*, 118.
39. Smout, *A History*, 28–29, 312; Macrae, *The Romance of a Royal Burgh*, 85–96. On Dingwall's market see Macrae, *The Romance of a Royal Burgh*, 89; Cromartie, *A Highland History*, 127–30.
40. Cromartie, *A Highland History*, 48–49, 135; Macrae, *The Romance of a Royal Burgh*, xi–xv, 33–37, 52–55, 75, 77, 79, 94, 154, 158.
41. Macrae, *The Romance of a Royal Burgh*, 161.
42. Cromartie, *A Highland History*, 237; Grant, *The Social and Economic Development of Scotland*, 557; Smout, *A History*, 150–53; Elizabeth Ewan, "'Hamperit in ane hony came': Sights, Sounds and Smells in the Medieval Town," in Edward Cowan and Lizanne Henderson, *A History of Everyday Life in Medieval Scotland, 1000–1600* (Edinburgh: Edinburgh University Press, 2011), 110–44.
43. Elizabeth Isichei, *The Ibo People and the Europeans: The Genesis of a Relationship—to 1906* (New York: St. Martin's Press, 1973), 59; Margaret Green, *Ibo Village Affairs* (New York: Frederick Praeger, 1964 [1947]), 140–42.
44. See for example Yvonne Brown and Rona Ferguson, Introduction," in Brown and Ferguson, *Twisted Sisters: Women, Crime and Deviance in Scotland Since 1400* (East Lothian, Scotland: Tuckwell Press, 2002), 1–9.
45. Smout, *A History*, 133.
46. Marjorie Plant supplies the answer, by way of Doctor Johnson's description of travels around Scotland: some women carried a knife and fork in their reticule. But usually the men cut their meat and then gave their knife and fork to the woman, while the men ate with their fingers. See Marjorie Plant, *The Domestic Life of Scotland in the Eighteenth Century* (Edinburgh: Edinburgh University Press, 1952), 45.
47. Norman Newton, *Lost Inverness* (Edinburgh: Birlinn, 2013), 210.
48. Maggie Craig, "The Fair Sex Turns Ugly: Female Involvement in the Jacobite Rising of 1745," in Brown and Ferguson, *Twisted Sisters: Women, Crime and Deviance in Scotland Since 1400*, 84–100, at 97–99.
49. For example Brown and Ferguson, *Twisted Sisters*; Elizabeth Ewan and Maureen Meikle, eds., *Women in Scotland c.1100–c.1750* (East Linton, UK: Tuckwell Press, 1999); Christina Larner, *Enemies of God: The Witch-Hunt in Scotland* (Edinburgh: John Donald, 2000 [1981]); Rosalind Marshall, *Virgins and Viragos: A History of Women in Scotland From 1080–1980* (Chicago: Academy Chicago, 1983). For a much earlier work which, while not focused on women, does have considerable information about their lives, see Plant, *The Domestic Life of Scotland*. There is much more information available about upper-class women than others.

50. Craig, "The Fair Sex Turns Ugly," 93–94; Dumhnall Stiùbhart, "Women and Gender in the Early Modern Western Gàidhealtachd," in Ewan and Meikle, *Women in Scotland c.1100–c.1750* 233–49, at 233–34.

51. Marshall, *Virgins and Viragos*, 18–21, 71.

52. Marshall, 25–26; David Sellar, "The Family," in Edward Cowan and Lizanne Henderson, *A History of Everyday Life in Medieval Scotland, 1000–1600* (Edinburgh: Edinburgh University Press, 2011), 89–108, at 99–100.

53. Marshall, *Virgins and Viragos*, 35; Alastair Mann, "Embroidery to Enterprise: the Role of Women in the Book Trade of Early Modern Scotland," in Ewan and Meikle, *Women in Scotland c.1100–c.1750*, 136–51, at 136.

54. Anne Frater, "Women of the Gàidhealtachd and Their Songs to 1750," in Ewan and Meikle, *Women in Scotland c.1100–c.1750*, 67–79, at 67.

55. Marshall, *Virgins and Viragos*, 28; Sellar, "The Family," 99–100.

56. Plant, *The Domestic Life of Scotland*, 131–58; Marshall, *Virgins and Viragos*, 41–60, 142–48.

57. Cromartie, *A Highland History*, 128–30; Macrae, *The Romance of a Royal Burgh*, 161–63.

58. Elizabeth Ewan, "'For Whatever Ales Ye': Women as Consumers and Producers in Late Medieval Scottish Towns," in Ewan and Meikle, *Women in Scotland c.1100–c.1750*, 125–35, at 131; Elizabeth Ewan, "Crime or Culture? Women and Daily Life in Late-Medieval Scotland," in Brown and Ferguson, *Twisted Sisters*, 117–136.

59. Ewan, "Crime or Culture?," 120; Nwando Achebe, *Farmers, Traders, Warriors, and Kings: Female Power and Authority in Northern Igboland 1900–1960* (Portsmouth, NH: Heinemann, 2005), 144–45. See also Green, *Ibo Village Affairs*, 133, 171.

60. Smout, *A History*, 113.

61. Whyte, *Agriculture and Society*, 162–68; Cromartie, *A Highland History*, 199; Smout, *A History*, 139–41; Plant, *The Domestic Life of Scotland*, 29–31, 33.

62. Whyte, *Agriculture and Society*, 38, 166.

63. Whyte, 71–72; Macleod, *Highlanders*, 101.

64. Macleod, *Highlanders*, 101, 143; Robert Dodgshon, "The Scottish Farming Township as Metaphor," in Leah Leneman, *Perspectives in Scottish Social History: Essays in Honour of Rosalind Mitchison* (Aberdeen: Aberdeen University Press, 1988), 69–82; Smout, *A History*, 113–15. For thorough discussion of farming and its transformation in Scotland see Whyte, *Agriculture and Society*; Smout, *A History*, 111–45; 282–310.

65. Stiùbhart, "Women and Gender," 234–35; Smout, *A History*, 298–99.

66. Gordon DesBrisay, "Wet Nurses and Unwed Mothers in Seventeenth-Century Aberdeen," in Ewan and Meikle, *Women in Scotland c.1100–c.1750*, 210–220; Larner, *Enemies of God*, 56. On the lives of young servant women

see Ian Whyte and Kathleen Whyte, "The Geographical Mobility of Women in Early Modern Scotland," in Leneman, *Perspectives in Scottish Social History*, 83–106.

67. Stiùbhart, "Women and Gender," 235; Marshall, *Virgins and Viragos*, 148–50.

68. Cullen, *Famine in Scotland*; Sanderson, *A Kindly Place?*, vii; Smout, *A History*, 137–41.

69. Macleod, *Highlanders*, 110. See also Gordon DesBrisay, "Twisted by Definition: Women Under Godly Discipline in Seventeenth-Century Scottish Towns," in Brown and Ferguson, *Twisted Sisters*, 138–55, at 138.

70. Michael Graham, "Women and the Church Courts in Reformation-Era Scotland," in Ewan and Meikle, *Women in Scotland c.1100–c.1750*, 187–98, at 188.

71. For example, Geoffrey Parker, "The 'Kirk by Law Established' and the Origins of 'The Taming of Scotland': St Andrews 1559–1600," in Leneman, *Perspectives in Scottish Social History: Essays in Honour of Rosalind Mitchison*, 1–32, at 5.

72. That power was abolished after the defeat of the last Jacobite Rebellion in 1745 in an attempt to break the power of the Highland chiefs, although many simply got themselves appointed in the new judicial system. See Livingstone, *Confess and Be Hanged*, 22.

73. Whyte, *Agriculture and Society*, 44–51; Grant, *The Social and Economic Development of Scotland*, 185; Smout, *A History*, 116–17. For an earlier period see Neville, *Land, Law, and People*, 15.

74. Grant, *The Social and Economic Development of Scotland*, 563–65; see also Rosalind Mitchison, *The Old Poor Law in Scotland: The Experience of Poverty, 1574–1845* (Edinburgh: Edinburgh University Press).

75. See Michel Foucault, *Discipline and Punish: The Birth of the Prison*, translated by Alan Sheridan (New York: Vintage Books, 1995 [1975]).

76. Macrae, *The Romance of a Royal Burgh*, 330, 322, 331. See also Parker, "The 'Kirk by Law Established.'" 3.

77. Macrae, *The Romance of a Royal Burgh*, 316–35. See also Graham, "Women and the Church Courts, 193; Parker, "The 'Kirk by Law Established,'" 3; DesBrisay, "Twisted by Definition," 137.

78. Parker, "The 'Kirk by Law Established,'" 18; see also Mitchison, *The Old Poor Law*.

79. DesBrisay, "Twisted by Definition,"138.

80. Parker, "The 'Kirk by Law Established,'" 5–6.

81. Parker, 12; Livingstone, *Confess and Be Hanged*, 121–23.

82. Macrae, *The Romance of a Royal Burgh*, 328–30.

83. Macrae, 324.

84. Livingstone, *Confess and Be Hanged*, 121; Larner, *Enemies of God*, 57.

85. See Neville, *Land, Law, and People,* 147–85; Grant, *The Social and Economic Development of Scotland,* 73–79; Smout, *A History,* 36, 168–70. For a Dingwall example see Macrae, *The Romance of a Royal Burgh,* 42.

86. On the role of sectarian differences in the Jacobite rebellions see Smout, *A History,* 57–66; Szechi, *1715,* 21–23.

87. I am particularly dependent on Larner's analysis of Scottish witch hunting in *Enemies of God* as a basis for this interpretation. On diarchy and punishment see Pem Davidson Buck, "Stating Punishment: The Struggle over the Right to Punish," *North American Dialogue* 17/1 (2014): 31–43.

88. Larner, *Enemies of God,* 196,199.

89. Larner, 1, 87–88.

90. See Maxwell-Stuart, *An Abundance of Witches,* 13–34.

91. Larner, *Enemies of God,* 54, 58.

92. Larner, 193. On the role of the devil as seen differently by class see 135–91.

93. Larner, 1, 80. Few of the discussions of the witchcraft panics address the question of why, in the Highland Gaelic areas, no witchcraft accusations were recorded, although the coastal Highlands—less heavily Gaelic, more under vhurch control—had many. Nevertheless, all agree this is the case. I'm attempting an explanation here. In the Highlands, the older Gaelic beliefs hung on much longer, though eventually overlaid with an Episcopalian veneer. The clan system, with its more communal ethic and the requirements of Highlands cooperative farming, along with the continued dominance of clan chiefs, may also have insulated Highlanders against the belief that individuals among them, on whom they depended, could make individual malicious pacts with the devil to individually advance themselves. Ideas such as fairies and the evil eye did abound—but the evil eye takes effect accidentally; it is not a purposeful act of malice. The idea of individually getting ahead through competition with others isn't built into a system where farmers exchange fields every few years and pay taxes jointly. Richard Lee's discussion of evil coming from outside the community, where people have to be able to cooperate, as Highlands cooperative farming required, is helpful in this regard, though relating to a very different kind of social structure. See Richard Lee, *The Dobe Ju/'hoansi,* 3rd ed. (Belmont, CA: Wadsworth, 2002), 137–40. And the Episcopalian version of Protestantism, to the extent that it did take hold, was closer to the old Catholicism and did not demand the individualized worship and commitment that was demanded by particularly Calvinistic Presbyterianism. All of this together may have meant that ideas about the devil had little purchase among Highlanders. In addition, the clan chiefs were able to defy the king generally, so perhaps to keep the king at bay they settled what accusations there were in-house and without executions.

94. See also Maxwell-Stuart, *An Abundance of Witches,* 224–28.

95. Larner, *Enemies of God,* 49; Sanderson, *A Kindly Place?,* vii. Smout,

however, sees parts of the 1600s as having less famine than parts of the 1500s. See Smout, *A History,* 143.

96. Cullen, *Famine in Scotland,* 138.
97. Cullen, 2, 18, 93, 191, 124; Smout, *A History,* 153.
98. Cullen, *Famine in Scotland,* 39; Richards and Clough, *Cromartie,* 40.
99. Richards and Clough, 30, 34, 41–42.
100. Richards and Clough, 47; Cromartie, *A Highland History,* 323. See Whyte, *Scotland Before the Industrial Revolution,* 270; Moffat, *The Highland Clans,* 114.
101. Richards and Clough, *Cromartie,* 48–49; Whyte, *Scotland Before the Industrial Revolution,* 253; Smout, *A History,* 129–34; Cromartie, *A Highland History,* 222.
102. Richards and Clough, *Cromartie,* 49.
103. Cullen, *Famine in Scotland,* 93, 92–96.
104. Cullen, 88. See also Richards and Clough, *Cromartie,* 34.
105. Richards and Clough, 43; Cromartie, *A Highland History,* 222. For improvers from their own perspective see Smout, *A History,* 271–81; Whyte, *Agriculture and Society*; Whyte, *Scotland Before the Industrial Revolution,* 143–49.
106. Whyte discusses this legislation in detail; however, he would not buy my interpretation, as he describes the improvement mentality as beneficial to the whole society, and takes little account of the fate of people who lost their rights to land use and the increased inequality this produced, although he does acknowledge that increase. Whyte, *Agriculture and Society,* 98–110, 168, 123, 145. On the Lowlands see Sanderson, *A Kindly Place?,* 31.
107. Moffat, *The Highland Clans,* 85; Dodgshon, "'Pretense of Blude,'" 193; Whyte, *Agriculture and Society,* 118, 124.
108. Smout, *A History,* 125. For the struggle over wages in other contexts see Peter Linebaugh, *The London Hanged: Crime and Civil Society in the Eighteenth Century* (New York: Cambridge University Press, 1992); Robert Steinfeld, *Coercion, Contract, and Free Labor in the Nineteenth Century* (New York: Cambridge University Press, 2001).
109. Macrae, *The Romance of a Royal Burgh,* 181.
110. Macleod, *Highlanders,* 112, 144. See also Macrae, *The Romance of a Royal Burgh,* 186. On varying overlapping labor types see Sanderson, *A Kindly Place?,* 36–39. On the rural hierarchy see Smout, *A History,* 126–45. By the mid-1700s, however, tacksmen began to disappear—landholders could keep more for themselves by removing the middleman. Whyte sees this as the real end of the clan system—commercialism had replaced kinship as the organizing principle. See Whyte, *Scotland Before the Industrial Revolution,* 263–64.
111. Smout, *A History,* 113; Whyte, *Scotland Before the Industrial Revolution,* 260.

112. Whyte, *Scotland Before the Industrial Revolution*, 254, 257; Dodgshon, "'Pretense of Blude,'" 181; Smout, *A History*, 137–38; Sanderson, *A Kindly Place?* 1–31, 203–5.
113. Whyte, *Scotland Before the Industrial Revolution*, 254.
114. Cullen, *Famine in Scotland*, 158.
115. Smout, *A History*, 263.
116. Cromartie, *A Highland History*, 247.
117. Presbyterian and Episcopalian churches are both Protestant; Presbyterians had broken away from the Church of England, rejecting the Anglican power of bishops; there were periods when the Presbyterian Church was the official Church of Scotland. Episcopalians maintained the Anglican Church hierarchy of bishops, with a structure much closer to that of the Catholic Church, which both sects rejected. *Kirk* is the term for the Scottish Church.
118. For a brief history of this period in the Highlands see Macleod, *Highlanders*, 127–47.
119. See Szechi, *1715*, 23, 54.
120. For varying analyses of Jacobite armies, tactics, demographics, and religious issues see Pittock, *The Myth of the Jacobite Clans;* Margaret Sankey, *Jacobite Prisoners of the 1715 Rebellion: Preventing and Punishing Insurrection in Early Hanoverian Britain* (Burlington VT: Ashgate, 2005); Szechi, *1715*.
121. Fitzroy Maclean, *Scotland: A Concise History* (New York: Thames and Hudson, 2000 [1970]), 139–140.
122. Maclean, 145–46; Moffat, *The Highland Clans*, 72–74; Macleod, *Highlanders*, 141–42.
123. Sankey, *Jacobite Prisoners*, x–xi.
124. Pittock, *The Myth of the Jacobite Clans*, 140–57.
125. Mt. Tabor Book Committee, *The History of Mt. Tabor*, 23. There is a claim that he was actually Irish or Scots-Irish; Irish people did join the rebellion. See Frank Gorin, *The Times of Long Ago: Barren County, Kentucky* (Glasgow, KY: South Central Kentucky Historical and Genealogical Society, 1992 [1929]), 138.
126. Cromartie, *A Highland History*, 222–23, 242–47; Dobson, *Original Scots Colonists*, 70–71; Dobson, *Directory of Scots Banished*, 36–37.
127. Macrae, *The Romance of a Royal Burgh*, 112.
128. See Dodson, *Original Scots Colonists*, 70–71.
129. Moffat, *The Highland Clans*, 80; Maclean, *Scotland*, 150–156. For a different perspective see Smout, *A History*, 199–200, 225–26.
130. Larner, *Enemies of God*, 49–51. See also Smout, *A History*, 303–10.
131. Smout, *A History*, 304; Linebaugh, *The London Hanged*, 195; Livingstone, *Confess and Be Hanged*, 184–85; Richards and Clough, *Cromartie*, 43.
132. Cromartie, *A Highland History*, 53, 75–76; Moffat, *The Highland Clans*, 43; Smout, *A History*, 36, 38.

133. Szechi, *1715*, 96, 110, 126.
134. Szechi, 123–25.
135. Quotes are respectively from Jean Elshtain, *Women and War, with a new Epilogue* (Chicago: University of Chicago Press, 1995), 206; and Brackette Williams, "A Class Act: Anthropology and the Race to Nation Across Ethnic Terrain," *Annual Review of Anthropology* 18 (1989): 401–44, at 436–438. See Szechi, *1715*, 125.
136. Pittock, *The Myth of the Jacobite Clans*, 3; Smout, *A History*, 206–207. Smout emphasizes English manipulation of inter-clan hostility and downplays the extent to which clan leaders were furthering their own interests.
137. Szechi, *1715*, 199–200. On Highland prisoners particularly see Sankey, *Jacobite Prisoners*, 21, 55–56, 59.
138. Sankey, *Jacobite Prisoners*, 151–52; Szechi, *1715*, 199, 203–4.
139. Sankey, *Jacobite Prisoners*, 99.
140. Sankey, 37, 55.
141. Szechi, *1715*, 230–36.
142. Sankey, *Jacobite Prisoners*, ix.
143. Sankey, xiv, 21, 48, 50–51, 56; Szechi, *1715*, 231.
144. Sankey, *Jacobite Prisoners*, 52–57; Szechi, *1715*, 207.
145. Sankey, *Jacobite Prisoners*, 62; John Thornton, *Africa and Africans in the Making of the Atlantic World, 1400–1800*, 2nd ed. (Cambridge: Cambridge University Press, 1998), 319; Szechi, *1715*, 207.
146. Sankey, *Jacobite Prisoners*, 63–64.

5: ANCESTOR TALES OF THE LOGIC OF A SLAVE SOCIETY

1. *Hezekiah Ellis*, Wikitree.com, citing *The Virginia Genealogist* 5 (1961), 107. https://www.wikitree.com/wiki/Ellis-3443. See also *Middlesex County, Virginia, Wills and Inventories 1673–1812 and Other Court Papers*, ed. William Hopkins (Richmond, VA: GEN-N-DEX, 1989), 85; *Parish Register of Christ Church, Middlesex County, Virginia, from 1653–1812*; The National Society of the Colonial Dames of America in the State of Virginia (Baltimore: Genealogical Publishing Company, 1964), 98.
2. *Middlesex County, Virginia, Wills and Inventories 1673–1812*, April 7, 1724, 256.
3. *Hezekiah Ellis*, Wikitree.com
4. Darrett Rutman and Anita Rutman, *A Place in Time: Middlesex County, Virginia 1650–1750* (New York: W. W. Norton, 1984).
5. Rutman and Rutman, 100.
6. Rutman and Rutman, 102; Joan Gundersen, "Kith and Kin: Women's Networks in Colonial Virginia," in Catherine Clinton and Michele Gillespie, *The Devil's Lane: Sex and Race in the Early South* (New York: Oxford University Press, 1997), 90–108.

7.   Rutman and Rutman, *A Place in Time*, 114.

8.   Rutman and Rutman, 114, 129.

9.   Rutman and Rutman, 114; *Spotsylvania County, Virginia, Will Book B*, October 3, 1752 (archived at Spotsylvania, Virginia, Office of the Circuit Court Clerk), 136.

10. *Spotsylvania County, Virginia, Will Book D*, August 4, 1766 (archived at Spotsylvania, Virginia, Office of the Circuit Court Clerk), 241–44.

11. Many family researchers say she was Elizabeth Beverley Chew, who was from one of the most elite families. However, I found no evidence of this, and some evidence that Elizabeth Chew married elsewhere.

12. Rutman and Rutman, *A Place in Time*, 104–5.

13. *Spotsylvania Will Book D*, August 4, 1766, 241–244.

14. For example, *Middlesex County Virginia Court Orders 1711–1713*, May 6, 1712 (Miami Beach, FL: T.L.C. Genealogy, n.d.), , 85.

15. *Middlesex County Virginia Court Orders 1711–1713*, May 6, 1712, 85; Kathleen Brown, *Good Wives, Nasty Wenches, and Anxious Patriarchs: Gender, Race, and Power in Colonial Virginia* (Chapel Hill: University of North Carolina Press, 1996), 128–35, 190, 196; Rutman and Rutman, *A Place in Time*, 90.

16. Rutman and Rutman, *A Place in Time*, 131.

17. Rutman and Rutman, 234; Brown, *Good Wives*, 248, 251.

18. Rutman and Rutman, *A Place in Time*, 189, 234–49; Darrett Rutman and Anita Rutman, *A Place in Time: Explicatus* (New York: W.W. Norton, 1984), 122–25, 153.

19. Edmund Morgan, *American Slavery American Freedom: The Ordeal of Colonial Virginia* (New York: W. W. Norton, 1975), 224; Paula Felder, *Forgotten Companions: The First Settlers of Spotsylvania County and Fredericksburgh Town (with notes on Early Land Use)* (Fredericksburg, VA: Historic Publications of Fredericksburg, 1982), 30, 77–79.

20. Don Jordan and Michael Walsh, *White Cargo: The Forgotten History of Britain's White Slaves in America* (New York: New York University Press, 2008), 176; Philip Bruce, *Economic History of Virginia in the Seventeenth Century,* vols. 1 and 2 (New York: Peter Smith, 1935), 2:42–44.

21. On the somewhat later development of the deerskin trade, see Wilma Dunaway, *The First American Frontier: Transition to Capitalism in Southern Appalachia, 1700–1860* (Chapel Hill: University of North Carolina Press, 1996), 23–50.

22. A group of Middlesex men were among the last to formally surrender. See Rutman and Rutman, *A Place in Time*, 81.

23. On the role of contracts see Robert Steinfeld, *Coercion, Contract, and Free Labor in the Nineteenth Century* (New York: Cambridge University Press, 2001).

24. Rutman and Rutman, *Explicatus*, 154.

25. Honorable manhood required land and wives—property and patriarchy. See Brown, *Good Wives*, 173; James Rice, *Tales from a Revolution: Bacon's Rebellion and the Transformation of Early America* (New York: Oxford University Press, 2012), 220.

26. Ira Berlin, *Many Thousands Gone: The First Two Centuries of Slavery in North America* (Cambridge, MA: Harvard University Press, 1998), 8–9. See also Brown, *Good Wives*; Anthony Parent, *Foul Means: The Formation of a Slave Society in Virginia, 1660–1740* (Chapel Hill: Omohundro Institute and University of North Carolina Press, 2003).

27. *Spotsylvania Will Book D*, August 4, 1766, 241–44. All his daughters and a son received one woman, with their increase, another son received a woman and boy, and another a man. This required the purchase of two additional people; all the rest, both men and women, went to his wife for her lifetime.

28. Rutman and Rutman, *A Place in Time*, 144.

29. Rice, *Tales from a Revolution*, 221–22; Brown, *Good Wives*, 9.

30. Rutman and Rutman, *A Place in Time*, 146, 189.

31. Rutman and Rutman, 184, 195–200.

32. Rutman and Rutman, 79–80, 203; Felder, *Forgotten Companions*, 49, 55. For the sake of comparison, guarding a prisoner for a night got you fifteen pounds of tobacco; doing some work as a constable got you between seventy and three hundred pounds for the year. The sheriff got 1,240 pounds. See *Spotsylvania County, Virginia Court Orders 1746–1748,* November, 1746 (Miami Beach, FL: T.L.C. Genealogy, 1999), 7.

33. Rutman and Rutman, *A Place in Time*, 236.

34. The deed describes William Ellis as "of Gloucester County." See *Spotsylvania County, Virginia, Deed Book D, 1742–1751*, August 1, 1743, 78. For Alexander, see *Spotsylvania County, Virginia Court Orders 1746–1748*, July 2, 1745, Part 2, 330. Both are archived at Spotsylvania, Virginia, Office of the Circuit Court Clerk.

35. Rutman and Rutman, *Explicatus*, 121, 130.

36. Rutman and Rutman, *A Place in Time*, 121.

37. Rutman and Rutman, *A Place in Time*, 77.

38. *Spotsylvania County, Virginia, Court Order Book, 1749–1755*, December 3, 1751 (archived at Spotsylvania, Virginia, Office of the Circuit Court Clerk), 141–42. For Bloomfield Long see James Mansfield, *A History of Early Spotsylvania* (Orange, VA: Green Publishers, 1977), 126; Laura Davidson Baird, 1901 letter available in Davidson file at South Central Kentucky Cultural Center, Glasgow, KY.

39. *Spotsylvania Will Book B*, 90.

40. *Spotsylvania Will Book B*, 136.

41. Peterson says that William and Philip were older, as do several other

sources. See Baird, 1901 letter; Patricia Peterson, *The Alexander Davidson Family*, handwritten genealogy available in Davidson file, South Central Kentucky Cultural Center, Glasgow KY, n.d.; Mt. Tabor Book Committee, *The History of Mt. Tabor Baptist Church: The Oldest Church in Barren County, Kentucky* (Glasgow, KY: South Central Kentucky Historical and Genealogical Society, 1988); Landon Chambliss, *Baird–Davidson–Rogers–Wood and Allied History*, typed ms. in Davidson file Hart County Historical Society, Munfordville, KY, 1989, 4, 15. That Alexander II had his father's name does not mean he was oldest. Although there were many exceptions, the Rutmans found a clear naming pattern, in which the oldest son was named for his paternal grandfather, and the father's name went to a younger son. See Rutman and Rutman, *Explicatus*, 90.

42.   The court document specifying the conditions of Sarah's administration of Alexander's estate refers to the lack of a will. See *Spotsylvania County, Virginia Will Book A*, February 7, 1748 (archived at Spotsylvania, Virginia, Office of the Circuit Court Clerk), 479–80.

43.   Rutman and Rutman, *A Place in Time*, 236–37.

44.   *Virginia County Records, Spotsylvania County, 1721–1800*, ed. William Crozier (New York: Fox, Duffield and Co., 1945), 185. Although Mansfield does not list Alexander as a blacksmith in Fredericksburg, he points out that some artisans never bought land and settled down, and thus don't show up in the records. See Mansfield, *A History*, 126.

45.   *Spotsylvania Court Orders 1746–1748* (archived), July 2, November 5, December 4, 1745, February 1746, 330, 344, 352, 399; *Spotsylvania County, Virginia Court Orders 1746–1748* (T.L.C.), November 1746, February 1746–47, 7, 10.

46.   *Spotsylvania Court Orders 1746–1748*, (T.L.C.), July 1747, 39. Spotsylvania County index of deeds contains no reference to Alexander.

47.   *Spotsylvania Will Book A*, February 13, 1748, 487. For the full inventory see Appendix 1. By the time Alexander and Sarah lived in Spotsylvania there were a few people who made their entire living from a craft such as shoe-making or tailoring. Previously the craft would have been combined with planting. See Rutman and Rutman, *Explicatus*, 154.

48.   Rutman and Rutman, *A Place in Time*, 193, 195.

49.   Rutman and Rutman, *A Place in Time*, 69.

50.   Rutman and Rutman, *Explicatus*, 155.

51.   Rutman and Rutman, *A Place in Time*, 236, 242–43.

52.   Rutman and Rutman, *Explicatus*, 122; see Appendix 1.

53.   Rutman and Rutman, *A Place in Time*, 147.

54.   *Spotsylvania County, Virginia Will Book A*, February 7, 1748, 479; *Spotsylvania Will Book B*, October 3, 1752, 136.

55.   Rutman and Rutman, *Explicatus*, 176.

56. Jennifer Morgan, *Laboring Women: Reproduction and Gender in New World Slavery* (Philadelphia: University of Pennsylvania Press, 2004), 89–92.

57. For example, Martin Klein, "Introduction: Modern European Expansion and Traditional Servitude in Africa and Asia," in Klein, *Breaking the Chains: Slavery, Bondage, and Emancipation in Modern Africa and Asia* (Madison: University of Wisconsin Press, 1993), 3–36, at 4; James Scott, *Against the Grain: A Deep History of the Earliest States* (New Haven: Yale University Press, 2017), 150–82.

58. See Robert Miles, *Capitalism and Unfree Labor: Anomaly or Necessity* (New York: Tavistock, 1987), 204; Klein, "Introduction," 4, 5; Richard Eaton, "Introduction," in Indrani Chatterjee and Richard M. Eaton, *Slavery and South Asian History* (Bloomington: Indiana University Press, 2006), 1–16, at 14; Joseph Miller, "A Theme in Variations: A Historical Schema of Slaving in the Atlantic and Indian Ocean Regions," in Gwyn Campbell, *The Structure of Slavery in Indian Ocean Africa and Asia* (London: Frank Cass, 2004), 169–94, at 171–72.

59. Miller, "A Theme in Variations," 171–72; Claude Meillassoux, *The Anthropology of Slavery: The Womb of Iron and Gold*, trans. Alide Dasnois (Chicago: University of Chicago Press, 1991 [1986]), 223–27, 92; Klein, "Introduction," 2.

60. See Cedric Robinson, *Black Marxism: The Making of the Black Radical Tradition* (Chapel Hill: University of North Carolina Press, 2000 [1983]), 23; Karen Fields and Barbara Fields, *Racecraft: The Soul of Inequality in American Life* (New York: Verso, 2014), 123–25.

61. Scotland's reinvention of slavery in mines is described in chapter 4.

62. Definitions of slavery have varied, with some including a wide range of types, such as pawned or bonded labor, while others limit the term to only those types based on the violent removal of people from their home polities to another where they have no rights. See Joseph Miller, *The Problem of Slavery as History: A Global Approach* (New Haven: Yale University Press, 2012), 90–96, 121–30; Gyan Prakash, "Terms of Servitude: The Colonial Discourse on Slavery and Bondage in India," in Klein, *Breaking the Chains,* 131–49; Suzanne Miers, "Slavery: A Question of Definition," in Campbell, *The Structure of Slavery in Indian Ocean Africa and Asia,* 1–16; Meillassoux, *The Anthropology of Slavery,* 67–77; Gwyn Campbell, "Introduction: Slavery and Other Forms of Unfree Labour in the Indian Ocean World," in Campbell, *The Structure of Slavery in Indian Ocean Africa and Asia,* vii–xxxii.

63. Miller, "A Theme in Variations," 180, 186–90. Women could also be a source of male slaves, since the babies they bore could be safely enslaved, unlike adult male war captives. See Campbell, "Introduction," xiii. Kings in South India apparently kept thousands of women for just that purpose. See

Daud Ali, "War, Servitude, and the Imperial Household: A Study of Palace Women in the Chola Empire," in Indrani Chatterjee and Richard M. Eaton, *Slavery and South Asian History* (Bloomington: Indiana University Press, 2006), 44–62, at 56–58; Meillassoux, *The Anthropology of Slavery*, 188–94.

64.   Miller particularly makes this point. See Miller, "A Theme in Variations," 185. See also Paul Lovejoy, *Transformations in Slavery: A History of Slavery in Africa*, 3rd ed. (Cambridge: Cambridge University Press, 2012), 8–14; John Thornton, *Africa and Africans in the Making of the Atlantic World, 1400–1800*, 2nd ed. (Cambridge: Cambridge University Press, 1998), 72–97; Meillassoux, *The Anthropology of Slavery*, 18, 85–90. Additional examples of this sort of organization, where the goal is "wealth in people," can be found in Indrani Chatterjee and Richard Eaton, eds., *Slavery and South Asian History* (Bloomington: Indiana University Press, 2006); Campbell, *The Structure of Slavery in Indian Ocean Africa and Asia*; Martin Klein, ed., *Breaking the Chains: Slavery, Bondage, and Emancipation in Modern Africa and Asia* (Madison: University of Wisconsin Press, 1993).

65.   Meillassoux, *The Anthropology of Slavery*, 74–75, 92, 157–202, 222–29; Klein, "Introduction,"12; Miller, *The Problem of Slavery as History*, 53–54, 96–100; Miers, "Slavery," 5.

66.   Meillassoux, *The Anthropology of Slavery*, 185–90.

67.   For discussion see Klein, "Introduction," 23; Miers, "Slavery,"10; Meillassoux, *The Anthropology of Slavery*, 289; Campbell, "Introduction," xxii– xxiv; Eaton, "Introduction," 5. Another perspective is that these were societies in which everyone was to some extent dependent on those above them in a "hierarchy of dependency," with slavery merely the most dependent status. See Campbell, "Introduction," xxii. Even the greatest lords were dependent on the king for their estates. Even the king could be defined as dependent on the gods and priests. Ironically, slaves, pawns, and bonded laborers were all protected by their master from the demands laid on peasants for tribute and labor by higher-ranking lords or kings. Their labor belonged to their master directly, not to the king, and the king had claims only on free people. Slaves were not his subjects; they were property. See Miller, *The Problem of Slavery as History*, 140; Eaton, "Introduction," 12.

68.   Silvia Federici, *Caliban and the Witch: Women, the Body and Primitive Accumulation*, 2nd rev. ed. (Brooklyn: Autonomedia, 2014 [2004]), 23–25; Max Weber, "The Social Causes of the Decay of Ancient Civilization," in Eugene Genovese, *The Slave Economies*, vol. 1 (New York: John Wiley and Sons, 1973 [1896]), 46-67, at 56-57; Meillassoux, *The Anthropology of Slavery*, 89–94, 118, 234–35, 280–83, 319–23.

69.   Meillassoux, *The Anthropology of Slavery*, 321.

70.   Miller, *The Problem of Slavery as History*, 149–50. Long pay periods, like those in sharecropping or in many early mines and factories, are a form

of unfree labor. On the long back-and-forth struggle between employers and employees over the length of time between pay periods, see Steinfeld, *Coercion, Contract, and Free Labor.*

71. Miles, *Capitalism and Unfree Labor*, 29; Meillassoux, *The Anthropology of Slavery*, 322.

72. For example Meillassoux, *The Anthropology of Slavery*, 95; see Edward Baptist, *The Half Has Never Been Told: Slavery and the Making of American Capitalism* (New York: Basic Books, 2014), 116, 128.

73. Baptist, *The Half Has Never Been Told*, 126–30.

74. Klein, "Introduction,"12.

75. Meillassoux, *The Anthropology of Slavery*, 88–90.

76. Miller, *The Problem of Slavery as History*, 123–25, 139; Meillassoux, *The Anthropology of Slavery*, 286–87.

77. See Sven Beckert, *Empire of Cotton: A Global History* (New York: Alfred A. Knopf, 2015), 174–98; Peter Linebaugh, *The London Hanged: Crime and Civil Society in the Eighteenth Century* (New York: Cambridge University Press, 1992).

78. For a description of the effect of tobacco production in shaping slavery in the Chesapeake see Berlin, *Many Thousands Gone*, 109–41.

79. See Meillassoux, *The Anthropology of Slavery*, 94.

80. Meillassoux, 294–313.

81. Baptist, *The Half Has Never Been Told*, for example, 315–25, 413; Sven Beckert and Seth Rockman, eds., *Slavery's Capitalism: A New History of American Economic Development* (Philadelphia: University of Pennsylvania Press, 2016); Pem Davidson Buck, "The Strange Birth and Continuing Life of the US as a Slaving Republic: Race, Unfree Labor, and the State," *Anthropological Theory* 17/2 (2017): 159–91.

82. Sally Hadden, *Slave Patrols: Law and Violence in Virginia and the Carolinas* (Cambridge, MA: Harvard University Press, 2003), 82–84.

83. On the changing patterns of lives of enslaved women in colonial Virginia see Gundersen, "Kith and Kin."

84. *Spotsylvania Will Book D,* August 4, 1766, 242.

85. Katherine Kendall, ed., *Caswell County, North Carolina Will Books 1774–1814,* November 1809 (Baltimore: Clearfield, 1979), 116,.

86. He signed a petition there in 1771. See William Powell, *When the Past Refused to Die: A History of Caswell County North Carolina, 1777–1977* (Durham, NC: Moore Publishing, 1977), 55–57.

87. Lewis Gray, *History of Agriculture in the Southern United States to 1860,* vol. 1 (Gloucester, MA: Peter Smith, 1958), 524–26; A. Leon Higginbotham, *In the Matter of Color: Race and the American Legal Process, The Colonial Period* (New York: Oxford University Press, 1978), 74; Bradford Wood and Larry Tise, "The Conundrum of Unfree Labor," in Tise and Jeffrey Crow,

New Voyages to Carolina: Reinterpreting North Carolina History (Chapel Hill: University of North Carolina Press, 2017), 85–109, at 95, 102.

6: ANCESTOR TALES OF THE BIRTH OF A SLAVING REPUBLIC

1. Stephen Aron, *How the West Was Lost: The Transformation of Kentucky from Daniel Boone to Henry Clay* (Baltimore: Johns Hopkins University Press, 1996), 3–4. See Alan Taylor, *American Revolutions: A Continental History, 1750–1804* (New York: W.W. Norton, 2016), 3–9, 351; Nicolas De Genova, *Working the Boundaries: Race, Space, and 'Illegality' in Mexican Chicago* (Durham, NC: Duke University Press, 2005), 98, 104.

2. On the Revolution as a civil war see Taylor, *American Revolutions*, 211–33; Ned Sublette and Constance Sublette, *The American Slave Coast: A History of the Slave-Breeding Industry* (Chicago: Lawrence Hill Books, 2016), 20.

3. James Mansfield, *A History of Early Spotsylvania* (Orange, VA: Green Publishers, 1977), 126. *Spotsylvania County, Virginia, Court Order Book, 1749–1755,* December 3, 1751 (archived at Spotsylvania, Virginia, Office of the Circuit Court Clerk), 141–42.

4. Mansfield, 1–2.

5. Mansfield, 29.

6. Mansfield, 1, 29.

7. Mansfield, 29. On the importance of the Haudenosaunee (the Iroquois) see for instance Taylor, *American Revolutions*, 255–57; Stephen Webb, *1676: The End of American Independence* (Syracuse, NY: Syracuse University Press, 1995 [1984]), 355–404; David Silverman, *Thundersticks: Firearms and the Violent Transformation of Native America* (Cambridge, MA: Harvard University Press, 2016), 50–51. On the role of Native nations in shaping colonial and US policy more generally see, for instance, Peter Silver, *Our Savage Neighbors: How Indian War Transformed America* (New York: W.W. Norton, 2008); Gregory Dowd, *A Spirited Resistance: The North American Indian Struggle for Unity, 1745–1815* (Baltimore: Johns Hopkins University Press, 1992); Silverman, *Thundersticks*; Alan Gallay, *The Indian Slave Trade: The Rise of the English Empire in the American South 1670–1717* (New Haven: Yale University Press, 2002).

8. On the long-term diplomacy conducted by both Cherokee and Haudenosaunee in negotiating with both British and then US and Canadian authorities, including diplomatic missions to London, see Jace Weaver, *The Red Atlantic: American Indigenes and the Making of the Modern World, 1000–1927* (Chapel Hill: University of North Carolina Press, 2014), 152–88.

9. For detailed analysis of these efforts see Dowd, *A Spirited Resistance*; Sami Lakomäki, *Gathering Together: The Shawnee People Through Diaspora and Nationhood, 1600–1870* (New Haven: Yale University Press, 2014).

10. Dowd, *A Spirited Resistance,* 27–46, 123–47; Lakomäki, *Gathering Together,* 143–46.

11. This is the English phrase used to translate names of the being in these visions from a variety of languages, including Tenskwakowa's Shawnee. Another phrase is "Great Spirit." See Dowd, *A Spirited Resistance,* 127; John Sugden, *Tecumseh: A Life* (New York: Henry Holt, 1997), 118.

12. For example, Dowd, *A Spirited Resistance,* 33–35, 128–29. For the later Shawnee version see Lakomäki, *Gathering Together,* 143–46.

13. Dowd, *A Spirited Resistance,* 126–28.

14. Ric Burns and Chris Eyre, directors, *Tecumseh's Vision,* in PBS *American Experience: We Shall Remain*(2009).

15. Dowd, *A Spirited Resistance,* 25–27; Sugden, *Tecumseh,* 22.

16. Ronald Turner, ed., *Prince William County Virginia, Bond Book 1732–1847,* December 7, 1767, http://www.pwcvirginia.com/documents/BondBook.pdf, 190–91. The assumption that Anna, James, and Moses Bridges were relatives, probably siblings, is based on the following documentation. Several serious efforts have been made by Bridges descendants to trace their ancestry through Prince William County in Virginia to Orange County and Rutherford/Cleveland County in North Carolina and just over what became the state line between Cleveland County, NC, and York County, SC. See Mrs. Ernest Newton and Roy Brooks, "Bridges to the Past," *Courier-Sun* (Forest City, NC), June 30, July 14, August 4, 1976. There were an incredible number of Bridges, with the same few first names used repeatedly. This research focuses on the male line, but rarely mentions women. So although James Bridges and Moses Bridges are tentatively identified, along with some of their brothers, there is no indication of whether they had sisters. I think they must have, and that one of them was Anna. I am basing this primarily on the fact that she and Alexander were closely associated with Moses and several of his brothers, and particularly that they were members of the same church, apparently changed churches together later, and then Alexander and his second wife, Mary Ellis, went on to Kentucky with them.

17. Milton Ready, *The Tarheel State: A History of North Carolina* (Columbia: University of South Carolina Press, 2005), 56. See Patricia Peterson, *The Alexander Davidson Family,* n.d., handwritten genealogy, Davidson file, South Central Kentucky Cultural Center, Glasgow, KY.

18. Paula Felder, *Forgotten Companions: The First Settlers of Spotsylvania County and Fredericksburgh Town (with notes on Early Land Use)* (Fredericksburg, VA: Historic Publications of Fredericksburg, 1982), 43, 146–47.

19. William Powell, *When the Past Refused to Die: A History of Caswell County, North Carolina, 1777–1977* (Durham, NC: Moore Publishing, 1977),

55–57; *Orange County North Carolina Deed Book 3*, ed. William Bennett (Raleigh, NC: privately published, 1990), March 24 and March 30, 1772, 93–94.

20. For an analysis of the Regulator movement see Marjoleine Kars, *Breaking Loose Together: The Regulator Rebellion in Pre-Revolutionary North Carolina* (Chapel Hill: University of North Carolina Press, 2002); Carole Troxler, *Farming Dissenters: The Regulator Movement in Piedmont North Carolina* (Raleigh: North Carolina Department of Cultural Resources, 2011); Ready, *The Tarheel State*, 89–101.

21. Kars, *Breaking Loose Together*, 60–73; Troxler, *Farming Dissenters*, 21–28; Powell, *When the Past Refused to Die*, 45.

22. On inequality throughout southern Appalachia, including western North Carolina and eastern Kentucky, see Wilma Dunaway, *The First American Frontier: Transition to Capitalism in Southern Appalachia, 1700–1860* (Chapel Hill: University of North Carolina Press, 1996), 84–121.

23. Kars, *Breaking Loose Together*, 72.

24. Troxler, *Farming Dissenters*, 159–66. My estimate of half is based on a total white population of 14,649 in Orange County in 1767. See Marvin Kay and Lorin Cary, *Slavery in North Carolina, 1748–1775* (Chapel Hill: University of North Carolina Press, 1995), 222. For a considerably lower population estimate see Joe Mobley, *The Way We Lived in North Carolina* (Chapel Hill: University of North Carolina Press, 2003), 89. Assuming half, 7,300, were male and that less than half were adult, so at most maybe 3,000 men, something under one-third of all adult white men, were among the 883 actually identified Regulators, so surely at least half the white men of Orange County were Regulators.

25. *Tax Lists, Caswell County, 1777*. North Carolina Digital Collections, 28, http://digital.ncdcr.gov/cdm/ref/collection/p16062coll33/id/2032; *North Carolina Taxpayers, 1679–1790*, vol. 2, ed. Clarence Ratcliff (Baltimore: Genealogical Publishing Co., 2003), 52.

26. See George Paschal, *History of North Carolina Baptists*, vol. 2 (Raleigh: The General Board, North Carolina State Convention, 1955), 63–71; Kars, *Breaking Loose Together*, 111–29, Troxler, *Farming Dissenters*, 32–33, 59–66.

27. Laura Davidson Baird, 1901 letter, Davidson File, South Central Kentucky Cultural Center, Glasgow, KY. See also Malory Huggins, *A History of North Carolina Baptists 1727–1932* (Raleigh: The General Board, Baptist State Convention of North Carolina, 1967), 50–62.

28. Kars, *Breaking Loose Together*, 68–70; Troxler, *Farming Dissenters*, 10–18, 85–87.

29. Kars, *Breaking Loose Together*, 23–26, 133, 135.

30. Troxler, *Farming Dissenters*, 91–93.

31. Ready, *The Tarheel State*, 98–99; Kars, *Breaking Loose Together*, 201–7; Troxler, *Farming Dissenters*, 103–13.

32. Paschal, *History of North Carolina Baptists*, 69–81, 71n11; Kars, *Breaking Loose Together*, 203–5; Troxler, *Farming Dissenters*, 115–21; Ready, *The Tarheel State*, 98; Powell, *When the Past Refused to Die*, 51. Both Kars and Troxler have detailed descriptions of the battle and the maneuvering before it.

33. Kars, *Breaking Loose Together*, 173, 171.

34. Kars, 171–73; Troxler, *Farming Dissenters*, 79–81. See also Mobley, *The Way We Lived*, 85–104.

35. See Mobley, *The Way We Lived*, 94.

36. See Kars, *Breaking Loose Together*, 195.

37. Ready, *The Tarheel State*, 75–77.

38. Troxler, *Farming Dissenters*, 25.

39. Parkinson particularly, but also Anderson and Silver make it clear that these attitudes, though perhaps genuinely felt, were consciously enflamed by careful manipulating by elite leaders who submitted editorials and exaggerated descriptions of events. See Robert Parkinson, *The Common Cause: Creating Race and Nation in the American Revolution* (Chapel Hill: University of North Carolina Press, 2016); Silver, *Our Savage Neighbors;* Gary Anderson, *Ethnic Cleansing and the Indian: The Crime That Should Haunt America* (Norman: University of Oklahoma Press, 2014). Land-grabbing by Separatist leaders is discussed by Taylor, *American Revolutions,* 72–77.

40. See David Harvey, "The 'New' Imperialism: Accumulation by Dispossession," *Socialist Register* 40 (2004): 63–87; Rosa Luxemburg, *The Accumulation of Capital*, trans. Agnes Schwarzschild (Mansfield Center, CT: Martino Publishing, 2015 [1913]), esp. 348–67; Jim Glassman, "Primitive accumulation, accumulation by dispossession, accumulation by 'extra-economic' means," *Progress in Human Geography* 30/5 (2006): 608–25; Sharryn Kasmir and August Carbonella, "Dispossession and the Anthropology of Labor," *Critique of Anthropology* 28/1 (2008): 5–25.

41. On the pressure toward wage labor resulting from the transition to capitalism, see Dunaway, *The First American Frontier*, 75–88.

42. Quoted respectively in Ready, *The Tarheel State*, 52; Taylor, *American Revolutions,* 67; Nancy Isenberg, *White Trash: The 400-Year Untold History of Class in America* (New York: Viking, 2016), 43, 55; Aron, *How the West Was Lost*, 21, 13–16. On the concept of "standing," see Judith Skhlar, *American Citizenship: The Quest for Inclusion* (Cambridge, MA: Harvard University Press, 1991), 1–23. See also Dwight Billings, Gurney Norman, and Katherine Ledford, eds., *Back Talk from Appalachia* (Lexington: University Press of Kentucky, 2013).

43. Kars, *Breaking Loose Together*, 192, 208–10. See also Mobley, *The Way We Lived*, 103–4; Ready, *The Tarheel State*, 117; Troxler, *Farming Dissenters*,

124. My discussion of the Regulators depends principally on Kars for analysis of the Piedmont social structure; Troxler contributes far more detail in relation to the political machinations involved. General North Carolina histories, such as those by Ready, *The Tarheel State,* and Mobley, *The Way We Lived,* were also helpful.

44. Ready, *The Tarheel State,* 120; Troxler, *Farming Dissenters,* 124.

45. Kars, *Breaking Loose Together,* 208–10.

46. Kars, *Breaking Loose Together,* 128, 211; Huggins, *A History of North Carolina Baptists,* 62–63.

47. Buffalo Church in York County, SC, is on the border of NC, two miles south of the border and seven miles west of Blacksburg, SC, and people from both states went there. According to his granddaughter, Alexander did have a brother William. See Baird, 1901 letter, Davidson file, South Central Kentucky Cultural Center; George Paschal, *History of North Carolina Baptists,* vol. 2 (Raleigh: The General Board, North Carolina State Convention, 1955), 339–40. Alexander joined Sandy Run, near Mooresboro, in what is now Cleveland County, partitioned off from Rutherford, by letter from Buffalo Church. The two are close enough that he would not have had to move, and according to DePriest, Sandy Run did have members from that area. He was a member of Sandy Run in 1782, as was Mary Ellis, whom he married the following year. See Peterson, *The Alexander Davidson Family;* Virginia DePriest, *The Sandy Run Settlement and Mooresboro* (n.p., 1976), https://archive.org/details/sandyrunsettle-me00depr; Landon Chambliss, *Baird–Davidson–Rogers–Wood and Allied History,* typed ms., Davidson file, Hart County Historical Society, 1989, 14. So this pretty well situates Alexander in the section of Rutherford County that later became Cleveland County, North Carolina. Alexander received a grant there in 1782, and owned land along Sandy Run. Moses Bridges had land in the same area. See *Rutherford County, North Carolina Abstracts of Deeds, 1773–1795,* May 1784, February 1791, July 1791, July 1792, ed. Caroline Davis (Rutherfordton, NC: Mrs. W.L.Davis, 1973), 46, 47, 54, 91, 93; on Bridges genealogy, see n.16.

I may be wrong about this William being the William who was Alexander II's brother. There were several William Davidsons—one of whom by family mythology was supposedly our relative, the William Davidson who was a general in the Revolution and was killed at the battle of Cowan's Gap and for whom Davidson County is named. However, this turns out to be incorrect—this was another line of Davidsons. See Chalmers Davidson, *Piedmont Partisan: The Life and Times of William Lee Davidson* (Davidson, NC: Davidson College, 1968 [1951]). There were other William Davidsons, but given the Buffalo Church and Bridges connection, it seems more likely that William, the deacon, was Alexander's brother. See Clarence Griffin, *History of Old Tryon and Rutherford Counties North Carolina, 1730–1936* (Asheville, NC: Miller Printing Co., 1937), 126–27. Additionally, Alexander's second wife is said to be the sister of William Davidson's wife—a quite possible marriage, referred to as part of family lore in an unidentified letter from Peggy to Lloyd, no longer available on line. There was also a William among the Davidsons and Bridges later in Kentucky; this could be Alexander's brother William. It could also be his son William, but if so William was on his own on the tax list of 1800 at the rather young age of twenty; Alexander III was also quite young on the 1790 census. See *First Census of the United States, North Carolina, 1790*, 119, https://www2.census.gov/library/publications/decennial/1790/heads_of_ families/north_carolina/1790h-04.pdf; *"Second Census" of Kentucky 1800*, ed. Glenn Clift (Baltimore: Genealogical Publishing Company, 1982).

48. Griffin, *History of Old Tryon*, 7, 10.
49. On the Shawnee see in particular Lakomäki, *Gathering Together*; Sugden, *Tecumseh*. On the Cherokee see Theda Perdue, *Cherokee Women: Gender and Culture Change, 1700–1835* (Lincoln: University of Nebraska Press, 1998); Carolyn Johnston, *Cherokee Women in Crisis: Trail of Tears, Civil War, and Allotment, 1838–1907* (Tuscaloosa: University of Alabama Press, 2003); Michael Oberg, *Native America: A History* (Malden, MA: Wiley-Blackwell, 2010); Theda Perdue and Christopher Oakley, *Native Carolinians: The Indians of North Carolina* (Raleigh: North Carolina Department of Cultural Resources, Office of Archives and History, 2010).
50. Lakomäki, *Gathering Together*, 60.
51. On the significance of treaties, and of the Proclamation in particular, see Pamela Klassen, "Spiritual Jurisdictions: Treaty People and the Queen of Canada," in Paul Johnson, Klassen, and Winifred Sullivan, *Ekklesia: Three Inquiries in Church and State* (Chicago: University of Chicago Press, 2018), 107–173.
52. Taylor, *American Revolutions*, 76; Dowd, *A Spirited Resistance*, 42–43, 52.
53. See Silverman, *Thundersticks*, 153.
54. Ready, *The Tarheel State*, 119–20; Griffin, *History of Old Tryon*, 93; *Roster of Soldiers from North Carolina in the American Revolution* (Daughters of the American Revolution, Durham, NC: Seeman Press, 1932), 375.
55. Hugh Lefler, *North Carolina History Told by Contemporaries* (Chapel Hill: University of North Carolina Press, 1965 [1934]), 72; see also Perdue, *Cherokee Women*, 94–95, 142, 149.
56. Kars, *Breaking Loose Together*, 166; Gerald Horne, *The Counter-Revolution of 1776: Slave Resistance and the Origins of the United States of America* (New York: New York University Press, 2014), 205–6.
57. Colin Calloway, *First Peoples: A Documentary Survey of American Indian History* (Boston: Bedford/St. Martin's, 2016 [2004]), 525, 613.

58. Mike Ferner, "Fourth of July Like You've Never Seen it Before," *Counterpunch*, June 30, 2017,https://www.counterpunch.org/2017/06/30/93804/.

59. On landholding patriarchy in backcountry and frontier areas, and on the conflict between would-be smallholders and large speculators and estate holders, see Aron, *How the West Was Lost*, 58–81.

60. Sublette and Sublette, *The American Slave Coast*, 267.

61. Kars, *Breaking Loose Together*, 135, 152; Ready, *The Tarheel State*, 97; Taylor, *American Revolutions*, 92–94, 115, 364; Sublette and Sublette, *The American Slave Coast*, 264, 293.

62. For example, Taylor, *American Revolutions*, 91–94, 100, 115. See also Ready, *The Tarheel State*, 92, 97.

63. Quoted in Ready, *The Tarheel State*, 97. See Kars, *Breaking Loose Together*, 135; Taylor, *American Revolutions*, 92, 115.

64. They weren't the only ones—a few years later, just before the Revolution, farmers in Massachusetts did much the same thing, and again in Shays' Rebellion, as did farmers in what later became Vermont. See Ray Raphael, *The First American Revolution: Before Lexington and Concord* (New York: New Press, 2002); Taylor, *American Revolutions*, 71–72, 366–68.

65. For extended discussion see Nicolas Guyatt, *Bind Us Apart: How Enlightened Americans Invented Racial Segregation* (New York: Basic Books, 2016); Simon Schama, *Rough Crossings: The Slaves, the British, and the American Revolution* (New York: HarperCollins, 2005); Gary Nash, *Race and Revolution* (Madison, WI: Madison House Publishers, 1990).

66. Horne, *The Counter-Revolution*; Taylor, *American Revolutions*, 228, 284–293.

67. On Spanish policies in relation to Africans see Berlin, *Many Thousands Gone*, 64–76; Jennifer Morgan, *Laboring Women: Reproduction and Gender in New World Slavery* (Philadelphia: University of Pennsylvania Press, 2004), 178–82; Taylor, *American Revolutions*, 22.

68. Horne, *The Counter-Revolution*, 14, 130–31,184–85; Taylor, *American Revolutions*, 266.

69. Horne, *The Counter-Revolution*, 14, 116.

70. Horne, 110–17; Jack Shuler, *Calling Out Liberty: The Stono Slave Rebellion and the Universal Struggle for Human Rights* (Jackson: University Press of Mississippi, 2009), 69, 73, 158.

71. Joseph Miller, *The Problem of Slavery as History: A Global Approach* (New Haven: Yale University Press, 2012), 62, 140–51; Joseph Miller, "A Theme in Variations: A Historical Schema of Slaving in the Atlantic and Indian Ocean Regions," in Gwyn Campbell, *The Structure of Slavery in Indian Ocean Africa and Asia* (London: Frank Cass, 2004), 169–94, at 75, 181; Claude Meillassoux, *The Anthropology of Slavery: The Womb of Iron and Gold*, trans. Alide Dasnois (Chicago: University of Chicago Press, 1991

[1986]), 241; Martin Klein, "Introduction: Modern European Expansion and Traditional Servitude in Africa and Asia," in Klein, *Breaking the Chains: Slavery, Bondage, and Emancipation in Modern Africa and Asia* (Madison: University of Wisconsin Press, 1993), 3–36, at 7–8.

72. For example, Miller, "A Theme in Variations," 179,183,190; Miller, *The Problem of Slavery as History*, 148; Suzanne Miers, "Slavery: A Question of Definition," in Campbell, *The Structure of Slavery in Indian Ocean Africa and Asia*, 1–16, at 5; Richard Eaton, "Introduction," in Indrani Chatterjee and Eaton, *Slavery and South Asian History*, 1–16 (Bloomington: Indiana University Press, 2006); Meillassoux, *The Anthropology of Slavery*, 185–200.

73. Klein, "Introduction," 7–8.

74. Miller, "A Theme in Variations," 174–75, 180–83.

75. Taylor, *American Revolutions*, 75. On the breakdown of colonial government in North Carolina by 1773 see Ready, *The Tarheel State*, 105–6.

76. See also Sven Beckert and Seth Rockman, eds., *Slavery's Capitalism: A New History of American Economic Development* (Philadelphia: University of Pennsylvania Press, 2016), 5; Sven Beckert, *Empire of Cotton: A Global History* (New York: Alfred A. Knopf, 2015), 92.

77. On the functioning of capitalism and the financializing of enslaved people themselves, rather than simply employing them as a productive labor force, see the articles collected in Beckert and Rockman, eds., *Slavery's Capitalism*, esp. Bonnie Martin, "Neighbor-to-Neighbor Capitalism: Local Credit Networks and the Mortgaging of Slaves," in Beckert and Rockman, *Slavery's Capitalism*, 107–21; Sublette and Sublette, *The American Slave Coast*, particularly 37–45, 464–65; Edward Baptist, *The Half Has Never Been Told: Slavery and the Making of American Capitalism* (New York: Basic Books, 2014), 90–91, 244–59; Miller, "A Theme in Variations," 190–91.

78. Horne, *The Counter-Revolution*, 5; Calvin Schermerhorn, "The Coastwise Slave Trade and a Mercantile Community of Interest," in Beckert and Rockman, *Slavery's Capitalism*, 209–24; Sublette and Sublette, *The American Slave Coast*, 65–70; Baptist, *The Half Has Never Been Told*, 317–22; Beckert, *Empire of Cotton*, 105.

79. Ira Berlin, *Many Thousands Gone: The First Two Centuries of Slavery in North America* (Cambridge MA: Harvard University Press, 1998), 10.

80. Quotes are respectively from Webb, *1676*, 66; Horne, *The Counter-Revolution*, 85. See also Miller, *The Problem of Slavery as History*, 141. Limiting slave trading and at times freeing slaves were tactics European colonial administrators had used to consolidate their control and to weaken local power holders. See Klein, "Introduction," 22; Richard Eaton, "Introduction," 12; Taylor, *American Revolutions*, 310.

81. Horne, *The Counter-Revolution*, 4–5; Taylor, *American Revolutions*, 56–57, 113–14.

82. Sublette and Sublette, *The American Slave Coast*, 255.
83. For the role of free and enslaved blacks in promoting abolitionism, and for connections between abolitionists on both sides of the Atlantic, see Manisha Sinha, *The Slave's Cause: A History of Abolition* (New Haven: Yale University Press, 2016); Horne, *The Counter-Revolution*, 209–33.
84. Taylor, *American Revolutions*, 135–41, 211–30, 353–61; Ready, *The Tarheel State*, 122.
85. Griffin, *History of Old Tryon*, 88; *Caswell County, North Carolina Land Grants, Tax Lists, State Census, Apprentice Bonds, Estate Records*, ed. Katherine Kendall (n.p., 1977), 27; *North Carolina Taxpayers, 1679–1790*, 2:52; *Tax Lists, Caswell County, 1777*, 28, http://digital.ncdcr.gov/cdm/ref/collection/p16062coll33/id/2032.
86. *Tax Lists, Rutherford County, 1782*. North Carolina Digital Collections, 15, http://digital.ncdcr.gov/cdm/ref/collection/p16062coll33/id/1097. For a description of North Carolina county governments during the Revolution and the continuity of the system immediately thereafter, including discussion of the role and power of justices of the peace, and the likely status of those appointed, see Troxler, *Farming Dissenters*, 10–18, 133–37, 147–48. On role of justice of the peace in Kentucky, showing continuity after the Revolution, see Joan Coward, *Kentucky in the New Republic: The Process of Constitution Making* (Lexington: University Press of Kentucky, 1979), 5–6.
87. Calculated from the Rutherford County section of the census. See *First Census of the United States, North Carolina, 1790*, 116–20.
88. Griffin, *History of Old Tryon*, 83; see also Lefler, *North Carolina History*, 111.
89. Troxler, *Farming Dissenters*, 149–50; in addition, persecution of Baptists was led by local elites, likely supporters of the Separatists. See John Ragosta, *Wellspring of Liberty: How Virginia's Religious Dissenters Helped Win the American Revolution and Secured Religious Liberty* (New York: Oxford University Press, 2010), 35. Both churches that Alexander joined in North Carolina were Separate Baptist, as were all the Baptist churches in the Sandy Creek Association in Orange County. See Huggins, *A History of North Carolina Baptists*, 51; Paschal, *History of North Carolina Baptists*, 2:338–40. On the difference between Baptist sects in North Carolina see Huggins, *A History of North Carolina Baptists*, 39–52.
90. Ragosta, *Wellspring of Liberty*, 7–13, 28–36, 40–42. On persecution of Baptists see also Mansfield, *A History of Early Spotsylvania*, 69–70; Kars, *Breaking Loose Together*, 98–110.
91. Of the known Orange County Regulators, there were 34 clear Royalists and an unknown number of Separatists, but the allegiance of the vast majority, 560 of them, is unknown. See Ready, *The Tarheel State*, 99. See also Troxler, *Farming Dissenters*, 124; Kars, *Breaking Loose Together*, 212.
92. See Taylor, *American Revolutions*, 135–37; Ready, *The Tarheel State*, 99;

Kars, *Breaking Loose Together*, 208; Ragosta, *Wellspring of Liberty*, 101–4. Such leaders included Samuel Johnston, author of the Johnston Act that legalized Tryon's use of force at Alamance; Richard Caswell, who led troops against them under Tryon; and Griffith Rutherford, one of the surveyors charging exorbitant fees. See Anna Bair, "Johnston, Samuel," in William Powell, *Dictionary of North Carolina Biographies*, 6 volumes (Chapel Hill: University of North Carolina Press, 1988), http://www.ncpedia.org/biography/johnston–samuel; Jerry Cashion, "Rutherford, Griffith," in Powell, ed., *Dictionary of North Carolina Biographies,*http://www.ncpedia.org/biography/rutherford–griffith; Charles Holloman, "Caswell, Richard," in Powell, *Dictionary of North Carolina Biographies*(,http://www.ncpedia.org/biography/caswell–richard–0.

93. On elite attitudes toward "peasants" see Paschal, *History of North Carolina Baptists*, 71n11. Governor Martin on bandits is quoted in Ready, *The Tarheel State*, 103.

94. Griffin, *History of Old Tryon*, 29.

95. Griffin, 93, 88.

96. Ready, *The Tarheel State*, 108–20; Taylor, *American Revolutions,* 154.

97. Powell, *When the Past Refused to Die*, 77–80; Ready, *The Tarheel State*, 120, 124. See also Taylor, *American Revolutions,*197–98.

98. Powell, *When the Past Refused to Die*, 78–80. See Kars, *Breaking Loose Together*, 156.

99. Ready, *TheTarheel State*, 126.

100. For details see Ready, *The Tarheel State*, 126–28; Taylor, *American Revolutions*, 237–38, 247; Griffin, *History of Old Tryon*, 81; *Battle of King's Mountain*, American Revolution website, http://theamericanrevolution.org/battledetail.aspx?battle=25. On the paucity of further fighting see Ready, *The Tarheel State*, 114–15, 122.

101. Baird, 1901 letter;Taylor, *American Revolutions,* 221–26, 244–48.

102. Taylor, *American Revolutions,* 245–46.

103. Taylor,, 247.

104. Perdue and Oakley, *Native Carolinians,* 39.

105. See Naomi Klein, *The Shock Doctrine: The Rise of Disaster Capitalism* (New York: Henry Holt, 2007); Naomi Murakawa, *The First Civil Right: How Liberals Built Prison America* (New York: Oxford University Press, 2014); Edward Herman and Noam Chomsky, *Manufacturing Consent: The Political Economy of the Mass Media* (New York: Random House/Vintage, 1995).

106. For discussion of the role of whiteness in the formation of the United States as a nation, see Charles Mills, *The Racial Contract* (Ithaca, NY: Cornell University Press, 1997).

107. Horne, *The Counter-Revolution*, 137–38.

108. Silver, *Our Savage Neighbors*, 114–23; Parkinson, *The Common Cause*, esp. 98–184; Horne, *The Counter-Revolution*, 240; Taylor, *American Revolutions*, 233. See also Pem Davidson Buck, *Worked to the Bone: Race, Class, Power, and Privilege in Kentucky* (New York: Monthly Review Press, 2001); Pem Davidson Buck, "Whither Whiteness? Empire, State, and the Re-Ordering of Whiteness," *Transforming Anthropology* 20/2 (2012):105–17.

109. Sublette and Sublette, *The American Slave Coast*, 257.

110. Nash, *Race and Revolution*, 57.

111. Taylor, *American Revolutions*, 231, 233, 320–23; Nash, *Race and Revolution*, 60–61; Guyatt, *Bind Us Apart*, 201; Horne, *The Counter-Revolution*, 246.

112. Taylor, *American Revolutions*, 320–23.

113. Schama, *Rough Crossings*, 44–55; Taylor, *American Revolutions*, 115–19.

114. Horne, *The Counter-Revolution*, 16; Silver, *Our Savage Neighbors*, 114–23; Parkinson, *The Common Cause*, 105, 108–9, 130.

115. Ready, *The Tarheel State*, 109; Parkinson, *The Common Cause*, 126–29, 153–76; Horne, *The Counter-Revolution*, 220–24, 230–33, 239; Sublette and Sublette, *The American Slave Coast*, 255–57. But, says Taylor, had the British taken that idea seriously and trained many more black soldiers, they might have won the war in the South. See Taylor, *American Revolutions*, 229–33.

116. Raphael, calling their action "The First American Revolution," describes this as revolt against the British. See Raphael, *The First American Revolution*. My interpretation from his details is that it was at least as much a revolt against local elites who were also part of the British colonial government, making it a relative of the Regulator revolt. See also Taylor, *American Revolutions*, 121.

117. Taylor, *American Revolutions*, 94–110.

118. For analysis that focuses less on taxation and more on the desire to protect slavery see Sublette and Sublette, *The American Slave Coast*, 20, 250, 255; Horne, *The Counter-Revolution*.

119. Taylor, *American Revolutions*, 212.

120. Taylor, 371–74.

121. Quoted in Taylor, 370; see also 87, 98–99, 138, 354; Alan Taylor, *The Internal Enemy: Slavery and War in Virginia, 1772–1832* (New York: W.W. Norton, 2013), 29.

122. Quoted in Griffin, *History of Old Tryon*, 17–18.

123. Taylor, *American Revolutions*, 13, 36, 50, 91–93, 100–106; Ready, *The Tarheel State*, 104–5.

124. Lefler, *North Carolina History*, 114; Griffin, *History of Old Tryon*, 83.

125. This assumes all the accused were male, since women had no legal standing. If that is correct, and if the estimate of 1,200 men "able to bear arms" made by a Rutherford County historian is correct, then in the neighborhood of

twenty percent of Rutherford County men were accused. Not all were convicted, and some might have been men too old to bear arms. See Griffin, *History of Old Tryon*, 83, 87, 91.

126. Griffin, 26.

127. Taylor, *American Revolutions*, 324-25.

128. Sublette and Sublette, *The American Slave Coast*, 257; Taylor, *American Revolutions*, 211-26. On the Revolution as a civil war see Taylor, *American Revolutions*, 211-33; Sublette and Sublette, *The American Slave Coast*, 20.

129. Parkinson, *The Common Cause*; Taylor, *American Revolutions*, 197-99, 216-19, 241-43, 314-15. On the dependence of newspapers on ads about slavery, suggesting a source of bias toward Separatism, see Sublette and Sublette, *The American Slave Coast*, 227-35.

130. Jack Shuler, *Calling Out Liberty*. For examples of authors supporting the reality of rebellion see Sublette and Sublette, *The American Slave Coast*, 63; Morgan, *Laboring Women*, 183-95; Anthony Parent, *Foul Means: The Formation of a Slave Society in Virginia, 1660-1740* (Chapel Hill: Omohundro Institute and University of North Carolina Press, 2003), 267-68. Philip Morgan, along with many others, supports the reality of resistance, but he also points out the difference between eighteenth-century slaveholders' fears of revolt versus its reality. Everyday resistance is not actual revolt. See Philip Morgan, *Slave Counterpoint: Black Culture in the Eighteenth-Century Chesapeake and Low Country* (Chapel Hill: University of North Carolina Press, 1998), xxii, 386-88. For examples of those emphasizing how rare actual rebellions were see Baptist, *The Half Has Never Been Told*, xviii, 281-84; Miller, *The Problem of Slavery as History*, 66-67, 147; Lawrence Goldstone, *Dark Bargain: Slavery, Profits, and the Struggle for the Constitution* (New York: Walker and Company, 2005), 40; Frederick Douglass as cited in Moses Finley, "Was Greek Civilization Based on Slave Labour?," in Eugene Genovese, *The Slave Economies*, vol. 1 (New York: John Wiley and Sons, 1973 [1959]), 19-45, at 37-38. This is in apparent contradiction to Horne and his insistence on the ubiquity of African resistance giving cause for fear. But what Horne is actually talking about is the fear of revolt, not revolt itself. See Horne, *The Counter-Revolution*.

131. Horne, *The Counter-Revolution*, 227.

132. Parkinson, *The Common Cause*, 249, also 1-25, 101-106, 327. See also Horne, *The Counter-Revolution*, 227. For the importance of fear of Native attacks in Pennsylvania, likewise pushed through lurid news reporting, see Silver, *Our Savage Neighbors*.

133. Parkinson, *The Common Cause*, 263.

134. Horne, *The Counter-Revolution*, 7.

135. Parkinson, *The Common Cause*, 128; Sally Hadden, *Slave Patrols: Law*

and Violence in Virginia and the Carolinas (Cambridge, MA: Harvard University Press, 2003), 156–57.

136. Taylor, *American Revolutions,* 26, 52–53, 104–5, 353. For examples, see Isenberg, *White Trash,* 55, 63.

137. Parkinson, *The Common Cause,* 17–19.

138. Taylor, *American Revolutions,* 77.

139. Taylor, *American Revolutions,* 199, 241.

140. Miller, *The Problem of Slavery as History,* 60; Horne, *The Counter-Revolution,* 248.

7: ANCESTOR TALES OF THE DISPOSSESSION OF WOMEN, THE DOMINATION OF MEN, AND THE DEFINITION OF LIBERTY

1.   Joseph Miller, *The Problem of Slavery as History: A Global Approach* (New Haven: Yale University Press, 2012), 60–63, 71.

2.   Max Weber, "The Social Causes of the Decay of Ancient Civilization," in Eugene Genovese, *The Slave Economies,* vol. 1 (New York: John Wiley and Sons, 1973 [1896]), 46–57, at 52; Moses Finley, "Was Greek Civilization Based on Slave Labour?" in Genovese, *The Slave Economies,* 19–45, at 45.

3.   Ned Sublette and Constance Sublette, *The American Slave Coast: A History of the Slave-Breeding Industry* (Chicago: Lawrence Hill Books, 2016), 134.

4.   Quoted in Alan Taylor, *American Revolutions: A Continental History, 1750–1804* (New York: W.W. Norton, 2016), 372. See also Lawrence Goldstone, *Dark Bargain: Slavery, Profits, and the Struggle for the Constitution* (New York: Walker and Company, 2005), 148; Taylor, *American Revolutions,* 353–93.

5.   Taylor says that the British learned their lesson from the US Revolution and in 1791 changed their policy toward Canada so that Canadian colonists would have far less reason to revolt, including largely giving them the right to manage their own affairs. Since this happened after the Revolution, it would not have prevented Canadians from revolting along with the other colonies. See Taylor, *American Revolutions,* 329–34. On Massachusetts farmers' rebellion, see Ray Raphael, *The First American Revolution: Before Lexington and Concord* (New York: New Press, 2002).

6.   For instance, Nova Scotia outlawed slavery in 1800 and the British Parliament abolished it in 1834. But slavery in England was seriously contested long before that, and was a major issue by the 1770s. Nash argues that sentiment for abolition was strong in the United States and in England before and shortly after the Revolution, as it was, as we shall see in chapter 8, in Kentucky in the 1790s. The Atlantic slave trade, though not slavery, was abolished by Britain in 1807, barely before the United States abolished importation of Africans in 1808. See Simon Schama, *Rough Crossings: The Slaves, the British, and the American Revolution* (New York: HarperCollins,

2005), 6; Gerald Horne, *The Counter-Revolution of 1776: Slave Resistance and the Origins of the United States of America* (New York: New York University Press, 2014), 219; Sublette and Sublette, *The American Slave Coast*, 374; Gary Nash, *Race and Revolution* (Madison, WI: Madison House Publishers, 1990).

7. Sublette and Sublette, *The American Slave Coast*, 16, 374.

8. For some indication of enslavement in Canada see Andrés Reséndez, *The Other Slavery: The Uncovered Story of Indian Enslavement in America* (Boston: Houghton, Mifflin, Harcourt, 2016), 172–73; Jace Weaver, *The Red Atlantic: American Indigenes and the Making of the Modern World, 1000–1927* (Chapel Hill: University of North Carolina Press, 2014), 65–66.

9. Mike Ferner, "Fourth of July Like You've Never Seen it Before," *Counterpunch*, June 30, 2017, https://www.counterpunch.org/2017/06/30/93804/.

10. On delegates' arguments about the role of slavery and about abolition of the slave trade from the perspectives of North, Upper South, and Deep South during the Constitutional Convention see Goldstone, *Dark Bargain*, 120–44; Sublette and Sublette, *The American Slave Coast*, 10–20, 287–305. More generally see Nash, *Race and Revolution*, 25–50. On black abolitionists see Manisha Sinha, *The Slave's Cause: A History of Abolition* (New Haven: Yale University Press, 2016).

11. Silvia Federici, *Caliban and the Witch: Women, the Body and Primitive Accumulation,* 2nd rev. ed. (Brooklyn, NY: Autonomedia, 2014 [2004]), 23–25; Weber, "The Social Causes of the Decay," 56–57; Claude Meillassoux, *The Anthropology of Slavery: The Womb of Iron and Gold,* trans. Alide Dasnois (Chicago: University of Chicago Press, 1991 [1986]), 89–94, 118, 234–35, 280–83, 319–23.

12. For example, Schama, *Rough Crossings*, 410. On Indian slavery see Alan Gallay, *The Indian Slave Trade: The Rise of the English Empire in the American South 1670–1717* (New Haven: Yale University Press, 2002); Reséndez, *The Other Slavery;* Pekka Hämäläinen, *The Comanche Empire* (New Haven: Yale University Press, 2008).

13. Goldstone, *Dark Bargain*, 46–47, 166; Edward Baptist, *The Half Has Never Been Told: Slavery and the Making of American Capitalism* (New York: Basic Books, 2014), 10; Sublette and Sublette, *The American Slave Coast*, 10–14, 107–43, 266.

14. Sublette and Sublette, *The American Slave Coast*, 3–65.

15. Sublette and Sublette, 39–40, 414–19. For example, Daniel Rood, "An International Harvest: The Second Slavery, the Virginia–Brazil Connection, and the Development of the McCormick Reaper," in Sven Beckert and Seth Rockman, *Slavery's Capitalism: A New History of American Economic Development* (Philadelphia: University of Pennsylvania Press, 2016), 87–104.

16. See Baptist, *The Half Has Never Been Told*, xxiii, 106, 122–23, 185; Jennifer Morgan, *Laboring Women: Reproduction and Gender in New World Slavery* (Philadelphia: University of Pennsylvania Press, 2004), 101–6; Sublette and Sublette, *The American Slave Coast*, 414–19.

17. Sublette and Sublette, *The American Slave Coast*, 38. Approximately two million were sold in total, including local sales.

18. Jennifer Morgan, *Laboring Women: Reproduction and Gender in New World Slavery* (Philadelphia: University of Pennsylvania Press, 2004), 83–104, 101–6, 138–40; Sublette and Sublette, *The American Slave Coast*, 31, 414–16.

19. Taylor, *American Revolutions*, 366–69; Goldstone, *Dark Bargain*, 148.

20. Baptist, *The Half Has Never Been Told*, 9, 312; Sven Beckert, *Empire of Cotton: A Global History* (New York: Alfred A. Knopf, 2015), 111–13; Steven Mintz, "Introduction to Part II," in Mintz and John Stauffer, *The Problem of Evil: Slavery, Freedom, and the Ambiguities of American Reform*, 127–37 (Amherst: University of Massachusetts Press, 2007), 24–25.

21. Beckert, *Empire of Cotton*, 105.

22. Gary Anderson, *Ethnic Cleansing and the Indian: The Crime That Should Haunt America* (Norman: University of Oklahoma Press, 2014).

23. On the colonial view of the alliance between Native peoples and the British and on Native management of their relations with the British, see Taylor, *American Revolutions*, 251–78. For an earlier period see Gallay, *The Indian Slave Trade*; Matthew Jennings, *New Worlds of Violence: Cultures and Conquests in the Early American Southeast* (Knoxville: University of Tennessee Press, 2011). On the logic behind the Proclamation see Taylor, *American Revolutions*, 60–62, 69–70, 86–89. For Comanche power in the West see Hämäläinen, *The Comanche Empire*.

24. Baptist, *The Half Has Never Been Told*, 178–79, 326–27; Sublette and Sublette, *The American Slave Coast*, 69; Beckert, *Empire of Cotton*, 102–10.

25. Extremely long contracts with long intervals between pay periods enable employers to create unfree labor legally enforced, even when entered into voluntarily. See Robert Steinfeld, *Coercion, Contract, and Free Labor in the Nineteenth Century* (New York: Cambridge University Press, 2001). For industrial slavery see Charles Dew, *Bond of Iron: Master and Slave at Buffalo Forge* (New York: W.W. Norton, 1994); Douglas Blackmon, *Slavery By Another Name: The Re-Enslavement of Black Americans from the Civil War to World War II* (Norwell, MA: Anchor, 2009), 19–22, 44–53; Sublette and Sublette, *The American Slave Coast*, 202–5; Stephen Aron, *How the West Was Lost: The Transformation of Kentucky from Daniel Boone to Henry Clay* (Baltimore: Johns Hopkins University Press, 1996), 144–45. For discussion of the degree of slavery's compatibility with an industrial economy see John Majewski, "Why Did Northerners Oppose the Expansion of Slavery?

Economic Development and Education in the Limestone South," in Beckert and Rockman, *Slavery's Capitalism*, 277–98; Andrew Shankman, "Capitalism, Slavery, and the New Epoch: Mathew Carey's 1819," Beckert and Rockman, *Slavery's Capitalism*, 243–61.

26. Baptist, *The Half Has Never Been Told*, 111–21, 141–43. See also Beckert, *Empire of Cotton*, 108; Morgan, *Laboring Women*, 131.

27. Baptist, *The Half Has Never Been Told*, 139–43, 262–65, 281–84.

28. Nicolas Guyatt, *Bind Us Apart: How Enlightened Americans Invented Racial Segregation* (New York: Basic Books, 2016), 128–39. On the history of abolition in the North, see Sinha, *The Slave's Cause*.

29. Guyatt, *Bind Us Apart*, 197–224, 247–80.

30. Anderson, *Ethnic Cleansing*; Taylor, *American Revolutions*, 251–78.

31. Hämäläinen, *The Comanche Empire*, 1, 292–93.

32. Wilma Dunaway, *The First American Frontier: Transition to Capitalism in Southern Appalachia, 1700–1860* (Chapel Hill: University of North Carolina Press, 1996), 23–50.

33. Michael Oberg, *Native America: A History* (Malden, MA: Wiley-Blackwell, 2010), 151.

34. Theda Perdue, *Cherokee Women: Gender and Culture Change, 1700–1835* (Lincoln: University of Nebraska Press, 1998), 119; Carolyn Johnston, *Cherokee Women in Crisis: Trail of Tears, Civil War, and Allotment, 1838–1907* (Tuscaloosa: University of Alabama Press, 2003), 50–51.

35. On Cherokee farming, gender roles, and white attitudes see Perdue, *Cherokee Women*, 13, 17–28; Johnston, *Cherokee Women in Crisis*, 11–14, 39.

36. See Aron, *How the West Was Lost*, 8–11.

37. See Perdue, *Cherokee Women*, 55–56; Theda Perdue, *Slavery and the Evolution of Cherokee Society, 1540–1866* (Knoxville: University of Tennessee Press, 1987), 157n2.

38. Perdue, *Cherokee Women*, 24, 152; Warbasse, speaking of a later time period, says Chickasaw law makes women's property separate from husbands', and may eventually have influenced lawmakers working on the Married Women's Property Act. See Elizabeth Warbasse, *The Changing Legal Rights of Married Women, 1800–1861* (New York: Garland Publishing, 1987), 140.

39. Quoted in Johnston, *Cherokee Women in Crisis*, 1; Perdue, *Cherokee Women*, 55.

40. Johnston, *Cherokee Women in Crisis*, 54–55.

41. Perdue, *Cherokee Women*, 77–78.

42. On the Civilization Program see Perdue, *Cherokee Women*, 109–34; Johnston, *Cherokee Women in Crisis*, 36–50.

43. Quoted in Perdue, *Cherokee Women*, 111.

44. Johnston, *Cherokee Women in Crisis*, 55.

45. Ronald Takaki, *A Different Mirror: A History of Multicultural America* (New York: Back Bay Books, 2008), 47–50; Perdue, *Cherokee Women*, 118–19; Guyatt, *Bind Us Apart*, 233–39.

46. Johnston, *Cherokee Women in Crisis*, 50–54; Perdue, *Cherokee Women*, 77–78, 116–22, 126–27, 133. See also Thurman Wilkins, *Cherokee Tragedy: The Ridge Family and the Decimation of a People*, 2nd rev. ed. (Norman: University of Oklahoma Press, 1986 [1970]), 119–31.

47. Johnston, *Cherokee Women in Crisis*, 77. On the Trail of Tears see Wilkins, *Cherokee Tragedy*, 316–28; Johnston, *Cherokee Women in Crisis*, 56–78. On Cherokee resistance to and white schemes for voluntary colonization beyond the Mississippi, see Guyatt, *Bind Us Apart*, 225–45, 281–305, 320–23.

48. Johnston, *Cherokee Women in Crisis*, 127–44.

49. Federici, *Caliban and the Witch*, 9, 14, 23–25, 61–115; see Peter Linebaugh, *The London Hanged: Crime and Civil Society in the Eighteenth Century* (New York: Cambridge University Press, 1992).

50. For example see Linebaugh, *The London Hanged*, 374–77.

51. Linebaugh, 378–82, 404–8, 170–76.

52. Linebaugh, 374–78. For analysis of the relationship between wages, economic coercion, and dispossession see Steinfeld, *Coercion, Contract, and Free Labor*, 8–19.

53. Rosa Luxemburg, *The Accumulation of Capital*, trans. Agnes Schwarzschild (Mansfield Center, CT: Martino Publishing, 2015 [1913]), esp. 348–67.

54. See also Robert Miles, *Capitalism and Unfree Labor: Anomaly or Necessity* (New York: Tavistock, 1987), 35–49.

55. David Harvey, "The 'New' Imperialism: Accumulation by Dispossession," *Socialist Register* 40 (2004): 63–87; Jim Glassman, "Primitive accumulation, accumulation by dispossession, accumulation by 'extra–economic' means," *Progress in Human Geography* 30/5 (2006): 608–25; Sharryn Kasmir and August Carbonella, "Dispossession and the Anthropology of Labor, *Critique of Anthropology* 28/1 (2008): 5–25.

56. Federici, *Caliban and the Witch*, 70–72; Janet Rifkin, "Toward a Theory of Law and Patriarchy," *Harvard Women's Law Journal* 3 (1980):83–95, at 93, 95.

57. Linebaugh, *The London Hanged*, xx–xxi.

58. Linebaugh, 16–19, 50, 404; Christina Larner, *Enemies of God: The Witch-hunt in Scotland* (Edinburgh: John Donald, 2000 [1981]), 60–61.

59. Linebaugh, *The London Hanged*, 425–36. See also Sam Mitrani, *The Rise of the Chicago Police Department: Class and Conflict, 1850–1894* (Urbana: University of Illinois Press, 2013).

60. For example see Linebaugh, *The London Hanged*, 390–96.

61. Linebaugh, 221–22, 285, 440–41.

62. Warbasse, *The Changing Legal Rights*, 5. On women's legal position in respect to property also see Marylynn Salmon, *Women and the Law of Property in Early America* (Chapel Hill: University of North Carolina Press, 1986).

63. Warbasse, *The Changing Legal Rights*, 5, 9, 14.

64. Claudia Zaher, "When a Woman's Marital Status Determined Her Legal Status: A Research Guide on the Common Law Doctrine of Coverture," *Law Library Journal* 94/3 (2002):459–86; Salmon, *Women and the Law of Property*, 14–18; Hendrik Hartog, *Man and Wife in America: A History* (Cambridge, MA: Harvard University Press, 2000), 96–103, 116–35; Warbasse, *The Changing Legal Rights*, 28–29. For detailed discussion of coverture and of dower rights and their variation with time and place see Salmon, *Women and the Law of Property*, esp. 3–18; Warbasse, *The Changing Legal Rights*, 1–56.

65. Salmon, *Women and the Law of Property*, 14–40; Hartog, *Man and Wife*, 146.

66. Hartog, 156.

67. Hartog, 165, 168.

68. Warbasse, *The Changing Legal Rights*, 10–13; Salmon, *Women and the Law of Property*, 142–47.

69. Salmon, *Women and the Law of Property*, 143.

70. *Hezekiah Ellis,* Wikitree.com, citing *The Virginia Genealogist* 5(1961), ed. John Fredrick Dorman, 107,https://www.wikitree.com/wiki/Ellis-3443; Salmon, *Women and the Law of Property*, 141; Hartog, *Man and Wife*, 145.

71. *Barren County Kentucky Will Book No.1,* archived at Office of the Barren County Clerk, June 15, 1811, 446. See also *Barren County Kentucky Will Book No.1,* Eva Peden, ed. (privately printed, 1979), 88.

72. Laura Davidson Baird, 1901 letter, Davidson File, South Central Kentucky Cultural Center, Glasgow, KY; Landon Chambliss, *Baird–Davidson–Rogers–Wood and Allied History,*1989, typed ms. in Davidson File, Hart County Historical Society, Munfordville, KY, 26.

73. Hartog, *Man and Wife*, 145; Salmon, *Women and the Law of Property*, 167–72. In the late 1830s the Southern states began passing the nation's first laws by which married women's land was automatically separate from their husbands. As Warbasse explains,, this was no move toward gender equality, despite the fact of giving women property rights. It simply gave men debt relief—the wife's property couldn't be taken to pay his debts, so he couldn't be totally dispossessed. See Warbasse, *The Changing Legal Rights*, vii–viii,140, 142–44.

74. Salmon speculates that women who could afford it were acting to keep control of their property, either by not remarrying or by insisting on a marriage settlement. See Salmon, *Women and the Law of Property*, 184.

75. *Spotsylvania County, Virginia, Court Orders, 1748–1750*, March 1749/50 (Miami Beach, FL: T.L.C. Genealogy, 1999), 90,.

76. Warbasse, *The Changing Legal Rights*, 1–56; Salmon, *Women and the Law of Property*, 183–84. On separation of estates giving married women control of the property they brought into a marriage or inherited later, see Salmon, *Women and the Law of Property*, 88–89. If a widow remarried, however, she would lose that right and her husband would take over. For an example of the havoc a new husband could wreak, against which his new wife was powerless, requiring intervention by the widow's son to save his own inheritance from the first husband, see *Middlesex County, Virginia, Court Orders, 1711–1713*, July 1711(T.L.C. Genealogy, n.d.), 36.

77. Salmon, *Women and the Law of Property*, 44–53, 81–119; Hartog, *Man and Wife*, 118; Warbasse, *The Changing Legal Rights*, 29–35, 47–48.

78. Kirsten Fischer, *Suspect Relations: Sex, Race, and Resistance in Colonial North Carolina* (Ithaca, NY: Cornell University Press, 2001), 112; Warbasse, *The Changing Legal Rights*, 167.

79. Hartog, *Man and Wife*, 93, 193.

80. Warbasse, *The Changing Legal Rights*, 26–27; Salmon, *Women and the Law of Property*, 58–66.

81. *Mt. Tabor Church Minutes, Barren County, Kentucky*, vol. 1:1798–1829, Sandra Gorin, transcriber (Glasgow KY: Gorin Genealogical Publishing, 1994), 71–72.

82. Salmon does not include North Carolina in her study, but she does make frequent statements about the South generally as compared to New England and to the Mid-Atlantic states. Fischer does mention coverture as applying in North Carolina during the colonial period. See Fischer, *Suspect Relations*, 112.

83. See chapter 6 on Alexander's status; Patricia Peterson, *The Alexander Davidson Family*, handwritten genealogy available in Davidson File, South Central Kentucky Cultural Center, Glasgow, KY, n.d.; Chambliss, *Baird–Davidson*, 14, 26. There is considerable disagreement about the date of Anna's death. The fact that she is not listed on the 1782 Sandy Run Church rolls might indicate the earlier death date. Virginia DePriest, *The Sandy Run Settlement and Mooresboro* (n.p., 1976), 6, https://archive.org/details/sandyrunsettleme00depr.

84. Sublette and Sublette, *The American Slave Coast*, 36; Annette Gordon-Reed, *The Hemingses of Monticello: An American Family* (New York: W.W. Norton, 2008), 146–48.

85. Patricia Bonomi, *Under the Cope of Heaven: Religion, Society, and Politics in Colonial America* (New York: Oxford University Press, 2003), 147–48, 153–57. For a discussion of the religious positions of preachers and attenders at meetings such as that at Cane Ridge, see Dickson Bruce, *And*

They All Sang Hallelujah: Plain–Folk Camp–Meeting Religion, 1800–1845 (Knoxville: University of Tennessee Press, 1974), 96–122.

86. Marjoleine Kars, *Breaking Loose Together: The Regulator Rebellion in Pre-Revolutionary North Carolina* (Chapel Hill: University of North Carolina Press, 2002), 106.

87. Bonomi, *Under the Cope of Heaven*, 108, 157; Bruce, *And They All Sang Hallelujah*, 111.

88. Marilyn Westerkamp, *Women in Early American Religion 1600–1850* (New York: Routledge, 1999), 95.

89. For example, *Mt. Tabor Church Minutes*, 65.

90. Jennifer McKinney, "Sects and Gender: Reaction and Resistance to Cultural Change," *Priscilla Papers* 29/4 (2015):15–25, at 15. Her view is backed up by Kars, *Breaking Loose Together*; Westerkamp, *Women in Early American Religion*; Bonomi, *Under the Cope of Heaven*; Bill Leonard, *Baptists in America* (New York: Columbia University Press, 2005), 185–86.

91. See Malory Huggins, *A History of North Carolina Baptists 1727–1932* (Raleigh: The General Board, Baptist State Convention of North Carolina, 1967), 50–62; Barry Hankins, *The Second Great Awakening and the Transcendentalists* (Westport, CT: Greenwood Press, 2004), 1–21. On revivals in North Carolina before Cane Ridge see Joe Mobley, *The Way We Lived in North Carolina* (Chapel Hill: University of North Carolina Press, 2003), 218–21. On Cane Ridge and on revivalism see also Craig Friend, *Along the Maysville Road: The Early American Republic in the Trans-Appalachian West* (Knoxville: University of Tennessee Press, 2005), 159–78; Westerkamp, *Women in Early American* Religion, 102–6; Bruce, *And They All Sang Hallelujah*, 52–56, 61–95.

92. Hartog, *Man and Wife*, 154, 153. See also Scott Stephan, *Redeeming the Southern Family: Evangelical Women and Domestic Devotion in the Antebellum South* (Athens: University of Georgia Press, 2008), 17; Bonomi, *Under the Cope of Heaven*, 157; Leonard, *Baptists in America*, 209.

93. Baird, 1901 letter.

94. Westerkamp, *Women in Early American Religion*, 101; Bonomi, *Under the Cope of Heaven*, xv; Huggins, *A History of North Carolina Baptists*, 68.

95. Baird, 1901 letter; Chambliss, *Baird-Davidson*, 14. Family lore in an unidentified letter from Peggy to Lloyd says Mary was the sister of William Davidson's wife, found online five years ago and no longer available.

96. DePriest, *The Sandy Run Settlement*, 6; Peterson, *The Alexander Davidson Family*; Chambliss, *Baird-Davidson*, 14, 26. According to Chambliss, Mary joined in 1788 also, but since she was on DePriest's membership rolls in 1782, this does not make sense.

97. Stephan, *Redeeming the Southern Family*, 18. See Leonard, *Baptists in America*, 209.

98. Ellen Eslinger, *Running Mad for Kentucky: Frontier Travel Accounts* (Lexington: University Press of Kentucky, 2004), 50; Aron, *How the West Was Lost*, 49–50. For a history of Native and white interaction in a cultural "middle ground" in early white entrance into Kentucky, see Aron, *How the West Was Lost*, 5–57.

99. *Deeds Before A&A, Barren County*, archived at the Office of the County Clerk, Barren County, KY, 35–37; *Old Surveys, Barren County, Kentucky, 1799–1835, of Edmund Rogers and Daniel Curd*, ed. Vivian Rousseau and Sandra Gorin (Glasgow, KY: private publication, 1990). Skaggs Creek, Beaver Creek, and Sinking Creek all go through the area just south of Glasgow, close to both Mt. Tabor and Sinking Creek Church. See also Baird, 1901 letter.

100. Eslinger, *Running Mad for Kentucky*, 58, 62, 177–79.

101. Joan Coward, *Kentucky in the New Republic: The Process of Constitution Making* (Lexington: University Press of Kentucky, 1979), 50–51; Aron, *How the West Was Lost*, 82–89.

102. Westerkamp, *Women in Early American Religion*, 115; Friend, *Along the Maysville Road*, 173.

103. Stephan, *Redeeming the Southern Family*; McKinney, "Sects and Gender," 16–18; Friend, *Along the Maysville Road*, 174; Ellen DuBois and Lynn Dumenil, *Through Women's Eyes: An American History with Documents* (Boston: Bedford/St. Martin's, 2005), 137–45. See also Joan Gundersen, "Kith and Kin: Women's Networks in Colonial Virginia," in Catherine Clinton and Michele Gillespie, *The Devil's Lane: Sex and Race in the Early South* (New York: Oxford University Press, 1997), 90–108, at 100.

104. Johnston, *Cherokee Women in Crisis*, 50.

105. For a description of this process for the area of Kentucky north and east of Lexington see Friend, *Along the Maysville Road*, 180–83, 193–205, 217–82.

106. Friend, 183; Thavolia Glymph, *Out of the House of Bondage: The Transformation of the Plantation Household* (New York: Cambridge University Press, 2008), 82.

107. On the gentry and the displays that marked their status, the development of a class structure, and the rising power of a local non–gentry intermediate class see Friend, *Along the Maysville Road*, 72–84, 124–30, 196–202.

108. Timothy Fitzgerald, "Negative Liberty, Liberal Faith Postulates and World Disorder," in Trevor Stack, Naomi Goldenberg, and Fitzgerald, *Religion as a Category of Governance and Sovereignty* (Boston: Brill, 2015), 248–79.

8: ANCESTOR TALES OF LIFE IN A CAPITALIST SLAVING SOCIETY

1. Mt. Tabor Book Committee, *The History of Mt. Tabor Baptist Church: The Oldest Church in Barren County, Kentucky* (Glasgow, KY: South Central Kentucky Historical and Genealogical Society, 1988), 23. His estate was not inventoried until late in 1818, however.

2. Lowell Harrison, "John Breckinridge and the Kentucky Constitution of 1799," *The Register of the Kentucky Historical Society* 57/3 (1958): 209–33, at 232; Joan Coward, *Kentucky in the New Republic: The Process of Constitution Making* (Lexington: University Press of Kentucky, 1979), 126. For the following statements refer to Kentucky's 1792 and 1797 constitutions, found in *Michie's Kentucky Revised Statutes, Certified Version*, vol. 1: *Constitutions* (Charlottesville, VA: Matthew Bender& Company, 2014), 905–17, 919–34.

3. Craig Friend, *Along* the *Maysville Road: The Early American Republic in the Trans-Appalachian West* (Knoxville: University of Tennessee Press, 2005), 80.

4. For analysis of the two constitutions and the politics involved in both see Coward, *Kentucky in the New Republic*.

5. Coward, 164, 44. See also Harrison, "John Breckinridge," 215.

6. Harrison, "John Breckinridge," 223; Asa Martin, *The Anti-Slavery Movement in Kentucky Prior to 1850* (New York: Negro Universities Press, 1970 [1918]), 13–16, 28–32; Coward, *Kentucky in the New Republic*, 36.

7. Martin, *The Anti-Slavery Movement*, 16.

8. Coward, *Kentucky in the New Republic*, 118. See also Harrison, "John Breckinridge," 215, 219, 222; Stephen Aron, *How the West Was Lost: The Transformation of Kentucky from Daniel Boone to Henry Clay* (Baltimore: Johns Hopkins University Press, 1996), 92–95.

9. Coward is quoting George Nicolas, a principle architect of the constitutions. See Coward, *Kentucky in the New Republic*, 32. See also Pem Davidson Buck, *Worked to the Bone: Race, Class, Power, and Privilege in Kentucky* (New York: Monthly Review Press, 2001), 32–33; Aron, *How the West Was Lost*, 94.

10. Coward, *Kentucky in the New Republic*, 126. See Harrison, "John Breckinridge," 225–26.

11. Coward, *Kentucky in the New Republic*, 54, 63. See Aron, *How the West Was Lost*, 127–28; Friend, *Along the Maysville Road*, 107; Lowell Harrison and James Klotter, *A New History of Kentucky* (Lexington: University Press of Kentucky, 1997), 71.

12. Harold Tallant, *Evil Necessity: Slavery and Political Culture in Antebellum Kentucky* (Lexington: University Press of Kentucky, 2003), 18.

13. Coward, *Kentucky in the New Republic*, 130, 136; Martin, *The Anti-Slavery Movement*, 16.

14. For voting analysis see Coward, *Kentucky in the New Republic*, 134–35.

15. Coward, 127.

16. Quoted in Harrison, "John Breckinridge," 209. For a more accurate appraisal of life south of the Green River see Aron, *How the West Was Lost*, 150–68.

17. Coward, *Kentucky in the New Republic*, 127.

18. Lowell Harrison, *The Antislavery Movement in Kentucky* (Lexington: University Press of Kentucky, 1978), 21–22. In the decade immediately following the convention the large Elkhorn Baptist Association advised that "ministers and churches in their religious capacities should have nothing to do with emancipation or any other political issue." See William Sweet, *Religion on the American Frontier: The Baptists, 1783–1830* (New York: Cooper Square Publishing, 1964), 82. See also Martin, *The Antislavery Movement*, 19.

19. John Boles, *Religion in Antebellum Kentucky* (Lexington: University Press of Kentucky, 1976), 116; Harrison, *The Antislavery Movement*, 22.

20. Mt. Tabor Book Committee, *The History of Mt. Tabor*, 61.

21. John Spencer, *A History of Kentucky Baptists From 1769–1885*, vols. 1 and 2 (London: Forgotten Books, 2017 [1886]), 385; *Mt. Tabor Church Minutes, Barren County, Kentucky*, vol. 1 [1798–1829], Sandra Gorin, transcriber (Glasgow, KY: Gorin Genealogical Publishing, 1994), 8–9.

22. Spencer, *A History of Kentucky Baptists*, 385; *Mt. Tabor Church Minutes*, 15.

23. Quotes are, respectively, from Boles, *Religion in Antebellum Kentucky*, 115; John Taylor, *A History of Ten Baptist Churches, Of Which the Author Has Been Alternately a Member* (Frankfort, KY: n.p., 1823), 79–80, http://baptisthistoryhomepage.com/taylor.ten.churches.title.html. See Martin, *The Antislavery Movement*, 20, 39–42.

24. Carter Tarrant, *History of the Baptised Ministers and Churches in Kentucky &c Friends of Humanity* (Frankfort, KY: Press of William Hunter, 1808), 23, http://baptisthistoryhomepage.com/tarrant.carter.history.html.

25. Spencer, *A History of Kentucky Baptists*, 384.

26. Harrison, *The Antislavery Movement*, 22; Sweet, *Religion on the American Frontier*, 86.

27. *Barren County Kentucky, Minister's Return Book, 1799–1825*, photocopy of original, ed. Sandra Gorin (Glasgow, KY: Gorin Genealogical Publishing, 1992), 5; Landon Chambliss, *Baird–Davidson–Rogers–Wood and Allied History*, typed ms. in Davidson File, Hart County Historical Society, 1989, 27, 53.

28. "Barren" refers to the open prairies of south central Kentucky, which Native people had created by generations of purposeful burning in order to create good hunting grounds. That Kentucky was seen as an incredibly bountiful hunters' paradise by astounded whites was no accident. See Aron, *How the West Was Lost*, 10–11.

29. *Mt. Tabor Church Minutes*, 22–23; James Brooks, *The Biography of Eld. Jacob Locke, of Barren County, KY* (Glasgow KY: Times Print, 1976 [1881]), 77. I have chosen to spell Lock's name without an *e*, following the usage of the Minutes.

30. Brooks, *The Biography*, 66; *Mt. Tabor Church Minutes*, 33.

31. Dickson Bruce, *And They All Sang Hallelujah: Plain–Folk Camp–Meeting Religion, 1800–1845* (Knoxville: University of Tennessee Press, 1974), 58–59; Martin, *The Anti-slavery Movement*, 34–35; Scott Stephan, *Redeeming the Southern Family: Evangelical Women and Domestic Devotion in the Antebellum South* (Athens: University of Georgia Press, 2008), 17; Jennifer McKinney, "Sects and Gender: Reaction and Resistance to Cultural Change," *Priscilla Papers* 29/ 4 (2015): 15–25.

32. Harrison, *The Anti-slavery Movement*, 20; Tallant, *Evil Necessity*, 100–101; Martin, *The Anti-slavery Movement*, 15, 38.

33. The query may have been prompted by the publication of David Barrow's powerful anti-slavery pamphlet. See Harrison, *The Antislavery Movement*, 28.

34. Brooks, *The Biography*, 66; *Mt. Tabor Church Minutes*, 33.

35. *Mt. Tabor Church Minutes*, 33; Martin, *The Anti-slavery Movement*, 38–39.

36. Tarrant, *History*, 23.

37. *Mt. Tabor Church Minutes*, 34.

38. *Mt. Tabor Church Minutes*, 41.

39. *Mt. Tabor Church Minutes*, 40; Brooks claims "emancipating brethren, who are orderly" could worship with them. Perhaps orderly" meant no mention of slavery. See Brooks, *The Biography*, 66.

40. *Mt. Tabor Church Minutes*, 42, 50, 51.

41. *Mt. Tabor Church Minutes*, 49–50.

42. Spencer, *A History of Kentucky Baptists*, 484.

43. Spencer implies he was already ordained, but according to the Mt. Tabor Minutes he was actually not ordained until 1824, at age fifty-six; Spencer says he was licensed to preach in 1820, and ordained later. See Spencer, *A History of Kentucky Baptists*, 385, 113; *Mt. Tabor Church Minutes*, 100–101.

44. On the distinction between abolitionism and antislavery, see Ned Sublette and Constance Sublette, *The American Slave Coast: A History of the Slave-Breeding Industry* (Chicago: Lawrence Hill Books, 2016), 439; Manisha Sinha, *The Slave's Cause: A History of Abolition* (New Haven: Yale University Press, 2016), 41. For the following description of antislavery attitudes I am dependent particularly on Tallant, *Evil Necessity;* Nicholas Guyatt, *Bind Us Apart: How Enlightened Americans Invented Racial Segregation* (New York: Basic Books, 2016); Harrison, *The Antislavery Movement*; Martin, *The Anti-slavery Movement*; and the articles collected in Lewis Perry and Michael Fellman, eds. *Antislavery Reconsidered: New Perspectives on the Abolitionists* (Baton Rouge: Louisiana State University Pres, 1979); Steven Mintz and John Stauffer, *The Problem of Evil: Slavery, Freedom, and the Ambiguities of American Reform* (Amherst: University of Massachusetts

Press, 2007). For detailed accounts of abolitionism see Andrew Delbanco, *The War Before the War: Fugitive Slaves and the Struggle of America's Soul from the Revolution to the Civil War* (New York: Penguin Press, 2018); Sinha, *The Slave's Cause*. On immediate emancipation attitudes after 1830 see Donald Scott, "Abolition as a Sacred Vocation," in Perry and Fellman, *Antislavery Reconsidered*, 51–74. See also Bill Leonard, *Baptists in America* (New York: Columbia University Press, 2005), 26–29.

45. On the logic of colonization see particularly Tallant, *Evil Necessity*, 27–57, 74–80; Guyatt, *Bind Us Apart*, 197–224, 247–80; Martin, *The Anti-slavery Movement*, 49–62.

46. Sweet, *Religion on the American Frontier*, 84, 569.

47. Hickman left the church six months later. Winney was restored to the church five years later. See Sweet, *Religion on the American Frontier*, 329–30, 338, 372.

48. Scott, "Abolition as a Sacred Vocation," 51.

49. On David Rice see Harrison, *The Antislavery Movement*, 18–20; 23; Martin, *The Anti-slavery Movement*, 12–17, 31; Boles, *Religion in Antebellum Kentucky*, 102–7; Guyatt, *Bind Us Apart*, 35–38.

50. On antislavery conservatives and disorder see Tallant, *Evil Necessity*, 59–90.

51. Tallant, *Evil Necessity*, 64.

52. *Third Census of the United States, 1810,* Barren, Kentucky, 59; *Fourth Census of the United States, 1820,* Barren, Kentucky, 157; *Fifth Census of the United States, 1830,* Hart, Kentucky, 173.

53. Tarrant, *History*, 39; Martin, *The Anti-slavery Movement*, 39–42. On the concept of limited terms of slavery, see Stephen Whitman, *The Price of Freedom: Slavery and Manumission in Baltimore and Early National Maryland* (New York: Routledge, 2000 [1997]).

54. William Thomas, "Some History of the People and Their Burial Places Located or Formerly Known To Be Located Near the Environs of Buck Creek," *Traces: Quarterly Publication of the South Central Kentucky Historical and Genealogical Society* 28/1 (2000):15–27, at 25; *Barren's Black Roots: A History of Black Families in Barren County*, Vol. 2, ed. Michelle Gorin (Glasgow KY: Gorin Genealogical Publishing, 1992), 1, 59–60, 86–87; *Order Book No. 4, Barren County Kentucky, May Court 1812–August Court 1818,* May 1815, ed. Eva Peden (Glasgow: private printing, 1979), 81; *Deeds, K, Barren County,* July 1825, archived at the Office of the Barren County Clerk, Glasgow, KY, 240. Although Thomas refers to Sampson as "Free Samuel," it is clear that this is actually Sampson. Hezekiah and Sampson were assigned to the same road crew, indicating that they lived along the same road. There are references to a court case concerning Sampson's land, and there is clearly much more to this story. See also Loren Schweninger, "The Fragile Nature of Freedom: Free Women

of Color in the U.S. South," in Darlene Hine and David Barry Gaspar, *Beyond Bondage: Free Women of Color in the Americas* (Urbana: University of Illinois Press, 2004), 106–24; Juliet Walker, "The Legal Status of Free Blacks in Early Kentucky, 1792–1825," *Filson Club Quarterly* 57(October 1983): 382–95.

55. Tallant, *Evil Necessity*, 10–14.

56. Tallant, 19.

57. Tallant, 14.

58. Paul Finkelman, "The Significance and Persistence of Proslavery Thought," in Steven Mintz and John Stauffer, *The Problem of Evil: Slavery, Freedom, and the Ambiguities of American Reform* (Amherst: University of Massachusetts Press, 2007), 95–114, at 105; Tallant, *Evil Necessity*, 98; Article VII of the 1799 Constitution required that laws be passed to treat slaves humanely, as did the Constitution of 1792. On Baptist attitudes and policies related to race nationally, see Leonard, *Baptists in America*, 26–29, 183–202.

59. Friend, *Along the Maysville Road*, 175; Sweet, *Religion on the American Frontier*, 320, 323–24.

60. *Mt. Tabor Church Minutes*, 90–91.

61. On the prevalence of renting (hiring out) enslaved workers see Aron, *How the West Was Lost*, 100, 144.

62. *Mt. Tabor Church Minutes*, 56.

63. *Mt. Tabor Church Minutes*, 45.

64. For examples of both using and not using the term see *Mt. Tabor Church Minutes*, 56, 60, 62, 64. See also Betty Wood, "'For their Satisfaction of Redress:' African Americans and Church Discipline in the Early South," in Catherine Clinton and Michele Gillespie, *The Devil's Lane: Sex and Race in the Early South* (New York: Oxford University Press, 1997), 109–23.

65. *Mt. Tabor Church Minutes*, 44, 46, 61.

66. *Mt. Tabor Church Minutes*, 59–60.

67. *Mt. Tabor Church Minutes*, 102, 103.

68. *Mt. Tabor Church Minutes*, 62, 88.

69. *Mt. Tabor Church Minutes*, 102–3.

70. For an explication of paternalistic interpretation see Yvonne Jones, "Dual Visions of History," *Current Anthropology* 58/2 (2017): 312–14.

71. *Barren County Will Book #1*, November,1818, archived at Office of Barren County Clerk, Glasgow, KY, 529–30; *Barren County Inventories and C. No.6*, July 1849, archived at Office of the Barren County Clerk, Glasgow, KY, 40–46; Appendices 2 and 3.

72. Aron, *How the West Was Lost*, 153, 168; Laura Davidson Baird, 1901 letter, available in Davidson file at South Central Kentucky Cultural Center, Glasgow, KY. On the 1850 census numbers, see Harrison and Klotter, *A New History*, 168.

73. *Barren County Inventories and C*, 45.

74. Walker, "The Legal Status of Free Blacks," 384, 392.

75. "Copper and Kings," *Kentucky Brandy Heritage*, 2016, http://www.copper-andkings.com/kentucky–brandy–heritage/.

76. Baird, 1901 letter.

77. For examples around the time of Alexander's death and of Mary's death later see the *Barren County Will Book 1* and *Barren County Inventories and C*.

78. For the economic argument see Tallant, *Evil Necessity*, 82–89.

79. Friend, *Along the Maysville Road*, 233–34.

80. Friend, 222; Aron, *How the West Was Lost*, 139–44; Steven Mintz, "Introduction to Part II," in Mintz and John Stauffer, *The Problem of Evil: Slavery, Freedom, and the Ambiguities of American Reform* (Amherst: University of Massachusetts Press, 2007), 127–37, esp. 130; Paul Knepper, "The Kentucky Penitentiary at Frankfort and the Origins of America's First Convict Lease System, 1798–1843," *The Filson Club Quarterly* 69/1 (1995): 41–66, at 57.

81. Tallant, *Evil Necessity*, 88; Friend, *Along the Maysville Road*, 178; Aron, *How the West Was Lost*, 99, 196.

82. Quoted in Tallant, *Evil Necessity*, 58.

83. Martin, *The Anti-Slavery Movement*, 28; Aron, *How the West Was Lost*, 91.

84. On free blacks in Lexington see Friend, *Along the Maysville Road*, 204–7, 230.

85. Knepper, "The Kentucky Penitentiary," 57.

86. Mintz, "Introduction," 130; Tallant, *Evil Necessity*, 82– 90; Friend, *Along the Maysville Road*, 231.

87. See Tallant, *Evil Necessity*, 86.

88. Martin, *The Anti-slavery Movement*, 28; Harrison, *The Antislavery Movement*, 19; Guyatt, *Bind Us Apart*, 35; Tallant, *Evil Necessity*, 82.

89. Tallant, *Evil Necessity*, 94.

90. Paul Knepper, "Thomas Jefferson, Criminal Code Reform, and the Founding of the Kentucky Penitentiary at Frankfort," *The Register of the Kentucky Historical Society* 91 (Spring 1993):129–49, at 135; Harrison and Klotter, *A New History*, 83.

91. Quoted in Knepper, "Thomas Jefferson," 135.

92. On proportionality and passage of the bill see Knepper, "Thomas Jefferson," 133, 135–40.

93. Harrison and Klotter, *A New History*, 83; Knepper, "Thomas Jefferson," 135.

94. Knepper, "Thomas Jefferson," 129; *Order Book No. 3, Barren County Kentucky, 1806–April Court 1812*, April 1809, ed. Eva Peden (Glasgow, KY: private printing, 1979), 75.

95. Knepper, "The Kentucky Penitentiary," 44.

96. Knepper, 48, 51.

97. Knepper, 43, 64–66.
98. For example see *Order Book No. 4*, 93.
99. Quoted in Knepper, "The Kentucky Penitentiary," 45.
100. Quoted in Knepper, 45–46.
101. For pictures of Kentucky's first prisons see Knepper, "Thomas Jefferson," 143, 145.
102. Aron, *How the West Was Lost*, 142–43.
103. Mintz, "Introduction," 130–31; Harrison and Klotter, *A New History*. 78.
104. Trevor Stack, "Introduction," in Stack, Naomi Goldenberg, and Timothy Fitzgerald, *Religion as a Category of Governance and Sovereignty* (Boston: Brill, 2015), 1–20, at 4, 12.
105. Naomi Goldenberg, "The Category of Religion in the Technology of Governance: An Argument for Understanding Religions as Vestigial States," in Stack, Goldenberg, and Fitzgerald, *Religion as a Category of Governance and Sovereignty*, 280–92, at 288.
106. The quotes come respectively from Christopher Krupa and David Nugent, "Off-Centered States: Rethinking State Theory Through the Andean Lens," in Krupa and Nugent, *State Theory and Andean Politics: New Approaches to the Study of Rule* (Philadelphia: University of Pennsylvania Press, 2015), 1–31, at 12, and from the title of Stack, Goldenberg, and Fitzgerald, *Religion as a Category of Governance and Sovereignty;* in that volume see especially the articles by Stack and by Goldenberg.
107. Bruce, *And They All Sang Hallelujah*, 123–24. In 1817 the Forks of Elkhorn had twenty-five white males, fifty-four white females, forty-seven slaves and persons of color. See Sweet, *Religion on the American Frontier*, 402.
108. Friend, *Along the Maysville Road*, 171, 104; Aron, *How the West Was Lost*, 171.
109. Buck, *Worked to the Bone*, 45–49; Mintz and Stauffer, *The Problem of Evil*, 174. See also Friend, *Along the Maysville Road*, 107–12, 221–28; Aron, *How the West Was Lost*, 140–43.
110. Macpherson, as described in Ronald Walters, "The Boundaries of Abolitionism," in Lewis Perry and Michael Fellman, *Antislavery Reconsidered: New Perspectives on the Abolitionists* (Baton Rouge: Louisiana State University Press, 1979), 3–23, at 9; Stack, "Introduction," 14; see Bruce, *And They All Sang Hallelujah*, 130–31.
111. Stephan, *Redeeming the Southern Family*, 5.
112. On growing inequality see Aron, *How the West Was Lost*, 127–28.
113. Bruce, *And They All Sang Hallelujah*, 47.
114. For a discussion of the interconnectedness of church and state, although not in terms of diarchy, see Paul Johnson, Pamela Klassen, and Winnifred Sullivan, *Ekklesia: Three Inquiries in Church and State* (Chicago: University of Chicago Press, 2018).

115. Bruce, *And They All Sang Hallelujah*, 48–49; Sweet, *Religion on the American Frontier*, 304, 310–11; *Mt. Tabor Church Minutes*, 15, 27, 31, 67–71.

116. *Mt. Tabor Church Minutes*, 35–36.

117. *Mt. Tabor Church Minutes*, 15, 21, 23, 25.

118. At Mt. Tabor, of the twenty-four months of 1802–1803, seventeen included some disciplinary action. See Bruce, *And They All Sang Hallelujah*, 50.

119. *Mt. Tabor Church Minutes*, 16–17.

120. Bruce, *And They All Sang Hallelujah*, 49, 123–24; *Mt. Tabor Church Minutes*, 97–98; Sweet, *Religion on the American Frontier*, 305.

121. *Mt. Tabor Church Minutes*, 16–17, 27, 68–69.

122. *Order Book No.4*, 124; *Order Book No. 3*, 75.

123. *Barren County Order Book I, 1799–1802*, ed. Eva Peden and Gladys Wilson (Glasgow, KY: Gorin Genealogical Publishing, 1976), 3.

124. For example, *Barren County Order Book No.3*, 139; Friend, *Along the Maysville Road*, 111–12, 129.

125. *Order Book No. 4*, 75. There is no further reference to the outcome.

126. *Order Book No. 4*, 93, 98.

127. For an anthropological history of this time period in central Kentucky see Buck, *Worked to the Bone*, 35–64.

128. Thavolia Glymph, *Out of the House of Bondage: The Transformation of the Plantation Household* (New York: Cambridge University Press, 2008), 2, 43.

129. *Kentucky Slave Narratives from the Federal Writers' Project, 1936–1938* (Bedford, MA: Applewood Books/ Library of Congress, n.d), 57–58.

130. Glymph, *Out of the House of Bondage*, 5, 6, 28, 30–31, 36–41.

131. Glymph, 49–52. For a somewhat later example of slavery for men close to where the Davidsons once lived, see Bertha Rogers, *Wounded, But Not Broken* (Columbus, GA: Abdal Publishing, 2004).

132. *Barren County Will Book #1*, 529–30; Baird, 1901 letter.

133. Friend, *Along the Maysville Road*, 135.

134. Aron, *How the West Was Lost*, 155–56, 206.

135. Glymph, *Out of the House of Bondage*, 6, 51–53, 78–82.

136. Glymph, 26.

137. Glymph, 6, 66. Glymph says these beliefs, particularly about dirtiness, became more common in the later antebellum years, so this attitude may have become more pronounced in Mary toward the end of her life.

138. *Kentucky Slave Narratives*, 33, 34, 72; Patrick Minges, ed., *Far More Terrible for Women: Personal Accounts of Women in Slavery* (Winston-Salem, NC: John F. Blair, Publisher, 2006), 10–14. See also Sublette and Sublette, *The American Slave Coast*, 24–28.

139. Minges, *Far More Terrible*, ix.

140. Chambliss, *Baird-Davidson*, 53.

141. Benjamin Radford, *The Autobiography of Benjamin Johnson Radford* (Eureka, IL: n.p., 1928), 14.

142. Aron, *How the West Was Lost*, 198.

143. Chambliss, *Baird-Davidson*, 27.

144. My description of Tecumseh's role and of Native and particularly Shawnee resistance depends heavily on John Sugden, *Tecumseh: A Life* (New York: Henry Holt, 1997); Sami Lakomäki, *Gathering Together: The Shawnee People Through Diaspora and Nationhood, 1600–1870* (New Haven: Yale University Press, 2014); Gregory Dowd, *A Spirited Resistance: The North American Indian Struggle for Unity, 1745–1815* (Baltimore: Johns Hopkins University Press, 1992).

145. Dowd, *A Spirited Resistance*, 185.

146. Alan Taylor, *The Internal Enemy: Slavery and War in Virginia, 1772–1832* (New York: W. W. Norton, 2013), 286.

147. Taylor, *The Internal Enemy*, 326.

148. Sugden, *Tecumseh*, 310–12.

149. Sugden, *Tecumseh*, 311–12, 385; Guyatt, *Bind Us Apart*, 239.

150. Guyatt, *Bind Us Apart*, 230–232, 284–286.

151. Sugden, *Tecumseh*, 398.

152. Dowd, *A Spirited Resistance*, 190.

153. Pekka Hämäläinen, *The Comanche Empire* (New Haven: Yale University Press, 2008), 3.

154. Jace Weaver, *The Red Atlantic: American Indigenes and the Making of the Modern World, 1000–1927* (Chapel Hill: University of North Carolina Press, 2014), 184–188; *Republic of Lakota* website, http://www.republicoflakotah.com/about-us/; Sam Levin, "'He's a political prisoner': Standing Rock Activists Face Years in Jail," *The Guardian*, June 22, 2018, https://www.theguardian.com/us-news/2018/jun/22/standing-rock-jailed-activists-water-protectors; Garet Bleir, Anya Zoledziowski, and News 21 Staff, "Murdered and Missing Native American Women Challenge Police and Courts," *Center for Public Integrity*, October 29, 2018, https://publicintegrity.org/federal-politics/murdered-and-missing-native-american-women-challenge-police-and-courts/; *Mending the Sacred Hoop*, website, https://mshoop.org/.

9: TALES OF THE PRESENT

1. For a general description of this period in Kentucky, particularly on the role of whiteness and on sharecropping see Pem Davidson Buck, *Worked to the Bone: Race, Class, Power, and Privilege in Kentucky* (New York: Monthly Review Press, 2001).

2. W. E. B. Du Bois, *Black Reconstruction in America* (New York: Russell and Russell, 1963 [1935]), 700.

3. Lerone Bennett, *The Shaping of Black America: The Struggles and Triumphs of African Americans, 1619–1990s,* rev. ed. (New York: Penguin Books, 1993 [1969]); Theodore Allen, *Invention of the White Race,* vol. 2: *The Origin of Racial Oppression in Anglo America* (New York: Verso, 1997); Du Bois, *Black Reconstruction.*

4. Pete Daniels, *The Shadow of Slavery: Peonage in the South, 1901–1969* (Urbana: University of Illinois Press, 1972).

5. *Lynching in America: Confronting the Legacy of Racial Terror* (Montgomery, AL: Equal Justice Initiative, 2015); George Wright, *Racial Violence in Kentucky, 1865–1940: Lynchings, Mob Rule, and "Legal Lynchings"* (Baton Rouge: Louisiana State University Press, 1990).

6. Wright, *Racial Violence*; Douglas Blackmon, *Slavery By Another Name: The Re-Enslavement of Black Americans from the Civil War to World War II* (Norwell, MA: Anchor, 2009); Mark Colvin, *Penitentiaries, Reformatories, and Chain Gangs: Social Theory and the History of Punishment in Nineteenth-Century America* (New York: St. Martin's Press, 1997), 233, 244.

7. Blackmon, *Slavery By Another Name*; Daniels, *The Shadow of Slavery*; Jacqueline Jones, *The Dispossessed: America's Underclasses from the Civil War to the Present* (New York: Basic Books, 1992).

8. Du Bois, *Black Reconstruction;* Bennett, *The Shaping of Black America.*

9. See Buck, *Worked to the Bone,* 65–88.

10. Wright, *Racial Violence.* On the state's complicity in both lynching and legal execution see Timothy Kaufman-Osborn, "Capital Punishment as Legal Lynching?," in Charles Ogletree and Austin Sarat, *From Lynch Mobs to the Killing State* (New York: New York University Press, 2006), 21–54.

11. Paul Knepper, "The Kentucky Penitentiary at Frankfort and the Origins of America's First Convict Lease System, 1798–1843," *The Filson Club Quarterly* 69/1 (1995), 41–66, at 43, 64, 66.

12. Dennis Childs, *Slaves of the State: Black Incarceration from the Chain Gang to the Penitentiary* (Minneapolis: University of Minnesota Press, 2015), 57–92.

13. On the legal targeting of blacks specifically see Blackmon, *Slavery By Another Name,* 64–69, 99.

14. Blackmon, *Slavery By Another Name,* 94–98, 351–52; Sarah Haley, *No Mercy Here: Gender, Punishment, and the Making of Jim Crow Modernity* (Chapel Hill: University of North Carolina Press, 2016), 4, 156–94, esp. 171.

15. Haley, 189.

16. *Mountain Goat Trail Alliance,* https://www.mountaingoattrail.org/history/. See Leichtenstein as cited in Angela Davis, *Are Prisons Obsolete?* (New York: Seven Stories Press, 2003), 34–35; Blackmon, *Slavery By Another Name,* 289–96, 386–90. Beckert sees cotton as the primary engine of the

earlier wave of industrialization, rather than steel mills or mines—also backed, indirectly, by the terrorism of convict leasing after the Civil War. Baptist also sees cotton as the enabler of Industrial Revolution built around cotton. Satia emphasizes the role of guns and their manufacture in both contributing to industrialization and in enabling what Beckert calls "war capitalism." All these approaches, however, involve the enforcement of various forms of unfree labor. See Sven Beckert, *Empire of Cotton: A Global History* (New York: Alfred A. Knopf, 2015); Edward Baptist, *The Half Has Never Been Told: Slavery and the Making of American Capitalism* (New York: Basic Books, 2014), xxi; Priya Satia, *Empire of Guns: The Violent Making of the Industrial Revolution* (New York: Penguin Press, 2018). See also Eric Williams, *Capitalism and Slavery* (Chapel Hill: University of North Carolina Press, 1994[1944]).

17. Haley, *No Mercy Here*, 157–58.

18. On white women's increasing violation of older norms of patriarchy see Haley, *No Mercy Here*, 160, 161–63, 188–89. On whites' relative impunity see Blackmon, *Slavery By Another Name*, 1; Haley, *No Mercy Here*, 163–64; Childs, *Slaves of the State*, 79–80.

19. Alan Gallay, *The Indian Slave Trade: The Rise of the English Empire in the American South 1670–1717* (New Haven: Yale University Press, 2002); Andrés Reséndez, *The Other Slavery: The Uncovered Story of Indian Enslavement in America* (Boston: Houghton, Mifflin, Harcourt, 2016); James Rice, *Tales from a Revolution: Bacon's Rebellion and the Transformation of Early America* (New York: Oxford University Press, 2012), 193–94.

20. Katherine Beckett and Steve Herbert, *Banished: The New Social Control in Urban America* (New York: Oxford University Press, 2010), 31; Jacob Kang-Brown, Oliver Hinds, Jasmine Heiss, and Olive Lu, *The New Dynamics of Mass Incarceration* (New York: Vera Institute of Justice, 2018), 5, https://storage.googleapis.com/vera-web-assets/downloads/Publications/the-new-dynamics-of-mass-incarceration/legacy_downloads/the-new-dynamics-of-mass-incarceration-report.pdf; Marie Gottschalk, *Caught: The Prison State and the Lockdown of American Politics* (Princeton: Princeton University Press, 2015), 1.

21. Kang-Brown et al., *The New Dynamics of Mass Incarceration*, 5–6, 30–31, 40n49.

22. Tyjen Tsai, and Paola Scommegna, "U.S. Has World's Highest Incarceration Rate," Population Reference Bureau,2012, http://www.prb.org/Articles/2012/us-incarceration.aspx?p=1; Gottschalk, *Caught*, 5, 121.

23. Gottschalk, 5, 128.

24. Gottschalk, 7–64. Gilmore, however, in rejecting the argument that imprisonment has grown in order to produce prison labor for corporations, also

rejected the argument that this constitutes a new form of slavery, saying that prison industries did not employ enough people to make this a reasonable explanation of increased incarceration. While she may well be right, that argument does not show that, regardless of the cause of the rise, prison labor is in fact unfree, dependent on the Thirteenth Amendment, and actually far more prevalent than she implies. She appears to be counting only those producing items for sale, not all work done by prisoners. See Ruth Gilmore, *Golden Gulag: Prisons, Surplus, Crisis, and Opposition in Globalizing California* (Berkeley: University of California Press, 2007), 21. Wacquant, while not addressing the question of prison slavery, does reject the importance of prison labor at present, while implying the possibility that it could regain the central role it once had. See Loïc Wacquant, *Punishing the Poor: The Neoliberal Government of Social Insecurity* (Durham, NC: Duke University Press, 2009), 177–86.

For an early exploration of the implications of prison labor see Pem Davidson Buck, "'Arbeit Macht Frei': Racism and Bound, Concentrated Labor in U.S. Prisons," *Urban Anthropology and Studies of Cultural Systems and World Economic Development* 23/4 (1994): 331–72. For more recent information see Pem Davidson Buck, "Carceral Logic: Race and Unfree Labor," *Anthropology News*, May 4, 2009; Susan Kang, "'The New Peculiar Institution': International Labor Standards, Human Rights and the Prison Labor in the Contemporary United States," paper presented at International Studies Association, San Diego, 2006; Vicky Peláez, "The Prison Industry in the United States: Big Business or a New Form of Slavery?" *Global Research*, March 10, 2008, 2006, http://www.alternet.org/story/41481/a_sweatshop_behind_bars. For analysis of the US prison system more generally, see Gottschalk, *Caught*; Gilmore, *Golden Gulag*; Wacquant, *Punishing the Poor*.

25. Whitney Benns, "American Slavery, Reinvented," *The Atlantic*, September 21, 2015, https://www.google.com/search?q=Benns%2C+American+Slavery%2C+reinvented&ie=utf-8&oe=utf-8&client=firefox-b-1; Bureau of Prisons, "Work Programs," BOP website, https://www.bop.gov/inmates/custody_and_care_programs.jsp; Gilmore, *Golden Gulag*, 21.

26. Wendy Sawyer, "How much do incarcerated people earn in each state?" *Prison Policy Initiative*, April 10, 2017, https://www.prisonpolicy.org/blog/2017/04/10/wages/; Bureau of Prisons, "Work Programs."

27. Becca Schimmel, "Daviess County Detention Center Work Program Restarting This Year," WKU Public Radio, April 10, 2018, https://www.google.com/search?q=schimmel+daviess+county+detention+center+work+program&ie=utf-8&oe=utf-8&client=firefox-b-1.

28. Rania Khalek, "21st-Century Slaves: How Corporations Exploit Prison Labor," *Alternet*, July 21, 2011, http://www.alternet.org/story/151732.

29. Lisa Autry, "Kentucky Working to Create a Prison-Industry Partnership," WKU Public Radio, September 7, 2018, http://www.wkyufm.org/post/kentucky-working-create-prison-industry-partnership#stream/0.

30. Kang, "The New Peculiar Institution"; Fizz Perkal, "Incarcerated Workers Strike"; Khalek, "21st-Century Slaves."

31. Gottschalk, *Caught*, 63–64; Amy Goodman and Nermeen Shaikh, "$1 an Hour to Fight Largest Fire in CA History: Are Prison Firefighting Programs Slave Labor?," *Democracy Now*, August 29, 2018, https://www.democracynow.org/2018/8/9/1_an_hour_to_fight_largest.

32. There is considerable variation in estimates of working inmates, depending on what kinds of jobs and what kinds of facilities are counted. See Gottschalk, *Caught*, 57; Fizz Perkal, "Incarcerated Workers Strike Against Dehumanizing Prison Conditions," *Inequality.org*, August 23, 2018, https://inequality.org/research/incarcerated-workers-strike-against-dehumanizing-prison-conditions/; Jessica Corbett, "Demanding an End to 'Modern Day Slavery,' Prisoners Launch Multi-Day Nationwide Strike," *Common Dreams*, August 22, 2018, https://www.commondreams.org/news/2018/08/21/demanding-end-moderm-day-slavery-prisoners-launch-multi-day-nationwide-strike. A proposed bill in Congress would have required 50-hour work weeks for all low-security inmates. See Khalek, "21st-Century Slaves."

33. Kang, "'The New Peculiar Institution,'" 14.

34. Corbett, "Demanding an End to 'Modern Day Slavery.'" For a former inmate perspective, maintaining that getting prison labor designated as employment rather than as slavery would be more productive, see Chandra Bozelko, "Give Working Prisoners Dignity—and Decent Wages," *National Review*, January 11, 2017, https://www.nationalreview.com/2017/01/prison-labor-laws-wages/.

35. Anita Mukherjee, "Impacts of Private Prison Contracting on Inmate Time Served and Recidivism," *SSRN*, August 20, 2017, https://ssrn.com/abstract=2523238.

36. Aviva Shen, "Private Prisons Spend $45 Million on Lobbying, Rake In $5.1 Billion for Immigrant Detention Alone," *Think Progress*, August 3, 2012, http://thinkprogress.org/justice/2012/08/03/627471/private-prisons-spend-45-million-on-lobbying--rake-in-51-billion-for-immigrant-detention-alone; Livia Luan, "Profiting from Enforcement: The Role of Private Prisons in U.S. Immigration Detention," *The Online Journal of the Migration Policy Institute*, May 2, 2018, https://www.migrationpolicy.org/article/profiting-enforcement-role-private-prisons-us-immigration-detention. See Saskia Sassen, *Expulsions: Brutality and Complexity in the Global Economy* (Cambridge, MA: Belknap Press, 2014), 68–79.

37. Noah Zatz, Tia Koonse, Theresa Zhen, Lucero Herrera, Han Lu, Steven

Shafer, and Blake Valenta, *Get to Work or Go to Jail*, UCLA Labor Center Research Brief, 2016, http://www.labor.ucla.edu/publication/get-to-work-or-go-to-jail/. See Robert Steinfeld, *Coercion, Contract, and Free Labor in the Nineteenth Century* (New York: Cambridge University Press, 2001), 26.

38. United States Department of Justice, *Investigation of the Ferguson Police Department,* Civil Rights Division, 2015, https://www.justice.gov/sites/default/files/opa/press-releases/attachments/2015/03/04/ferguson_police_department_report.pdf; "Policing and Profit," *Harvard Law Review*, April 10, 2015, https://harvardlawreview.org/2015/04/policing-and-profit/; Donna Murch, "Paying for Punishment: The New Debtors' Prison," *Boston Review*, August 1, 2016, http://bostonreview.net/editors-picks-us/donna-murch-paying-punishment; Khalek, "21st-Century Slaves"; Alexandra Natapoff, *Punishment Without Crime: How Our Massive Misdemeanor System Traps the Innocent and Makes America More Unequal* (New York: Basic Books, 2018).

39. Katherine Beckett and Naomi Murakawa, "Mapping the shadow carceral state: Toward an institutionally capacious approach to punishment," *Theoretical Criminology* 16/2 (2012): 221–44, at 222, 224, 235.

40. "Policing and Profit."

41. For discussion of the laws and policies that have created a disproportionately black and brown prison population from a variety of perspectives see Elizabeth Hinton, *From the War on Poverty to the War on Crime: The Making of Mass Incarceration in America* (Cambridge, MA: Harvard University Press, 2016); Michelle Alexander, *The New Jim Crow: Mass Incarceration in the Age of Colorblindness* (New York: New Press, 2010); Jordan Camp, *Incarcerating the Crisis: Freedom Struggles and the Rise of the Neoliberal State* (Oakland: University of California Press, 2016); Tony Whitehead, "Barriers to Successful Reentry and Perceptions of Such Barriers," *Final Report for the Violence Reduction Program Ethnography,* vol. 3 (College Park MD: Cultural Systems Analysis Group, University of Maryland, 2007); Robert Perkinson, *Texas Tough: The Rise of America's Prison Empire* (New York: Metropolitan Books, Henry Holt, 2010); Wacquant, *Punishing the Poor*; Naomi Murakawa, *The First Civil Right: How Liberals Built Prison America* (New York: Oxford University Press, 2014).

42. Federal Bureau of Investigation, "Crime in the US, 2017," https://ucr.fbi.gov/crime-in-the-u.s/2017/crime-in-the-u.s.-2017/topic-pages/tables/table-70; Bureau of Labor Statistics, "Correctional Officers and Bailiffs," https://www.bls.gov/ooh/protective-service/correctional-officers.htm. In 2017 there were a total of 1,011,239 employees in corrections and law enforcement. This number does not count the myriad jobs that go to support the industry. Levister points out that in 2006 the prison industry alone was the country's second-largest employer, after General Motors. See Levister, "A Sweatshop Behind Bars."

43. For example, Andrea Morrell, "Hometown Prison: Whiteness, Safety, and Prison Work in Upstate New York State," paper presented at the American Anthropological Association, November 30, 2017; Andrea Morrell, "'Municipal Welfare' and the Neoliberal Prison Town: The Political Economy of Prison Closures in New York State," *North American Dialogue*, 15/2 (2012): 43–50; Nick Szuberla and Amelia Kirby, directors, *Up the Ridge* (Whitesburg, KY: Appalshop Films, 2006).

44. Robert Miles, *Capitalism and Unfree Labor: Anomaly or Necessity?* (New York: Tavistock, 1987), 159–66.

45. On the importance of captive immigrant labor, deportation and detention and its consequences see Martha Escobar, *Captivity Beyond Prisons: Criminalization Experiences of Latina (Im)migrants* (Austin: University of Texas Press, 2016); Aviva Chomsky, *Undocumented: How Immigration Became Illegal* (Boston: Beacon Press, 2014); Tanya Golash-Boza, *Deported: Immigrant Policing, Disposable Labor, and Global Capitalism* (New York: New York University Press, 2015). See also Nicolas De Genova, *Working the Boundaries: Race, Space, and "Illegality" in Mexican Chicago* (Durham, NC: Duke University Press, 2005). On contract guest-worker labor see Mary Bauer, *Close to Slavery: Guestworker Programs in the United States* (Montgomery, AL: Southern Poverty Law Center, c. 2008), https://www.splcenter.org/20130218/close-slavery-guestworker-programs-united-states. On immigrant labor in the chicken industry see Michael Grabell, "Exploitation and Abuse at the Chicken Plant," *The New Yorker*, May 5, 2017, http://www.newyorker.com/magazine/2017/05/08/exploitation-and-abuse-at-the-chicken-plant.

46. Gottschalk, *Caught*, 216, 218, 220, 225; Teresa Wiltz, "What Crimes Are Eligible for Deportation?," *Stateline*, Pew Charitable Trusts, December 21, 2016, https://www.pewtrusts.org/en/research-and-analysis/blogs/stateline/2016/12/21/what-crimes-are-eligible-for-deportation; Gretchen Gavett, "The U.S. Immigration Detention Boom," PBS *Frontline*, October 18, 2011, https://www.pbs.org/wgbh/frontline/article/map-the-u-s-immigration-detention-boom/; Erin Rosa, "GEO Group, Inc: Despite a Crashing Economy, Private Prison Firm Turns a Handsome Profit," *CorpWatch*, March 1, 2009, https://corpwatch.org/article/geo-group-inc-despite-crashing-economy-private-prison-firm-turns-handsome-profit; Yana Kunichoff, "A Long Stay," *Truthout.org*. August 1, 2010, http://www.truth-out.org/a-long-stay61888. On legal changes that have made this possible see Gottschalk, *Caught*, 215–32. For extended analysis see, among others, De Genova, *Working the Boundaries*; Chomsky, *Undocumented;* Golash-Boza, *Deported;* Escobar, *Captivity Beyond Prisons*. On the privatization of detention and its profitability see Gottschalk, *Caught*, 233–39; Mark Dow, *American Gulag: Inside U.S. Immigration Prisons* (Berkeley: University of California Press, 2004),

89–109; Tom Barry, "Imprisoning Immigrants for Profit: The New National Imperative," *Counterpunch,* March 13, 2009, https://www.counterpunch. org/2009/03/13/imprisoning-immigrants-for-profit/; Leslie Berestein, "Detention Dollars," *San Diego Union-Tribune,* May 4, 2008, http://legacy. sandiegouniontribune.com/uniontrib/20080504/news_lz1b4dollars.html; Shen, "Private Prisons." For analysis of Trump administration policies increasing detention and support for them from private detention industry see Luan, "Profiting from Enforcement."

47. Sassen, *Expulsions,* 10, 29; De Genova, *Working the Boundaries,* 124–26; Escobar, *Captivity Beyond Prisons*; Wacquant, *Punishing the Poor.*

48. Ian Urbina, "Using Jailed Migrants as a Pool of Cheap Labor," *New York Times.* May 25, 2014, https://www.nytimes.com/2014/05/25/us/using-jailed-migrants-as-a-pool-of-cheap-labor.html; Alexandra Levy, "Who has the most to gain from Trump's immigration policies? Private prisons," *Washington Post,* June 29, 2018, https://www.washingtonpost.com/ opinions/who-has-most-to-gain-from-trumps-immigration-policies-private-prisons/2018/06/29/4ae9c6a8-7a4d-11e8-aeee-4d04c8ac6158_story. html?noredirect=on&utm_term=.ab3a0a70c5ea.

49. Kristine Phillips, "Thousands of ICE Detainees Claim They Were Forced into Labor, A Violation of Anti-Slavery Laws," *Washington Post,* March 5, 2017, https://www.washingtonpost.com/news/post-nation/wp/2017/03/05/ thousands-of-ice-detainees-claim-they-were-forced-into-labor-a-violation-of-anti-slavery-laws/?utm_term=.c79677602b00; Mia Steinle, "Slave Labor Widespread at ICE Detention Centers, Lawyers Say," Project on Government Oversight, https://www.pogo.org/investigation/2017/09/ slave-labor-widespread-at-ice-detention-centers-lawyers-say/.

50. Chomsky, *Undocumented,* 113–51;Wacquant, *Punishing the Poor,* 1–75.

51. On the racialization of Mexicans, see De Genova, *Working the Boundaries,* particularly 136–43. On gendered racialization of blacks and Latinx see Escobar, *Captivity Beyond Prisons,* 103–6.

52. Michael Omi and Howard Winant, *Racial Formation in the United States: From the 1960s to the 1990s,* 2nd ed. (New York: Routledge, 1994). Many scholars have pointed out that the construction of internal "Others" is basic to the formation of a nation and thus of the nation-state. The nation is defined as a "people" in contrast to these Others, who are not of the people. See for example Begona Aretxaga, "Maddening States," *Annual Review of Anthropology* 32 (2003): 393–410; Brackette Williams, "A Class Act: Anthropology and the Race to Nation Across Ethnic Terrain," *Annual Review of Anthropology* 18 (1989): 401–44; Charles Mills, *The Racial Contract* (Ithaca, NY: Cornell University Press, 1997); Pem Davidson Buck, "Whither Whiteness? Empire, State, and the Re-Ordering of Whiteness," *Transforming Anthropology* 20/ 2 (2012):105–17; David Theo Goldberg,

The Racial State (Malden MA: Blackwell Publishing, 2002); Anthony Marx, *Making Race and Nation: A Comparison of South Africa, The United States, and Brazil* (New York: Cambridge University Press, 1998), 267–78; Benedict Anderson, *Imagined Communities: Reflections on the Origin and Spread of Nationalism*, rev. ed. (New York: Verso, 1991).

53. See Escobar, *Captivity Beyond Prisons*, 25–61.

54. Beckett and Herbert, *Banished*, 168n52.

55. Mike Davis, "Foreword," in Joseph Nevins, *Operation Gatekeeper: The Rise of the "Illegal Alien" and the Making of the U.S.-Mexico Boundary* (New York: Routledge, 2001), ix–xi. See Chomsky, *Undocumented*; Nevins, *Operation Gatekeeper*, 63, 119; De Genova, *Working the Boundaries*, 213–49.

56. Otto Santa Ana, *Brown Tide Rising: Metaphors of Latinos in Contemporary American Public Discourse* (Austin: University of Texas Press, 2002), esp. 49–56; Nevins, *Operation Gatekeeper*, esp. 63–67, 119–22. See also Michael Tonry, *Thinking About Crime: Sense and Sensibility in American Penal Cultures* (New York: Oxford University Press, 2004), 14–20; Kate Pickert, "Dispelling 'Anchor Baby' Myths," *Swampland blog, Time.com*, August 11, 2010, http://swampland.time.com/2010/08/11/ dispelling-anchor-baby-myths/.

57. Sang Hea Kil and Cecilia Menjivar, "The 'War on the Border': Criminalizing Immigrants and Militarizing the U.S.-Mexico Border," in Ramiro Martinez and Abel Valenzuela, *Immigration and Crime: Ethnicity, Race, and Violence* (New York: New York University Press, 2006), 164–88.

58. Wajahat Ali, Eli Clifton, Matthew Duss, Lee Fang, Scott Keyes, Faiz Shakir, *Fear, Inc: The Roots of the Islamophobic Network in America,* Center for American Progress, October 8, 2011, https://www.americanprogress.org/ issues/religion/reports/2011/08/26/10165/fear-inc/. See Murakawa, *The First Civil Right.*

59. On strategies by which people avoid knowing about atrocities see Stanley Cohen, *States of Denial: Knowing About Atrocities and Suffering* (Malden, MA: Polity Press, 2001). Tellingly, Cohen seems himself to be in denial concerning atrocities and suffering in the United States.

60. Philip Alston, "Report of the Special Rapporteur on extreme poverty and human rights on his mission to the United States," United Nations Human Rights Council, 2018, https://digitallibrary.un.org/record/1629536?ln=en.

61. For examples on urban restructuring see David Harvey, *Rebel Cities: From the Right to the City to the Urban Revolution* (New York: Verso, 2013); Ayse Cağlar and Nina Glick Schiller, *Migrants and City-Making: Multiscalar Perspectives on Dispossession* (Durham, NC: Duke University Press, 2018), 1–32. On the "new constitutionalism" by which elites "legally or constitutionally insulate economic institutions and agents from popular scrutiny or political accountability" see Stephen Gill; "Economic Globalization and

the Internationalization of Authority: Limits and Contradictions" *Geoforum* 23/3 (1992): 269–83, at 279.

62. On the role of contracts see Steinfeld, *Coercion, Contract, and Free Labor.*

63. Thus I am arguing, following Luxemburg, that ongoing accumulation by dispossession not only provides the "something outside of capitalism" in terms of resources that capitalism continuously requires, but also, carried far enough, creates and maintains, also by noneconomic forces outside of capitalism, the Others, that necessary super-exploitable labor force, the dispossessed. See Rosa Luxemburg, *The Accumulation of Capital,* trans. Agnes Schwarzschild (Mansfield Center, CT: Martino Publishing, 2015 [1913]), esp. 348–67. See also Sassen, *Expulsions;* Ann Kingsolver, "Farmers and Farmworkers: Two Centuries of Strategic Alterity in Kentucky's Tobacco Fields," *Critique of Anthropology* 27/1 (2007): 87–102. On accumulation by dispossession see David Harvey, "The 'New' Imperialism: Accumulation by Dispossession," *Socialist Register* 40 (2004): 63–87; Sharryn Kasmir and August Carbonella, "Dispossession and the Anthropology of Labor," *Critique of Anthropology* 28/1 (2008): 5–25; Jim Glassman, "Primitive accumulation, accumulation by dispossession, accumulation by 'extra-economic' means," *Progress in Human Geography* 30/5 (2006): 608–25. See also Cedric Robinson, *Black Marxism: The Making of the Black Radical Tradition* (Chapel Hill: University of North Carolina Press, 2000 [1983]); Jones, *The Dispossessed;* Sharryn Kasmir and August Carbonella, eds., *Blood and Fire: Toward a Global Anthropology of Labor* (New York: Berghahn Books, 2014).

Legitimation of this process is provided by outsider status which allows the denial of rights—perhaps to immigrants, perhaps by racialization, perhaps by race-like designations such as "trailer trash," or most powerfully by a combination of these. See Judith Skhlar, *American Citizenship: The Quest for Inclusion* (Cambridge, MA: Harvard University Press, 1991); Buck, "Whither Whiteness"; Mills, *The Racial Contract*; Williams, "A Class Act." On the raced and gendered effects of these policies see the articles collected in Nandini Gunewardena and Ann Kingsolver, eds., *The Gender of Globalization: Women Navigating Cultural and Economic Marginalities* (Santa Fe, NM: School for Advanced Research Press, 2007). On the global interconnections in these processes see Ann Kingsolver, *NAFTA Stories: Fears and Hopes in Mexico and the United States* (Boulder, CO: Lynne Rienner Publishers, 2001); Ann Kingsolver, "In the Fields of Free Trade: Gender and Plurinational En/Countering of Neoliberal Agricultural Policies," in Gunewardena and Kingsolver, *The Gender of Globalization,* 235–55.

64. In my years of community college teaching in a largely white rural and small-town working-class environment, I found very little awareness of how the state uses force to punish and to maintain sovereignty. Particularly unjust situations were seen largely as individual cases, perhaps enacted by "bad

apples," and only rarely as part of a system; the systemic perception was most likely to be voiced by black or quite poor white students, and occasionally by disillusioned veterans.

65. For this framing of care and coercion distributed in a hierarchy of dosages I am indebted to Mieka Polanco, Maggie Dickinson, Karen Williams, and Harmony Goldberg, participants in a session on "The Political Economy of Care, Coercion, and Consent" at the American Anthropological Association Annual Meetings, Washington, DC, December 4, 2014.

66. Patricia Collins discusses the "matrix of domination," explaining how these hierarchies interact, so that all of them are operating on each other, thus producing a social structure in which all of them always matter at once for each person, although often operating differentially in differing situations and combinations. See Patricia Collins, *Black Feminist Thought: Knowledge, Consciousness, and the Politics of Empowerment*, 2nd ed. (New York: Routledge, 1999 [1990]).

67. On the buffer social control class see Pem Davidson Buck, "Keeping the Collaborators on Board as the Ship Sinks: Toward a Theory of Fascism and the U.S. 'Middle Class,'" *Rethinking Marxism* 20/1 (2008): 68–90; Pem Davidson Buck, "When the White Picket Fence Needs Whitewash: Fascism and the Middle Class," *Dialogue and Initiative* (Summer/Fall)(2004): 9–12; Allen, *Invention of the White Race*.

68. Judah Schept, *Progressive Punishment: Job Loss, Jail Growth, and the Neoliberal Logic of Carceral Expansion* (New York: New York University Press, 2015), 96–118 in particular.

69. Murakawa, *The First Civil Right*.

70. Maggie Dickinson, "Working for food stamps: Economic citizenship and the post-Fordist welfare state in New York City," *American Ethnologist* 43/2 (2016): 270–81.

71. Khiara Bridges, *The Poverty of Privacy Rights* (Stanford, CA: Stanford University Press, 2017); Alex Vitale, *The End of Policing* (New York: Verso, 2017).

72. Vitale, *The End of Policing;* Jordan Camp and Christina Heatherton, eds., *Policing the Planet: Why the Policing Crisis Led to Black Lives Matter* (New York: Verso, 2016); Beckett and Murakawa, "Mapping the shadow carceral state," 225–32; Beckett and Herbert, *Banished*.

73. Vitale, *The End of Policing;* Bridges, *The Poverty of Privacy Rights*.

74. Faye Harrison, "Introduction: Global Perspectives on Human Rights and Interlocking Inequalities of Race, Gender, and Related Dimensions of Power," in Harrison, *Resisting Racism and Xenophobia: Global Perspectives on Race, Gender, and Human Rights* (Walnut Creek, CA: Altimira Press, 2005), 1–31 at 12.

75. Alston, "Report of the Special Rapporteur."

76. Grabell, "Exploitation and Abuse."

77. Abstract for the session "Centering Prisons: Reframing Analysis of the State, Relations of Power and Resistance" at the American Anthropological Meetings, Washington, DC, November 30, 2017. My thanks to Karen Williams, Orisanmi Burton, Melissa Burch, Andrea Morrell, and Damien Sojoyner for their framing of the topic and for the ethnographic work on which this section of the chapter depends. See also Davis, *Are Prisons Obsolete?*; Angela Davis, *Abolition Democracy: Beyond Empire, Prisons, and Torture* (New York: Seven Stories Press, 2005); Escobar, *Captivity Beyond Prisons,* 25–29; Gottschalk, *Caught*; Perkinson, *Texas Tough*, 370; Jackie Wang, *Carceral Capitalism* (South Pasadena, CA: Semiotext(e), 2018).

78. The following description depends on the ethnographic fieldwork of Karen Williams, "'Worthy Ladies Don't Behave Badly': Addiction and Sobriety Inside Prisons"; and Orisanmi Burton, "Fugitive Masculinity: Confrontation and Compliance in New York State Prisons," both papers presented at the American Anthropological Association Meetings, Washington, DC, November 30, 2017.

79. On this discourse as presented by counselors see Melissa Burch, "Scripting the Conviction: Power and Resistance in the Management of Criminal Stigma," presented at the American Anthropological Association Meetings, Washington DC, November 30, 2017.

80. Damien Sojoyner, "You Are Going to Get Us Killed: Mapping Political Genealogies Against the Carceral State," presented at the American Anthropological Association Meetings, Washington DC, November 30, 2017; Orisanmi Burton, "Fugitive Masculinity"; Karen Williams, "From Coercion to Consent?: Governing the Formerly Incarcerated in 21st-Century United States" (PhD diss., City University of New York Graduate Center, 2016). On the development of habitus—an ingrained and sub-conscious understanding of the world that impacts one's perception and interpretation of events, people, and situations—in relation to the normal-ization of prison expansion, see Schept, *Progressive Punishment.*

81. Morrell, "Hometown Prison."

82. See Wacquant, *Punishing the Poor*, 185–86.

83. Christopher Krupa and David Nugent, "Off-Centered States: Rethinking State Theory Through the Andean Lens," in Krupa and Nugent, *State Theory and Andean Politics: New Approaches to the Study of Rule* (Philadelphia: University of Pennsylvania Press, 2015), 1–31, at 2, 9, 14; see also articles collected in Krupa and Nugent, *State Theory*; Sharma and Gupta, *Anthropology of the State.*

84. For example, Aradhana Sharma and Akhil Gupta, "Introduction: Rethinking Theories of the State in an Age of Globalization," in Sharma and Gupta, *The Anthropology of the State: A Reader* (Malden, MA: Blackwell Publishing,

2006), 1–41; Philip Abrams, "Notes on the Difficulty of Studying the State," also in Sharma and Gupta, *The Anthropology of the State,* 112–30; Begoña Aretxaga, "Maddening States," *Annual Review of Anthropology 32* (2003): 393–410.

85. Respectively, Abrams, "Notes," 122–23; Charles Tilly, "War Making and State Making as Organized Crime," in Peter Evans, Dietrich Rueschemeyer, and Theda Skocpol, *Bringing the State Back In* (New York: Cambridge University Press, 1985), 169–91.

86. Abrams, "Notes," 122–23; Krupa and Nugent, "Off-Centered States, 18; Gyanendra Pandey, "Off-Centered States: An Appreciation," in Krupa and Nugent, *State Theory and Andean Politics,* 257–66, at 266. On the connection between sovereignty and the state's power to deport across borders see Natalie Peutz and Nicolas De Genova, "Introduction," in De Genova and Peutz, *The Deportation Regime: Sovereignty, Space, and the Freedom of Movement* (Durham, NC: Duke University Press, 2010), 1–29; Nicolas De Genova, "The Deportation Regime: Sovereignty, Space, and the Freedom of Movement," in De Genova and Peutz, *The Deportation Regime,* 33–65.

87. Edward Herman and Noam Chomsky, *Manufacturing Consent: The Political Economy of the Mass Media* (New York: Random House/Vintage, 1995).

88. For example, David Theo Goldberg, *The Racial State* (Malden, MA: Blackwell Publishing, 2002); Jacqueline Stevens, *Reproducing the State* (Princeton: Princeton University Press, 1999); Pem Davidson Buck, "Whither Whiteness? Empire, State, and the Re-Ordering of Whiteness," *Transforming Anthropology* 20/2 (2012): 105–17; Pem Davidson Buck, "Stating Punishment: The Struggle over the Right to Punish," *North American Dialogue* 17/1 (2014): 31–43; Anthony Giddens, *The Nation-State and Violence,* vol. 2 of *A Contemporary Critique of Historical Materialism* (Berkeley: University of California Press, 1987); Judith Skhlar, *American Citizenship: The Quest for Inclusion* (Cambridge, MA: Harvard University Press, 1991). Faye Harrison points out that the state's "role in social control and security, with the political will and technologies to repress and to inflict lethal regimes of violence, has clearly not [declined]." For her analysis of the role anthropologists have played in the understanding of state, power, and politics, see Faye Harrison, "Anthropology Interrogating Power and Politics," in *Ethnology, Ethnography and Cultural Anthropology, Encyclopedia of Life Support Systems,* ed. Paolo Barbaro (Oxford, UK: UNESCO/EOLSS Publishers, 2016), http://greenplanet.eolss.net/Eolss Logn/mss/C04/E6-20D/E6-20D-68/E6-20d-68-17/E6-20D-68-17-TXT-04.aspx#citation.

89. See Camp, *Incarcerating the Crisis,* 1–20.

90. For example, Hinton, *From the War on Poverty to the War on Drugs;* Murakawa, *The First Civil Right;* Camp, *Incarcerating the Crisis.*

91. For discussion of the effect of US decline from hegemonic power in rela-
    tion to the "greatest nation on earth" ideology see Emmanuel Wallerstein,
    "An American Dilemma of the 21st Century?," *Societies without Borders* 1/1
    (2006): 7–20, at 17, 20.

92. For a discussion of exclusion from the post-Fordist formal economy see
    Thomas Holt, *The Problem of Race in the 21st Century* (Cambridge, MA:
    Harvard University Press, 2000), 102–105; Alexander, *The New Jim Crow.*
    More generally on "surplus" workers see Sassen, *Expulsions.*

93. See Escobar, *Captivity Beyond Prisons,* 96–106. On militarization of
    the border see Kil and Menjivar, "The 'War on the Border'"; Nevins,
    Operation Gatekeeper, 62–74. On the militarization of policing see ACLU,
    War Comes Home: The Excessive Militarization of American Policing (New
    York: American Civil Liberties Union, 2014), https://www.aclu.org/issues/
    criminal-law-reform/reforming-police-practices/war-comes-home; Radley
    Balko, *Rise of the Warrior Cop: The Militarization of America's Police Forces*
    (New York: Public Affairs, 2014).

94. See also Buck, "Whither Whiteness"; Nevins, *Operation Gatekeeper,*
    151–64.

95. Ferguson Commission, *Forward Through Ferguson: A Path Toward Racial
    Equity,* Forwardthroughferguson.org, October 14, 2015, https://3680or2kh
    mk3bzkp33juiea1 -wpengine.netdna-ssl.com/wp-content/uploads/2015/09/
    101415_FergusonCommissionReport.pdf; United States Department of
    Justice, *Investigation of the Ferguson Police Department.*

96. InterAmerican Commission on Human Rights, *Hearing on Reports of
    Impunity for Extrajudicial Executions in The United States,* December 7,
    2017, http://civilrightsdocs.info/pdf/policy/letters/2017/ Final-Statement
    -of-The-Leadership-Conference-for-IACHR-Hearing-on-Law-Enforce-
    ment-Accountability-166th-Period-of-Sessions-12.7.17.pdf.

97. Faye V. Harrison's work provides a clear-eyed stare at the race, class, and
    gendered implementation of and consequences of the structural violence
    produced by the policies of structural adjustment, which, as she points out,
    applies to the United States as well as to the Caribbean context in which
    she developed her analysis. See Faye Harrison, *Outsider Within: Reworking
    Anthropology in the Global Age* (Urbana: University of Illinois Press, 2008),
    196, 201–57.

Bibliography

Abrams, Philip. "Notes on the Difficulty of Studying the State," in Aradhana Sharma and Akhil Gupta, *The Anthropology of the State: A Reader*, 112–130 (Malden MA: Blackwell Publishing, 2006).

Achebe, Nwando. *Farmers, Traders, Warriors, and Kings: Female Power and Authority in Northern Igboland 1900–1960* (Portsmouth NH: Heinemann, 2005).

_____. *The Female King of Colonial Nigeria: Ahebi Ugbabe* (Bloomington: Indiana University Press, 2011).

ACLU. *War Comes Home: The Excessive Militarization of American Policing* (New York: American Civil Liberties Union, 2014), https://www.aclu.org/issues/criminal-law-reform/reforming-police-practices/war-comes-home.

Agamben, Giorgio. *State of Exception,* translated by Kevin Attell (Chicago: University of Chicago Press, 2005).

Alexander, Michelle. *The New Jim Crow: Mass Incarceration in the Age of Colorblindness* (New York: The New Press, 2010).

Ali, Daud. "War, Servitude, and the Imperial Household: A Study of Palace Women in the Chola Empire," in Indrani Chatterjee and Richard M. Eaton, *Slavery and South Asian History*, 44–62 (Bloomington: Indiana University Press, 2006).

Ali, Wajahat, Eli Clifton, Matthew Duss, Lee Fang, Scott Keyes, Faiz Shakir. *Fear, Inc: The Roots of the Islamophobic Network in America*, Center for American Progress, October 8, 2011, https://www.americanprogress.org/issues/religion/reports/2011/08/26/10165/fear-inc/.

Allen, Theodore. *Invention of the White Race, Vol II, The Origin of Racial Oppression in Anglo America* (New York: Verso, 1997).

Alpers, Edward. "Flight to Freedom: Escape from Slavery among Bonded
    Africans in the Indian Ocean World, c. 1750–1962," in Gwyn Campbell,
    The Structure of Slavery in Indian Ocean Africa and Asia, 51–68 (Portland
    OR: Frank Cass, 2004).

Alston, Philip. "Report of the Special Rapporteur on extreme poverty and
    human rights on his mission to the United States," United Nations Human
    Rights Council, 2018, https://digitallibrary.un.org/record/1629536?ln=en.

Amadiume, Ifi. *Male Daughters, Female Husbands: Gender and Sex in an
    African Society* (London: Zed Books, 1987).

Anderson, Benedict. *Imagined Communities: Reflections on the Origin and
    Spread of Nationalism,* rev.ed. (New York: Verso, 1991).

Anderson, Gary. *Ethnic Cleansing and the Indian: The Crime That Should
    Haunt America* (Norman: University of Oklahoma Press, 2014).

Aretxaga, Begona. "Maddening States," *Annual Review of Anthropology,* 32:393–
    410, 2003.

Aron, Stephen. *How the West Was Lost: The Transformation of Kentucky from
    Daniel Boone to Henry Clay* (Baltimore: Johns Hopkins University Press,
    1996).

Autry, Lisa. "Kentucky Working to Create a Prison-Industry Partnership,"
    WKU Public Radio, September 7, 2018, http://www.wkyufm.org/post/
    kentucky-working-create-prison-industry-partnership#stream/0.

Bair, Anna. "Johnston, Samuel," in William Powell, *Dictionary of North Carolina
    Biographies,* 6 volumes (Chapel Hill: University of North Carolina Press,
    1988), http://www.ncpedia.org/biography/johnston-samuel.

Baird, Laura Davidson. Letter (available in Davidson file at South Central
    Kentucky Cultural Center, Glasgow, KY, 1901).

Balandier, Georges. *Political Anthropology,* translated by A. M.Sheridan Smith
    (New York: Pantheon Books, 1970).

Balko, Radley. *Rise of the Warrior Cop: The Militarization of America's Police
    Forces* (New York: Public Affairs, 2014).

Bannerman, John. "MacDuff of Fife," in Alexander Grant and Keith Stringer,
    Medieval Scotland: Crown, Lordship and Community, 20–38 (Edinburgh:
    Edinburgh University Press, 1998).

Baptist, Edward. *The Half Has Never Been Told: Slavery and the Making of
    American Capitalism* (New York: Basic Books, 2014).

Barker, Alex. "Powhatan's Pursestrings: On the Meaning of Surplus in a
    Seventeenth Century Algonquin Chiefdom," in Barker and Timothy
    Pauketat, 61–80, *Lords of the Southeast: Social Inequality and Native Elites
    of Southeastern North America,* Archaeological Papers of the American
    Anthropological Association (Hoboken, NJ: Wiley–Blackwell, 1992).

Barrell, A.D.M. *Medieval Scotland* (Cambridge: Cambridge University Press,
    2000).

Barren County Inventories and C. No.6. (archived at Office of the Barren County Clerk, Glasgow, KY).

Barren County Kentucky, Minister's Return Book, 1799–1825, photocopy of original, Sandra Gorin, ed. (Glasgow, KY: Gorin Genealogical Publishing, 1992).

Barren County Kentucky Will Book No. 1. Eva Peden, ed. (Glasgow, KY: private printing, 1979).

Barren County Order Book I, 1799–1802, Eva Peden and Gladys Wilson, eds. (Glasgow, KY: Gorin Genealogical Publishing, 1976).

Barren County Order Book No.3, 1806–1812, Eva Peden, ed. (Glasgow, KY: Gorin Genealogical Publishing, 1977).

Barren County Will Book #1 (archived at Office of Barren County Clerk, Glasgow, KY).

Barren's Black Roots: A History of Black Families in Barren County, Vol.2, Michelle Gorin, ed. (Glasgow, KY: Gorin Genealogical Publishing, 1992).

Barry, Tom. "Imprisoning Immigrants for Profit: The New National Imperative," *Counterpunch* March 13/15, 2009, https://www.counterpunch.org/2009/03/13/imprisoning-immigrants-for-profit/.

Battle of King's Mountain. The American Revolution, website, http://theamericanrevolution.org/battledetail.aspx?battle=25.

Bauer, Mary. *Close to Slavery: Guestworker Programs in the United States* (Montgomery, Alabama: Southern Poverty Law Center, c.2008, https://www.splcenter.org/20130218/close-slavery-guestworker-programs-united-states.

Beckett, Katherine and Steve Herbert. *Banished: The New Social Control in Urban America* (New York: Oxford University Press, 2010).

_____ and Naomi Murakawa. "Mapping the shadow carceral state: Toward an institutionally capacious approach to punishment," *Theoretical Criminology,* 16(2):221–244, 2012.

Beckert, Sven. *Empire of Cotton: A Global History* (New York: Alfred A. Knopf, 2015).

_____ and Seth Rockman, eds. *Slavery's Capitalism: A New History of American Economic Development* (Philadelphia: University of Pennsylvania Press, 2016).

Bellamy, John. *Crime and Public Order in England in the Later Middle Ages* (Toronto: University of Toronto Press/Routledge & Kegan Paul, 1973).

Bennett, Lerone. *The Shaping of Black America: The Struggles and Triumphs of African-Americans, 1619–1990s,* rev.ed. (New York: Penguin Books, 1993 [1969]).

Benns, Whitney. "American Slavery, Reinvented," *The Atlantic,* September 21, 2015, https://www.google.com/search?q=Benns%2C+American+Slavery%2C+reinvented&ie=utf-8&oe=utf-8&client=firefox-b-1.

Berestein, Leslie. "Detention Dollars," *San Diego Union-Tribune*, May 4, 2008, http://legacy.sandiegouniontribune.com/uniontrib/20080504/news_lz1b-4dollars.html.

Berlin, Ira. *Many Thousands Gone: The First Two Centuries of Slavery in North America* (Cambridge MA: Harvard University Press, 1998).

Billings, Dwight, Gurney Norman, and Kathering Ledford, eds., *Back Talk from Appalachia* (Lexington: The University Press of Kentucky, 2013).

Blackmon, Douglas. *Slavery By Another Name: The Re-Enslavement of Black Americans from the Civil War to World War II* (Norwell MA: Anchor, 2009).

Bleir, Garet, Anya Zoledziowski, and News 21 Staff. "Murdered and Missing Native American Women Challenge Police and Courts," *Center for Public Integrity,* October 29, 2018, https://publicintegrity.org/federal-politics/murdered-and-missing-native-american-women-challenge-police-and-courts/.

Boles, John. *Religion in Antebellum Kentucky* (Lexington: The University Press of Kentucky, 1976).

Bonomi, Patricia. *Under the Cope of Heaven: Religion, Society, and Politics in Colonial America* (New York: Oxford University Press, 2003).

Boomgaard, Peter. "Human Capital, Slavery and Low Rates of Economic and Population Growth in Indonesia, 1600–1910," in Gwyn Campbell, *The Structure of Slavery in Indian Ocean Africa and Asia,* 83–96 (Portland, OR: Frank Cass, 2004).

Bozelko, Chandra. "Give Working Prisoners Dignity—and Decent Wages," *National Review,* January 11, 2017, https://www.nationalreview.com/2017/01/prison-labor-laws-wages/.

Bredwa-Mensah, Yaw. "Slavery and Resistance on Nineteenth Century Danish Plantations in Southeastern Gold Coast, Ghana," *African Study Monographs,* 29(3):133–145, September 2008.

Bridges, Khiara. *The Poverty of Privacy Rights* (Stanford: Stanford University Press, 2017).

Brooks, James. *The Biography of Eld. Jacob Locke, of Barren County, Kentucky* (Glasgow, KY: Times Print, 1976 [1881]).

Brown, Kathleen. *Good Wives, Nasty Wenches, and Anxious Patriarchs: Gender, Race, and Power in Colonial Virginia* (Chapel Hill: University of North Carolina Press, 1996).

Brown, Michael and Steve Boardman. "Survival and Revival: Late Medieval Scotland," in Jenny Wormald, *Scotland: A History,* 69–92 (New York: Oxford University Press, 2005).

Brown, Yvonne and Rona Ferguson. "Introduction, Twisted Sisters: Women, Crime and Deviance in Scotland Since 1400," in Brown and Ferguson, *Twisted Sisters: Women, Crime and Deviance in Scotland Since 1400,* 1–9 (East Lothian, Scotland: Tuckwell Press, 2002).

Brown, Yvonne and Rona Ferguson, eds. *Twisted Sisters: Women, Crime and Deviance in Scotland Since 1400*, 1–9 (East Lothian, Scotland: Tuckwell Press, 2002).

Bruce, Dickson. *And They All Sang Hallelujah: Plain-Folk Camp-Meeting Religion, 1800–1845* (Knoxville: University of Tennessee Press, 1974).

Bruce, Philip. *Economic History of Virginia in the Seventeenth Century*, Vol. I and II (New York: Peter Smith, 1935).

Buck, Pem Davidson. "'Arbeit Macht Frei': Racism and Bound, Concentrated Labor in U.S. Prisons," *Urban Anthropology and Studies of Cultural Systems and World Economic Development*, 23(4): 331–372, 1994.

_____. "Carceral Logic: Race and Unfree Labor," *Anthropology News*, May: 4, 2009.

_____. "Colonized Anthropology: Cargo-Cult Discourse," in Faye Harrison, *Decolonizing Anthropology*, 24–41 (Washington DC: American Anthropological Association, 1991).

_____. *In/Equality: An Alternative Anthropology*, 4th ed. (Palo Cedro, CA: CAT Publishing, 2016).

_____. "Keeping the Collaborators on Board as the Ship Sinks: Toward a Theory of Fascism and the U.S. 'Middle Class,'" *Rethinking Marxism*, 20(1):68–90, 2008.

_____. "Stating Punishment: The Struggle over the Right to Punish," *North American Dialogue*, 17(1):31–43, 2014.

_____. "The Strange Birth and Continuing Life of the US as a Slaving Republic: Race, Unfree Labor, and the State," *Anthropological Theory*, 17(2):159–191, 2017.

_____. "When the White Picket Fence Needs Whitewash: Fascism and the Middle Class," *Dialogue and Initiative*, Summer/Fall: 9–12, 2004.

_____. "Whither Whiteness? Empire, State, and the Re-Ordering of Whiteness," *Transforming Anthropology*, 20(2):105–117, 2012.

_____. *Worked to the Bone: Race, Class, Power, and Privilege in Kentucky* (New York: Monthly Review Press, 2001).

Burch, Melissa. "Scripting the Conviction: Power and Resistance in the Management of Criminal Stigma," presented at the American Anthropological Association Meetings, Washington DC, November 30, 2017.

Bureau of Labor Statistics. "Correctional Officers and Bailiffs," https://www.bls.gov/ooh/protective-service/correctional-officers.htm.

Bureau of Prisons. "Work Programs," BOP website, https://www.bop.gov/inmates/custody_and_care_programs.jsp.

Burns, Ric and Chris Eyre, directors, *Tecumseh's Vision* (American Experience: We Shall Remain, 2009).

Burton, Orisanmi. "Fugitive Masculinity: Confrontation and Compliance in

New York State Prisons," presented at the American Anthropological
    Association Meetings, Washington DC, November 30, 2017.

Cağlar, Ayse and Nina Glick Schiller. *Migrants and City-Making: Multiscalar
    Perspectives on Dispossession* (Durham, NC: Duke University Press, 2018).

Calloway, Colin. *First Peoples: A Documentary Survey of American Indian
    History* (Boston: Bedford/St. Martin's, 2016 [2004]).

_____. *The World Turned Upside Down: Indian Voices from Early America*
    (New York: Bedford/St. Martin, 1994).

Camp, Jordan. *Incarcerating the Crisis: Freedom Struggles and the Rise of the
    Neoliberal State* (Oakland: University of California Press, 2016).

Camp, Jordan and Christina Heatherton, eds. *Policing the Planet: Why the
    Policing Crisis Led to Black Lives Matter* (New York: Verso, 2016).

Campbell, Gwyn. "Introduction: Slavery and other forms of Unfree Labour in
    the Indian Ocean World," in Campbell, *The Structure of Slavery in Indian
    Ocean Africa and Asia,* vii–xxxii (London: Frank Cass, 2004).

_____, ed. *The Structure of Slavery in Indian Ocean Africa and Asia,* vii–
    xxxii (London: Frank Cass, 2004).

Carson, Jane. *Bacon's Rebellion: 1676–1976* (Jamestown: Jamestown
    Foundation, 1976).

Cashion, Jerry. "Rutherford, Griffith," in William Powell, ed., *Dictionary
    of North Carolina Biographies,* 6 volumes (Chapel Hill: University
    of North Carolina Press, 1994), http://www.ncpedia.org/biography/
    rutherford-griffith.

Caswell County, North Carolina Will Books 1774–1814, Katherine Kendall, ed.
    (Baltimore: Clearfield, 1979).

*Caswell County, North Carolina Land Grants, Tax Lists, State Census,
    Apprentice Bonds, Estate Records,* Katherine Kendall, ed. (n.p., 1977).

"Centering Prisons: Reframing Analysis of the State, Relations of Power and
    Resistance," session abstract, American Anthropological Meetings,
    Washington DC, November 30, 2017.

Chambliss, Landon. *Baird-Davidson-Rogers-Wood and Allied History* (typed ms.
    in Davidson file, Hart County Historical Society, 1989).

Chatterjee, Indrani and Richard Eaton, eds. *Slavery and South Asian History*
    (Bloomington: Indiana University Press, 2006).

Childs, Dennis. *Slaves of the State: Black Incarceration from the Chain Gang to
    the Penitentiary* (Minneapolis: University of Minnesota Press, 2015).

Chomsky, Aviva. *Undocumented: How Immigration Became Illegal* (Boston:
    Beacon Press, 2014).

Clan Davidson touring information, http://www.ancestralscotland.com/plan/
    itineraries/davidson.

Clancy, M. T. "Law, Government, and Society in Medieval England," *History,*
    59(196):73–78, 1974.

Cohen, Stanley. *States of Denial: Knowing About Atrocities and Suffering* (Malden MA: Polity Press, 2001).

Collins, Patricia. *Black Feminist Thought: Knowledge, Consciousness, and the Politics of Empowerment*, 2nd ed. (New York: Routledge, 1999 [1990]).

Colvin, Mark. *Penitentiaries, Reformatories, and Chain Gangs: Social Theory and the History of Punishment in Nineteenth-Century America* (New York: St. Martin's Press, 1997).

Coomaraswamy, Ananda. *Spiritual Authority and Temporal Power in the Indian Theory of Government* (New Haven: American Oriental Society, 1942).

"Copper and Kings," *Kentucky Brandy Heritage*, 2016, http://www.copperandkings.com/kentucky-brandy-heritage/.

Coquery-Vidrovitch, Catherine. *The History of African Cities South of the Sahara: From the Origins to Colonization*, translated by Mary Baker (Princeton: Marcus Wiener Publications, 2005 [1993]).

Corbett, Jessica. "Demanding an End to 'Modern Day Slavery,' Prisoners Launch Multi-Day Nationwide Strike," *Common Dreams,* August 22, 2018, https://www.commondreams.org/news/2018/08/21/demanding-end-moderm-day-slavery-prisoners-launch-multi-day-nationwide-strike.

Coward, Joan. *Kentucky in the New Republic: The Process of Constitution Making* (The University Press of Kentucky, 1979).

Craig, Maggie. "The Fair Sex Turns Ugly: Female Involvement in the Jacobite Rising of 1745," in Yvonne Brown and Rona Ferguson, *Twisted Sisters: Women, Crime and Deviance in Scotland Since 1400*, 84–100 (East Lothian, Scotland: Tuckwell Press, 2002).

"Criminal: How Lock Up Quotas and 'Low Crime Taxes' Guarantee Profits for Private Prisons Corporations," *Public Interest*, September, 2013, https://www.inthepublicinterest.org/criminal-how-lockup-quotas-and-low-crime-taxes-guarantee-profits-for-private-prison-corporations/.

Cromartie, Earl of. *A Highland History* (Berkhamsted, Hertfordshire: The Gavin Press, 1979).

Cullen, Karen. *Famine in Scotland: The 'Ill Years' of the 1690s* (Edinburgh: Edinburgh University Press, 2010).

Curtin, Philip. *Africa Remembered: Narratives of West Africans from the Era of the Slave Trade* (Prospect Heights, Ill: Waveland Press, 1997 [1967]).

Daniels, Pete. *The Shadow of Slavery: Peonage in the South, 1901–1969* (Urbana: University of Illinois Press, 1972).

Davidson, Chalmers. *Piedmont Partisan: The Life and Times of William Lee Davidson* (Davidson, NC: Davidson College, 1968 [1951]).

Davidson/Davison/Davisson Research DNA Study Project, http://www.tqsi.com/davidsongenes2/results.php.

Davis, Angela. *Abolition Democracy: Beyond Empire, Prisons, and Torture* (New York: Seven Stories Press, 2005).

_____. *Are Prisons Obsolete?* (New York: Seven Stories Press, 2003).

Davis, Mike. "Foreword," in Joseph Nevins, *Operation Gatekeeper: The Rise of the 'Illegal Alien' and the Making of the U.S.-Mexico Boundary,* ix–xi (New York: Routledge, 2001).

Dawson, Jane. *Scotland Re-Formed 1488-1587* (Edinburgh: Edinburgh University Press, 2007).

Dawson, Matthew. "Battles of Invernhaven and Perth-1300s," Clan Davidson Society of North America, https://clandavidson.org/the-clan/history-of-clan-davidson/battles-of-invernhaven-and-perth-1300s/2/.

Deeds Before A &A, Barren County (archived at the Office of the County Clerk, Barren County, KY).

Deeds, K, Barren County (archived at the Office of the Barren County Clerk, Glasgow, Kentucky).

De Genova, Nicolas. *Working the Boundaries: Race, Space, and "Illegality" in Mexican Chicago* (Durham: Duke University Press, 2005).

Delbanco, Andrew. *The War Before the War: Fugitive Slaves and the Struggle of America's Soul from the Revolution to the Civil War* (New York: Penguin Press, 2018).

_____. "The Deportation Regime: Sovereignty, Space, and the Freedom of Movement," in De Genova and Nathalie Peutz, *The Deportation Regime: Sovereignty, Space, and the Freedom of Movement,* 33–65 (Durham: Duke University Press, 2010).

_____ and Nathalie Peutz, eds. *The Deportation Regime: Sovereignty, Space, and the Freedom of Movement* (Durham: Duke University Press, 2010).

DePriest, Virginia. *The Sandy Run Settlement and Mooresboro,* (n.p:n.p., 1976), https://archive.org/details/sandyrunsettleme00depr.

DesBrisay, Gordon. "Twisted by Definition: Women Under Godly Discipline in Seventeenth-Century Scottish Towns," in Yvonne Brown and Rona Ferguson, *Twisted Sisters: Women, Crime and Deviance in Scotland Since 1400,* 138–155 (East Lothian, Scotland: Tuckwell Press, 2002).

_____. "Wet Nurses and Unwed Mothers in Seventeenth-Century Aberdeen," in Elizabeth Ewan and Maureen Meikle, *Women in Scotland c.1100–c.1750,* 210–220 (East Linton, GB: Tuckwell Press, 1999).

Dew, Charles. *Bond of Iron: Master and Slave at Buffalo Forge* (New York: W.W. Norton and Company, 1994).

Dickinson, Maggie. "Working for food stamps: Economic citizenship and the post-Fordist welfare state in New York City," *American Ethnologist,* 43(2):270–281, 2016.

Dingwall, Helen. "The Power Behind the Merchant? Women and the Economy in Late-Seventeenth Century Edinburgh," in Elizabeth Ewan and Maureen Meikle, *Women in Scotland c.1100–c.1750,* 152–162 (East Linton, UK: Tuckwell Press, 1999).

Dobson, David. *Directory of Scots Banished to the American Plantations* (Baltimore: Genealogical Publishing Company, 1983).

_____. *The Original Scots Colonists of Early America, 1612–1783* (Baltimore: Genealogical Publishing Company, 1995.

Dodgshon, Robert. "Everyday Structures, Rhythms and Spaces of the Scottish Countryside," in Elizabeth Foyster and Christopher Whatley, *A History of Everyday Life in Scotland, 1600–1800*, 27–50 (Edinburgh: Edinburgh University Press, 2010).

_____. " 'Pretense of Blude' and 'Place of Thair Duelling': The Nature of Scottish Clans, 1500–1745," in Robert Houston and Ian Whyte, *Scottish Society 1500–1800*, 169–198 (New York: Cambridge University Press, 1989).

_____. "The Scottish Farming Township as Metaphor," in Leah Leneman, *Perspectives in Scottish Social History: Essays in Honour of Rosalind Mitchison*, 69–82 (Aberdeen: The Aberdeen University Press, 1988).

Dow, Mark. *American Gulag: Inside U.S. Immigration Prisons* (Berkeley: University of California Press, 2004).

Dowd, Gregory. *A Spirited Resistance: The North American Indian Struggle for Unity, 1745–1815* (Baltimore: The Johns Hopkins University Press, 1992).

Drake, St Clair. *Black Folk Here and There,* Vol. II (Los Angeles: Center for Afro-American Studies, University of California, 1990).

DuBois, Ellen and Lynn Dumenil. *Through Women's Eyes: An American History with Documents* (Boston: Bedford/St. Martin's, 2005).

Du Bois, W.E.B. *Black Reconstruction in America* (New York: Russell and Russell, 1963 [1935]).

Dunaway, Wilma. *The First American Frontier: Transition to Capitalism in Southern Appalachia, 1700–1860* (Chapel Hill: University of North Carolina Press, 1996).

Eaton, Richard. "Introduction," in Indrani Chatterjee and Eaton, *Slavery and South Asian History*, 1–16 (Bloomington: Indiana University Press, 2006).

Elshtain, Jean. *Women and War, with a new Epilogue* (Chicago: University of Chicago Press, 1995).

Empiricus, Sextus. "Critias Fragment" from *Adversus Mathematicos*, ix, 54, translated by R. G. Bury, revised by J. Garrett, 2009 [n.d], https://people.wku.edu/jan.garrett/302/critias.htm.

Equiano, Olaudah. "The Early Travels of Olaudah Equiano," in Philip Curtin, *Africa Remembered: Narratives of West Africans from the Era of the Slave Trade*, 69–98 (Prospect Heights, Ill: Waveland Press, 1997 [1967]).

Escobar, Martha. *Captivity Beyond Prisons: Criminalization Experiences of Latina (Im)migrants* (Austin: University of Texas Press, 2016).

Eslinger, Ellen. *Running Mad for Kentucky: Frontier Travel Accounts* (Lexington: University Press of Kentucky, 2004).

Ewan, Elizabeth. "Crime or Culture? Women and Daily Life in Late-Medieval Scotland," in Yvonne Brown and Rona Ferguson, *Twisted Sisters: Women, Crime and Deviance in Scotland Since 1400*, 117–136 (East Lothian, Scotland: Tuckwell Press, 2002).

_____. "'For Whatever Ales Ye': Women as Consumers and Producers in Late Medieval Scottish Towns," in Elizabeth Ewan and Maureen Meikle, *Women in Scotland c.1100–c.1750*, 125–135 (East Linton, UK: Tuckwell Press, 1999).

_____. "'Hamperit in ane hony came': Sights, Sounds and Smells in the Medieval Town," in Edward Cowan and Lizanne Henderson, *A History of Everyday Life in Medieval Scotland, 1000–1600*, 110–144 (Edinburgh: Edinburgh University Press, 2011).

Ewan, Elizabeth and Maureen Meikle, eds. *Women in Scotland c.1100–c.1750*, 125–135 (East Linton, GB: Tuckwell Press, 1999).

Fagan, Brian. *World Prehistory: A Brief Introduction,* 8th ed. (Upper Saddle River, NJ: Prentice Hall, 2011).

Federal Bureau of Investigation. "Crime in the US, 2017, https://ucr.fbi.gov/crime-in-the-u.s/2017/crime-in-the-u.s.-2017/topic-pages/tables/table-70.

Federici, Silvia. *Caliban and the Witch: Women, the Body and Primitive Accumulation,* 2nd rev. ed. (Brooklyn: Autonomedia, 2014 [2004]).

Felder, Paula. *Forgotten Companions: The First Settlers of Spotsylvania County and FredericksburghTown (with notes on Early Land Use)* (Fredericksburg, VA: Historic Publications of Fredericksburg, 1982).

Feldman, Allen. *Formations of Violence: The Narrative of the Body and Political Terror in Northern Ireland* (Chicago: University of Chicago Press, 1991).

Ferguson Commission. *Forward Through Ferguson: A Path Toward Racial Equity* (Forwardthroughferguson.org, October 14, 2015), https://3680or2khmk3bzkp33juiea1-wpengine.netdna-ssl.com/wp-content/uploads/2015/09/101415_FergusonCommissionReport.pdf.

Ferner, Mike. "Fourth of July Like You've Never Seen it Before," *Counterpunch*, June 30, 2017, https://www.counterpunch.org/2017/06/30/93804/.

Fields, Karen and Barbara Fields. *Racecraft: The Soul of Inequality in American Life* (New York: Verso, 2014).

Fifth Census of the United States, 1830, Barren, Kentucky.

Fifth Census of the United States, 1830, Hart, Kentucky.

Finkelman, Paul. "Crimes of Love, Misdemeanors of Passion: The Regulation of Race and Sex in Colonial Virginia," in Catherine Clinton and Michele Gillespie, *The Devil's Lane: Sex and Race in the Early South*, 124–135 (New York: Oxford University Press, 1997).

_____. "The Significance and Persistence of Proslavery Thought," in Steven

Mintz and John Stauffer, *The Problem of Evil: Slavery, Freedom, and the Ambiguities of American Reform*, 95–114 (University of Massachusetts Press, 2007).

Finley, Moses. "Was Greek Civilization Based on Slave Labour?" in Eugene Genovese, *The Slave Economies*, Vol. I, 19–45 (New York: John Wiley and Sons, 1973 [1959]).

First Census of the United States, North Carolina, 1790, https://www2.census. gov/library/publications/decennial/1790/heads_of_families/north_ carolina/1790h-04.pdf.

Fischer, Kirsten. *Suspect Relations: Sex, Race, and Resistance in Colonial North Carolina* (Ithaca: Cornell University Press, 2001).

Fitzgerald, Timothy. "Negative Liberty, Liberal Faith Postulates and World Disorder," in Trevor Stack, Naomi Goldenberg, Fitzgerald, *Religion as a Category of Governance and Sovereignty*, 248–279 (Boston: Brill, 2015).

Fixico, Donald, ed. *Rethinking American Indian History* (Albuquerque: University of New Mexico Press, 1997).

Foucault, Michel. *Discipline and Punish: The Birth of the Prison*, translated by Alan Sheridan (New York: Vintage Books,1995 [1975]).

Fourth Census of the United States, 1820, Barren, Kentucky.

Frater, Anne. "Women of the Gàidhealtachd and their Songs to 1750," in Elizabeth Ewan and Maureen Meikle, *Women in Scotland c.1100–c.1750*, 67–79 (East Linton, UK: Tuckwell Press, 1999).

Friedman, Jonathan, ed. *Globalization, the State, and Violence* (Walnut Creek: AltaMira Press 2003).

Friend, Craig. *Along the Maysville Road: The Early American Republic in the Trans-Appalachian West* (Knoxville: University of Tennessee Press, 2005).

Gallay, Alan. *The Indian Slave Trade: The Rise of the English Empire in the American South 1670–1717* (New Haven: Yale University Press, 2002).

Gavett, Gretchen. "The U.S. Immigration Detention Boom," *Frontline*, October 18, 2011, https://www.pbs.org/wgbh/frontline/article/ map-the-u-s-immigration-detention-boom/.

Giddens, Anthony. *The Nation-State and Violence: Volume Two of a Contemporary Critique of Historical Materialism* (Berkeley: University of California Press, 1987).

Gill, Stephen. "Economic Globalization and the Internationalization of Authority: Limits and Contradictions," *Geoforum*, 23(3): 269–283, 1992.

Gilmore, Ruth. *Golden Gulag: Prisons, Surplus, Crisis, and Opposition in Globalizing California* (Berkeley: University of California Press, 2007).

Glassman, Jim. "Primitive accumulation, accumulation by dispossession, accumulation by 'extra-economic' means," *Progress in Human Geography*, 30(5): 608–625, 2006.

Gleach, Frederic. *Powhatan's World and Colonial Virginia* (Lincoln: University of Nebraska Press, 1997).

Gledhill, John. *Power and its Disguises: Anthropological Perspectives on Politics,* 2nd ed. (London: Pluto Press, 2000).

Glymph, Thavolia. *Out of the House of Bondage: The Transformation of the Plantation Household* (New York: Cambridge University Press, 2008).

Golash-Boza, Tanya. *Deported: Immigrant Policing, Disposable Labor, and Global Capitalism* (New York: New York University Press, 2015).

Goldberg, David. *The Racial State* (Malden MA: Blackwell Publishing, 2002).

Goldenberg, Naomi. "The Category of Religion in the Technology of Governance: An Argument for Understanding Religions as Vestigial States," in Trevor Stack, Goldenberg, and Timothy Fitzgerald, *Religion as a Category of Governance and Sovereignty,* 280–292 (Boston: Brill, 2015).

Goldstone, Lawrence. *Dark Bargain: Slavery, Profits, and the Struggle for the Constitution* (New York: Walker and Company, 2005).

Goodman, Amy and Nermeen Shaikh. "$1 an Hour to Fight Largest Fire in CA History: Are Prison Firefighting Programs Slave Labor?" *Democracy Now,* August 29, 2018, https://www.democracynow. org/2018/8/9/1_an_hour_to_fight_largest.

Gordon-Reed, Annette. *The Hemingses of Monticello: An American Family* (New York: W.W. Norton, 2008).

Gorin, Frank. *The Times of Long Ago: Barren County, Kentucky* (Glasgow, KY: South Central Kentucky Historical and Genealogical Society, 1992 [1929]).

Gottschalk, Marie. *Caught: The Prison State and the Lockdown of American Politics* (Princeton: Princeton University Press, 2015).

Grabell, Michael. "Exploitation and Abuse at the Chicken Plant," *New Yorker,* May 5, 2017, http://www.newyorker.com/magazine/2017/05/08/ exploitation-and-abuse-at-the-chicken-plant.

Gradie, Charlotte. "The Powhatans in the Context of the Spanish Empire," in Helen Rountree, *Powhatan Foreign Relations1500–1722,* 154–172 (Charlottesville: University Press of Virginia, 1993).

Graham, Michael. "Women and the Church Courts in Reformation-Era Scotland," in Elizabeth Ewan and Maureen Meikle, *Women in Scotland c.1100–c.1750,* 187–198 (East Linton, GB: Tuckwell Press, 1999).

Grant, Alexander. "Crown and Nobility in Late Medieval Britain," in Roger Mason, *Scotland and England 1286–1815,* 34–59 (Edinburgh: John Donald Publishers LTD, 1987).

Grant, I.F. *The Social and Economic Development of Scotland before 1603* (Edinburgh: Oliver and Boyd, 1930).

Gray, Lewis. *History of Agriculture in the Southern United States to 1860,* Vols.I and II (Gloucester, MA: Peter Smith, 1958).

Green, Margaret. *Ibo Village Affairs* (New York: Frederick Praeger, 1964 [1947]).

Greene, Beth. "The Institution of Woman-Marriage in Africa: A Cross-cultural Analysis," *Ethnology,* 37(4):395–413,1998.

Griffin, Clarence. *History of Old Tryon and Rutherford Counties, North Carolina, 1730–1936* (Asheville, NC: Miller Printing Co, 1937).

Grizzard, Frank and D. Boyd Smith. *Jamestown Colony: A Political, Social, and Cultural History* (Santa Barbara: ABC-CLIO, 2007).

Gundersen, Joan. "Kith and Kin: Women's Networks in Colonial Virginia," in Catherine Clinton and Michele Gillespie, *The Devil's Lane: Sex and Race in the Early South,* 90–108 (New York: Oxford University Press, 1997).

Gunewardena, Nandini and Ann Kingsolver, eds. *The Gender of Globalization: Women Navigating Cultural and Economic Marginalities* (Santa Fe: School for Advanced Research Press, 2007).

Guyatt, Nicholas. *Bind Us Apart: How Enlightened Americans Invented Racial Segregation* (New York: Basic Books, 2016).

Hadden, Sally. *Slave Patrols: Law and Violence in Virginia and the Carolinas* (Cambridge: Harvard University Press, 2003).

Haley, Sarah. *No Mercy Here: Gender, Punishment, and the Making of Jim Crow Modernity* (Chapel Hill: University of North Carolina Press, 2016).

Hämäläinen, Pekka. *The Comanche Empire* (New Haven: Yale University Press, 2008).

Haney Lopez, Ian. *White By Law: The Legal Construction of Race,* revised and updated (New York: New York University Press, 2006).

Hankins, Barry. *The Second Great Awakening and the Transcendentalists* (Westport, Conn.: Greenwood Press, 2004).

Hantman, Jeffrey. "Powhatan's Relations with the Piedmont Monacans," in Helen Rountree, *Powhatan Foreign Relations1500–1722,* 94–111 (Charlottesville: University Press of Virginia, 1993).

Harrison, Faye. "Anthropology Interrogating Power and Politics," in Paolo Barbaro, *Ethnology, Ethnography and Cultural Anthropology, Encyclopedia of Life Support Systems* (UNESCO/EOLSS Publishers, Oxford, UK, 2016), [http://www.eolss.net] http://greenplanet.eolss.net/EolssLogn/mss/C04/E6–20D/E6-20D-68/E6-20d-68-17/E6-20D-68-17-TXT-04.aspx#citation.

_____. "Introduction: Global Perspectives on Human Rights and Interlocking Inequalities of Race, Gender, and Related Dimensions of Power," in Harrison, *Resisting Racism and Xenophobia: Global Perspectives on Race, Gender, and Human Rights,* 1–31 (Walnut Creek, CA: Altimira Press, 2005).

_____. *Outsider Within: Reworking Anthropology in the Global Age* (Urbana: University of Illinois Press, 2008).

Harrison, Lowell. *The Antislavery Movement in Kentucky* (Lexington: The University Press of Kentucky, 1978).

_____. "John Breckinridge and the Kentucky Constitution of 1799," *The Register of the Kentucky Historical Society* 57(3):209–233, 1958.

_____. and James Klotter. *A New History of Kentucky* (Lexington: The University Press of Kentucky, 1997).

Hartog, Hendrik. *Man and Wife in America: A History* (Cambridge: Harvard University Press, 2000).

Harvey, David. "The 'New' Imperialism: Accumulation by Dispossession," *Socialist Register* 40: 63–87, 2004.

_____. *Rebel Cities: From the Right to the City to the Urban Revolution* (New York: Verso, 2013).

Hashaw, Tim. *The Birth of Black America: The First African Americans and the Pursuit of Freedom at Jamestown* (New York: Carroll & Graf Publishers, 2007).

Herman, Edward and Noam Chomsky. *Manufacturing Consent: The Political Economy of the Mass Media* (New York: Random House/Vintage, 1995).

Hezekiah Ellis. Wikitree.com. citing John Fredrick Dorman, ed., *The Virginia Genealogist*, Volume 5, 1961, 107, https://www.wikitree.com/wiki/Ellis-3443.

Higginbotham, A. Leon. *In the Matter of Color: Race and the American Legal Process, the Colonial Period* (New York: Oxford University Press, 1978).

Hinton, Elizabeth. *From the War on Poverty to the War on Crime: The Making of Mass Incarceration in America* (Cambridge: Harvard University Press: 2016).

Hobsbawm, Eric. "The Seventeenth Century in the Development of Capitalism," in Eugene Genovese, *The Slave Economies*, Vol. I (New York: John Wiley and Sons, 145–160, 1973 [1959]).

Hodge, Derrick. Personal Communication, October 2018.

Holloman, Charles. "Caswell, Richard," in William Powell, ed., *Dictionary of North Carolina Biographies*, 6 volumes (Chapel Hill: University of North Carolina Press, 1979), http://www.ncpedia.org/biography/caswell-richard-0.

Holt, Thomas. *The Problem of Race in the 21st Century* (Cambridge: Harvard University Press, 2000).

Horn, James. *Adapting to a New World: English Society in the Seventeenth-Century Chesapeake* (Chapel Hill: University of North Carolina Press, 1994).

Horne, Gerald. *The Counter-Revolution of 1776: Slave Resistance and the Origins of the United States of America* (New York: New York University Press, 2014).

Huggins, Malory. *A History of North Carolina Baptists 1727–1932* (Raleigh: The General Board, Baptist State Convention of North Carolina, 1967).

Inter-American Commission on Human Rights, *Hearing on Reports of Impunity For Extrajudicial Executions In the United States,* December 7, 2017, http://civilrightsdocs.info/pdf/policy/letters/2017/ Final-Statement-of-The-Leadership-Conference-for-IACHR-Hearing-on-Law-Enforcement-Accountability-166th-Period-of-Sessions-12.7.17.pdf.

Isenberg, Nancy. *White Trash: The 400–Year Untold History of Class in America* (New York: Viking, 2016).

Isichei, Elizabeth. *The Ibo People and the Europeans: The Genesis of a Relationship—to 1906* (New York: St. Martin's Press, 1973).

Jamestown Rediscovery, Original Settlers (Association for the Preservation of Virginia Antiquities, 2000), http://www.apva.org/history/orig.html.

Jennings, Matthew. *New Worlds of Violence: Cultures and Conquests in the Early American Southeast* (Knoxville: University of Tennessee Press, 2011).

Johnson, Paul, Pamela Klassen, and Winnifred Sullivan. *Ekklesia: Three Inquiries in Church and State* (Chicago: University of Chicago Press, 2018).

Johnston, Carolyn. *Cherokee Women in Crisis: Trail of Tears, Civil War, and Allotment, 1838–1907* (Tuscaloosa: University of Alabama Press, 2003).

Jones, G.I. "Olaudah Equiano of the Niger Ibo: Introduction," in Philip Curtin, *Africa Remembered: Narratives of West Africans from the Era of the Slave Trade,* 60–69 (Prospect Heights, Ill.: Waveland Press, 1997 [1967]).

Jones, Jacqueline. *The Dispossessed: America's Underclasses from the Civil War to the Present* (New York: Basic Books, 1992).

Jones, Yvonne. "Dual Visions of History," *Current Anthropology* 58(2):312–314, 2017.

———. Personal communication, April 2014.

Jordan, Don and Michael Walsh. *White Cargo: The Forgotten History of Britain's White Slaves in America* (New York: New York University Press, 2008).

Kang, Susan. "'The New Peculiar Institution': International Labor Standards, Human Rights and the Prison Labor in the Contemporary United States," presented at International Studies Association, San Diego, 2006.

Kang-Brown, Jacob, Oliver Hinds, Jasmine Heiss, and Olive Lu. *The New Dynamics of Mass Incarceration* (New York: Vera Institute of Justice, 2018), https://storage.googleapis.com/vera-web-assets/downloads/ Publications/the-new-dynamics-of-mass-incarceration/legacy_downloads/ the-new-dynamics-of-mass-incarceration-report.pdf .

Kantorowicz, Ernst. *The King's Two Bodies: A Study in Mediaeval Political Theology* (Princeton: Princeton University Press, 1957).

Kapferer, Bruce, ed. *State, Sovereignty, War: Civil Violence in Emerging Global Realities* (New York: Berghahn Books, 2004).

Kars, Marjoleine. *Breaking Loose Together: The Regulator Rebellion in Pre-Revolutionary North Carolina* (Chapel Hill: University of North Carolina Press, 2002).

Kasmir, Sharryn and August Carbonella, eds. *Blood and Fire: Toward a Global Anthropology of Labor* (New York: Berghahn Books, 2014).

_____ and _____. "Dispossession and the Anthropology of Labor," *Critique of Anthropology,* 28(1): 5–25, 2008.

Kaufman-Osborn, Timothy. "Capital Punishment as Legal Lynching?" in Charles Ogletree and Austin Sarat, *From Lynch Mobs to the Killing State,* 21–54. (New York: New York University Press, 2006).

Kay, Marvin and Lorin Cary. *Slavery in North Carolina, 1748–1775* (Chapel Hill: University of North Carolina Press, 1995).

Kelso, William. *Jamestown: The Buried Truth* (Charlottesville: University of Virginia Press, 2006).

Kentucky Slave Narratives from the Federal Writers' Project, 1936–1938 (Bedford, MA: Applewood Books/ Library of Congress. n.d).

Khalek, Rania. "21st Century Slaves: How Corporations Exploit Prison Labor," *Alternet,* July 21, 2011. http://www.alternet.org/story/151732.

Kil, Sang Hea and Cecilia Menjivar. "The 'War on the Border': Criminalizing Immigrants and Militarizing the U.S.–Mexico Border," in Ramiro Martinez and Abel Valenzuela, *Immigration and Crime: Ethnicity, Race, and Violence,* 164–188 (New York: New York University Press, 2006).

Kingsolver, Ann. "Farmers and Farmworkers: Two Centuries of Strategic Alterity in Kentucky's Tobacco Fields," *Critique of Anthropology,* 27(1):87–102, 2007.

_____. "In the Fields of Free Trade: Gender and Plurinational En/Countering of Neoliberal Agricultural Policies," in Nandini Gunewardena and Kingsolver, *The Gender of Globalization: Women Navigating Cultural and Economic Marginalities,* 235–255 (Santa Fe: School for Advanced Research Press, 2007).

_____. *NAFTA Stories: Fears and Hopes in Mexico and the United States* (Boulder, CO: Lynne Rienner Publishers, 2001).

Kirch, Patrick. *A Shark Going Inland Is My Chief: The Island Civilization of Ancient Hawai'i* (Berkeley: University of California Press, 2012).

Klassen, Pamela. "Spiritual Jurisdictions: Treaty People and the Queen of Canada," in Paul Johnson, Klassen, and Winnifred Sullivan, *Ekklesia: Three Inquiries in Church and State,* 107–173 (Chicago: University of Chicago Press, 2018).

Klein, Herbert. *The Atlantic Slave Trade* (New York: Cambridge University Press, 1999).

Klein, Martin, ed. *Breaking the Chains: Slavery, Bondage, and Emancipation in Modern Africa and Asia* (Madison: University of Wisconsin Press, 1993).

_____. "Introduction: Modern European Expansion and Traditional Servitude in Africa and Asia," in Klein, *Breaking the Chains: Slavery, Bondage, and Emancipation in Modern Africa and Asia,* 3–36 (Madison: University of Wisconsin Press, 1993).

Klein, Naomi. *The Shock Doctrine: The Rise of Disaster Capitalism* (New York: Henry Holt, 2007).

Knepper, Paul. "The Kentucky Penitentiary at Frankfort and the Origins of America's First Convict Lease System, 1798-1843," *The Filson Club Quarterly* 69(1): 41-66, 1995.

_____."Thomas Jefferson, Criminal Code Reform, and the Founding of the Kentucky Penitentiary at Frankfort," *The Register of the Kentucky Historical Society* 91(Spring):129-149, 1993.

Kolp, John. *Gentlemen and Freeholders: Electoral Politics in Colonial Virginia* (Baltimore: Johns Hopkins University Press, 1998).

Kulikoff, Allan. *Tobacco and Slaves: The Development of Southern Culture in the Chesapeake 1680-1800* (Chapel Hill: University of North Carolina Press, 1986).

Kunichoff, Yana. "A Long Stay," *Truthout.org.*, August 1, 2010, http://www.truth-out.org/a-long-stay61888.

Kupperman, Karen. *Indians and English: Facing Off in Early America* (Ithaca: Cornell University Press, 2000).

_____. *The Jamestown Project* (Cambridge MA: The Belknap Press of Harvard University Press, 2007).

Krupa, Christopher and David Nugent. "Off-Centered States: Rethinking State Theory Through the Andean Lens," in Krupa and Nugent, *State Theory and Andean Politics: New Approaches to the Study of Rule,* 1-31 (Philadelphia: University of Pennsylvania Press, 2015).

Lakomäki, Sami. *Gathering Together: The Shawnee People Through Diaspora and Nationhood, 1600-1870* (New Haven: Yale University Press, 2014).

Lancaster County, Virginia Deeds and Will Abstracts, Vol I, 1652-1657, Ruth and Sam Spartico, eds. (McLean, VA: The Antient Press, 1991).

Larner, Christina. *Enemies of God: The Witch-hunt in Scotland* (Edinburgh: John Donald, 2000 [1981]).

Lee, Richard. *The Dobe Ju/'hoansi*, 3rd ed. (Belmont CA: Wadsworth, 2002).

Lefler, Hugh. *North Carolina History Told by Contemporaries* (Chapel Hill: University of North Carolina Press, 1965 [1934]).

Leneman, Leah. "A New Role for a Lost Cause: Lowland Romanticisation of the Jacobite Highlander," in Leneman, *Perspectives in Scottish Social History: Essays in Honour of Rosalind Mitchison,* 107-124 (Aberdeen: The Aberdeen University Press,1988).

Leonard, Bill. *Baptists in America* (New York: Columbia University Press, 2005).

Levin, Sam. "'He's a political prisoner:' Standing Rock Activists Face Years in Jail," *The Guardian,* June 22, 2018, https://www.theguardian.com/us-news/2018/jun/22/standing-rock-jailed-activists-water-protectors.

Levister, Chris. "A Sweatshop Behind Bars," *Alternet,* September 12, 2006. http://www.alternet.org/story/41481/a_sweatshop_behind_bars .

Levtzion, Nehemia and Jay Spaulding, eds. *Medieval West Africa: Views from Arab Scholars and Merchants* (Princeton: Marcus Wiener Publications, 2003).

Levy, Alexandra. "Who has the most to gain from Trump's immigration policies? Private prisons," *Washington Post*, June 29, 2018, https://www. washingtonpost.com/opinions/who-has-most-to-gain-from-trumps-immigration-policies-private-prisons/2018/06/29/4ae9c6a8-7a4d-11e8-aeee-4d04c8ac6158_story.html?noredirect=on&utm_term=.ab3a0a70c5ea.

Linebaugh, Peter. *The London Hanged: Crime and Civil Society in the Eighteenth Century* (New York: Cambridge University Press, 1992).

Livingstone, Sheila. *Confess and Be Hanged: Scottish Crime and Punishment Through the Ages* (Edinburgh: Birlinn, 2000).

Lovejoy, Paul. *Transformations in Slavery: A History of Slavery in Africa*, 3rd ed. (Cambridge University Press, 2012).

Luan, Livia. "Profiting from Enforcement: The Role of Private Prisons in U.S. Immigration Detention," *The Online Journal of the Migration Policy Institute*, May 2, 2018, https://www.migrationpolicy.org/article/profiting-enforcement-role-private-prisons-us-immigration-detention.

Luxemburg, Rosa. *The Accumulation of Capital*, translated by Agnes Schwarzschild (Mansfield Center, CT: Martino Publishing, 2015 [1913]).

Lynching in America: Confronting the Legacy of Racial Terror (Equal Justice Initiative: Montgomery, Alabama, 2015).

Maclean, Fitzroy. *Scotland: A Concise History* (New York: Thames and Hudson, 2000 [1970]).

Macleod, John. *Highlanders: A History of the Gaels* (London: Hodder and Stoughton, 1996).

Macrae, Norman. *The Romance of a Royal Burgh: Dingwall's Story of a Thousand Years.* (Dingwall: The North Star Proprietors. Republished by EP Publishing Ltd., East Ardsley, Wakefield, Yorkshire, England, 1974 [1923]).

Majewski, John. "Why Did Northerners Oppose the Expansion of Slavery? Economic Development and Education in the Limestone South," in Sven Beckert and Seth Rockman, *Slavery's Capitalism: A New History of American Economic Development,* 277–298 (Philadelphia: University of Pennsylvania Press, 2016).

Mann, Alastair. "Embroidery to Enterprise: The Role of Women in the Book Trade of Early Modern Scotland," in Elizabeth Ewan and Maureen Meikle, *Women in Scotland c.1100–c.1750*, 136–151 (East Linton, UK: Tuckwell Press, 1999).

Mansfield, James. *A History of Early Spotsylvania* (Orange, VA: Green Publishers, 1977).

Marshall, Rosalind. *Virgins and Viragos: A History of Women in Scotland From 1080–1980* (Chicago: Academy Chicago, 1983).

Martin, Asa. *The Anti-slavery Movement in Kentucky Prior to 1850* (New York: Negro Universities Press, 1970 [1918]).

Martin, Bonnie. "Neighbor-to-Neighbor Capitalism: Local Credit Networks and the Mortgaging of Slaves," in Sven Beckert and Seth Rockman, *Slavery's Capitalism: A New History of American Economic Development*, 107–121 (Philadelphia: University of Pennsylvania Press, 2016).

Martinot, Steve. *The Rule of Racialization* (Philadelphia: Temple University Press, 2003).

Maxwell-Stuart, P.G. *An Abundance of Witches: The Great Scottish Witch-Hunt* (Stroud, Gloucestershire, England: Tempus Publishing Ltd, 2005).

Mbembe, Achille. "Necropolitics," *Public Culture*, 15(1):11–40, 2003.

McKerracher, Archie. *Davidson* (Newtongrange, Midlothian: LangSyne Publishing, n.d.).

McKinney, Jennifer. "Sects and Gender: Reaction and Resistance to Cultural Change," *Priscilla Papers* 29(4):15–25, 2015.

McNie, Alan. *Clan Davidson*, rev. ed. (Jedburgh Scotland: Cascade Publishing Company, 1989).

Meacham, Charles. *A History of Christian County, Kentucky: From Oxcart to Airplane* (Markham, VA: Apple Manor Press, 2016 [1930]).

Meillassoux, Claude. *The Anthropology of Slavery: The Womb of Iron and Gold*, translated by. Alide Dasnois (Chicago: University of Chicago Press, 1991 [1986]).

Mending the Sacred Hoop, website, https://mshoop.org/.

Merrill, James. "'The Customes of Our Countrey:' Indians and Colonists in Early America," in Bernard Bailyn and Philip Morgan, *Strangers within the Realm*, 117–156 (Chapel Hill: University of North Carolina Press, 1991).

Michie's Kentucky Revised Statutes, Certified Version, Vol.I, Constitutions (Charlottesville, VA: LexusNexus, Matthew Bender & Company, Inc, 2014).

Middlesex County Virginia Court Orders 1711–1713 (Miami Beach, FL: T.L.C. Genealogy, n.d.).

Middlesex County, Virginia, Wills and Inventories 1673–1812 and Other Court Papers, William Hopkins, ed. (Richmond, VA: GEN-N-DEX, 1989).

Miers, Suzanne. "Slavery: A Question of Definition," in Gwyn Campbell, *The Structure of Slavery in Indian Ocean Africa and Asia*, 1–16 (London: Frank Cass, 2004).

Miles, Robert. *Capitalism and Unfree Labor: Anomaly or Necessity?* (New York: Tavistock, 1987).

Miller, Joseph. *The Problem of Slavery as History: A Global Approach* (New Haven: Yale University Press, 2012).

_____. "A Theme in Variations: A Historical Schema of Slaving in the Atlantic and Indian Ocean Regions," in Gwyn Campbell, *The Structure of*

Slavery in Indian Ocean Africa and Asia, 169–194 (London: Frank Cass, 2004).

Mills, Charles. *The Racial Contract* (Ithaca: Cornell University Press, 1997).

Minges, Patrick, ed. *Far More Terrible for Women: Personal Accounts of Women in Slavery* (Winston-Salem: John F. Blair, Publisher, 2006).

Mintz, Steven. "Introduction to Part II," in Mintz and John Stauffer, *The Problem of Evil: Slavery, Freedom, and the Ambiguities of American Reform*, 127–137 (University of Massachusetts Press, 2007).

_____ and John Stauffer. *The Problem of Evil: Slavery, Freedom, and the Ambiguities of American Reform* (University of Massachusetts Press, 2007).

Mitchison, Rosalind. *The Old Poor Law in Scotland: The Experience of Poverty, 1574–1845* (Edinburgh: Edinburgh University Press).

Mitrani, Sam. *The Rise of the Chicago Police Department: Class and Conflict, 1850–1894* (Urbana: University of Illinois Press, 2013).

Mobley, Joe. *The Way We Lived in North Carolina* (Chapel Hill: University of North Carolina Press, 2003).

Moffat, Allistair. *The Highland Clans* (New York: Thames and Hudson, 2010).

Morgan, Edmund. *American Slavery American Freedom: The Ordeal of Colonial Virginia* (New York: W.W. Norton and Company, 1975).

Morgan, Jennifer. *Laboring Women: Reproduction and Gender in New World Slavery* (Philadelphia: University of Pennsylvania Press, 2004).

Morgan, Philip. "British encounters with Africans and African Americans," in Bernard Bailyn and Morgan, *Strangers within the Realm*, 157–219 (Chapel Hill: University of North Carolina Press, 1991).

_____. *Slave Counterpoint: Black Culture in the Eighteenth-Century Chesapeake and Low Country* (Chapel Hill: University of North Carolina Press, 1998).

Morrell, Andrea. "Hometown Prison: Whiteness, Safety, and Prison Work in Upstate New York State," presented at the American Anthropological Association, November 30, 2017, Washington, DC, November 30, 2017.

_____. "'Municipal Welfare' and the Neoliberal Prison Town: The Political Economy of Prison Closures in New York State," *North American Dialogue* 15(2):43–50, 2012.

Moss, Bobby. *Roster of the Loyalists at King's Mountain* (Blacksburg, SC: Scotia-Hibernia Press, 1998).

_____. *Roster of the Patriots in the Battle of Moore's Creek Bridge* (Blacksburg, SC: Scotia-Hibernia Press, 1992).

_____. *The Patriots at King's Mountain* (Blacksburg, SC: Scotia-Hibernia Press, 1990).

Mountain Goat Trail Alliance. https://www.mountaingoattrail.org/history/.

Mt. Tabor Book Committee. *The History of Mt. Tabor Baptist Church: The*

Oldest Church in Barren County, Kentucky (Glasgow, KY: South Central Kentucky Historical and Genealogical Society, 1988).

Mt. Tabor Church Minutes, Barren County, Kentucky, Vol. 1 [1798–1829]. Sandra Gorin, transcriber (Glasgow, KY: Gorin Genealogical Publishing, 1994).

Mukherjee, Anita, "Impacts of Private Prison Contracting on Inmate Time Served and Recidivism," *SSRN,* August 20, 2017, https://ssrn.com/abstract=2523238.

Murakawa, Naomi. *The First Civil Right: How Liberals Built Prison America* (New York: Oxford University Press, 2014).

Murch, Donna. "Paying for Punishment: The New Debtors' Prison," *Boston Review,* August 1, 2016, http://bostonreview.net/editors-picks-us/donna-murch-paying-punishment.

Nash, Gary. *Race and Revolution* (Madison: Madison House Publishers, 1990).

Natapoff, Alexandra. *Punishment Without Crime: How Our Massive Misdemeanor System Traps the Innocent and Makes America More Unequal* (New York: Basic Books, 2018).

Needham, Rodney. *Reconnaissances* (Toronto: University of Toronto Press, 1980).

Nelson, John. *A Blessed Company: Parishes, Parsons, and Parishioners in Anglican Virginia 1690–1776* (Chapel Hill: University of North Carolina Press, 2014).

Neville, Cynthia. *Land, Law, and People in Medieval Scotland* (Edinburgh: Edinburgh University Press, 2010).

Nevins, Joseph. *Operation Gatekeeper: The Rise of the "Illegal Alien"and the Making of the U.S.–Mexico Boundary* (New York: Routledge, 2001).

Newton, Mrs. Ernest and Roy Brooks. "Bridges to the Past," *Courier-Sun* (Forest City, NC), June 30, July 14, August 4, 1976.

Newton, Norman. *Lost Inverness* (Edinburgh: Birlinn, 2013).

Nordstrom, Carolyn. *Global Outlaws: Crime, Money, and Power in the Contemporary World* (Berkeley: University of California Press, 2007).

North Carolina Taxpayers, 1679–1790, vol. 2, Clarence Ratcliff, ed. (Baltimore: Genealogical Publishing Co, 2003).

Northrup, David. *Trade without Rulers: Pre-Colonial Economic Development in South-Eastern Nigeria* (Oxford: Clarendon Press, 1978).

Nugent, David. "Appearances to the Contrary: Fantasy, Fear, and Displacement in Twentieth-Century Peruvian State Formation," in Christopher Krupa and Nugent, *State Theory and Andean Politics: New Approaches to the Study of Rule,* 186–209 (Philadelphia: University of Pennsylvania Press, 2015).

Nwokeji, G. Ugo. *The Slave Trade and Culture in the Bight of Biafra: An African Society in the Atlantic World* (New York: Cambridge University Press, 2010).

Oberg, Michael. *Native America: A History* (Malden, MA: Wiley-Blackwell, 2010).

Ojiaku, Mazi. *Yesteryear in Umu-Akha: History and Evolution of an Igbo Community (1665-1999)* (North Charleston, SC:Booksurge Publishing, 2008).

Okonjo, Kamene. "The Dual-Sex System in Operation: Igbo Women and Community Politics in Midwestern Nigeria," in Nancy Hafkin and Edna Bay, *Women in Africa: Studies in Social and Economic Change*, 45–58 (Stanford: Stanford University Press, 1976).

Omi, Michael and Howard Winant. *Racial Formation in the United States: From the 1960s to the 1990s*, 2nd ed. (New York: Routledge, 1994).

Orange County North Carolina Deed Book 3, William Bennett, ed. (Raleigh, NC: Privately Published, 1990).

Order Book No. 3, Barren County Kentucky, 1806 April Court 1812, Eva Peden, ed. (Glasgow: private printing, 1979).

Order Book No. 4, Barren County Kentucky, May Court 1812–August Court 1818, Eva Peden, ed. (Glasgow: private printing, 1979).

Ottenberg, Simon. *Leadership and Authority in an Africa Society: The Afikpo Village-Group* (Seattle: University of Washington Press, 1971).

Pandey, Gyanendra. "Off-Centered States: An Appreciation," in Christopher Krupa and David Nugent, *State Theory and Andean Politics: New Approaches to the Study of Rule*, 257–266 (Philadelphia: University of Pennsylvania Press, 2015).

Parent, Anthony. *Foul Means: The Formation of a Slave Society in Virginia, 1660–1740* (Chapel Hill: Omohundro Institute and University of North Carolina Press, 2003).

Parish register of Christ Church, Middlesex County, Virginia, from 1653–1812, The National Society of the Colonial Dames of America in the State of Virginia (Baltimore: Genealogical Publishing Company, 1964).

Parker, Geoffrey. "The 'Kirk by Law Established' and the Origins of 'The Taming of Scotland': St Andrew 1559–1600," in Leah Leneman, *Perspectives in Scottish Social History: Essays in Honour of Rosalind Mitchison*, 1–32 (Aberdeen: The Aberdeen University Press, 1988).

Parkinson, Robert. *The Common Cause: Creating Race and Nation in the American Revolution* (Chapel Hill: University of North Carolina Press, 2016).

Paschal, George. *History of North Carolina Baptists*, Vol. II (Raleigh: The General Board, North Carolina State Convention, 1955).

Patterson, Thomas. *Archaeology: The Historical Development of Civilizations*, 2nd ed. (Englewood Cliffs, NJ: Prentice Hall, 1993).

Peláez, Vicky. "The Prison Industry in the United States: Big Business or a New Form of Slavery?," *Global Research*, March 10, 2008, https://www.globalresearch.ca/

the-prison-industry-in-the-united-states-big-business-or-a-new-form-of-slavery/8289.

Peutz, Natalie and Nicolas De Genova. "Introduction," in De Genova and Peutz, *The Deportation Regime: Sovereignty, Space, and the Freedom of Movement*, 1–29 (Durham: Duke University Press, 2010).

Perdue, Theda. *Cherokee Women: Gender and Culture Change, 1700–1835* (Lincoln: University of Nebraska Press, 1998).

_____. *Slavery and the Evolution of Cherokee Society, 1540–1866* (Knoxville: University of Tennessee Press, 1987).

_____. and Christopher Oakley. *Native Carolinians: The Indians of North Carolina* (Raleigh: North Carolina Department of Cultural Resources, Office of Archives and History, 2010).

Perkal, Fizz. "Incarcerated Workers Strike Against Dehumanizing Prison Conditions,"*Inequality.org*, August 23, 2018, https://inequality.org/research/incarcerated-workers-strike-against-dehumanizing -prison-conditions/.

Perkinson, Robert. *Texas Tough: The Rise of America's Prison Empire* (New York: Metropolitan Books, Henry Holt and Co, 2010).

Perry, Lewis and Michael Fellman, eds. *Antislavery Reconsidered: New Perspectives on the Abolitionists*, 51–74 (Baton Rouge: Louisiana State University Pres, 1979).

Peterson, Patricia. *The Alexander Davidson Family* (handwritten genealogy available in Davidson file, South Central Kentucky Cultural Center, Glasgow, KY, n.d.).

Phillips, Kristine. "Thousands of ICE Detainees Claim They Were Forced into Labor, A Violation of Anti-Slavery Laws," *Washington Post*, March 5, 2017, https://www.washingtonpost.com/news/post-nation/wp/2017/03/05/thousands-of-ice-detainees-claim-they-were-forced-into-labor-a-violation-of-anti-slavery-laws/?utm_term=.c79677602b00.

Pickert, Kate. "Dispelling 'Anchor Baby' Myths," *Swampland blog, Time.com*, August 11, 2010, http://swampland.time.com/2010/08/11/dispelling-anchor-baby-myths/.

Pittock, Murray. *The Myth of the Jacobite Clans: The Jacobite Army in 1745*, 2nd rev. ed. (Edinburgh: Edinburgh University Press, 2009).

Plant, Marjorie. *The Domestic Life of Scotland in the Eighteenth Century* (Edinburgh: Edinburgh University Press, 1952).

"Policing and Profit." *Harvard Law Review*, April 10, 2015, https://harvardlaw-review.org/2015/04/policing-and-profit/.

Potter, Stephen. *Commoners, Tribute, and Chiefs: The Development of Algonquian Culture in the Potomac Valley* (Charlottesville: University Press of Virginia, 1993).

Powell, William. *When the Past Refused to Die: A History of Caswell County, North Carolina, 1777–1977* (Durham: Moore Publishing Co, 1977).

Prakash, Gyan. "Terms of Servitude: The Colonial Discourse on Slavery and
    Bondage in India," in Martin Klein, *Breaking the Chains: Slavery, Bondage,
    and Emancipation in Modern Africa and Asia,* 131–149 (Madison:
    University of Wisconsin Press, 1993).
Prince William County Virginia, Bond Book 1732–1847, Ronald Turner, ed.,
    190–191 (pdf published online), www.pwcvirginia.com/documents/
    BondBook.pdf.
Radford, Benjamin. *The Autobiography of Benjamin Johnson Radford* (Eureka,
    Ill: n.p., 1928).
Ragosta, John. *Wellspring of Liberty: How Virginia's Religious Dissenters Helped
    Win the American Revolution and Secured Religious Liberty* (New York:
    Oxford University Press, 2010).
Raphael, Ray. *The First American Revolution: Before Lexington and Concord*
    (New York: The New Press, 2002).
Ready, Milton. *The Tarheel State: A History of North Carolina,* (Columbia:
    University of South Carolina Press, 2005).
Records of Colonial Gloucester County, Virginia, Polly Cary Mason, ed.
    (Baltimore: Genealogical Publishing Co, 2003 [1946]).
Republic of Lakota, website, http://www.republicoflakotah.com/about-us/.
Reséndez, Andrés. *The Other Slavery: The Uncovered Story of Indian
    Enslavement in America* (Boston: Houghton, Mifflin, Harcourt, 2016).
Rice, James. *Tales from a Revolution: Bacon's Rebellion and the Transformation
    of Early America* (New York: Oxford University Press, 2012).
Richards, Eric and Monica Clough. *Cromartie: Highland Life 1650–1914*
    (Aberdeen: Aberdeen University Press, 1989).
Rifkin, Janet. "Toward a Theory of Law and Patriarchy," *Harvard Women's Law
    Journal.* 3:83–95, 1980.
Robinson, Cedric. *Black Marxism: The Making of the Black Radical Tradition*
    (Chapel Hill: University of North Carolina Press, 2000 [1983]).
Rogers, Bertha. *Wounded, But Not Broken* (Columbus, GA: Abdal Publishing, 2004).
Rood, Daniel. "An International Harvest: The Second Slavery, the Virginia-
    Brazil Connection, and the Development of the McCormick Reaper," in
    Sven Beckert and Seth Rockman, *Slavery's Capitalism: A New History of
    American Economic Development,* 87–104 (Philadelphia: University of
    Pennsylvania Press, 2016).
Rosa, Erin. "GEO Group, Inc: Despite a Crashing Economy, Private Prison
    Firm Turns a Handsome Profit," *CorpWatch,* March 1, 2009, https://
    corpwatch.org/article/geo-group-inc-despite-crashing-economy-private
    -prison-firm-turns-handsome-profit.
Roster of Soldiers from North Carolina in the American Revolution (Daughters of
    the American Revolution, Durham NC: The Seeman Press, 1932).
Rountree, Helen. "Introduction: Who Were the Powhatans, and Did They Have

a Unified 'Foreign Policy'?" in Rountree, *Powhatan Foreign Relations 1500–1722*, 1–19 (Charlottesville: University Press of Virginia, 1993).

_____. *The Powhatan Indians of Virginia: Their Traditional Culture* (University of Oklahoma Press, 1989).

Rountree, Helen. "The Powhatans and the English: A Case of Multiple Conflicting Agendas," in Rountree, *Powhatan Foreign Relations1500–1722*, 173–205 (Charlottesville:University Press of Virginia, 1993).

Rutherford County, North Carolina Abstracts of Deeds, 1773–1795, Caroline Davis, ed. (Rutherfordton, NC: Mrs. W.L. Davis, 1973).

Rutman, Darrett and Anita Rutman. *A Place in Time: Explicatus* (New York: W.W. Norton, 1984).

_____. *A Place in Time: Middlesex County, Virginia 1650–1750* (New York: W.W. Norton, 1984).

Sanderson, Margaret. *A Kindly Place? Living in Sixteenth Century Scotland* (East Linton, UK: Tuckwell Press, 2002).

Salmon, Marylynn. *Women and the Law of Property in Early America* (Chapel Hill: University of North Carolina Press, 1986).

Sankey, Margaret. *Jacobite Prisoners of the 1715 Rebellion: Preventing and Punishing Insurrection in Early Hanoverian Britain* (Burlington, VT: Ashgate, 2005).

Santa Ana, Otto. *Brown Tide Rising: Metaphors of Latinos in Contemporary American Public Discourse* (Austin: University of Texas Press, 2002).

Sassen, Saskia. *Expulsions: Brutality and Complexity in the Global Economy* (Cambridge, MA: Belknap Press, 2014).

Satia, Priya. *Empire of Guns: The Violent Making of the Industrial Revolution* (New York: Penguin Press, 2018).

Sawyer, Wendy. "How much do incarcerated people earn in each state?" *Prison Policy Initiative*, April 10, 2017, https://www.prisonpolicy.org/blog/2017/04/10/wages/.

Schama, Simon. *Rough Crossings: The Slaves, the British, and the American Revolution* (New York: HarperCollins Books, 2005).

Schept, Judah. *Progressive Punishment: Job Loss, Jail Growth, and the Neoliberal Logic of Carceral Expansion* (New York: New York University Press, 2015).

Schermerhorn, Calvin. "The Coastwise Slave Trade and a Mercantile Community of Interest," in Sven Beckert and Seth Rockman, *Slavery's Capitalism: A New History of American Economic Development*, 209–224 (Philadelphia: University of Pennsylvania Press, 2016).

Schimmel, Becca. "Daviess County Detention Center Work Program Restarting This Year," *WKU Public Radio*, April 10, 2018, https://www.google.com/search?q=schimmel+daviess+county+detention+center+work+program&ie=utf-8&oe=utf-8&client=firefox-b-1.

Schweninger, Loren. "The Fragile Nature of Freedom: Free Women of Color in the U.S. South," in Darlene Hine and David Barry Gaspar, *Beyond Bondage: Free Women of Color in the Americas*, 106–124 (Urbana: University of Illinois Press, 2004).

Scott, Donald. "Abolition as a Sacred Vocation," in Lewis Perry and Michael Fellman, *Antislavery Reconsidered: New Perspectives on the Abolitionists*, 51–74 (Baton Rouge: Louisiana State University Pres, 1979).

Scott, James. *Against the Grain: A Deep History of the Earliest States* (New Haven: Yale University Press, 2017).

"Second Census" of Kentucky 1800, Glenn Clift, ed. (Baltimore: Genealogical Publishing Company, 1982).

Sellar, David. "The Family," in Edward Cowan and Lizanne Henderson, *A History of Everyday Life in Medieval Scotland, 1000–1600*, 89–108 (Edinburgh: Edinburgh University Press, 2011).

Shankman, Andrew. "Capitalism, Slavery, and the New Epoch: Mathew Carey's 1819," in Sven Beckert and Seth Rockman, *Slavery's Capitalism: A New History of American Economic Development*, 243–261 (Philadelphia: University of Pennsylvania Press, 2016).

Sharma, Aradhana and Akhil Gupta, eds. *The Anthropology of the State: A Reader* (Malden, MA: Blackwell Publishing, 2006).

_____ and _____. "Introduction: Rethinking Theories of the State in an Age of Globalization," in Sharma and Gupta, *The Anthropology of the State: A Reader*, 1–41 (Malden MA: Blackwell Publishing, 2006).

Shen, Aviva. "Private Prisons Spend $45 Million on Lobbying, Rake in $5.1 Billion for Immigrant Detention Alone," *Think Progress*, August 3, 2012, http://thinkprogress.org/justice/2012/08/03/627471/private-prisons-spend-45-million-on-lobbying--rake-in-51-billion-for-immigrant-detention-alone.

Sinha, Manisha. *The Slave's Cause: A History of Abolition* (New Haven: Yale University Press, 2016).

Shuler, Jack. *Calling Out Liberty: The Stono Slave Rebellion and the Universal Struggle for Human Rights* (Jackson: University Press of Mississippi, 2009).

Silver, Peter. *Our Savage Neighbors: How Indian War Transformed America* (New York: W.W. Norton, 2008).

Silverman, David. *Thundersticks: Firearms and the Violent Transformation of Native America* (Cambridge, MA: Harvard University Press, 2016).

Skhlar, Judith. *American Citizenship: The Quest for Inclusion* (Cambridge: Harvard University Press, 1991).

Skinner, Quentin. *The Foundations of Modern Political Thought*, Vols. I and II (Cambridge: Cambridge University Press, 1978).

Smout, T.C. *A History of the Scottish People 1560–1830* (Glasgow, Scotland: Fontana/Collins, 1969).

Sojoyner, Damien. "You Are Going to Get Us Killed: Mapping Political Genealogies Against the Carceral State," presented at the American Anthropological Association Meetings, Washington DC, November 30, 2017.

Spencer, John. *A History of Kentucky Baptists From 1769–1885*, Vols. I and II (London: Forgotten Books, 2017 [1886]).

Spotsylvania County, Virginia Court Orders 1746–1748 (archived at Spotsylvania, Virginia, Office of the Circuit Court Clerk).

Spotsylvania County, Virginia, Court Order Book, 1749–1755 (archived at Spotsylvania, Virginia, Office of the Circuit Court Clerk).

Spotsylvania County, Virginia Court Orders 1746–1748 (Miami Beach, FL: T.L.C. Genealogy, 1999).

Spotsylvania County, Virginia, Deed Book D, 1742–1751 (archived at Spotsylvania, Virginia, Office of the Circuit Court Clerk).

Spotsylvania County, Virginia Will Book A, (archived at Spotsylvania, Virginia, Office of the Circuit Court Clerk).

Spotsylvania County, Virginia, Will Book B (archived at Spotsylvania, Virginia, Office of the Circuit Court Clerk).

Spotsylvania County, Virginia, Will Book D (archived at Spotsylvania, Virginia, Office of the Circuit Court Clerk).

Stack, Trevor. "Introduction," in Stack, Naomi Goldenberg, Timothy Fitzgerald, *Religion as a Category of Governance and Sovereignty*, 1–20 (Boston: Brill, 2015).

———, Naomi Goldenberg, Timothy Fitzgerald, eds. *Religion as a Category of Governance and Sovereignty*, 1–20 (Boston: Brill, 2015).

Steinfeld, Robert. *Coercion, Contract, and Free Labor in the Nineteenth Century* (New York: Cambridge University Press, 2001).

Steinle, Mia. "Slave Labor Widespread at ICE Detention Centers, Lawyers Say," Project on Government Oversight, https://www.pogo.org/investigation/2017/09/slave-labor-widespread-at-ice-detention-centers-lawyers-say/.

Stephan, Scott. *Redeeming the Southern Family: Evangelical Women and Domestic Devotion in the Antebellum South* (Athens: University of Georgia Press, 2008).

Stiùbhart, Dumhnall. "Women and Gender in the Early Modern Western Gàidhealtachd," in Elizabeth Ewan and Maureen Meikle, *Women in Scotland c.1100–c.1750, 233–249* (East Linton, UK: Tuckwell Press, 1999).

Sublette, Ned and Constance Sublette. *The American Slave Coast: A History of the Slave-Breeding Industry* (Chicago: Lawrence Hill Books, 2016).

Sugden, John. *Tecumseh: A Life* (New York: Henry Holt and Co, 1997).

Sweet, William. *Religion on the American Frontier: The Baptists, 1783–1830* (New York: Cooper Square Publishing, 1964).

Szechi, Daniel. *1715: The Great Jacobite Rebellion* (New Haven: Yale University Press, 2006).

Szuberla, Nick and Amelia Kirby, directors. *Up the Ridge* (Whitesburg, KY: Appalshop Films, 2006).

Takaki, Ronald. *A Different Mirror: A History of Multicultural America* (New York: Back Bay Books, 2008).

Tallant, Harold. *Evil Necessity: Slavery and Political Culture in Antebellum Kentucky* (Lexington: The University Press of Kentucky, 2003).

Tarrant, Carter. *History of the Baptised Ministers and Churches in Kentucky &c Friends of Humanity* (Frankfort KY: Press of William Hunter, 1808), http://baptisthistoryhomepage.com/tarrant.carter.history.html.

Tax Lists, Caswell County, 1777. North Carolina Digital Collections, http://digital.ncdcr.gov/cdm/ref/collection/p16062coll33/id/2032.

Tax Lists, Rutherford County, 1782. North Carolina Digital Collections, http://digital.ncdcr.gov/cdm/ref/collection/p16062coll33/id/1097.

Taylor, Alan. *American Revolutions: A Continental History, 1750–1804* (New York: W.W. Norton, 2016).

_____. *The Internal Enemy: Slavery and War in Virginia, 1772–1832* (New York: W. W. Norton, 2013).

Taylor, John. *A History of Ten Baptist Churches, Of Which the Author has been Alternately a Member* (Frankfort, KY: n.p., 1823), http://baptisthistoryhomepage.com/taylor.ten.churches.title.html.

Third Census of the United States, 1810, Barren, Kentucky.

Thomas, William. "Some History of the People and Their Burial Places Located or Formerly Known To Be Located Near the Environs of Buck Creek," *Traces: Quarterly Publication of the South Central Kentucky Historical and Genealogical Society*, 28(1):15–27, 2000.

Thornton, John. *Africa and Africans in the Making of the Atlantic World, 1400–1800*, 2nd ed. (Cambridge: Cambridge University Press, 1998).

Tilly, Charles. *Coercion, Capital, and European States, AD 990–1992* (Malden, MA: Blackwell Publishers, 1992).

_____. "War Making and State Making as Organized Crime," in Peter Evans, Dietrich Rueschemeyer, and Theda Skocpol, *Bringing the State Back In*, 169–191 (New York: Cambridge University Press, 1985).

Tonry, Michael. *Thinking About Crime: Sense and Sensibility in American Penal Cultures* (New York: Oxford University Press, 2004).

Troxler, Carole. *Farming Dissenters: The Regulator Movement in Piedmont North Carolina* (Raleigh: North Carolina Department of Cultural Resources, 2011).

Turner, E. Randolph. "Native American Protohistoric Interactions in the Powhatan Core Area," in Helen Rountree, *Powhatan Foreign Relations 1500–1722*, 76–93 (Charlottesville: University Press of Virginia, 1993).

Uchendo, Victor. "Ezi Na Ulo: The Extended Family in Igbo Civilization," *Dialectical Anthropology* 31:167–219, 2007.

United States Department of Justice. *Investigation of the Ferguson Police Department.* Civil Rights Division, 2015, https://www.justice.gov/sites/default/files/opa/press-releases/attachments/2015/03/04/ferguson_police_department_report.pdf.

Urbina, Ian. "Using Jailed Migrants as a Pool of Cheap Labor," *New York Times,* May 25, 2014. https://www.nytimes.com/2014/05/25/us/using-jailed-migrants-as-a-pool-of-cheap-labor.html.

Van Allen, Judith. "'Aba Riots' or Igbo 'Women's War'? Ideology, Stratification, and the Invisibility of Women," in Nancy Hafkin and Edna Bay, *Women in Africa: Studies in Social and Economic Change,* 59–85 (Stanford: Stanford University Press, 1976).

_____. "'Sitting on a Man': Colonialism and the Lost Political Institutions of Igbo Women," *Canadian Journal of African Studies,* VI (ii):165–181, 1972.

Vitale, Alex. *The End of Policing* (New York: Verso, 2017).

Virginia Colonial Abstracts. Beverly Fleet, ed. (Genealogical Publishing Company, 1988).

Virginia County Court Records, Deed Abstracts of Middlesex County, VA, 1679–1688, Deed Book 2, Part1, Ruth and Sam Spartico, eds. (McLean, VA: The Antient Press, 1989).

Virginia County Court Records, Order Book Abstracts of Middlesex County, VA, 1673–1677, Ruth and Sam Spartico, eds. (McLean, VA: The Antient Press, 1989).

Virginia County Court Records, Order Book Abstracts of Middlesex County, VA, 1680–1686, Ruth and Sam Spartico, eds. (McLean, VA: The Antient Press, 1994).

Virginia County Court Records, Deed Abstracts of (Old) Rappahannock County, Virginia, 1686–1688 , Ruth and Sam Sparico, eds. (McLean, VA: The Antient Press, 1990).

Virginia County Records, Spotsylvania County, 1721–1800, William Crozier, ed. (New York: Fox, Duffield and Co., 1945).

Wacquant, Loïc. *Punishing the Poor: The Neoliberal Government of Social Insecurity* (Durham: Duke University Press, 2009).

Walker, Juliet. "The Legal Status of Free Blacks in Early Kentucky, 1792–1825," *Filson Club Quarterly,* 57(October): 382–395, 1983.

Wallerstein, Immanuel. "An American Dilemma of the 21st Century?" *Societies without Borders* 1(1): 7– 20, 2006.

_____. *The Modern World System II: Mercantilism and the Consolidation of the European World-Economy 1600–1750* (Berkeley: University of California Press, 2011).

Walters, Ronald. "The Boundaries of Abolitionism," in Lewis Perry and Michael

Fellman, *Antislavery Reconsidered: New Perspectives on the Abolitionists*, 3–23 (Baton Rouge: Louisiana State University Pres, 1979).

Wang, Jackie. *Carceral Capitalism* (South Pasadena CA: Semiotext(e), 2018).

Warbasse, Elizabeth. *The Changing Legal Rights of Married Women, 1800–1861* (New York: Garland Publishing Inc, 1987).

Warner, Thomas. *History of Old Rappahannock Co VA 1656–1692, Including Present Counties of Essex and Richmond and Parts of Westmoreland, King George, Stafford, Caroline, and Spotsylvania* (Tappahannock, VA: Pauline Pearce Warner Publisher, c.1965).

Weaver, Jace. *The Red Atlantic: American Indigenes and the Making of the Modern World, 1000–1927* (Chapel Hill: University of North Carolina Press, 2014).

Webb, Stephen. *1676: The End of American Independence* (Syracuse: Syracuse University Press, 1995 [1984]).

Weber, Max. "Politics as a Vocation," in Weber, *Rationalism and Modern Society,* translated and edited by Tony Waters and Dagmar Waters, 129–198 (New York: Palgrave Books, 2015 [1919]).

————. "The Social Causes of the Decay of Ancient Civilization," in Eugene Genovese, *The Slave Economies,* Vol. I (New York: John Wiley and Sons, 46–67, 1973.

Wenger, Morton and Pem Davidson Buck. "Farms, Families, and Super-exploitation: An Integrative Reappraisal," *Rural Sociology* 53(4):460–472, 1988.

Westerkamp, Marilyn. *Women in Early American Religion 1600–1850* (New York: Routledge, 1999).

Westmoreland County, Virginia, Order Book, 1675/6-1688/9, John Dorman, ed. (Washington DC: J.F. Dorman, 1988).

Whatley, Christopher. "Order and Disorder," in Whatley and Elizabeth Foyster, *A History of Everyday Life in Scotland: 1600–1800,* 191–216 (Edinburgh: Edinburgh University Press, 2010).

Whitehead, Tony. "Barriers to Successful Reentry and Perceptions of Such Barriers," *Final Report for the Violence Reduction Program Ethnography,* Vol. 3. (College Park, MD: The Cultural Systems Analysis Group, University of Maryland, 2007).

Whiteside, Heustis. "Ashe, John," in William Powell, *Dictionary of North Carolina Biographies,* 6 volumes (Chapel Hill: University of North Carolina Press, 1979), http://www.ncpedia.org/biography/ashe-john.

Whitman, Stephen . *The Price of Freedom: Slavery and Manumission in Baltimore and Early National Maryland* (New York: Routledge, 2000 [1997]).

Whyte, Ian. *Agriculture and Society in Seventeenth–Century Scotland* (Edinburgh: John Donald Publishers Ltd, 1979).

————. *Scotland Before the Industrial Revolution, c 1500–c.1750* (New York: Longman, 1995).

_____ and Kathleen Whyte. "The Geographical Mobility of Women in Early Modern Scotland," in Leah Leneman, *Perspectives in Scottish Social History: Essays in Honour of Rosalind Mitchison*, 83–106 (Aberdeen: The Aberdeen University Press, 1988).

Wilkins, Thurman. *Cherokee Tragedy: The Ridge Family and the Decimation of a People*, 2nd rev. ed. (Norman: University of Oklahoma Press, 1986 [1970]).

Will of William Ellis. RootsWeb.com, copied from Spotsylvania Will Book D, 241–244. https://sites.rootsweb.com/~bianco/Resources/wellis66.html.

Williamson, Margaret. *Powhatan Lords of Life and Death: Command and Consent in Seventeenth Century Virginia* (Lincoln: University of Nebraska Press, 2003).

Williams, Eric. *Capitalism and Slavery* (Chapel Hill: University of North Carolina Press, 1994[1944]).

Williams, Karen G. *From Coercion to Consent? Governing the Formerly Incarcerated in 21st Century United States* (PhD diss., City University of New York Graduate Center, 2016).

_____. "'Worthy Ladies' Don't Behave Badly: Addiction and Sobriety inside Prisons," presented at the American Anthropological Association Meetings, Washington DC, November 30, 2017.

Williams, Brackette. "A Class Act: Anthropology and the Race to Nation Across Ethnic Terrain," *Annual Review of Anthropology*, 18:401–444, 1989.

Wiltz, Teresa. "What Crimes Are Eligible for Deportation? *Stateline*, Pew Charitable Trusts, December 21, 2016, https://www.pewtrusts. org/en/research-and-analysis/blogs/stateline/2016/12/21/ what-crimes-are-eligible-for-deportation.

Wolf, Eric. *Europe and the People Without History* (Berkeley: University of California Press, 1982).

Wood, Betty. "'For their Satisfaction of Redress': African Americans and Church Discipline in the Early South," in Catherine Clinton and Michele Gillespie, *The Devil's Lane: Sex and Race in the Early South*, 109–123 (New York: Oxford University Press, 1997).

Wood, Bradford and Larry Tise. "The Conundrum of Unfree Labor," in Tise and Jeffrey Crow, *New Voyages to Carolina: Reinterpreting North Carolina History*, 85–109 (Chapel Hill: University of North Carolina Press, 2017).

Woodward, Grace. *The Cherokees* (Norman: University of Oklahoma Press, 1963).

Woolley, Benjamin. *Savage Kingdom: The True Story of Jamestown, 1607, and the Settlement of America* (New York: HarperCollins, 2007).

Wright, George. *Racial Violence in Kentucky, 1865–1940: Lynchings, Mob Rule, and 'Legal Lynchings'* (Baton Rouge: Louisiana State University Press, 1990).

Wright, J. Leitch. *The Only Land They Knew: American Indians in the Old South* (Lincoln: University of Nebraska Press, 1999 [1981]).

Young, Alan. "The Earls and Earldom of Buchan in the Thirteenth Century," in
    Alexander Grant and Keith Stringer, *Medieval Scotland: Crown, Lordship
    and Community,* 174–202 (Edinburgh: Edinburgh University Press,
    1998).
Zaher, Claudia. "When a Woman's Marital Status Determined Her Legal Status:
    A Research Guide on the Common Law Doctrine of Coverture," *Law
    Library Journal* 94(3):459–486, 2002.
Zatz , Noah, Tia Koonse, Theresa Zhen, Lucero Herrera, Han Lu, Steven
    Shafer, and Blake Valenta. *Get to Work or Go to Jail,* UCLA Labor
    Center Research Brief, 2016. http://www.labor.ucla.edu/publication/
    get-to-work-or-go-to-jail/.

Index

abolitionism: in England, 188–92, 198; in Kentucky, 234, 235–41, 249–50; during Revolution, 199; slaveholding abolitionists, 241–47; in United States, 207, 211

Adam (enslaved person), 12, 84, 155–56, 304; life in slavery of, 167–68, 170, 175; owned by Davidson, 85–86, 193

African Americans, *see* blacks

Africans: in British and Spanish armies, 189; domestic slavery among, 159–60; enslavement of, 88–89; Igbo and Aro, 93–107; medieval kingdoms of, 91; during Revolution, 198; slavery among, 90; in Virginia social structure, 81; *see also* blacks

Alamance, Battle of, 178, 183

Ali, Wajahat, 287

American Indian Movement (AIM), 268

American Revolution (Revolutionary War), 190, 192, 195–204; Alexander Davidson, II, during, 192–95; sovereignty as issue in, 186

Anderson, Gary, 210

Anglican Church: authority of, 67–68; dissenters from, 194; marriage fees of, 175; monarchy and, 68; property rights controlled by, 58–59; women's disrespect for, 227

Aro (African people), 90, 100, 103–7

Attakullakulla (Cherokee leader), 213

Bacon, Nathaniel, 69, 77–78, 135

Bacon's Rebellion (1676), 69, 74–80, 138; consequences of, 83; Bruen Radford in, 71; slavery as consequence of, 15, 139–40, 147

Bailey, John, 238

Baird, Laura Davidson, 228, 249

Baptist, Edward, 163, 167, 210

Baptists, 177, 227–31; behavior prohibited for, 259–60; class equality among, 258–59; Separate Baptists, 194; on slavery, 238–41, 244–45
Bayne, Annie, 124
Bayne, Kenneth, 124
Beckert, Sven, 106, 210, 287
Beckett, Katherine, 282
Bennett, Lerone, 81–82
Berkeley, Sir William (governor, Virginia), 63–64, 71, 75, 77–79, 138
Berlin, Ira, 149
Blackmon, Douglas, 277
blacks (African Americans): after Bacon's Rebellion, 84; Bacon's Rebellion among, 77; creation of racial identity of, 81–82; debt peonage of, 274; executions of, 276; as indentured servants, 57; media perceptions of, 302; after Reconstruction, 272; during Revolution, 201–2; slaveholding abolitionists on, 241–46; as waged workers, 273; during War of 1812, 267; *see also* Africans
Boston Marathon bombing (2013), 305
Bracero Program, 283
Breckinridge, John, 252, 254
Bridges, Anna, 171, 174, 230–31; becomes Baptist, 228–29; death of, 226–27; inheritance of, 224; marries Alexander Davidson, 175; slaves owned by, 248–50
Bridges, James, 175
Bridges, Moses, 168, 175, 193, 230
Britain, *see* England
Brown, Michael, 281–82, 302

burglary, 219
Burnet, Archibald, 20
Burnham, John, 61, 62, 69, 71
Burnham, Rowland, 61

Canada, 206; during War of 1812, 267
capitalism: development of working class under, 215; dispossession of women needed for, 221; enclosure movement and, 41; Luxemburg on, 22; monarchy power and, 68; private property necessary for, 291; productive slavery in, 166; religion under, 256; religion and ideology of, 257–61; in Scotland, 121, 129–30; slavery and, 216–18, 251–52; slave trade and, 106
Caswell County (North Carolina), 176
chain gangs, 277–78
Charles I (king, England), 66
Charles II (king, England), 137, 138
Charles III (king, Scotland; Bonnie Prince Charlie), 132
Cherokees (Native Americans), 179, 184–86, 231; gender among, 211–14; during Revolution, 196
children: as cheap labor, 262; in Jamestown, 42–43; Powhatan, 50–51; removed from families, 294; sale of, 101; as slaves, 89–90, 208–9
Chomsky, Aviva, 287
Chomsky, Noam, 18
Church, *see* Anglican Church
civil rights movement, 276
Clan Davidson, 110–11
clans (Scottish), 111–15
class, *see* social class

Cole, Francys, 61

Cole, Martin, 56, 60–62, 142

Comanches (Native Americans), 211; Comanche Empire of, 268

Committees of Safety, 195, 201

Constitution (U.S.), 207; liberty in, 234; Thirteenth Amendment on abolition of slavery in, 276–77, 281; three-fifths compromise in, 209–10

convict leasing, 278–81

cotton, 163, 208; slavery used for, 210–11

coverture laws, 221–26

Coward, Joan, 236–38

Craig, Maggie, 117–18

Cromwell, Oliver, 67

Cullen, Karen, 130

Cult of True Womanhood (Cult of Domesticity), 231–33, 257, 258, 264

Dale, Sir Thomas, 45, 46

Davidson, Alexander I (1690?- 1748), 11–12, 20, 66, 304; arrives in Virginia, 139, 140; class position of, 154–55; death of, 170; as indentured servant, 15–16, 85–86, 107, 108; in Jackobite rebellions, 133–34, 136; marries Sarah Ellis, 13, 84, 151–53, 158–59; in Scotland, 109–11, 116; slaves owned by, 167–70; in Spotsylvania, 153–54

Davidson, Alexander II (1744- 1817), 13, 143, 152, 171, 304, 305; on Anna's conversion to Baptism, 228–29; birth of, 110; in Kentucky, 230–31, 234, 236–41; as licensed minister, 261–62;

marriages of, 226–27; marries Anna Bridges, 175; marries Mary Ellis, 229–30; in North Carolina, 174, 176–77, 180, 183–85; during Revolution, 192–96, 201, 202; slaves owned by, 168, 235, 244, 247–50, 263; will of, 224

Davidson, Caleb, 265

Davidson, Elijah, 239–41, 243, 265; as abolitionist, 235, 249–50; as Church official, 260

Davidson, Hezekiah, 224, 243, 250, 261, 265

Davidson, Philip, 152, 153, 168

Davidson, Thomas, 55, 142, 265

Davidson, William (son of Alexander Davidson I), 152, 153, 168

Davidson, X, 110, 124

death penalty, 42

debt peonage, 274

Declaration on the Rights of Indigenous Peoples (2007), 269

De Genova, Nicolas, 287

Depha (enslaved person), 12, 247, 263–65, 304

diarchies (dual sovereignty), 28–31; under capitalism, 256; sacrificial victims of, 38; in Scotland, 122

Dickinson, Maggie, 293

Dingwall (Scotland), 109–10, 116– 17, 124–25

dispossession, 289–91

divorce, 226

domestic slavery, 159–60, 162–63

Dowd, Gregory, 174, 267, 268

dual-sex systems, 97–99

Du Bois, W. E. B., 271

Dunaway, Wilma, 211

Earl of Cromartie, 114

Elkhorn Church, 256
Ellis, Hezekiah, 141–43, 150
Ellis, Mary, 141–43, 196, 224,
    228–33; in Kentucky, 234; slaves
    owned by, 247–48, 250, 263–65
Ellis, Rachel, 229
Ellis, Sarah, 12–13, 16, 305; birth
    and childhood of, 141–45;
    death of, 170; marries Davidson,
    84, 151–53, 158–59; slaves
    owned by family of, 150, 167; in
    Spotsylvania, 154; as widow, 225
Ellis, William, 143, 149, 150–55,
    168, 170, 193
enclosure movement, 40–41
England (Britain): abolitionism in,
    188–92; American Revolution
    against, 192, 195–204; centraliza-
    tion of colonial power by, 190;
    conflicts between monarchy and
    church in, 66–69; development of
    working class in, 80–81; Glorious
    Revolution (1688) in, 139–40;
    Jacobite rebellions against, 135–
    39; poverty in (1500s and 1600s),
    41–42; Scotland gains indepen-
    dence from, 112; Scotland in
    union with, 1, 115, 133; Scotland
    under, 131–32; slave trade of,
    100, 106, 107; Virginia placed
    under direct control by, 83–84; in
    War of 1812, 266–68
English colonists, 26–28; Bacon's
    Rebellion among, 76–80; driven
    by poverty, 42; privilege associ-
    ated with, 57; rebellion of 1676
    by, 64; religious authority for,
    30–31; see also Jamestown
Episcopalianism, 115, 136
Equiano, Olaudah, 92, 100

Eureka College, 265

Fallen Timbers, Battle of, 266
Farmers' Alliance, 271
Federici, Silvia, 214, 218
Ferguson Commission, 302
food stamps, 293–94
Fort Stanwix, Treaty of (1770), 185
Foucault, Michel, 20, 21
Friends of Humanity Association of
    Churches, 242

gender: among Cherokees, 212–14;
    among Igbo, 97–100; see also
    men; women
George I (king, England), 132, 134,
    138
Ghent, Treaty of, 268
Glencoe (Scotland), 132
Glorious Revolution (1688), 139, 140
Glymph, Thavolia, 263, 264
Gordon, Margaret Tennant, 225
Gordon-Reed, Annette, 226
Gottschalk, Marie, 280
government: diarchies, 28–31; see
    also states
Grayham, William, 168, 169
Great Awakening (religious move-
    ment), 177
guns, 82–83

Haley, Sarah, 277, 278
Hämäläinen, Pekka, 268
Harrison, Faye, 294–95
Hartog, Hendrik, 223
Haudenosaunee (Native Americans),
    172–73, 185
headrights, 43, 47, 65; land dis-
    tributed through, 146; of John
    Radford, 56, 58, 60

Henry VIII (king, England), 68, 69
Herbert, Steve, 287
Herman, Edward, 18
Hickman, William, 238, 239, 242, 256
Horne, Gerald, 139, 188, 191, 202
human rights, 295
hunting, 214

Igbo (African people), 87, 90–107, 118, 120
Igboland, 93–99, 101–2, 104, 106
immigration and immigrants, 286, 287
incarceration rates, 287
indentured servants, 66; blacks as, 57; Davidson as, 107, 152; in Jamestown, 42–43, 46–47; land given to, 73; mortality among, 56; slaves and, 15–16; slaves compared with, 149; women as, 49, 70
Indians, *see* Native Americans
individualism, 258
Iroquois (Native Americans), 63, 65, 172
Islamophobia, 287

Jacobite rebellions, 25, 115, 135–39; first (1690), 132; second (1715), 133–35
Jacobs, Harriet, 265
James VI (king, Scotland; James I, king, England), 115, 121–22, 128
James VII (king, Scotland; James II, King, England), 110, 131, 132
James VIII (king, Scotland), 132, 134
Jamestown (Virginia), 24; Bacon's Rebellion in, 76–77; death rates in, 41; indentured servants in, 42–43, 46–47; Powhatan and, 25–28, 39–40, 45–46; Powhatan attack on (1622), 50–51; punishment in, 43–45; religious beliefs of English settlers in, 69; state power in, 52–53; tobacco grown at, 48; women sent to, 49
Jefferson, Thomas, 156, 214, 226–27
Johnston, Carolyn, 214
Judah (enslaved person), 12, 247, 263–65, 304

Kars, Marjolene, 179
Keystone XL pipeline, 269
Kil, Sang Hea, 287
King Philip's War, 64
Knepper, Paul, 253, 276
Ku Klux Klan, 271

Lakomäki, Sami, 174
Lakota Nation, 269
Larner, Christina, 125–27, 135
Leigh, Alice, 66
liberty, 234
Lincoln, Abraham, 13, 55, 265
Linebaugh, Peter, 42, 220
Livingston, Susan, 225
Lock, Jacob, 239
Long, Bloomfield, Jr., 152
Luxemburg, Rosa, 22, 217, 218, 231
lynchings, 274; laws against, 275–76

MacDonald, Flora, 117–18
Mackenzie, George (Earl of Cromartie), 129
Mackenzie, John, 115–16
Madison, James, 205
Malinda (enslaved person), 247

Manahoacs (Native Americans), 172

Manifest Destiny, 268, 269

Mariah (enslaved person), 247

Martin, Josiah, 199, 202

Martinot, Steve, 19

Mary (queen, England), 132

Mary II (queen, England), 132

Massey, Ann, 84

Mbembe, Achille, 19, 78, 179

McDavid, Sarah, 109, 110, 117, 119–21, 124, 304

McKinney, Jennifer, 228

McNie, Alan, 111

Meillassoux, Claude, 162, 167

men: Cherokee, 212–14; coverture laws on, 222–26; Igbo, 94–96, 99; as laborers, in Middlesex, 148; male privilege of, 221–22; religiously prohibited behavior of, 260

Menjivar, Cecilia, 287

Mercat Cross, 116–17

Mexico: border between United States and, 287, 301; Bracero Program importing workers from, 283

Middlesex County (Virginia): death rates in, 147; slavery in, 149–51; society in, 145–49

Miller, Joseph, 190

Morgan, Jennifer, 156, 209

Mt. Tabor Church, 230, 238–40, 244–47, 260–61

Murakawa, Naomi, 282, 293

Murphy, John, 238–40, 250

Murphy, Margaret (Davidson), 239, 240, 249–50

Murray, John, 199

Nancy (enslaved person), 247

Nash, Gary, 198

Native Americans (American Indians), 211; attacks by, leading to Bacon's Rebellion, 75; after Bacon's Rebellion, 84; Cherokees, 212–14; in colonial history, 64–65; English policy of extermination of, 51; enslavement of, 279; Haudenosaunee, 172–73; pan-Indian confederacy among, 173–74, 184–85, 265–67; resistance of, 211–12, 268–69; sovereignty rights claimed by, 21–22; during War of 1812, 267–68; see also Powhatan

Nelson, John, 59

Nevins, Joseph, 287

New Hope Church, 239, 242, 243

Newport, Christopher, 39

Northrup, David, 104

Nwokeji, Ugo, 99, 100, 104, 105

Opechancanough (Powhatan chief), 50

Orange County (North Carolina), 176

Pamunkeys (Native Americans), 63

Parker, Geoffrey, 124

Parkinson, Robert, 201, 202

patriarchy, 48; in capitalism, 221; coverture laws for, 222–26; post-Reconstruction, 275

pawning people, 101

penitentiaries, 253–55, 262, 276

People's Party, 271

Personal Responsibility and Work Opportunity Act, 293

Pocahontas, 26, 39

policing, 219–20

polity, 15
Poor Laws (England, 1500s), 41
poverty, 289, 292; as cause of
    Bacon's Rebellion, 74; in England
    of 1500s and 1600s, 41–42,
    67; among English settlers, 58;
    as human rights issue, 295; in
    Igboland, 101; among Powhatan,
    51; among whites in Middlesex,
    151
Powhatan (Native Americans),
    12; canoe travel by, 60; contact
    between Europeans and, 32–33;
    diarchy governance of, 29–31;
    English control over, 52; execu-
    tions of, 20; Jamestown attacked
    by (1622), 50–51; Jamestown set-
    tlers and, 25–28, 39–40, 45–46,
    63; punishment among, 34–38,
    44–45; Wahunsonacock as chief
    of, 33–34; women among, 48
primitive accumulation, 218
prisons, 296–98; leasing of convicts
    from, 278–81; penitentiaries,
    253–55, 262, 276; prison labor,
    253–55
private property, 58–59, 186–87,
    291; necessary for capitalism, 219
Proclamation of 1763 (England),
    210
productive slavery, 159, 165–67
Protestant Reformation, 127
punishment: chain gangs for,
    277–78; in diarchies, 29, 38;
    in feudal Scotland, 112; among
    Igbo, 93, 102–4; in Jamestown,
    43–45, 52–53; Kentucky laws on,
    252–53; lynchings as, 275–76; in
    post-Reconstruction period, 274;
    among Powhatan, 34–37; prison

labor as, 253–55; of servants,
    50; states' power of, 18–21, 78;
    Thirteenth Amendment on, 276–
    77; of witches, 219; of women in
    Virginia (1700s)0, 144–45

race: creation of identity tied to,
    81–82; in Davidson family history,
    13; mixing of, in 1600s, 57; *see
    also* blacks; whites
Radford, Benjamin (mythical),
    24–25
Radford, Benjamin J., II (1797-
    1857), 265
Radford, Benjamn, III (1838-1933;
    Uncle Ben), 13, 265
Radford, Bruen, 57, 61–63, 69–71,
    75
Radford, Elizabeth Ann (1827-
    1901), 55, 142, 265
Radford, George (1665-1739), 57,
    62–63, 69–71, 75; white privilege
    inherited by, 84
Radford, John (1595?-1675), 11–12,
    24–25, 62–63, 304; arrives in
    Virginia, 55–58; in Chesapeake,
    65–66; headright of, 60; land pur-
    chased by, 61, 142
Radford, Robert, 66
Radford, Roger, 60, 61
Radford, X (name unknown), 39,
    49–50, 54; arrives in Jamestown,
    25, 40; in Jamestown, 27–28;
    leaves England, 69; refuses to
    work, 43
Reconstruction, 275
Regulator movement, 176–83, 188,
    259; during Revolution, 194
religion: among Aro, 104, 105; of
    Baptists, 227–31; as cause of

Jacobite rebellions, 135–37; in diarchies, 28–31; Great Awakening in, 177; ideology of capitalism and, 257–61; among Igbo, 96, 102; in Jamestown, 45; as part of states' technology, 255–57; of Powhatan, 35–37; in Scotland, 115, 123–24, 131; war legitimated by, 37–38; on witchcraft, in Scotland, 126–27

republics, slavery compatible with, 205–6

Revolutionary War, *see* American Revolution

Rice, David, 240, 242

Roanoke (Virginia), 27

Roman Catholic Church, in Scotland, 115, 122, 131

Rose (enslaved person), 247

Rountree, Helen, 48

Royal Africa Company, 107, 139

Rutman, Anita, 60, 142, 145, 154; on buying indentured servants, 72; on Middlesex County death rates, 58

Rutman, Darrett, 60, 142, 145, 154; on buying indentured servants, 72; on Middlesex County death rates, 58

Sam (enslaved person), 247

Sampson, 243, 250

Sandy Creek Baptist Association, 228

Sandy Run Church, 229–30

Sankey, Margaret, 138

Santa Ana, Otto, 287

Schept, Judah, 293

Scotland, 109–11; development of capitalism in, 129–30; feudal power and clans in, 111–16; historic rights of women in, 215–16; Jacobite rebellions in, 132–39; witchcraft in, 125–27; women in, 117–24

Second Great Awakening, 256–57

Separate Baptists (sect), 194, 227–30, 238

serfdom, 275

sharecropping, 271, 273–75

Shawnee (Native Americans), 173, 184–85, 266

Shay's Rebellion (1786), 209

Shen, Aviva, 281

Sinking Creek Church, 239

slaves and slavery, 156–65, 186–88; arrival in Chesapeake of, 12; British abolitionist movement and, 188–92; capitalism and, 216–18, 251–52; deregulation of slave trade, 139; domestic, 162–63; end of trade in, 207–8; within households, 262–65; among Igbo and Aro, 99, 100, 103–7; indentured servants and, 15–16; in Kentucky, 235–41; laws regulating, 83; lives of whites shaped by, 174–75; in Middlesex, 149–51; names given to, 88; owned by Alexander Davidson, II, 247–49; productive slavery, 165–67; reproduction of, 208–9; republics compatible with, 205–6; during Revolution, 196–97, 201–2; in Scotland, 124–25; Thirteenth Amendment on abolition of, 276–77; trade in, from Bight of Biafra, 87–88; used in cotton production, 210–11; Venis and Adam as, 167–70; in Virginia social structure,

80–81; war captives sold as, 89;
see also abolitionism
Smith, John, 25, 26, 39–40, 43, 172
Smith, Thomas, 153
Smout, Thomas, 117
social class, 288–89; privilege
associated with, in 1600s, 57; in
Scotland, 114, 119–21, 130–31;
in Tsenacommacoh, 33; in
Virginia (1700s), 145–46; witchcraft and, 126–27
social contract, 18–19
Spain: explorers and colonists from,
26–27; Savannah invaded by, 189
Spotswood, Alexander (governor), 84
Spotsylvania (Virginia), 172
Stack, Trevor, 255
states, 299–301; definitions of,
16–17; evolution of powers of,
83–84; among Igbo and Aro,
106–7; monopoly on use of force
by, 13, 17–18, 22; polities and,
15; punishment enforced by,
18–21; religion as part of technology of, 255–57; social contract
on, 291; taxing powers of, 181–82
Stiuĺbhart, Dumhnall, 121
Stono Revolt (1739), 189, 202
Stuart, Charles Edward (Bonnie
Prince Charlie), 117–18
Sublette, Constance, 208, 226
Sublette, Ned, 208, 226
Sugden, John, 268
Susquehanna (Native Americans), 75

tacksmen (Scottish gentry class),
114, 130
Tallant, Harold, 244
Tarrant, Carter, 238–40, 242, 243,
250

taxes: as cause of Bacon's Rebellion,
74; Regulators movement against,
177; sovereignty and, 187; as state
power, 181–82
Taylor, Alan, 201, 267
Tecumseh, 21–22, 174, 266–68
Tennessee Coal and Railroad
Company, 278
Tenskwatawa, 266, 267
Thames, Battle of, 268
Tilly, Charles, 18, 37
tobacco: as export crop, 58, 59;
investment in, 48; as revenue for
Crown, 147; slavery in produc-
tion of, 166; used as currency,
40, 49
Todd, Thomas, 56, 58, 60
Trafficking Victims Protection Act,
285
Trump, Donald, 276
Trump administration, 269, 301
Tryon, William, 178, 194–95
Tsenacommacoh, 27, 29; class struc-
ture in, 33; decline of, 52

United Nations, 269
United States: border with Mexico,
287, 301; Constitution of, 207;
creation of, 171; extreme poverty
in, 295; highest incarceration
in, 279–80; Revolution against
England by, 192, 195–204; in War
of 1812, 265–68

Venis (enslaved person), 12, 86–88,
175, 212, 304, 305; African life
of, 92, 94–96, 98, 100, 101, 105;
arrives in Virginia, 140; forced
into slavery, 106, 108; lack of
legal protections for, 226; life in

slavery of, 167–70, 175; owned by
Davidson, 84, 85–86, 155, 159,
193
Virginia Company, 15, 28, 41–42,
46–49
Virginia House of Burgesses, 50

Wahunsonacock (Powhatan chief),
32–34; Jamestown English settlers
and, 27–28; as Powhatan chief,
12; Powhatan empire expanded
under, 36–37; Smith and, 39–40
War of 1812, 265–68
Washington, George, 200, 213
Wayne, Anthony, 266
Webb, Stephen, 75, 190–91
Weber, Max, 16
Webster, Noah, 200
West Indies, 139
white privilege, 56–57, 81–83, 271,
273
whites: creation of racial identity of,
81–82; Du Bois on psychological
wage of, 271; labor of, 251–52;
in Middlesex, 148–49; Native
Americans' view of, 173–74;
as prison labor, 253–55; in
Regulator movement, 179–80;
slavery shaping lives of, 174–75
William of Orange (king, England),
13, 132, 136
Williamson, Margaret, 38
Winney (enslaved person), 242
witchcraft and witch hunts, 125–27,
214–15, 219, 304
women: as Baptists and Separate
Baptists, 227–31; Cherokee, 212–
14; coverture laws on, 222–26;
Cult of True Womanhood on,
231–33; dispossession of, 218–
21; in English colonies, 69–71;
historic rights of, 215–16; Igbo,
95–100; as indentured servants,
in Virginia, 148; in Jamestown,
53; Powhatan, 45, 48; religion
on role of, in capitalism, 257–58;
in Scotland, 117–24; sent to
Jamestown, 49; serving on chain
gangs, 277–78; as slaves, 89–90,
149, 150, 163–64, 263–65; in
Virginia (1700s), 143–44
working class: development of, in
Europe, 215, 216; dispossession
of women needed for, 220–21; in
England, development of, 165; in
England, rights of, 80–81
Wounded Knee, 268

Zebra Law, 278
Zinn, Howard, 186, 206